PENGUIN BOOKS

NATIONAL LIBERATION

Nigel Harris lives in London with his wife and two grown-up children. He is a member of a small unit specializing in developing countries at University College London and works extensively in developing countries. He has lived in Malaysia, Nigeria and India and frequently visits Mexico and East Asia. A former editor of *International Socialism*, his previous works include *Beliefs in Society* (1967), *Competition and the Corporate Society* (1972), *India–China: Underdevelopment and Revolution* (1974), *The Mandate of Heaven: Marx and Mao in Modern China* (1978), *Economic Development, Cities and Planning* (1978), *Of Bread and Guns: The World Economy in Crisis* (Penguin 1983), *The End of the Third World* (Penguin 1990) and *City, Class and Trade* (1991).

NIGEL HARRIS

NATIONAL LIBERATION

PENGUIN BOOKS

PENGUIN BOOKS

Published by the Penguin Group
Penguin Books Ltd, 27 Wrights Lane, London W8 5TZ, England
Penguin Books USA Inc., 375 Hudson Street, New York, New York 10014, USA
Penguin Books Australia Ltd, Ringwood, Victoria, Australia
Penguin Books Canada Ltd, 10 Alcorn Avenue, Toronto, Ontario, Canada M4V 3B2
Penguin Books (NZ) Ltd, 182–190 Wairau Road, Auckland 10, New Zealand

Penguin Books Ltd, Registered Offices: Harmondsworth, Middlesex, England

First published by I. B. Tauris, by arrangement with Penguin Books, 1990
Published in Penguin Books 1992
1 3 5 7 9 10 8 6 4 2

Printed in England by Clays Ltd, St Ives plc

CONTENTS

PREFACE

> The conception of an interdependent, interacting, global manufacturing system cuts across the old view of a world consisting of nation-States, as well as one of groups of countries, More or Less Developed and Centrally Planned, the First, the Third and the Second World . . .
>
> Yet the world order is still dominated by the culture, politics and ideology of the old pattern, a world of national egotisms where States determine what is important . . . The concepts of nationalism thus organize our perceptions and our consciousness, and so predetermine our view of what is reality. (*The End of the Third World*, p.200)

This book began as a preoccupation with the future relationships of economic nationalism and an integrating world economy. Each theme had been explored in my earlier *Of Bread and Guns* (Penguin, 1983) and *The End of the Third World* (Tauris/Penguin, 1986). However, economic nationalism is only a fragment of nationalism in general, so that the present account was drawn to consider this much larger theme, seeking in particular to assess the viability of nationalism. Nationalism in general is far too large and heterogeneous a category to allow one to say much that is useful. It spans the politics of established States (which account for overwhelmingly the largest part of nationalist politics) as well as those of rebellion. Furthermore, it covers both these 'public' themes, as well as relating to an element of personality, something known as a sense of national identity (which is what, mistakenly in my view, many people identify as nationalism proper). I have tried to avoid this second element, but it has inevitably been necessary to discuss it at some points.

The remedy for this unwieldy size was to narrow the main discussion to examine the conditions for the creation of nationalism, hence the title of national liberation. Secondly, this discussion has been related to the most uncompromising form of modern secular internationalism, Marxism. How did the Marxists come to be so closely identified with national liberation, how did the internationalists become nationalists?

These topics have been well worked by a number of hands before, but I hope the context presented here may afford some fresh insights, and, in particular, a more direct confrontation with the central question concerning the long-term viability of nationalism in an increasingly integrated world. The starting point – economic nationalism – now becomes a penultimate chapter of summary after the main discussion of political nationalisms.

The topics account for the structure of the book. First are some general propositions concerning nationalism as a feature of a world system, not individual nations. There is then an examination of the origins of the first attempts at nationalism in Europe; nationalism may have been European in origin, but, like gunpowder and China, or maize and Mexico, it has long since become the property of the world. From there we move to examining how the Marxists reacted to European nationalism, the grave tactical difficulties that arose in reconciling national liberation and internationalism, as a prelude to examining the complete transformation of the issues as a result of the Russian revolution and the establishment of the Soviet Union. The account then looks at what happened to this tradition in China, before examining a series of other cases in South Asia. The last part looks at a counter-example, a 'perverse' national liberation, before trying to relate the themes back to the starting point, the relationship of nationalism and a world economy.

I cannot claim complete success in the original enterprise. It is not possible to predict with any assurance the end of nationalism. Indeed, events in Eastern Europe and the Soviet Union as the manuscript for this book was being completed make any such suggestion ridiculous. We have plenty of warnings of how grandly wrong many Marxists were before the First World War in pronouncing the end of the nation-State and nationalism. Nonetheless some of the conditions for slow decline can be identified.

The book – as will be apparent – has gained immeasurably from the labours of others, not all of them, I fear, adequately acknowledged. The work of the historians of Marxism, of the Soviet Union, of China and of South Asia, have been ransacked, not necessarily in ways, or with properly scholarly reservations, that are appropriate. The only justification is in the task of seeking to draw out some general conclusions concerning national liberation. I have also gained much from John Breuilly's *Nationalism and the State* (Manchester University

Press, 1985), although he may not recognize this since we disagree on some important issues.

A number of people have read the work closely and contributed enormously in the clarification of themes and detail – Alasdair McAuley, Duncan Hallas, Tirril Harris, Colin Barker. Pervaiz Nazir was illuminating on South Asia, and John Rose on Zionism. Ajit Kumar Jha was very helpful on bringing me up to date on the history of British India, and Akiva Orr – despite our disagreements – on illuminating the contradictory character of modern Israel. My warmest thanks are also due to Professor Robert Brenner of the Center for Social Theory and Comparative History, University of California at Los Angeles, and to the Regents of the University for providing a stimulating three months in which I could complete the manuscript in singularly privileged circumstances. Ms Valerie Hoare was particularly helpful in preparing the final manuscript.

Nobody else, I fear, except the author is responsible for errors of fact and judgement.

Notes

Chinese names have been rendered in the now archaic Giles-Wade system since this is how they appear in the original English sources of the interwar period. However, for those versed in Pinyin this will pose difficulties of identification: my apologies.

Abbreviations:
ECCI: Executive Committee, Communist International
Comintern: Communist International
CPSU: Communist Party of the Soviet Union
RCP(B): Russian Communist Party (Bolsheviks)
USSR: Union of Soviet Socialist Republics (Soviet Union)
RSFSR: Russian Socialist Federation of Soviet Republics
RSDLP: Russian Social Democratic Labour Party

1

INTRODUCTION

IN 1939, the Royal Institute of International Affairs in London published a survey of nationalism in the world. It was possible to do this. Nationalism was still the concern of a relatively small part of the globe. Since then, the vast European world empires which so simplified the political map have gone, leaving behind something over 170 governments and well over 170 nationalisms. It would not now be possible in one volume to do any kind of justice to so many. Even after listing the existing States and their associated nationalisms, there would still be the nations without States whose warriors and militants occasionally fill the daily newspapers with their exploits – the Basques and Bretons, Scots and Welsh, Kurds, Catalans, Crimean Tatars, Corsicans, Québecois, Baluchis, Balts and Georgians, Tibetans, Serbs and Albanians of Yugoslavia, Timorese, Gurkhas, Biafrans, Eritreans, Pushtos, Shans and Karens, and countless others. At the outer rim of awareness, the known and declared nationalists fade into a host that have still to declare themselves. And there are yet others to be invented.

Even where the media report sightings of what are apparently other phenomena, they often turn out to be the same species. The Polish Solidarnosc, an unequivocal worker movement, opposed the regime not only as a class force but as the authentic voice of the Polish nation. In Angola and Mozambique, there are strange creatures called 'Marxist-Leninist States' when Marx and Lenin had both spent much time denouncing the State as intrinsically oppressive, but the media mean no more by this phrase than radical nationalists. In Iran, the regime that replaced the Shah appears as militantly Islamic (and, in theory, internationalist, for Shi-ism acknowledges no secular boundaries), and yet is more easily seen as the spearhead of Iranian nationalism. In Nicaragua – like Cuba – the overthrow of the local dictatorship was *national* liberation. And the demand of American black people for equality appears as black nationalism.

There has never been a time, it seems, when the world has been so dominated by the politics of nationalism. The idea has become axiomatic to politics, so much so that people are hardly conscious of it any longer. For many, their own loyalty to a particular nation is so much an unspoken element of personal identity (as opposed to the public world of politics) that it is impossible to discuss; nationalism is only what foreigners believe in. National loyalty becomes a component of personal honour, and any analysis is as much an affront for many people as a discussion of any other items of the sacred.

In such a perception, the world is not physical geography but an arena inhabited by individual countries. Each supposedly embodies a nation with a unique culture and language, its people the product of a common ethnic descent. The characters of the world drama are unified vertical slices of the globe's inhabitants – 'the United States', 'Guatemala', 'Burma' – not horizontal ones (beekeepers, engineers, bird lovers etc.). Thus have governments and their interests pre-empted perception, even to the point of dragooning the commodities of the world's markets into nationality – Japanese cars, Pakistani cricket bats, German steel.

The simplifications convert all concepts into issues of national power and prestige. They allow us to escape the vast and growing area of ambiguity – for that 'Japanese car' is assembled in the United States by Mexican and Korean workers, from parts made in twenty other countries, by a corporation whose parent is registered in Tokyo but owned by a consortium of companies registered in five other countries, and the general manager is a German. Such complexities tire the mind. The nationalist knee-jerk is easier and orders the world into the good and the bad. Two car bombs in Karachi kill 72 and injure 250; the authorities blame 'saboteurs of foreign origin' (in the presence of such disasters, it takes a certain frivolity to care whether those who perpetrated the act were natives or not).

Opinion takes a world of countries so much for granted, it is mildly shocking to discover how recent the concept is. The overwhelming majority of the world's people have lived until recently without the need to be members of national groups. Most West Europeans and North Americans found no need for strict national alignments up to the late eighteenth century; the East Europeans the late nineteenth century; much of the rest of the world, the present century. There were those who promoted the idea much earlier, but they had a limited following.

The idea of a nation, however, is not very helpful. In real circumstances, the 'nation' summarizes very complicated social and economic interests and classes which are not the same at different times, nor in different places. Knowing that a conflict is about nationalism tells one very little – whether Ukrainian peasants face Polish landlords,

French grape growers Algerian wine exporters, Chinese workers British employers. This specificity and complexity often robs general discussions of nationalism of much sense – the concept is not just a chameleon, but a different creature altogether in different contexts and times. Indeed, the national is often a concept used deliberately to conceal conflict over the issues, to force one kind of unity around an existing *status quo* (and if the arguments do not achieve unity, troops can be used to enforce it on the recalcitrants).

Of course, nationalism is not all simple illusion, for real material differences do exist and have existed for a long time between different countries. This was particularly so in late-nineteenth-century Europe among workers – levels of employment, income, education, trade union organization, social insurance, political rights and so on were very different, and what country a worker belonged to could be of vital importance. Thus, the defence of the superiority of one nation against another had then a material dimension. The same is true today, nowhere more starkly, for example, than on the border between Mexico and the United States (where the inhabitants on both sides are of the same origin, culture and language). Peasants were much less differentiated, and thus in the past always less engaged in nationalist alignments. As more and more peoples have become involved in the modern world, the perception of the unevenness of social and economic conditions has grown more extreme.

However, many discussions of nationalism assume that the topic remains the same regardless of time and place, so that explanations are equally applicable to all cases. Such an approach does not usually analyse nationalism so much as confirm the claims of the nationalist. Often, anti-nationalists are, in fact, opposed only to new nationalisms that threaten the position of the old, those of the Great Powers. The critics are thus half in love with the concept – in condemning anti-British nationalism, by implication they accept British nationalism. Yet others may deplore British nationalism while taking it for granted that there is some homogeneous group called the British, thus conceding the basic premise for a British nationalism.

Even on the supposedly internationalist Left, the same problem arises. From Otto Bauer[1] to Tom Nairn,[2] the claims of the nationalist to the unequivocal existence of nations are honoured without challenge. Consider the argument of Nicos Poulantzas[3] who asserts that nations are as old as or older than class society (as if the two modes of analysis are not mutually reinforcing), will persist after the State disappears, and possess a 'transhistorical irreducibility'. Nations are, he says, the basis of the State, and national struggles derive not from social classes but from historical entities called nations. The case can make no pretension to scientific detachment: it is a declaration of nationalist faith, a recommendation of how we ought to see the world, not how it is. Régis Debray does something similar in an even more pretentious form:[4]

> We must locate the national phenomenon within general laws regulating the survival of the human species ... against death. Against entropy.

Why must we do this? How *does* nationalism relate to human survival? There are no answers, for this is not analysis, but a manifesto. It is part of the nationalist fantasy world where, as Zubaida,[5] commenting upon Nairn and Gellner,[6] puts it:

> 'Nations' seem to be historically supersubjects with attributes of agency and action: they 'mobilize', 'aspire', 'propel themselves forward', 'react' and they even have atavistic, irrational 'ideas' with traumas which explode periodically.

The nationalist presses the case to encompass all the world's people. Thus, by now, no one is supposed to exist without being firmly bonded to one or other nation, or, in legal terms, State. It is a kind of modern serfdom: all are tied, usually by the accident of birth, to the national abstraction. Having achieved this enormous distribution of people (with all its many and continuing cruelties), the nationalist can point proudly to the result as itself the evidence for the prior existence of nations. All that has been achieved, he or she now claims, is no more than a revelation of some primordial ordering of humanity. A legion of policemen and border officials are required to preserve this happy feature of a benevolent nature.

Culture and nationalism

There are several criteria proposed for the ordering of mankind in national groups. One of the most important is culture, the proposition that the world's peoples are divided by discrete cultures. The value of the proposition is the greater because, outside anecdote, the word is sufficiently vague to give room for any prejudice. Approached systematically, however, it would be difficult to show that, before the coming of States which enforced degrees of uniformity upon their citizens, what was common to a people living in a particular territory was greater than what they had in common with people outside the territory. The criteria of sameness and difference offer few ways of separating out peoples once we rise above the level of locality.

Moreover, we also know that what modern nations identify as their national culture is a quite recent invention. For Europe, the nineteenth century was the great time when languages were identified and codified in single forms, minority languages in part eliminated, consciously national literatures and musics invented, and the territory mapped (appropriately described as a 'father' or 'mother' land, even though very few peoples have occupied the same territory for more than a thousand years). Above all, the historians were inspired to carve out of the record of the past an exclusive nationalist slice. Suddenly, the common achievements of unknown people in the past were seized as the artefacts of a national genius, part of a struggle to invent and impose a cultural consistency both on the past and on the present inhabitants, in contrast to the heterogeneity of benighted foreigners.

It is the work of minorities, not nations. What becomes the English language starts as the dialect of a minority and is imposed upon the majority, usually by force, with legal punishments for those who refuse the schooling which will induct them in the national language. Thus, the definition of what is the national culture is the result of a preemptive strike by only one group of people. In India, a tiny minority of caste Hindus, usually Brahmins, appropriated 'Indianness' in one narrow form, thus rendering, for example, Muslims and, to a lesser extent, scheduled castes and tribes, foreign. A pre-emptive strike by a minority of non-Jewish Germans turned German Jews into foreigners in their own homeland. In a similar way, the white newcomers to South Africa turned the older Bantu newcomers into aliens. Force is the precondition for compelling the majority of people to accept this pretension. Thus, the appearance of the nation is not the revelation of some continuous culture, but an invention of the struggle for power and prestige.

The struggle does not end, for each age must reaffirm the continuity of the nation in the face of powerful discontinuities and the appearance of striking similarities between members of different nations. An English grocer in south London, for example, seems to have more in common with a grocer in Berlin or Delhi or Yokohama than one in sixteenth-century London; such common sense is politically dangerous in a nationalist world. Thus, governments are endlessly seeking to shore up the erosion of the national idea which a world economy inflicts upon them. The British must refine a new history curriculum to show the national genius and thus the inferiority of all others, and do so in the face of the sleepy yawns of the poor pupils. The Education Deliberation Committee on Textbooks of National History has submitted guidelines to the South Korean Ministry of Education on how the history of the inhabitants of the Korean Peninsula can be doctored into a saga of the heroic descent of a single people from time immemorial, the overture to an entirely modern symphony.[7]

In sum, culture provides no secure foundation for defining a national group. Insofar as there is uniformity between the members of a nation, it is the result of nationalism (and usually the creation of a State to enforce uniformity) not the cause.

A common descent

Culture is so often used to justify nationalism today perhaps because people are a little embarrassed to give the more traditional grounds for believing in the existence of nations: the idea that nations are characterized by common biological descent, ethnic origin or race. Each nation is seen as a kind of family, clan or tribe, assuming these entities denote common descent. This common descent transmits an historical genius, the membership of which – like that, in theory, of the old nobility of Europe – is by birth, and so beyond the striving of those without the required descent. By now, this essentially moral theory controls citizenship and who is admitted across borders, and the rights accruing to the 'sons of the soil'.

However, the claim to a common ethnic descent is in principle very unlikely for all except the most tiny and isolated groups. Where the information is available, it shows that each modern nation is descended from a wide diversity of peoples, leaving aside all those who have joined or left down the years. There can be no serious defensible pedigrees here (even if we could decide what characteristics had to be inherited to ensure pure descent). Most ancient peoples have disappeared. Consider the fate, for example, of the Jutes, Scythians, Medes, Phoenicians, Etruscans, Gauls, Picts, Arameans, Babylonians, Sumerians, Akkadians, Elamites, Canaanites, Philistines, Alamans, Burgondes, Franks, Lombards, Normans, Cahorsins, Mercians and innumerable others. The names that survived provided no evidence of past links; and the fact of disappearance shows no inferior civilization. On the evidence, assimilation, constant making, unmaking and remaking of groups, appears to be the norm – nations are, before the coming of the modern State, the precise opposite of those indestructible building blocks of humanity. And what we have today are entirely modern creations, syntheses, the result of countless unrecorded accidents rather than the national spirit seeking to realise itself.

The idea of the organization of peoples according to descent was one of the most common in the past. But even then, the claim to ethnic identity was more often fictional. Groups were created by political or material need, and once created, granted each other quasi-familial status (complete, for literate societies, with swiftly constructed genealogies; thus, the descendants of the Prophet in Islam have down the ages offered much work for the imagination and ingenuity of the genealogical archivists).

Take, for example, David Morgan's comment on the Mongols, just prior to their advance to domination in the Middle East:[8]

> We shall misunderstand nomadic society if we think of it as composed of tribes whose membership is determined exclusively by blood relationships. Theoretically, they were so determined and this is no doubt the explanation of the plethora of patently spurious genealogies that litter the contemporary and later literature. In reality, however, the tribe was rather an 'open' institution, its membership created more by shared political interests than by descent from a common ancestor. It is only in this way that it is possible to explain the fact that Chingis Khan was able to organize the nomads of Central Asia, an extraordinarily disparate collection of groupings whether considered 'racially' or 'linguistically', into a unified and effective war machine.

Something similar seems to have occurred among the tribes of East Africa. They were pre-eminently political formations which families joined and left, and by no means exclusive (families could claim simultaneously to belong to more than one tribe).[9] It was the Europeans who, in establishing their power, made tribes into exclusive and ethnic descent groups, the basic building blocks of empire. John Breuilly[10] provides interesting examples of the way in which this happened in certain parts of central Africa under British and Belgian rule. The French did something not dissimilar by inventing a people, the Berbers, from the groups that inhabited the highlands of north Africa.[11]

However, regardless of the fictional character of the claim to a common ancestor, the concept had and continues to have a powerful hold on people's perceptions. At its most extreme, it leads to their protesting against those who marry foreigners (and discriminating against the resultant offspring). Furthermore, the same attitudes can become attached to concepts which, in origin, laid no claim to common ethnicity. In a north Indian town recently, a Hindu woman was prevented from marrying a Muslim and forced to marry a Hindu by an alliance of Hindu and Muslim militants. Confessional status had become the basis for an exclusive descent group. In China, during the Cultural Revolution, something similar happened to class membership. The child might never have known his or her grandfather nor seen the small piece of land that made him a landlord, yet the child remained stubbornly a landlord in official eyes decades after land reform. Landlords, like workers, peasants and capitalists, had become translated into parallel descent groups, not functional elements of a single social structure.

Why is a common descent so frequently suggested, when the claim can scarcely ever be substantiated? The fiction of the family is the most powerful one in terms of unquestioned loyalties – children, parents, grandparents, siblings and spouses are traditionally expected to conform to codes of duty and right without question or gain. Of course, in practice, things are more complicated, as the Moroccan Swasa saying has it on brothers running a grocer shop:[12]

> We are brothers.
> But when we evaluate the inventory,
> We are enemies.

The moral code remained an ideal even if the performance was inferior, and for tribes and clans the aspiration was what counted: those who fought, sacrificed and died together became brothers, their leaders fathers. The modern State is no less opportunistic in seeking to highjack the fiction of the family as a model for national loyalty, making all citizens brothers and sisters, and the territory a parent.

However, once detached from the tangible relationships of a real family, there is nothing to discipline the imagination. Aristocratic families in Europe defended the purity of their descent (the basis of their legitimate right to rule), and now, by an heroic leap of imagination, racial purity comes to be attached to whole peoples for certain political purposes. Ex-Prime Minister Yasuhiro Nakasone recently, in all innocence, explained that Japan was an 'intelligent society', in contrast to the United States, because 'in America there are many Blacks, Puerto Ricans and Mexicans'. 'Homogeneity' was the source of Japan's high level of literacy; peoples, like animals in the wild, should live in separate locations (that is, different peoples are different species, and, presumably, should not miscegenate). Nakasone was unmoved in this breathtakingly preposterous nonsense either by common sense, the protests of the many minorities living in Japan (Ainu, Okinawans, Koreans, Chinese, Filipinos and others), or the judgements of historians on the melange of different peoples who provide the ancestors of the modern Japanese. On the contrary, at government expense, he set up a Kyoto institute of nationalist historical anthropology to demonstrate the spiritual civilization that supposedly provides the source of the modern Japanese. Nakasone thus highjacked the concept of 'Japanese' for his private – or rather, class – definition.

Other Criteria

Culture and common descent provide the main claims for national differences, but other criteria have also been used. If nations imply national States, there can be no State without a territory to administer, so a common territory is the precondition for asserting a claim to the right of national self-determination. However, the occupation of territory is very recent for most peoples, and very often has entailed excluding the inhabitants already there. Thus, a certain historical myopia is required to substantiate territorial claims. When the Malay leaders of Malaysia assert that the Malays are 'bumiputras', sons of the soil, and therefore to be accorded privileges as against the Chinese and Indian Malaysians, only the unkind would point out that the Malays were also immigrants from an earlier period, and that no-one has paid attention to the claims of the real indigenous peoples, the Dayak and other tribes of the forestland.

Where a minority lacks a territory – for example, the Jews for much of their history, black people in the United States, the Indian Dalit Panthers (an organization of untouchable caste members) – then the practical struggle can be only for equality of treatment, not national independence. Some Jews went in the opposite direction by expropriating a territory in Palestine (on the grounds of an historical occupation) to substantiate their claim to being a nation. The national claim came before the land to which the claim related. Some of India's Muslims followed the same course in migrating to Pakistan in 1947. America's black nationalism, on the other hand, was an identification with independence struggles in Africa, not a demand for a separate territory. The nationalism is by way of analogy.

Some writers have stressed the importance in the struggle to create an independent national State of the use – or the attempt to establish the use – of one language in a given territory, 'unified fields of exchange' as Benedict Anderson puts it.[13] Gellner[14] stresses that nationalism becomes important when linguistic communication becomes vital for the State. This may be true in the rise of European nationalism, although the need for a uniform language arises also because of the competition between States and therefore the drive to establish single national markets. More often, the establishment of a uniform language is not the motive so much as the result – and not invariably so – of national independence. Today there are numerous multi-lingual States, without this necessarily weakening national unity.

The use of a particular language does not necessarily coincide either with a group that claims common descent, or a geographical area or what is supposedly a culture. The black inhabitants of Haiti speak French, as do the Indians of Mauritius. The French speak a language derived from that small group of speakers of Latin who conquered Gaul at the beginning of the first millennium AD, although they suppose they are descended more from the Gauls than the Romans.[15]

The use of one language rather than another has always been a highly political matter. The use of Latin in medieval Europe excluded the laity, just as the use of English in India today excludes the majority of Indians. Thus the use of the vernacular is a great step forward in permitting participation by the majority. On the other hand, establishing the vernacular as the main medium of government and instruction can be a way of excluding competition by outsiders for public employment. The ban on other languages operates like import controls to give a domestic monopoly to local people.

The reverse phenomenon, forcing a language on people, can be a different means to eliminate competition by establishing linguistic inequality. In India, the northern language, Hindi (spoken by the largest number of Indians, but all in the north), has the effect of disqualifying southerners from public employment. The small current campaign in California to prevent the use of Spanish is probably less about jobs, more about enforcing a single uniformity to the advantage of those who regard themselves as of English descent. During the French revolution, the revolutionaries tried to eliminate the minority languages (Provençal, Basque, Corsican, Flemish, Alsatian, Celtic) as the instruments of reaction and superstition. The Tsars, as we shall see, tried something similar: if nations required linguistic uniformity, then the power of the State should be used to create it.

In the nineteenth century, religion was not admitted as a legitimate basis for national independence. Today, it has become an important one. Yet it was often an element in earlier national struggles – in the Low Countries, between the Protestant north and the Catholic south (where the Spanish Crown ensured, through the Inquisition, that the Catholic faith remained the religion of the loyalists). In our own times, in Northern Ireland, Protestant vigilantes and a Catholic IRA confront each other, Christian Armenians and Bulgars face Muslim Turks and Azeris; Muslims in south Thailand and the south Philippines face Buddhist and Christian majorities. In Lebanon, a patchwork quilt of religious loyalties paralyses the State. In India and Cyprus, the religious divide broke the old British territory in two.

However, it is as naive to regard religious divisions as self-explanatory as it is to see nationalisms so. Both summarize complicated interests and classes, and we need constantly to remind ourselves that the overwhelming majority of people of different religions live together in peace. Religion *per se* is rarely the cause, rather the language, of strife. States and ruling orders continually seek to manipulate religion to political advantage. Furthermore, the activists in political movements that fly religious banners are rarely religious in any serious sense; indeed, they may have only the haziest idea of the doctrines they claim to champion. Many other forces of much more secular significance are at stake.

In sum, it seems, the principle which is supposed to underlie the formation of groups, of which nationalists are one, is of much less importance than the existence of the groups. That the grounds claimed are fictional, matters little compared to the fact that the group exists; the symbols do not explain its existence.

The question of membership

Let us look at the issue of national and other groups from a different angle: how do people join them? Most people today are members of a nationality without choosing it, and that membership in the short term usually excludes by law the possibility of belonging to another nationality. People are born and raised within one country, without considering the question of choice. But this is a relatively new situation. In the past, choice was more important, and then national groups were much like many other groups of which one might be a member. For people are members of many groups – by inheritance, adherence, occupation, residence, origin, language, appearance and so on. Adding a generation or two can vastly extend the possible claims.

The choice of which group it is relevant to claim membership of turns on specific circumstances. Sometimes, we are forced to be members of one group rather than another; in the British colony, Kenyans were all those inhabitants excluded by the British from a share in political and administrative power, or at least that was the appearance. In practice, the ambiguities of class blurred the theory; rich Kenyans had privileges that made them virtually equal to the British, and a large number of the British – including the instruments of power, the soldiers – were not accepted as equals by the Establishment. In conditions of disorder, the alignments became sharper and memberships inescapable. Even more sharply, it is impossible for the majority of people to be other than black in South Africa as it became impossible to be other than Jewish for Jews in Nazi Germany. When the former ruling order of Ethiopia defined itself as Amhara, it thus imposed on all other Ethiopians non-Amharaness.

For the subordinate, then, the definition may be inescapable. For the dominant, there may be a more flexible perimeter, depending upon the political tactics of the time. In up-country British Nigeria, the

British proper were too small a group to be British, so they became 'Europeans' and let in the Lebanese traders.

Where politics forces one identification, it also dissolves others – prior social groupings that may be of much greater age. The struggle for independence forced the 'homogenization' of the national liberation movement relative to the imperial power. For example, the Guinean leader, Amilcar Cabral, notes how the Guineans created their own nationality:[16]

> Ten years ago we were Fula, Mandjak, Madinka, Balante, Pepel and others. Now we are a nation of Guineans.

Thus, in a colonial situation, subordinate peoples have a particular group identity forced upon them by the operation of power, rather than by some prior common features. Quite often, this forced identity does not fit those prior features. Take, for example, the invention of the 'Muslims' as a political force in British India. The British expressed a fear of the Muslims since the imperial dynasty which they had replaced had been Muslim. However, the overwhelming majority of those inhabitants of the subcontinent who adhered to Islam had no sense of identification with the dynasty (even when they knew it existed) and the fact that the dynasty was Muslim had little to do with its exercise of power. Nonetheless, it was British fears that began the process of creating a *political* group (rather than a religious one), and British political tactics to safeguard their continued power that gave it national significance.

However, in other circumstances, people also choose to claim membership of one group rather than another for specific purposes – from the trivial (jumping the queue because the shopkeeper is from the same village) to the momentous. The choice may be quite temporary and for limited purposes – using contingent loyalties as strategies for action. But while the choice is individual, it does not take place in isolation, but within a framework of given options.

Thus, the individual is undertaking a gamble about what action is required to defend or advance an interest: what is the right way to describe the problem, what is to be done, and who are the most appropriate allies; whether to say that the Ministry of Education has not provided enough school places (and all 'parents' should unite to press the government for more) or there are not enough places because the Ammanites have stolen them (so all non-Ammanites must unite to resist the theft). The choice of label, of group, is a strategic one, not a passive recognition of ancient primordial alignments. Whether I decide to be, for current purposes, pre-eminently a parent or a child, a woman, a teacher, a part-time sempstress, a member of the

Patel family or caste, a Gujerati, a Briton or an Indian, a citizen of Leicester, a taxpayer, a chess player and so on depends upon the task in hand rather than some inherent singularity, for I can be all these things simultaneously and without discomfort. In general, opportunism rather than predetermination is the key.

However, to repeat, the historical context presents the options, not a solitary individual freely sorting the name cards of group membership. But choice it is, choice of alignments with the social or political forces presented at the time. Take, for example, the class struggle in Bohemia-Moravia (what later became the core of Czechoslovakia) between the end of the last century and the 1930s. The conflict between nationalism and socialism aligned different classes. The urban lower middle class was broadly nationalist, while class-conscious workers, with the support of the majority, were deliberately anti-nationalist (the Czech Communist Party declared itself the party of Czech, German, Slovak, Hungarian, Ruthenian and Polish workers). There was no inevitable alignment with nationalism but the choice, for and against, involved a choice of many other things, including revolution and classes.

The options which define the framework of choice are closely related to the available leadership and organization. In the anti-colonial struggle, the speed with which these options were created was remarkable. The nationalist leader often had to invent a unifying culture as well as lead. He played the role of a kind of intellectual version of Lévi-Strauss' *bricoleur*.[17] A *bricoleur* was a handyman who, by using bits of machinery or equipment, the original purpose of which had been forgotten or never known, was able to solve immediate mechanical problems. The nationalist leader did something similar with the cultural detritus of the past to create a new national group. In doing so, he pre-empted the choice of others on what the nation was. But also he learned the parameters of what was acceptable. Consider the case of Abdellatif Sbili who led the first Moroccan nationalist campaign against the French in 1930:[18]

> Soon he saw that his way of presenting the threat in terms of a single territory that should not be torn apart was not understood by the people. For them, he had to say: 'Islam is being violated in its very being.'

The creation of a new culture, in this case a kind of Islamic secularism, is easiest for those slightly alienated from the customs of the society. It was the educated and Westernized who were most important as nationalist leaders, and these were almost invariably drawn from the urban middle class or the Western-educated children of rural landlords. Many were adventurers, seeking any opportunity to advance themselves, and little constrained by either principle or higher political commitment: slogans and culture were means to advancement. But for much of the time, without the right circumstances, they remained hungry, prophets without followings.

Even the demand for independence might be advanced as primarily a bargaining counter. In the fluid political context, nationalism was not necessarily an overriding objective, but a tentative foray, a provisional objective that, in the right circumstances, might be relinquished. The struggle for national independence was thus a peculiar context where the normal sets of interests and classes appeared not to bind the leaders: the skilful adventurer could almost create his or her own outcome.

Furthermore, the creation and leadership of a movement against a colonial power required different abilities from those needed to run a new State. The vision of the future country mixed the aim of liberating the new State (and those who would direct it) with the emancipation of the inhabitants of the country: an end to exploitation, hunger and hardship. In power, the second part of the programme usually needed radical revision. It was one thing to lead an alliance of interests and classes for independence, another to run a system consisting of interests and classes in conflict. The utopian vision of Gandhi ceased to have practical significance with the formation of the Government of India, and he handed power to the practical man of affairs, Nehru. Partha Chatterjee[19] notes the layers of contradiction in 1947 India between

> a nationalism which stood upon a critique of the very idea of civil society, a movement supported by the bourgeoisie which rejected the idea of progress, the ideology of a political organisation fighting for the creation of a modern national State which accepted at the same time the ideology of 'enlightened anarchy'.

Internal and external pressures

The degree to which 'internal' factors – as opposed to external pressures – lead to the emergence of a separate nationality obviously varies in emphasis between cases, and the first were possibly of greater significance in the seventeenth and eighteenth centuries in the emergence of the first national groups in Europe. But in the anti-colonial revolutions and the Soviet Union today external oppression is as commonly the fundamental source of the creation of a national group, no matter how much that group defines itself in relationship to inherited cultural symbols or a supposedly common past. National liberation is thus reactive. Nigerian nationalism in the first instance was a reaction to British imperialism and took its form from the nature of British rule, as mediated by different social strata. For those preoccupied with culture, the defence of a brand new African culture arose because the British denied the validity of all except British culture. A defence of indigenous languages flows from a rejection of all except English, and so on. But even this overestimates the degree of homogeneity: some Nigerians were rich enough to escape being 'black'; some whites were always too poor ever to be 'white'.

The nationalists do not see the emergence of nationalism in this way. They 'discover' what is supposedly pre-existing, an ancient collective identity. In the same way, in religious conversion people 'discover' God, a pre-existing reality. For the nationalist, the voyage of discovery is a profound spiritual experience. A nineteenth-century German writer observes:[20]

In the whole history of a people its holiest moment is when it awakens from its unconsciousness and for the first time thinks of its old holy rights. A people which grasps its sense of nationality with pleasure and love can always celebrate its rebirth.

A rebirth, a rediscovery, a reawakening: the imagery of a predetermined reality persists. Nehru, at the declaration of Indian independence, doubly stressed the image, with an awakened India and a sleeping world:[21]

Long years ago, we made a tryst with destiny, and now the time comes when we shall redeem our pledge, not wholly or in full measure, but very substantially. At the stroke of the midnight hour, when the world sleeps, India will awake to life and freedom. A moment comes, which comes but rarely in history, when we step out from the old to the new, when an age ends, and when the soul of a nation, long oppressed, finds utterance.

It was appropriate that, given India had no indigenous language accessible to all Indians, English should be used for the solemn and archaic style of this speech.

Once awakened, as in religious conversion or falling in love, the nationalist finds a new family from which he or she derives pride, dignity, the opportunity for unimagined courage, contact with a supposed eternity, and 'humanity' (as opposed to the mechanical arrangements of an alien bureaucracy and the market). Above all, war inspires the simplification of normal complexities into the heroism of folklore. A suddenly discovered national identity can indeed be what Marx described religious belief as, 'the heart of a heartless world'.

But this is at the level of nationalist discourse. It leaves out place and circumstance, the powerful and unconscious drive of material interests and class identity. In reality, for a Chinese peasant, his sons conscripted for forced labour in the Japanese army, his women seized for their brothels, his land destroyed, the power of nationalism does not add an extra dimension to his anguish and anger. In isolation from these underlying realities, we are tempted to fill in the explanatory gap with imagination:[22]

> The tremendous emotional energies released when men break their bonds with the village, the kin group and the family are all available for a new focus on politics. More frequently, this focus is nationalism.

Do people search for emotional attachments when they migrate to cities? Many of the nationalists had long since passed beyond the kin–village axis. On the other hand, many millions of people have left and are leaving villages, kin and family without becoming either emotional or nationalist. Only a small minority correpond to the image. They may be willing to die for the motherland; conscription or the threat of sanctions may be required for everyone else.

Nationalism creates a morality. It offers criteria to decide who is rightfully a member of the nation, and the duties and rights which attach to membership. It lays down that loyalty to the nation – and in established States, the State – ought to take priority over all other loyalties, including that to the family, and that the crime of disloyalty is treason, the punishment for which is frequently death (that is, the nation has the power of life and death over its members). National interest also allows a member to disregard moral principles in defence of the nation – it is permissible to lie, to steal and to murder. Foreigners are, as an abstract category, enemies.

In established States, less serious forms of bad behaviour are also permitted. Nationalism encourages a collective vanity, paeans of self-praise ('We are the greatest'), which would be considered childish in an adult. It also promotes a neurotic insecurity, reflected in the sillier newspaper headlines – 'Briton insulted on the Costa Brava' or vicarious triumphs of infantile egotism ('Krauts firmly put down'). It is difficult to identify the personality that might give rise to this energetic emotional life, so full of fears and petty triumphs; it is a kind of vainglorious fool, a *miles gloriosus*. Nationalism provides an *alter ego* and an *id*, a means to export all anger and frustration on to outsiders. Thus is the *status quo* preserved.

The paradox of national liberation

The nationalism of national liberation thus includes, for the minority of the national group involved, a paradox: a loyalty to the idea of the national group which is most intense, emotional and committed, to the point of sacrificing one's life, but which is also, on other criteria, quite shallow, apparently founded upon intellectually erroneous grounds. The paradox arises partly because the emotional force derives from external oppression, not internal unities, but the external oppression seems to identify an internal essence, the junction point between what is imagined as a national group and personal integrity, self-respect. There are more mundane explanations, as we have suggested earlier. The national summarizes complex social and economic issues where the sources of fury are more obvious.

However, for much of the time, these violent commitments are relatively rare. The majority at best are passive and, given the opportunity, may well be happy or at least indifferent about shedding their membership of a national group. The massed emigrants to the United States were (and still are) in many cases American patriots well before they arrived or could speak English. So it has been with other countries of immigration – the immigrants embraced a new nationality with, if the nationalist fictions are to be believed, unseemly eagerness. Perhaps the child or the grandchild will invent a nostalgia, a personal explanation of current unhappiness, which will make of special significance the origin of the parent or grandparent. But these private fictions are rarely of much significance, nor do they affect most people – despite much American talk of 'roots'. Nor do they survive the passing of many generations. The ease of shedding national identity is more impressive than its retention.

If nationality is so speedily abandoned, it is also – as we shall see later – no less speedily invented. Contrary to European perceptions, it takes months rather than centuries (as European emigrants to the United States demonstrated). Passionate national commitment seems rather like falling in love – obsessive, emotional, violent, but often swiftly forgotten. Fickle it may be but, while in its intense form, it can lead to the greatest heights of courage and self-sacrifice.

What provides stability to the fickleness of love is the material framework of marriage. What turns national liberation into a stable nationalism is the accomplishment of State power. As a political, rather than psychological, phenomenon, national liberation and nationalism concern first and foremost the State – the aspiration to create a State, or the defence or expansion of an existing State. Once created, the State enforces on all a common nationalism, so that in the end the 'nation' becomes a kind of ideational shadow to the operation of public power; what the government decides defines the will of the nation.

For national liberation, greater emphasis must fall upon the independent existence of a nation. But even here, the creation of an armed wing – or the fact that the nationalists are armed guerrillas – is a kind of proto-State. The armed bodies of men and women indicate that national liberation is no longer a world of private sentiment but a serious aspiration.

It is the first step on the road to the creation of a new State. But it is still very far. The militants of national liberation, single-mindedly focused upon the conquest of State power, see their end as opening the doors to freedom. But States in general – and new poor States in particular – are part of a competing system and one marked by profound inequalities. The defence of a newly won national independence against actual or potential threats from other States imposes an entirely new discipline upon society. Military power requires the capacity to purchase the equipment abroad and usually a measure of industrialization at home. Ensuring the loyalty of the population entails all-round development. To achieve these goals usually entails a much higher degree of centralization and a much more interventionist role for the government in focusing national resources.

Economic development imposes upon society unprecedented social strains. Thus, what begins in the springtime of national liberation as a great sense of popular emancipation becomes a range of new and often heightened oppressions, those required for economic development. The reality of independence is distant from the hopes of national liberation. For, it becomes apparent, the terms of the competition between States are constantly changing, and therefore the struggle for national independence is never complete.

In earlier times, the pressure of a system of competing States was perhaps less all-encompassing, and the agenda of economic development much more sketchy. There was time for domestic forces to shape a new nation without the same constant vigilance of the behaviour of neighbours. Since the later years of the nineteenth century, however, national liberation has become defensive, reactive, and the new States continually aware of their vulnerability and therefore of the necessity, at whatever tolerable speed, of economic development. The transition perhaps partly explains why representative democracy is so much less associated with national liberation today than in the late eighteenth and the first half of the nineteenth centuries. Participation in the affairs of State and open discussions of political matters must now be tempered by the need for survival between the testing conditions of competition abroad and what results from the State's reactions to these conditions, the resentments of the population at home. The national liberationists of Jharkhand may cry: 'What kind of Jharkhand do we want? We want a Jharkhand free of exploitation, a Jharkhand where those who work will eat and those who loot will go.'[23] But the terms to achieve this end are not in Jharkhand, and not within the grasp of an independent Jharkhand State.

Many people, of course, do gain in the achievement of independence. Those that inherit the new State and come to constitute its new ruling order are some. The ragged guerrillas become a new regular army with housing and pensions. Capital may flourish from limitations on imports, curbs on, or the expropriation of, foreign companies, and the expansion the State may initiate to secure its power. The intelligentsia has an enhanced role in creating and transmitting the new national culture through a national educational system. In certain circumstances, cultivators may gain some land from the break-up of large estates, and often workers are rewarded with new regulations on conditions and pay. But once the State settles to the task of development, the majority of people may find conditions distant from the rhetorical promise of independence. Class struggle emerges from the supposed common interest, and the invitation to sacrifice for the nation is directed by one class at another. Ultimately, the government says, all will benefit from development, but that is a remote promise for the present generation.

As we shall see subsequently, many of the revolts that become nationalist start as a reaction to increased centralization – administrative (with increased taxation) by the State and economic, by external markets. The pressures that force these two processes do not cease after a national liberation movement attains power. On the contrary, they may increase. Thus the new State finds it necessary to accommodate precisely those processes which were one of the sources of the original movement of national liberation. The cry of 'neocolonialism' attacks a real issue: the persistence of a world economy and political order that imposes upon its constituent elements quite strict forms of behaviour. To refuse to conform is to risk threats to national independence.

The theme of resistance to increased centralization is persistent, linking the formation of both European States and those in the rest of the world. We shall note cases later in the Austro-Hungarian Empire, in the Russias of the Tsars, in British India. Benedict Anderson notes another case in the Spanish empire of the late eighteenth century. Madrid was driven by its competition with the more advanced States of north-western Europe (and shortly to be overwhelmed by the Napoleonic wars), and failed to draw salutary lessons from Britain's loss of its North American colonies. The Spanish Crown endeavoured to rationalize the administration of its dependencies, to tighten control, centralize and increase taxation. Its clients who bore the brunt of administering Spanish America, the creoles, reacted with fury and resisted.[24] It was an important starting point for the anger which under later pressures inspired movements of independence. Thus, the enlightenment of the enlightened despot, the attempt to modernize and make the administration more systematic (as well as relieve the royal purse), produced precisely the opposite reaction.

The empires have gone (with the exception, as anti-Communists have since the 1940s been fond of saying, of the Soviet Union). The world is now parcelled up in independent States which claim a monopoly in the employment of nationalism. The system of States does not now easily permit further fracturing, even though the associated processes of national economic development and administrative centralization continually stimulate forms of resistance, some of which are nationalist. Thus, national liberation today is usually defensive, resisting the domestic effects of greater integration in, or competition with, a world order, rather than itself being the spearhead of 'modernization'.

Furthermore, what is meant by economic development has also changed. Since the mid-nineteenth century, the content of development – creating the capacity to defend national independence – changed radically. But today it is again radically different. Formerly, the process was supposed to focus upon national accumulation, capital held in local hands, production focused upon the domestic market and designed to displace all imports. The nation was thus both a discrete political and economic concept. Today, it seems, domestic development is much more effectively promoted by integration in a world economy: accepting foreign capital into the domestic economy, with production specialized for a world market (and relying upon imports). Thus the national economic programme departs from the political; national independence does not include economic independence. The nation-alists promised to end the drain of resources out of the country, to industrialize in order to supply home consumption. Yet the current logic implies a greater role for foreign capital (and greater repatriation of profits), directing output to foreign consumption, greater dependence upon the rest of the world.

The argument that there is no long-term viability for a country which is economically isolated from the rest of the world is not new. Before the First World War, many Marxists believed, as we shall see, that world capitalism had become so internationalized that even the political struggle for national independence made no sense (or worse, it was reactionary). The elements of national life which were consistent with the new world order were solely cultural, not political or economic. Even the existing States were too small for the emerging economy. Thus, for example, Leon Trotsky described the First World

War as 'at bottom, a revolt of the forces of production against the political forms of the nation and the State'. The War heralded 'the collapse of the national State as an independent economic unit'; henceforth, the nation would be only 'a cultural, ideological and psychological fact'.[25] Yet the high tide of nationalism was still to come, from two World Wars and the colonial revolution.

The error was to project the growth trends of the world economy from 1870 to 1914 and see the political order as not much more than a reflex of these trends. Modern empires, it was thought, showed the internationalization of a world economy in a distorted form; once the empires could be overthrown, the world's productive forces would create a single economy. The reality was far different. The long-term stagnation and the Great Depression of the interwar years, not to mention the two World Wars themselves, separated the Great Powers economically in clear-cut economic empires. The imperial States, as political entities, seemed to dominate all economic matters. The economic separation itself then did profound damage to the world payments and trade systems.

Even if this outcome had not occurred, and by some miracle the world economy had continued to grow after 1918, it is not possible that States would merely have accommodated to the requirements of growing world trade. Their rivalries were not washed away by the flows of commerce and finance. Indeed, as we shall see, in certain circumstances economic integration can heighten nationalism.

The real outcome was at striking variance with Marx's original prognosis. There, capitalism dissolved social differentiation – families, castes, clans, tribes, provinces, religions, gender, nationality. Capitalism forced all into equality, the equality of a common subordination. Only functional distinctions would remain. In the end, the sociology of a world economy would find a world bourgeoisie confronting a world proletariat. Yet reality went in the reverse direction; the world cake was sliced vertically, not horizontally. Daily life might lead people to interact internationally – through the goods they handled, collaborative work, consumption patterns, even culture. But the shadow of the national State fell over all these items, dividing humanity into the territorial patches administered by national governments.

The Marxists were wrong. But their error was more fruitful than those who might have been right. It was precisely their uncompromising, simplistic internationalism which collided so directly with growing nationalism and so illuminated the sources of national feeling in a way nationalists could not. The first part of this book is therefore preoccupied with the case that Marx developed, what later Marxists made of it, and how this tradition was transformed in the history of the Soviet Union. From there, we move to examine the inheritance

China received from the Soviet Union, before looking at a series of other cases in South Asia and Israel. The argument then returns to the starting point – the conditions for the survival of nationalism in an integrated world economy.

In summary, the main points this chapter has attempted to make are the following:

(i) In the European origins of the formation of modern States, nationalism was a means to establish the loyalty of populations and enforce some measure of homogeneity (against the local particularisms of earlier times). However, with the spread of European imperial power throughout the world – and the fierce competition of the Great Powers – in the late nineteenth century, national liberation became essentially defensive. Imperialism forced all to be nationalist in response.

(ii) National liberation was thus a reaction both to the political domination of the Great Powers and to integration into a wider capitalist system (the two were not always distinguishable). The movement thus required economic programmes to parallel political ambitions, which would end what was seen as the domination of capitalism. In the post-1945 period, national liberation has been seen as the first line of rebellion against capitalism.

(iii) National liberation invariably takes its form from the nature of the force oppressing those to be liberated. Thus, the traditional grounds for identifying genuine nationalisms are either derived from the oppressive context or established by the independent State (even if, in both cases, symbols are borrowed from the past, albeit transformed to modern purposes).

(iv) Individuals choose to belong to national groups (even if the oppressing force reduces the range of choice to a very narrow one) and do so as the selection of a strategy for action, not the passive recognition of some primordial ordering. They are opportunistic, and national identification is simultaneously intense and shallow.

(v) National claims summarize complex economic and social interests and classes, a coalition that is rarely the same in different times and places; so 'nationalism' does not, in and of itself, indicate any self-evident aims.

(vi) In conditions of rapid social change, the role of adventurers, guided by the search for power without being committed in loyalty to any interest or class, is important in the creation of a national liberation movement.

(vii) The achievement of a new State transforms a national liberation movement into something quite different, necessitating quite often a change of leadership, of support groups, of style and programme. This is because the central disciplines over a new State derive from the world system of competitive and unequal States and the continuing struggle to preserve national independence.

(viii) Finally, the terms under which economic development can be undertaken by new States have been radically changed, so that today the programme of economic liberation has become separated from that of political freedom.

The rest of this book is an extended exploration of these themes.

Part I

MARXISM AND NATIONALISM

2

THE EUROPEAN
ORIGINS OF THE
NATIONAL IDEA

*T*HE social order of the European high Middle Ages was characterized by an immense number of local subsistence economies, with relatively little intercommunication for much of the time. Villages and towns might occasionally war with each other, but the fundamental basis of life was local. There was intense suspicion of the 'foreigner' (although he was as likely to be a trader from the nearby town as a native of another land), but the ordinary inhabitants of the territories which were to become the modern States of Europe had no sense of common identity, of membership of national groups.

Above this local base, there were all-European social groups – nobles, knights, priests, lawyers, with changing sets of loyalties to their overlords and to different dynasties. None of this included identification with a national entity; indeed, 'a French knight, like a French priest, had more in common with a knight or a priest from Italy or Germany than with a French peasant'.[1] In fact, even this formulation is doubtful, since, at the time, the concepts of 'French', 'Italian' or 'German' were insecurely anchored in reality. Even the great diversity of dialects did not allow linguistic grouping; it took the nineteenth century to invent the demarcations that created separate languages corresponding to the nations which had by then been created.

Furthermore, power – the subsequent basis of the national State – was personal, attached to the person of the ruler, not to an impersonal agency like the State. Loyalty had to be reaffirmed each time it was required; it could not be assumed merely by reason of inhabiting a particular locality. Treason therefore was a crime no greater than being disloyal to one who claimed to be an overlord. Since it was perfectly possible for an individual to have loyalties to several overlords, betrayal was not uncommon. There were no 'international affairs', only relations between ruling dynasties (who were not members or representatives of different nations, but part of a single class). Kings had 'possessions' and 'subjects'; the majority of subjects were not citizens and had no automatic rights.

Of course, this description is very schematic, covering not only a variety of situations but differences at different times. There were also rebellions, the creation of groups that cut across localities – from religious heresies to occupational strata (fishermen, peasants, artisans). Oppressed groups – the Welsh, for example – possibly retained some sense of a common group experience. The Lombard bankers, when they were abroad, also did, and the Jews were obliged to do so. Wars, famine, plagues were catastrophes that tore people out of their local niches. Nonetheless, for much of the time and for many places, local particularism was a dominant motif.

What changed the picture were two related processes: commercialization and the formation of modern States, the second of which has most immediate importance for nationalism.

(i) *Commercialization*. The growth of merchant and banking capitalism, as well as the spread of rural manufacturing (from 1400), began processes of change in a series of connected districts – from the leading area, northern Italy, to Flanders and the Baltic. It was a development taking place outside the immediate purview of the great all-European social strata and, to some extent, establishing the sinews of economic life which cut across the areas of dynastic concern. Trading stimulated urbanization, and thus a population less trapped in village particularisms and dealing geographically with much more distant areas. Capital came to provide rulers with sources of power other than direct taxation, and this introduced a new factor into political affairs, allowing overlords to put down rivals and oblige priests to anoint them as rulers. Interactions over longer distances encouraged the development of common conventions, of measures of security, of a *lingua franca* in which business could be conducted.

(ii) *The modern State*. Outside the immediate area of commercialization, however, another phenomenon appeared. Stretching over a long period, a number of important rulers began to seek to secure much greater power over their dominions as the means to extend their power abroad – particularly in what was to become known as France, but also in England, Sweden, Spain and, somewhat later, Brandenburg-Prussia. The creation of a powerful State thus preceded the creation of a popular nationalism for these countries (in contrast to most later cases), and, indeed, one could say that the manufacture of a popular patriotism was an instrument for the consolidation of State power here.

The process was driven by intensified competition between the participants. In particular, the two separate processes of State formation in France and England, and the rivalries between France and the Habsburg empire (with, simultaneously, the rivalry between the Habsburgs and the Ottomans, with the French on occasions allied to the Ottomans), were important constituents. Unlike much of Europe, England had long been a territory ruled by one dynasty, and was protected by the Channel from invasion by the great land powers of the Continent. France, with four to five times as many people in the late Middle Ages and twice the territory (when unification was complete), consisted of a series of virtually independent and equal principalities – Normandy, Brittany, Burgundy, Gascony, Aquitaine, each capable of entering into dynastic relationships with other powers. Furthermore, the open land borders made France subject to direct attack. The two contexts produced two remedies. France created a powerful centralized bureaucracy to override local power and ensure a direct supply of resources to sustain the armies of the Crown; England's monarchy was dependent upon a gentry that supplied the armed forces, administered local justice, sat in Parliament and paid the taxes upon which the royal armies depended. The only limits to the capacity of the French Crown to tax its inhabitants was the capacity to pay (and the means to appropriate the surplus); between 1537 and 1642, the per capita fiscal burden in France was ten times that in England.[2] The English Crown was trapped at every stage by the gentry, to the point where the king was beheaded and a military dictatorship established (with, for the first time, a standing army, accompanied by a five-fold increase in the tax burden). However, the Channel still allowed the English to escape what was forced upon the French kings, continual modernization of the military forces; in its place, the English concentrated on naval power.

The French State was fashioned in a Europe with a wide variety of political forms but, once it was created, it changed the terms of competition and of survival for lesser powers and for the ramshackle empires that in part covered these principalities. The creation of States posed an immediate threat to the freedom of action of lesser rulers. The political entities of the twentieth century are the survivors of a ferocious rivalry. Most of the 500 or so independent political units of Europe in 1500 disappeared, absorbed by their more powerful neighbours, leaving some 25 or so victors.

The outcome of this process was in no way predetermined. No French nation was waiting in 1500 to emerge in the concept of France; and it could just as well have been Burgundy which assumed that role.

In the first and longest phase, those who directed the process had no sense of the final outcome. They were driven by domestic challenge and external threat to build a powerful State, with the mechanisms for raising resources to finance it, but without a powerful State being the intention (let alone what was to come later, popular participation and a general nationalism).

Rivalries and domestic threats meant war: 'War made the State, and the State made war'.[3] War, whether against domestic rebels or external threats, meant armed forces and armaments, and the financing of these prodigious costs meant that much of the time and energy of the Monarch's developing bureaucracies were devoted to raising funds for this purpose, securing access to the surplus generated within society. In the first instance, this was exceedingly difficult. Labour productivity in the overwhelmingly preponderant sector of society, subsistence agriculture, was very low, so any net surplus was small. Furthermore, it was difficult both to secure part of the surplus from self-supporting peasant households (with a rather low participation in any monetary economy) and to do so on a fair basis, that is, one which did not provoke revolt. In the early days, transport was difficult and expensive, markets too constrained to dispose of taxes in kind, and there were few outside sources of funding (external borrowing, assets to be expropriated). Moreover, even when funds were available, the peasantry refused to fight for the monarch: and this was true even with the growth of an expropriated landless labouring class. Royal armies thus depended upon mercenaries – even as late as the battle of Waterloo in 1815, over half the army of Napoleon was not French, and half that of Wellington (excluding the forces of Blücher) was not English.

The growth of labour productivity and commercialization eased some of these problems. But it was the industrial revolution which transformed the situation, by its effect on the size of the surplus, by the completion of a monetary economy (so making the surplus accessible to State appropriation), and also by making possible a popular participation in which people resented tax-paying less and were willing to fight. Arms spending and the size of armies soared.

The process of securing resources for war obsessed monarchs and their officers in the earlier periods. It was an unremitting struggle that led to the overriding, abolition, co-optation or subordination of the inherited liberties and assemblies of society – vested in manors, villages, communities, provinces and estates – to achieve an unprecedented degree of centralization in the leading power in this respect, France. The State allied with different segments of the population against the rest, all the time increasing its control, until it had funds sufficient to exercise direct coercion. Where it could, it expropriated resources by simple edict. It promoted economic activities to free or create resources for its own purposes, bribed and was bribed, all with the continuing preoccupation of creating an independent public force, loyal solely to the Crown, and of an effectiveness capable of matching any rival force in Europe. Innovations in military and naval technology – of which there were an increasing number as time passed – further increased the burdens to be imposed upon the population at large.

The alliances and compromises, the sales of offices and titles, all the shifts and feints required of the Crown to secure a continuing coalition had, however, an important adverse effect: corruption, the leakage of the resources garnered with such painful persistence (and often brutality) into private hands. Trevor-Roper puts it in this way:[4]

> The Renaissance State consisted, at bottom, of an ever-expanding bureaucracy which, although at first a working bureaucracy, had by the end of the sixteenth century become a parasitic bureaucracy; and this ever expanding bureaucracy was sustained on an equally expanding margin of 'waste': 'waste' which lay between the taxes imposed on the subjects and the revenue collected by the Crown. Since the Crown could not afford an absolute loss of revenue, it is clear that this expansion of the waste had to be at the expense of society. It is clear that it could be borne only if society itself were expanding in wealth and numbers.

Although kings made sporadic efforts to reform, to purge and reorganize, again ultimately only the nineteenth century brought the abundance which permitted a system to organize the State and curb some of the worst excesses.

People resisted these attempts. Increases in taxation and steps in the centralization of royal power (which usually went together) were the most important factors promoting rebellion. Thus, the English Tudors faced six major rebellions and countless minor revolts. The pace then slackened, perhaps because rising prosperity eased some of the burdens (and Henry VIII's expropriation of the Church lands and assets eased the constraints on the king). After 1600, there was a pause before the same issues emerged even more violently in the Civil War and led to the beheading of the king. In France, the bloody religious wars of the sixteenth century were fought partly against the arbitrary exercise of the royal prerogative. Richelieu faced some hundreds of mutinies and riots against royal innovations. Indeed, rebellion was intrinsic to the growth of State power up to the nineteenth century. There were times, however, when the difficulties were eased – when religious inspiration or tangible threats from abroad led people to commit both their resources and their persons to fight. But for most States, that only became feasible in the nineteenth century with the development of popular participation. Then resources and manpower became available on a scale coercion could never match – and one of government's major preoccupations became to control and guide popular attitudes and the process of socialization in order to ensure an adequate tax base and flow of manpower.

What began as a blind struggle to stabilize and expand the power of a small group of competitive monarchs in Western Europe threatened the rest of the principalities. The contest forced all to copy the process in part or whole sooner or later; State formation spread eastwards. The more power in Europe lay in the hands of a few strong States, the more a State system emerged in which the position of each was established through the recognition of the others. Perhaps the 1648 Treaty of Westphalia which ended the Thirty Years War was the first to acknowledge the emergence of an international order which legitimated State sovereignty. By the time of the Treaty of Vienna and the Concert of Europe, such a system had become formalized, and the Treaty of Versailles following the First World War brought in many more participants (and took power to create new States, like Czechoslovakia and Yugoslavia).

In the eighteenth and nineteenth centuries, the European powers forced the State system on the rest of the world, scooping up all available territories into empires. They did so, in the main, by mutual agreement, despite the simultaneous fierce rivalries. Finally, in the mid-twentieth century, the empires fragmented into a new and much wider State system. Thus, one could almost describe the period since the Roman Empire as one of alternating fusion and fission, each phase extending the geographical reach of the system more and more widely.

The later the process of formation of States, the less the importance of domestic factors in determining their creation. The aggressive creation of nation-States as part of a blind process of self-modernization, that ultimately produced popular nationalisms, could not be repeated. All others, in Europe and the rest of the world, reacted to this first step – national liberation became defensive, reactive. In the first phase, nationalism emerged as the result of State formation; in the second, the State was created as the result of a nationalist opposition to external competition or oppression. In the first phase, States created themselves in, as it were, a vacuum, a State-less environment. In all subsequent cases, national liberation was the route to enter an established system of States (which sanctioned the newcomer). In the end, the State system of our own times scarcely permits the fashioning of new territorial entities. The whole burden of competition now takes the form of rivalry for military and economic superiority and – with some exceptions – political domination short of expropriation.

Origins in Europe

The process of creating a nation was not simply the imposition of a single political authority over a territory. The sinews of political and economic integration required to enable the expanded raising of resources by the Crown took a long time to create. They included the extension of land communications, the establishment of an exchange economy, with markets and a single accepted currency, the standardization of the law and of a single language. The language had to be one accessible to more than the ruling elite, so it became one or other dialect of the vernacular. While this permitted access to public life by more of the natives (standard national education was required to give access to all), it excluded the Europe of Latin-speakers and the immediate inheritance of religion. The unity of medieval Catholicism began to dissolve in sub-European States and national churches. New commercial and urban classes emerged with a view of markets and polities going well beyond the district and, with the king's changing need for allies and finance, a degree of participation in public affairs. The stage was set for some alignment between the individual, a single political authority, and a single territory, culture and language: a passive patriotism that was defined by the existence of clear enemies abroad.

Whether the king's subjects were patriotic or not was, for the king, of marginal significance. What changed passive patriotism, an incidental by-product of the emerging political and economic order, into an important political factor was the need for popular support to wage war. This seems to have emerged with greatest sharpness in an area marked simultaneously by the most advanced commercial wealth in Europe and the absence of an established State: the seventeen provinces of the Low Countries, the possessions of the Habsburg dynasty. The long struggle of the provinces against the most powerful ruler in Europe has perhaps the best claim to be the first war of national liberation. It was half defeated for, in the end, only the seven northern provinces secured national independence in the Dutch Republic.

The eighty years of war in the Netherlands were a turning point in European history. For they created, through struggle, something approaching a nation. Philip II, whose most important possession was Spain, endeavoured to reform his administration through greater centralization and to raise much greater funds from the prosperous trading cities of the Low Countries (particularly for his continuing struggle against the Ottoman Sultans, and secondarily, against the French monarchs). This task entailed a reduction – and even abolition – of the traditional corporate liberties of the cities. Philip thus forced upon the Netherlanders a degree of unity which had hitherto not existed. Part of the process was interwoven with the Counter-Reformation: Philip's Catholicism, his court and his Spanish armies and administrators became a further instrument of oppression that unified and heightened the Protestantism of the rebels (the Inquisition was thus a means of imposing a homogeneity upon Philip's subjects, the better to subordinate them to a uniform governance). Finally, the exigencies of the struggle forced the conservative burghers of the Netherland cities to involve an increasing number of people in the provision of manpower and funds, so that they in turn claimed the right to participate in political life. The nature of the conflict obliged the city fathers to extend the membership of the 'nation' far beyond those who would customarily have been considered. In turn, this inhibited the power of the aristocracy and the urban oligarchies. Thus was a popular nationalism created, not by intention or design, but out of the exigencies of the struggle. In the end, to general astonishment, Europe's most powerful ruler was defeated by the vulgar city mobs.

Even before the struggle in the Low Countries was complete, yet another type of revolt took place in economically much more backward England (but an England closely preoccupied with the revolt across the sea since it affected the position of Protestant England relative to Catholic Spain and France). Once again, the immediate issues were the royal prerogative and the high tax burdens entailed by the monarch's profligate spending. Under the leadership of part of the gentry, the forces of Parliament, the urban classes and part of the better-off peasantry defeated – and executed – the king. More than ever before, this was a war in which one side was strongly supported by the mass of the population at large, sufficiently so for the New Model Army to be recruited from the mass of the peasantry in selected regions and to aspire to a meritocratic, rather than aristocratic, officer corps.

The struggle for unification of the opposition in the Netherlands had been difficult, but at least there a much more substantial commercial class could simultaneously fight the Habsburgs and prevent the outbreak of class war. In England, a military dictatorship was required to protect the existing social order. It left no heirs. Only a king could inherit what Cromwell had defended, albeit a king under much closer restrictions than ever before.

The revolts in the Low Countries and in England challenged the nature of dynastic power and the modernizing State. They also raised the issues of religious freedom and popular participation (although the participation was limited to the propertied). The struggle, however, was most often seen as a defence of traditional liberties, not of 'liberty' itself. Over a century later, in Britain's American colonies, what began as a defence of traditional rights against the attempts by the British Crown to impose new taxation, became an affirmation of universal and secular liberty – the rights of man.

The doctrine of now universal liberation received its most dramatic affirmation in the French revolution of 1789. Its prophet, Jean-Jacques Rousseau, proclaimed the right of all people to express their *national* character through the exercise of political sovereignty in a government of their own. The nation existed prior to the State, was the source of its authority and the independent judge of its actions. Of course, by 'nation' Rousseau meant no more than the people in a locality as opposed to what the word came to mean, the inhabitants of an established State. However, the claim to universal liberty was the justification of Napoleon's attempt to conquer Europe, not the right of France to control the Continent (on the other hand, Napoleon's armies did little to change the inherited social structure of the areas they conquered).

In the French revolution, as in its American and English forerunners, a new revolutionary current was emerging in the opposition to the dynasty. This was opposed, not simply to kings and aristocrats, but to the propertied minority. In all three revolutions, however, the established order was able to curb such communist aspirations. In practice, it was not the majority of the people who were to inherit power, but those who qualified by the ownership of property; the 'people' had not yet come to include all inhabitants. And by 1830 in France the two currents had parted – the powerful and propertied recognized the unpropertied as a graver threat than what was left of the old order. The causes of bourgeois democracy and socialism parted company.

In the principalities of what, under the hegemony of Prussia, was to become Germany, the impact of the French revolution and of Napoleon was considerable. On the one hand, the doctrine of the rights of man raised high hopes of universal freedom. On the other, the French threat made urgent the need to create a united German State, regardless of popular freedom. Indeed, Herder could argue for a popular State without democratic mechanisms.

Almost simultaneous with the outbreak of the French revolution, the three Great Powers of East and Central Europe, the Tsar, the Austro-Hungarian Emperor and the King of Prussia, repartitioned Poland. For the tiny minority of nationalist rebels in Europe at that time, this was a horrifying act of dynastic power, imposed on what had been an ancient and important State with no reference to the wishes of the inhabitants. The French revolution and the Napoleonic armies helped to spread the concepts and values required to constitute a Polish nationalism among a section of the Polish nobility in exile. Throughout the nineteenth century, the struggle to reconstitute Poland was a touchstone for liberals and socialists alike, a focus for national liberation in general. Lord Acton, writing much later in a significant nationalist metaphor, deplored a partition which created a nation demanding to be united in a State, 'a soul, as it were, wandering in search of a body in which to begin life over again'.[5] The truth was a little more prosaic. When, in 1846, the Polish aristocracy in Western Galicia, pre-eminent representatives of the *ancien régime*, endeavoured to interest their peasant tenants in the national struggle, the latter rose in revolt and slaughtered nearly one thousand of the nobles. For them class remained the decisive issue.

The contradictory currents of national liberation reached a crescendo in the great European upsurge of 1848. The challenge to the accepted claims of the major national liberation movements came not only from the unpropertied, but also from lesser movements; the Germans, the Poles, the Hungarians, the Italians found their claims undermined by those who felt themselves oppressed by these dominant peoples. Many of the nationalists abandoned the hopes of a popular movement, and in subsequent years came to rely upon forces other than popular struggle: Bismarck and the rulers of Prussia, and the House of Savoy.

Thus, at what seemed its moment of greatest triumph, popular national liberation foundered. The Frankfurt Assembly showed less the strength of the German middle class, more its vulnerability to the demands of the unpropertied and therefore its equivocation on the issue of democracy and its dependence on the armed power of Prussia and Austria. The princes of the German principalities saw no reason why a shared set of dialects should be grounds for superseding their sovereignty. Friedrich Wilhelm of Prussia refused the German Crown offered him by the Frankfurt Assembly because it was offered by 'Liberals and Jews' and because he felt his cousin in Vienna had a better claim.

After 1848, the popular movement declined. Ambitious princes began to recognize the value of nationalism for an extension of their own claims, rather than those of popular democracy. Thus, German unification was achieved not by revolution, but by the political ingenuity of Bismarck and the arms of Prussia. The *Realpolitik* of Berlin detached the definition of the new Germany from Germanism – it did not include all Germans nor did it exclude non-Germans. The Reich, the Lesser Germany, was primarily a concept of power, unified by the Hohenzollern dynasty, not of language, culture or any supposed common descent.

For much of the period and up to the First World War, the targets of the largest movements of national liberation were the two great empires of Eastern and Central Europe – that of the Romanovs in the Russias and of the Habsburgs in Austro-Hungary. In both cases, the nineteenth century witnessed movements for the cultural identification and assertion of many of the subject peoples, without these inevitably producing demands for secession. That was almost invariably provoked by the actions of the dynasts themselves. One can thus trace the development of the first waves of nationalism in Austro-Hungary to the reforms of Joseph II (reigning from 1760 to 1790). With heightened competition between the Great Powers, the emperor, in an effort to rationalize his ramshackle domains, instituted a greater degree of centralization by overriding traditional claims, and enhanced the tax base of the imperial government. Part of the process of creating a modern State was to replace the *lingua franca*, Latin, with a vernacular, and German, the language of Vienna, was selected. But German was the speech of the ruling minority and therefore coincided with power and privilege. In particular, the Magyar gentry saw themselves placed at a disadvantage compared with German-speakers at the same time as their historic liberties were threatened. Thus, the reforms started a course which was the precise opposite of the emperor's intention – moves to resist centralization, indeed, to secure greater decentralization, a process which ultimately led to the division of the empire in a Dual Monarchy, and ultimately its disintegration in the First World War.

The Magyar gentry itself ruled many peoples whose native tongue was not Hungarian. It also ruled a Hungarian peasantry whose tongue might be Hungarian, but whose material conditions were no less wretched than those of their Croat, Serb, Slovak and Romanian counterparts. The Magyar response to Vienna's imposition of German was to try to enforce upon their non-Hungarian-speaking subjects the use of Hungarian. Louis Kossuth (1802–94), the Magyar leader, combined, in Seton-Watson's words, 'unrealistic benevolence and national intolerance':[6] since the non-Hungarians possessed a culture inferior to the Hungarian, they could not be accorded the same privileges as the Magyars; however, they should be encouraged to become Hungarian as swiftly as possible.

The non-Hungarians, inspired by a considerable and ancient hostility towards their Magyar overlords, were obliged to defend the use of their own languages against the Magyar attempt to eliminate them. Kossuth in turn endeavoured to create a much stronger popular nationalist alliance of classes on the basis of radical reforms. He promised an end to serfdom, reform of landholdings and an extension of the suffrage, a programme which in turn alienated an important part of the Magyar gentry and rendered them much more favourably disposed to suspending national demands in favour of outside intervention to protect existing social relationships. The intervention of the Tsar's armies closed the issue, and despatched Kossuth to exile.

There was a further intervention – by the Prussians – in 1866. It achieved the worst of all worlds, paralysing the empire without liberating new forces. The Dual Monarchy provided the Magyar gentry with self-government under a Habsburg ruler, leaving the subject peoples – the southern Slavs – as before.

The class issues at stake in Hungary were only one illustration of the conflict throughout the empires and in Europe generally. The middle classes led a host of new national movements – the large ones of the Germans, Poles, Magyars, Italians, but also now including a host of smaller peoples: Irish, Schleswig Danes, Czechs, Slovaks, Croats and Ruthenians. Other classes – peasants and now workers – were accepted only on the terms laid down by the leaders. Few peasants became involved, and the workers were frequently indifferent – or positively hostile, feeling that national struggles were ways of evading their own class demands. Class-based social democracy also grew during the period.

In the last two decades of the century, the context changed. The rivalry of the Great Powers now led all contenders to pursue the British, French and Dutch to the world beyond Europe, spreading empires to the limits of the globe. The right of national self-determination in Europe now rested upon the emphatic denial of that right to all lesser peoples. Nationalism now became imperialism.

Furthermore, within the Great Powers the contest coincided with the process of incorporating wider and wider sections of the population in the nation. The new methods of production now emerging required an educated labour force, who participated consciously in the process of production rather than playing the role of brute labour. Advance in labour productivity was beginning to depend upon the quality and involvement of the worker. Mass education, a popular press for the much larger literate audiences, extensions of the suffrage, the increasing political influence of trade unions and social democratic parties (with resulting public regulation of social and working conditions, health and safety), all drew the working classes into the mainstream of national life. Workers had to push hard to win these advances, but they could be won short of revolution. Right-wing social democrats drew the conclusion that material advances could be won indefinitely and therefore nothing extra was to be gained by open class struggle. A growing proportion of politically active workers were no longer without a country, as the Communist Manifesto had proclaimed. While this change was not the immediate source of the popular jingoism that swept the lower middle classes in Britain at the time of the Boer War, or later in all the Great Powers in 1914, nonetheless popular nationalism and imperialism were becoming factors in national politics.

The social democrats generally were not isolated from these changes. Despite disclaimers, Social Democracy in Germany was *German* Social Democracy, not simply a German component of an international class organization (as theory and the French maintained). It had come to represent important sections of socialized nations, mass societies, and in this responsible role social democrats were required to do their patriotic duty when war threatened 'their' ruling order. Thus did the social democrats betray their promise of a new world without war, and come to act as instruments for each ruling order: nationalism was the key ideological means of breaking the workers' challenge to the *status quo*. In fact, the social democrats secured the compliance of workers rather than their zealous support, but that was enough to safeguard the Establishments of most of Europe.

However, before the First World War it was not at all clear how far the social democratic movements had been subverted. The outbreak of war exposed the reality. The shock was greatest for those socialists who had believed the rhetoric of the International. Even elementary fraternity, the demand of the French revolution, let alone class solidarity, proved no match for loyalty to one or other State. Only on the ill-colonized perimeter of Europe were there exceptions (Russia, Bulgaria, Serbia, Ireland). In the empire of the Tsars, the twin revolutions offered such a strikingly different alternative that they overshadowed the remarkable changes elsewhere – the disintegration of the Habsburg and Ottoman empires, and the appearance of a host of new States. With those States came new nations, languages, and lovingly created cultures. For a moment, the world seemed less heartless.

3

MARX–ENGELS: THE SPRINGTIME OF NATIONALISM

*I*N comparison with our own times, Marx and Engels lived in a pre-nationalist age. (For the sake of simplicity, the two will be referred to here as 'Marx' unless otherwise specified.) European movements of national liberation were the most important forms of popular rebellion during their lifetime, but the intellectual atmosphere of mid-nineteenth-century London as well as their own convictions made it seem that nationalism was a temporary phase, and that internationalism was the norm, or at least the force that would grow most powerfully in the future. For capitalism daily unified the globe and created an international working class. Marx's internationalism paralleled what was identified by him as the leading sector of capitalism, the international.

However, he assumed that capitalism could not finally achieve an integrated world, that the bourgeoisie could never transcend nationality. That required the end of existing property relations which were national (and which involved 'the exploitation of some nations by others'). At most the bourgeoisie could embrace the 'hypocritical private cosmopolitanism of free trade'. Only the proletariat had no material interest in nationality; they possessed a 'brotherhood of the oppressed against the oppressors':[1]

> the proletarians of all countries have one and the same interest, one and the same enemy, and one and the same struggle. The great mass of the proletarians are, by their nature, free from national prejudice and their whole disposition and movement is essentially humanitarian, anti-nationalist. Only the proletarians

can destroy nationality.

Marx's starting point for both analysis and strategy was a world system, not one or other country. National movements were never ends in themselves, only stepping-stones to a liberated world order. The task of the proletariat was to emancipate humanity, not a particular country. And the progress of capitalism itself eliminated all intermediate divisions between the individual and his or her world class; nations, like estates, provinces, religions, families, would all be superseded:[2]

> only then will the separate individuals be liberated from the various national and local barriers, be brought into practical connection with the material and intellectual product of the whole world and be put in a position to acquire the capacity to enjoy this all-sided product of the whole earth, the creations of man. All-round dependence, this natural form of the world historical co-operation of individuals, will be transformed by this communist revolution into control and conscious mastery of these powers.

However, much of Europe, let alone the world at large, was economically backward. Neither bourgeoisie nor working class was significant. Here the immediate struggle was to establish the political form, the national State, within which capitalism could flourish. This required the break-up of the multinational empires of East and Central Europe which not only controlled their own peoples but intervened throughout Europe to protect the *ancien régime*.

The aim, therefore, was both to create new centres of national capitalism and to neutralize the capacity to obstruct this process of the three dominant powers of backward Europe – the Tsars, the Habsburg emperors, and the monarchs of Prussia (the three were interlocked in the tripartite division of Poland). To stand against the old order, the new national States would have to be strong – 'The very first conditions of national existence [are] large numbers and compactness of territory,' along with resources, ability and a favourable social organization.[3] Engels elaborated:[4]

> There could, indeed, be no two opinions as to the right of every one of the great national subdivisions of Europe to dispose of itself, independently of its neighbours in all internal matters, so long as it did not encroach upon the liberty of others. The right was, in fact, one of the fundamental conditions of the internal liberty of all.

Thus, the right of national self-determination applied only to 'the large and well-defined historical nations of Europe . . . Italy, Poland, Germany, Hungary'.[5]

No such right generally applied to the rest. The selection of those who might have the right varied according to immediate tactics but, in general, Engels reserved his most withering scorn – and violent prejudice – for 'non-historical peoples',[6]

> the ruins of peoples which are still found here and there and which are no longer capable of a national existence, are absorbed by the larger nations and either become part of them or maintain themselves as ethnographic monuments without political significance.

Thus, the right of the large nation could deny that of the small. In the same way, the capacity of the British to accelerate development vindicated their expropriation of India (the same principle justified the French seizure of Algeria and the North American annexation of northern Mexico). Marx was merciless in his indictment of the horrors inflicted upon subject peoples by British imperialism, but without repudiating the general right of the more advanced to develop the backward. However, he also argued that, under imperial initiative, the process of social transformation in India could not be complete without either a proletarian revolution in Britain or 'the Hindoos themselves . . . grown strong enough to throw off the English yoke altogether'.[7]

The viable nations of Europe were constituted by a line of cultural or linguistic descent, without this being an overriding principle or implying complete ethnic homogeneity. For Poland to be effective and block the Tsar's advance on Central Europe, it needed to be large. If restored to its 1772 boundaries, it would encompass a plurality of peoples (including some millions of Ukrainians and White Russians). Lands historically occupied by Germans would be included, but in time they would become Polish. In fact, all European countries were likely to have more than one nationality within their frontiers and often people of the same nationality would live in several countries. There were no grounds for redrawing borders; 'The Germans of Switzerland and Alsace do not desire to be reunited to Germany any more than the French in Belgium and Switzerland wish to become attached politically to France'.[8] Indeed, on occasions, the word 'nation' was used by Engels to refer to the inhabitants of a State regardless of language, culture or ethnicity.[9]

Furthermore, while the support for the national claims of the large peoples of Europe might imply supporting social forces quite other than those of the proletariat – for example, the Polish aristocracy or the Magyar gentry – the national claims could not be won without revolution:[10]

> The great agricultural countries between the Baltic and the Black Sea can free themselves from patriarchal–feudal barbarism only through an agrarian revolution which will transform the peasants from their condition of serfdom or of subjection to the *corvée* into the free owners of the land – a revolution which will be exactly the same as the French revolution of 1789 in the countryside.

Moreover, insofar as a nationalist aristocracy fought for democracy, so they undermined their own privilege:[11]

> The men who led the Cracow revolutionary movement [the Polish insurrection of 1830] were deeply convinced that only a democratic Poland could be independent, and a democratic Poland was impossible without the abolition of feudal rights, without the agrarian movement which would transform the tied peasants into free proprietors.

This emphasis upon the revolutionary character of the struggle for national liberation raised other questions. Initially, Marx saw the establishment of proletarian power in Britain as the means to prosecute reforms in all other fields. The Chartist movement was therefore vital not just for power in Britain but throughout Europe and in India – 'Hence, Poland must be liberated not in Poland, but in England'.[12]

Marx and Engels were initially unsympathetic towards the cause of Irish freedom. The Chartists would liberate the Irish as a byproduct of their struggle for power in Britain. The English might have created the form of Irish oppression, Engels wrote in 1848, but the poverty was due to the temperament of the people. Thus the agitation to end the union with Britain would not achieve useful results:[13]

> Irish distress cannot be removed by any Act of Repeal. Such an Act would, however, at once lay bare the fact that the cause of Irish misery, which now seems to come from abroad, is really to be found at home.

Continuous oppression had made the Irish[14]

> a completely wretched nation, and now, as everyone knows, they have the job of providing England, America and Australia

etc. with whores, day labourers, pimps, pickpockets, swindlers, beggars and other wretches.

Even in 1848, the prejudice of the Irish – rather than the behaviour of the British – is blamed for their reluctance to see the Chartist movement as the means to their liberation:[15]

> there is a better chance now than ever before to break down that prejudice which prompted the Irish people to confound in one common hatred the oppressed classes of England with the oppressors of both countries.

There was, however, another principle at work. In 1843, Marx – writing on the Jewish question – argued that 'we must emancipate ourselves before we can emancipate others'.[16] He applied the same principle to the Germans, who had participated through the Prussians in the dismemberment of Poland. And it applied also to the Chartists – 'A nation cannot become free and at the same time continue to oppress other nations'. Once admitted, however, the principle could then also be applied to the Magyar treatment of the Croats, the Polish of Ruthenians, etc. The door was opened to a much more generalized right of national self-determination.

In the specific case of Ireland, the Chartists failed, but the Fenian movement for Irish independence burst out anew in the 1860s. Now, it seemed, the Irish struggle might ignite the British rather than vice versa. Marx reversed his position:[17]

> The English workers . . . must make the *Repeal of the Union* . . . an article of their *pronunziamento*. This is the only legal and therefore only possible form of Irish emancipation which can be admitted in the programme of an *English* party.

This was not primarily a gesture of support for, or solidarity with, the Irish. It was necessary if the English were to emancipate themselves:[18]

> the English working class . . . can never do anything decisive here in England until it separates its policy with regard to Ireland in the most definite way from the policy of the ruling class, until it not only makes common cause with the Irish, but actually takes the initiative in dissolving the Union established in 1801, and replacing it by a federal relationship. And, indeed, this must be done, not as a matter of sympathy with Ireland, but as a demand made in the interest of the English proletariat.

Or again:[19]

It is in the direct and absolute interest of the English working class to get rid of their present connection with Ireland . . . For a long time, I believed that it would be possible to overthrow the Irish regime by English working class ascendancy . . . Deeper study has convinced me of the opposite. The English working class will never accomplish anything before it has got rid of Ireland . . . The lever must be applied in Ireland.

Thus the more backward could liberate the advanced (a point subsequently of great importance for the Bolsheviks), a 'non-historical' people an historical one. Now the national and agrarian revolution, the transition to capitalism, could set off the proletarian revolution, the transition to socialism. The change was profound. The reasons for it were several – the overthrow of world capitalism depended upon an English proletarian revolution which, it was now argued, could only be initiated at Britain's weakest point, Ireland. Here, the agrarian issue was explosive, a matter of life and death for the Irish peasantry and crucial for Anglo-Irish landlordism. Thus, revolution on the land was interwoven with the issue of Irish liberation from the English gentry. However, it was also vital to free the English workers from the effect of the British control of Ireland:[20]

The ordinary English worker hates the Irish worker as a competitor who lowers his standard of life. In relation to the Irish worker, he feels himself a member of the *ruling nation* and so turns himself into a tool of the aristocrats and capitalists of his country *against Ireland*, thus strengthening their domination *over himself*. He cherishes religious, social and national prejudices against the Irish worker. His attitude towards him is much the same as that of the 'poor white' to the 'niggers' in the former slave states of the U.S.A. . . . This *antagonism* is the *secret of the impotence of the English working class*, despite its organisation. It is the secret by which the capitalist class maintains its power. And that class is fully aware of it.

Thus Marx identified the already well-advanced process of the 'nationalization' of English workers which was to cause such a shock in 1914.

In sum, 'any nation that oppresses another, forges its own chains'.[21] Colonialism enslaved the colonialist. Or as Engels meditated, 'Irish history shows one what a misfortune it is for a nation to have subjugated another nation. All the abominations of the English have their origin in the Irish Pale'.[22]

Poland and Ireland were therefore the two key points for the transformation of the European system of power, each a battering ram against the most backward and the most advanced Great Power, at opposite ends of Europe. Internationalism required that two thoroughly nationalistic and non-socialist movements be given complete support. For, as Engels wrote to Kautsky in 1882, both movements had 'not only the right but even the duty to be nationalistic before they become internationalistic ... they are most internationalistic when they are genuinely nationalistic'.[23]

The attitude to national liberation, however, remained entirely instrumental. Support for the Irish as a means to liberate the English remained consistent. But not so for the Magyars who had been so praised in 1848, 'an obscure semibarbarous people ... still standing in the half-civilization of the sixteenth century'.[24] And even the Polish issue was a contingent one:[25]

> The Poles are *une nation foutue* who can only continue to serve a purpose until such time as Russia herself becomes caught up into the agrarian revolution. From that moment Poland will have absolutely no *raison d'être* any more. The Poles' sole contribution to history has been to indulge in foolish pranks, at once valiant and provocative. Nor can a single moment be cited when Poland, even if only in comparison with Russia, has successfully represented progress or done anything of historical significance.

Engels always found it difficult to control the wild swings of his enthusiasms.

In the same light, Marx opposed national independence when it came through non- or anti-revolutionary means. Thus, despite all the effort he had devoted to the cause of German unification, he opposed it when it came through the force of Prussian arms and Bismarckian diplomacy. For the Kaiser's Germany, he said, would strengthen both the position of the Tsar and reaction in Europe generally.[26]

Marx was also sensitive – as in the case of the English and Irish – to the affirmation of Great Power nationalism in the guise of internationalism. It was, as we shall see, a recurrent problem among social democrats. Thus, at one stage in the meetings of the first International (September 1864), the followers of the French socialist, Proudhon, opposed any movements for national independence on the grounds that the concept of the nation was already obsolete. When Lafargue, a Proudhonist, argued later that nationalities were 'antiquated superstitions', Marx teased him gently by replying that 'by his denial of nationalities, he quite unconsciously understood their absorption in a model French nation'.[27] Engels elaborated the case:[28]

If members of a conquering nation called upon the nation they had conquered and continued to hold down to forget their specific nationality and position, to 'sink national differences' and so forth, that was not internationalism, it was nothing else but preaching to them submission to the yoke, and attempting to justify and perpetuate the domination of the conqueror under the cloak of internationalism.

On the other hand, the internationalism of the patriot, Lassalle's approach, Marx denounced as the 'international brotherhood of peoples' (that is, nations were primary), not class solidarity across borders.

In their long lives, Marx and Engels faced many different contexts and drew necessarily different tactical conclusions. The danger in quoting fragments of their writings out of context is that this may distort their intention and produce a static picture. But change they did, and quite radically. In 1848, Engels was completely insensitive to the complicated class issues of the Austro-Hungarian empire, subordinating all to the fate of Magyars, Poles and Italians and the need to stop Russia. All others were reduced to the 'non-historical', the rubbish of ages bound to be swept into one or other Great Power but, in the short term, dangerous instruments of the Tsar or the Habsburgs. All Slavs except the Poles became 'Panslavists'. Perversely, it was Marx's anarchist adversary, Michael Bakunin, who displayed greater sensitivity not only to the position of the Slavs in 1848, but also to the close relationship of nationalism and peasant radicalism at that time – 'I demand only one thing: that every people, that every tribe, great and small, be given the full opportunity and right to act according to its will'.[29] And to Engels' accusation of Panslavism, he replied:[30]

Panslavs are, in the eyes of Germans, all Slavs who, with anger and contrariness refuse the culture which they (the Germans) wish to force upon them. If that is the sense they give to the word 'Panslavism', oh! then I am a Panslav.

However, by about 1870, the differences had grown very much less. In 1848, Engels had viewed Europe as a general, deploying as his armies subject peoples to lock up the gendarme of Europe, Tsarist Russia. After 1848, the Tsar's forces were, relative to his rivals, increasingly technically backward; he was less and less able to intervene as gendarme. But for Marx and Engels the discovery of Ireland changed the motivation, not simply the strategic balance. The principle of the right of national self-determination was then extended much more widely. For now Great Nations must free themselves by releasing peoples they oppressed, not simply assimilate them, and that would have to include Engels' non-historic peoples. At the age of 70 (in 1890), Engels reflected on the coming break-up of the European empires and the liberation of many of those for whom, in 1848, he had seen only assimilation:[31]

> Magyars, Roumanians, Serbs, Bulgars, Arnauts (Albanians), Greeks and Turks will then finally be in a position to settle their own mutual disputes without the intervention of foreign powers, to settle among themselves the bounds of their individual national territories, to manage their internal affairs according to their own judgement.

The issues at stake – the strategic balance of forces in Europe, both States and classes – were complex; so also were Marx's purposes. In his lifetime, nationalism was appropriated by the ruling orders as imperialism, a denial of democracy. The national independence of both Germany and Italy came not through agrarian revolution, but through the force of arms of established powers. Nationalism did not now overthrow orders, it seemed to make them stronger. Thus, the political approach had to be changed.

Even so, it was never again to be so easy. For later generations, the nationalism of the established powers contended with a host of rebellions of the 'non-historic peoples' in an extraordinarily complicated national mixture, the surface of even more complex and divergent class and other interests. The closer the revolutionaries came to immediate issues and tactics in such a context, the greater the strain in reconciling internationalism and nationalism.

4

THE HEYDAY
OF THEORY

*T*HE world of the second half of the nineteenth century was very different from that which had existed before 1848. Then it might have seemed that, despite the setbacks of that year, popular national liberation would ultimately lead to a Europe modelled on the most advanced powers, Britain, France, Holland and the rest: nation States, administered by popularly elected governments and founded in free-trade capitalism. The reality was the creation of competitive world empires, the essence of which was a *denial* of the right of the majority of the peoples of the world to national self-determination, let alone to popularly elected governments. Perversely progress had brought the leading powers back to the position of the backward, the empires of the Romanovs and Habsburgs: 'prisons of peoples'. If Marx were right – that colonialism enslaved the colonizing power – then the slaves had come to be loaded with even heavier chains.

There was a further result of much greater importance for the future. The Great Powers had been continually driven by the competition among themselves, but in the last decades of the nineteenth century their intensified rivalries included a host of newcomers – Germany and Italy, the two newest Great Powers in Europe, and, close behind, the United States and, in the Far East, Japan. This led to an extension of Great Power domination to much of the rest of the world. Furthermore, even the archaic powers that had not started from the position of being nation-States were forced to compete; the Tsars thrust their reach eastwards to block the British advance in Asia, to stop the other Europeans in China, and finally to try to halt the westward movement of Japan. The Great Powers thus pressed their territorial control outwards to encompass for the first time virtually the whole surface of the globe, to centralize the world on a few centres of power.

Not all were convinced that empire was the right policy. Leading politicians in Britain, particularly in the mid-nineteenth century Liberal Party, scorned the imperial enterprise as no more than a way of offering the unemployable aristocracy a means to enrich itself at heavy cost to the innocent. The young Disraeli, later to be the chief manager of the Victorian imperial pageant, deplored the colonies as 'millstones round our neck'. But by 1890 the competition imposed on the world by Britain and its nearest rivals in north-western Europe had returned a hundredfold, and there no longer seemed a possibility of escape: if the British did not colonize, others would, and at British expense. Like the theory of the market in which firms have no choice but to compete if they are to survive, now States were similarly obliged to emulate each other.

Furthermore, empire now had a domestic political function. The incorporation of the mass of the population in the nation supplied an appreciative audience and, in certain circumstances, enthusiastic recruits for imperial adventures, provided they could be presented as noble rather than money-making enterprises. If every inhabitant was now to become a citizen and without the former property qualification, empire provided a vicarious property qualification for the Master Race. In addition, the social imperialists held that empire was the means to secure and enhance working-class living standards and employment in the metropolitan country, and so deflect revolution. It was not merely a Bolshevik view that empire was the source of a quiescent working class.

There was yet another result, of even greater importance for the future. The Great Powers imposed upon countless peoples demarcated territories with separate administrations, authorities which ultimately created quite new identities. Furthermore, with the conquerors came an aggressive nationalism (and racialism) to justify their right to rule. This in turn invoked a defensive nationalism in the subordinate peoples. It was the same in the old empires. The Tsars, the Habsburgs and the Ottomans sought to rationalize and industrialize their ramshackle empires in order to protect themselves against the expansionism of the modern West European State. They thus invoked a host of resistances, the nucleus for new nationalisms. There seemed no end to the knock-on effects – the Magyar attempt to resist Vienna provoked the development of nationalism among Croats, Serbs, Roumanians and more. In Russia, the 1905 revolution served notice of many more newcomers, restless beneath the yoke of the Tsars – Finns, Poles, Ukrainians, Byelorussians, Georgians, Armenians. There were also the first beginnings of an Islamic nationalism in the Russian Middle East. This last force emerged parallel to the revolt of the Young Turks in the heart of the Ottoman domains, the Persian Constitutional revolution of 1906 and the beginnings of national feeling among some of the Arabs. Further afield, the Indian National Congress was already beginning to grope towards a national identity, as was the Sarekat Islam in the great Dutch empire of the East Indies. The fall of the Manchus in China hinted at the far wider rebellion that would mark the first half of the twentieth century, transforming world political geography from a handful of empires, maps on which only the primary colours were needed to show each domain, to a mass of independent States, more numerous than the ingenuity of any distinguishable colour range.

All that was for the future. Few envisaged what was to come, for there were more pressing problems. As the socialists ceased to be politically irrelevant sects and emerged as worker armies, the violence in the air reflected the contest both of the classes and of the Great Powers, set, it seemed, inexorably on the lunatic road to 1914. The system seemed doomed. For the Left, imperialism was the decomposing form of a capitalism no longer capable of its historic role of forcing progress on humanity.

The socialists of the Great Powers dominated the second International. Internationalist rhetoric prevailed, providing a cover for an increasingly nationalist reality. After the establishment of an independent Germany and Italy, it was assumed that the national question, as a progressive issue, was now past in Europe; only reactionaries would continue to try to resurrect it. For the colonies of the European empires it was not over, but independence there would come after the victory of the working classes in Europe. Some even promoted the idea of an enlightened socialist administration of the colonies – 'until the Federation of the world becomes an accomplished fact, we must accept the most responsible imperial federations available as a substitute for it'(George Bernard Shaw).[1]

It was in Poland, part of the uncompleted business of the old empires, that this complacency was challenged. By the 1870s, the aristocratic leadership of Polish nationalism had been finally defeated. Poland was becoming the most industrialized part of the Tsar's empire, and the business classes, as represented in the National Democrats, were strongly committed to remaining part of this imperial market. Only the intelligentsia remained loyal to the idea of an independent Poland.

In 1881 a socialist organization was formed with a mainly intellectual leadership, and it was obliged to confront the possibility of the recreation of Poland out of the territories held by the Tsar (the part known as the Kingdom of Poland), the Habsburgs and the Hohenzollerns of Prussia. There were plenty of supporting arguments in the works of Marx and Engels for such an endeavour. In 1892, the party majority led by Pilsudski opted for opposition to capitalism *and* support for an independent Poland. A small minority, led by

Rosa Luxemburg, Radek and Leo Jogiches, opposed the second demand.

The two groups undertook preliminary skirmishes at the Zurich Congress of the International in 1893. The Luxemburg group was defeated and its claim to the official affiliation to the International rejected; it became the Social Democratic Party of the Kingdom of Poland, as opposed to the majority, the Polish Socialist Party, PSP. To clinch its victory, the PSP tabled a resolution for the London Congress of the International in 1896, affirming the right of Poland to national self-determination. The British chairman, George Lansbury, closed the issue for the moment with a compromise resolution which settled nothing; it affirmed 'the full right of all nations to self-determination' and urged workers of all countries to 'join together to defeat international capitalism and achieve social democracy'.

Social democracy and colonialism

The Polish quarrel served notice that the national question in Europe was by no means over. However, even where it was acknowledged to be still relevant – in the colonies of the European empires – the Congress of the International was no more clear. The traditional position was a straight condemnation of colonialism as robbery (as in resolutions to be passed at Mainz in 1900 and Paris in 1901). But the growing tempo of competition between the Great Powers, particularly for imperial possessions, changed the atmosphere. When the British were attacked for their role in the Boer War, Hyndman and Quelch for the British Social Democratic Federation prepared a dossier on the crimes of other imperial powers as the basis for condemning all – and so exonerating the British as no worse than the rest.

Others began to develop a countercase. At Amsterdam in 1904, a Dutch delegate, Van Kol, threw down the gauntlet – 'The new needs which will make themselves felt after the victory of the working class and its economic emancipation will make the possession of colonies necessary, even under the future socialist system of government.' The need for tropical products, for outlets for exports and surplus population and to offset 'the deadly competition of colonial labour', all entailed rethinking the old position. 'Can we abandon half the globe to the caprice of peoples still in their infancy . . .? Must we not understand by socialization of the means of production that the means of living and working belong to everyone?'[2] His report was not accepted.

Within the German Social Democratic Party the issue had been in dispute for some time. In 1887, Kautsky, who was to become the most authoritative exponent of Marxism, gave what became the official account of the economic basis for modern nationalism – the drive to create a unified market for capitalist development. He also reaffirmed the continuing need to oppose German expansionism. Another famous Marxist, Edouard Bernstein – who was to lead the right wing of Social Democracy – began to challenge this position in 1890. It was at this stage that he sought to qualify the right of national self-determination even in the colonies – 'to support savages and barbarians', he wrote in *Neue Zeit*,[3] 'who resist the penetration of capitalist civilization would be romantic'. Later he praised the role of the British in India as a civilizing force; Indian poverty was the result of excessive breeding.[4] A subsequent collection of writings affirmed the right of the more civilized to appropriate the lands of the less:[5]

> It is neither necessary that the occupation of tropical lands by Europeans should injure the natives in their enjoyment of life nor has it hitherto usually been the case. Moreover, only a conditional right of savages to the land occupied by them could be recognized. The higher civilization ultimately can claim a higher right. Not the conquest but the cultivation of the land gives the historical legal title to its use.

Later on, for example at the Party Congress of 1907, the right-wing faction, of which Bernstein was one of the leading members, proposed to approve German colonial expansion on the grounds that this promoted a progressive capitalism and harmonized relationships between classes in Germany. The faction never won a majority, but the party was increasingly circumspect in appearing unpatriotic. In substance, if not in theory, the German Social Democrats had by 1912 become a patriotic party, with only moderate criticisms of German expansionism.

Efforts were made to nudge the International in the same direction. A special committee was created for the 1907 Congress, and the irrepressible Van Kol again proposed a 'positive colonial policy', affirming that 'under a socialist regime, colonization can be a work of civilization'. A German delegate, Edouard David, accepted the principle of colonization on the apparently sound internationalist basis that 'the occupation and exploitation of the entire world are indispensable for the well-being of humanity . . . Europe needs colonies. It does not have enough of them.'

Another delegate objected that all colonization was 'necessarily capitalistic and thus exploitative', but a French delegate, Rouanet, reproached him: 'it is all too easy to blame everything on capitalism and to saddle it with all the crimes of colonization. This is not a capitalistic but an historical phenomenon.' Van Kol's resolution won a majority of the committee, but not of the Congress. There it was defeated by 127 to 108 votes (with ten abstentions), but with the benefit of hindsight the size of the opposition showed the way opinion was moving.[6]

The Austro-Marxists

A different approach to the reconciliation of socialism and empire occurred in the Austrian Social Democratic Party. As we have seen, the internal nationalist tensions of the Austro-Hungarian empire became severe in the second half of the nineteenth century. To this were added the effects of the transformation of the social structure by industrialization and urbanization in the more advanced areas (Austria, the Czech lands, etc.). Vienna's population of half a million in 1864 had become 2 million by 1914. Industrialization created for the first time a new political force in the mass of factory workers. Fierce repression failed to eliminate the growing strength of the Social Democrats, and in 1887, after decades of faction fighting, the groups came together at the Hainfeld Congress to form a single multinational party under the foremost Social Democrat, Victor Adler. With unity and growing legal tolerance, the party, like its fraternal party in Germany, grew swiftly. At the first May Day demonstration in Vienna in 1890, 200,000 marchers emerged into the public arena. Furthermore, in the great flowering of Viennese intellectual life which occurred in the last decade of the nineteenth century, the party contributed a galaxy of famous intellectuals – Karl Kautsky (who, through his journal, *Neue Zeit*, and his role in the German party, became the most influential Marxist of his time), Victor Adler himself and his mentor, Carl Gruneberg, Max Adler, Otto Bauer, Rudolf Hilferding, Karl Renner etc.

However, the national issue was a continuing line of sharp rocks for the frail craft of Social Democracy. Separate national autonomies had appeal for those with some stake in society, the lower-middle classes, craft and some skilled workers; the right wing gravitated towards peaceful reform and nationalism, while the left endeavoured to hold hard to revolution and a working-class unity that would cut horizontally across the empire. However, what the emperor could not achieve in neutralizing the working-class challenge, the right-wing Social Democrats did for him.

Nor, as theory suggested, was it the industrially more backward parts that resisted a Viennese leadership. From the beginning, many of the Czechs, with strong links to the trade unions of skilled and craft workers, resented both the German domination of the heart of the empire and the close links of the Czech bourgeoisie to Vienna (just as the Polish Socialists attacked the links of Polish employers to St Petersburg). A majority of the Czech party called for autonomy, and when Adler resisted this, split away. (Kautsky warned them that capitalism now required large international markets with a single language which, in the Habsburg domains, would best be German; retaining Czech would lead to the economic decline of the Czech people.) The break was a signal to the rest, the Poles, Ukrainians, Italians, Slovenes and others. Only the Germans remained 'internationalist'.

The frictions grew steadily worse, and in an attempt to accommodate them the 1897 Vienna Congress resolved that the party become a federation of six national parties. A joint central committee and joint congresses endeavoured to secure some co-ordination. Whatever the pleasure at 'new experiments', the party in effect gave in to nationalism and the social forces it represented. However, the remedy did not settle the issue, and at the 1899 Brno Congress it was again in hot dispute. By now few proposals could be judged on their merits, only according to which national group put them forward (or rather, each proposal was identified as if it were no more than the product of a national group). The Germans argued for increased centralization in order to fight the empire. The Southern Slavs argued for 'personal cultural autonomy' – that is, the inhabitants of the empire would be grouped according to culture (regardless of where they lived), and their cultural–educational affairs directed by an elected national council.[7] The final compromise proposed a federation of self-governing territories, defined by nationality, the scattered territories of each nationality to be united in a national council with complete authority in the affairs of that nationality (which were defined as cultural and linguistic). Economic and political matters remained at the level of the imperial government.

The compromise only fuelled national frictions. After the 1907 elections, the national components of the party operated increasingly independently. Thus, the workers' movement was already showing the disintegration which was fully accomplished in the destruction of the empire in the First World War.

There were two leading theoreticians of nationalism in the German section of the party (although both published their main works well after the Brno Congress). Karl Renner (1870–1950) was on the right of the party. For him, nations were the fundamental building blocks of society, 'both indestructible and undeserving of destruction . . . Far from being unnational or anti-national, [Social Democracy] places nations at the foundation of its world structure.' Nations would not dissolve with the coming of socialism and the abolition of the bourgeoisie. However, in the short term there was a problem because economic development led necessarily to the integration of territories, and this threatened the much smaller areas which coincided with nationalities. The economy demanded multinational States, so that nationality could no longer be a 'State-forming' principle. Nonetheless, nationalism continued and incited collisions between nations instead of 'the orderly procedure of court and parliamentary transactions'.[8] This blocked the advance to socialism – 'the awakening proletariat is seized by a naive nationalism, fortified by class hatred, and this obstructs, for a long time, the penetration of socialist ideas'.[9] It also fortified imperialist competition: each Great Power rival was now backed by popular support. The remedy was to separate the essence of national life (a language and a culture) from the organization of economic activity, and embody it in a separate institution. For Austria, Renner proposed eight national governments in Vienna to administer the cultural affairs of each nationality, eight socio-economic bodies administering economic regions (covering several nationalities), four agricultural administrations and a supreme federal power under the Crown (responsible for foreign and military affairs, joint finance, economic and social welfare and justice). Implicitly, the programme was one for the reform of the existing empire rather than its overthrow.

Otto Bauer (1881–1938) was much the most important thinker on the national question among the Austro-Marxists.[10] Bauer was on the Left, so, unlike Renner, his central preoccupation was with the creation of a united working-class movement for the achievement of a socialist State, but undertaken in conditions where nationalism continually divided the workers. Like Renner, he saw the system as driving towards increased international economic integration which ought to create an internationally united working class, yet seemed only to strengthen national separatism. What accounted for this stubborn resistance of nationalities to the predicted assimilation?

Bauer argued that nations were not, as Marx argued, temporary historical formations produced by the rise and rule of the bourgeoisie, but of great antiquity, capable of outlasting all economic change, the residue of the history of a people, 'the totality of men bound, together through a common destiny in a community of character'.[11] The cultural community of the feudal nobility created a national culture; the peasants did not participate because their membership of this community was concealed by a mass of local particularisms. However, 'Capitalism and its attendant, the modern State, effected everywhere a widening of the cultural community in that it freed the masses from the fetters of an all-powerful tradition and called them to participate in the regeneration of a national culture'.[12]

But the lower classes of different nations were separated from each other, 'for they, too, gain a share in national education, national cultural life, and the national standard language'. Engels' 'non-historical peoples' now emerged also with a legitimate claim to a national existence. However, capitalism forced upon people the collision of classes and this prevented the full development of national culture; socialism would allow the full development of a 'community of education, work and culture', rising above narrow local loyalties. Alongside this flourishing of national cultures, for the first time a real international economic division of labour would emerge, covering multinational economic regions in which each nation would play a specialized role for all other:[13]

> Through the international division of labour, the whole of civilized humanity becomes a great organism; and precisely by this means, the political freedom and unity of all nations becomes possible. In a society in which each community is supposed to be autarchic and to supply its own needs, the full implementation of the nationality principle is impossible; national freedom is necessarily denied to small nations, the nations whose territory provides less favourable conditions for production.

Thus, Bauer's analysis led to a sharp possible separation of the economic and the cultural, each supposedly expressing the international and the national.

In the event, the schemes of Renner for a 'great central European Catholic peace community' and of Bauer for a model socialist State with a cultural federation could not save the empire. And, with its disintegration, both were driven to an increasing identification with German nationalism and the proposal for a merger of Austria and Germany. Culture now coincided with a large economic region. The Versailles Treaty forbade the unification of the two countries, so they were obliged, with great misgivings, to settle for a little Austria (until the Third Reich simultaneously achieved the forbidden merger and the destruction of the Social Democrats).

The Austro-Marxists seemed to carry the argument so far into the nationalist camp that only the distinction between the cultural and the economic preserved internationalism. Yet they attached the greatest importance to the economic (and its organization, the State), so that ultimately they denied the right of national self-determination (that is, the right to an independent State). The argument was in any case flawed. For in practice there was little validity in the distinction: the nationalist pursued not culture but power, and above all the power of the State, which, once won, it was thought, would then protect a national culture.

Furthermore, the idea that nations were indestructible components of social life was an historical fantasy. More peoples, 'nations', had disappeared through assimilation than had survived. Indeed, what had survived were names, not peoples. The modern inhabitants of Europe had little in common with the ancestors they claimed. Even for the peoples of the empire, it was not clear how far a majority of them were committed in any serious sense to a separate cultural identity. To oblige them to belong to a national group was as likely to imprison them in an identity from which they wanted to escape as to liberate them. It was to block the normal processes of assimilation.

Rosa Luxemburg and the Left

Rosa Luxemburg started from a reconsideration of Marx's argument for Polish independence. Russia, she argued, was no longer the gendarme of Europe; increasingly ramshackle and transformed by rapid industrialization, it was itself faced with the threat of revolution. It was no longer necessary to block Russia's advance with an independent Poland and a strong Turkey to control the Dardanelles; nor was it necessary to oppose the national struggles of the Czechs and the Southern Slavs.

Furthermore, the Polish nobility that had led the national movement in Marx's time had yielded power in Poland to a new rising capitalist class and settled for privileges guaranteed by the Tsar. On the other hand, the Polish bourgeoisie was of mainly foreign origin (it did not therefore identify with the nationalist tradition) and constituted the leading segment of the empire's industry, dependent upon the markets of the whole empire, not a lesser Poland. Finally, the new working class had no interest in a separate nation; their natural allies were the workers of Petrograd, Moscow and other cities of the empire. Only the intelligentsia remained loyal, but their social importance was far too slight for the task of achieving an independent Poland. 'The recognizable direction of social development', she concluded, 'has made it clear to me that there is no social class in Poland that has at one and the same time both an interest in, and an ability to achieve, the restoration of Poland'.[14]

However, Luxemburg did not limit her case to Poland. It became an argument about Europe as a whole. Vigorous national movements were no longer the instrument of rising capitalist classes, for capital accumulation now required markets far larger than individual countries could provide. Class, the product of the new economic order of society, now cut across the unity of nations:[15]

In a society based on classes, the nation as a uniform social-political whole does not exist. Instead, there exist within each nation classes with antagonistic interests and 'rights'. There is literally no social arena – from the strongest material relationship to the most subtle moral one – in which the possessing classes and a self-conscious proletariat could take one and the same position and figure as an undifferentiated whole.

If the development of capitalism, for Bauer, allowed nations to escape the internal fragmentation of local loyalties, imperialism for Rosa Luxemburg forced the integration of nations and the emergence of horizontal class loyalties that cut across nationality. To attempt to resurrect – or, more likely in her view, invent – the old national groups was entirely reactionary, to turn the clock back to a past economic system, and to attempt by this means to frustrate the proletarian revolution.

Marxists were generally agreed on the internationalization of the economic system. In Rosa Luxemburg's view this forced nations either to be assimilated into an existing empire or to create their own empire. In an imperialist world, there was no third alternative. Thus the call for an independent Poland was a demand for a new imperialist power. There were no longer *national* interests:[16]

> In the era of rampaging imperialism, there can be no more national wars. [The assertion of] national interests can serve only as a means of deception, of betraying the working masses of the people to their deadly enemy, imperialism.

Nationalism had now become incompatible with socialism, a profound enemy, not an ally.

Existing smaller powers that were supposedly independent had little real power. World markets dominated their economies, and they lacked the means for independent national economic development. Aspirations to independence parted from the reality of dependence. For socialists to champion the aspiration when there was no objective possibility of its being realized was to be both reactionary and utopian. Only with the end of capitalism, the domination of the world market, would it be possible to attain national independence:[17]

> society will win the ability to freely determine its national existence when it has the ability to determine its political being and the conditions of its creation. 'Nations' will control their historical existence when human society controls its social process.

But under socialism all oppression would have been ended: there would then be no need for national independence.

This uncompromising case was qualified in two respects. First, the old programme of the right for national self-determination still applied to the territories of the European overseas empires (because of their backwardness). 'In India', Rosa Luxemburg wrote, 'nationalism is an expression of the rising indigenous bourgeoisie which seeks to exploit the country for its own ends rather than to be drained by English capital'.[18] Second, Luxemburg accepted, as did the Austro-Marxists, a cultural–linguistic nationality. For Poles, the programme of her party promised 'The equality of all national groups that live in Russia; assurance of their cultural development; national schools and freedom in the use of native languages; provincial self-government, that is to say, autonomy'.[19] It was on this ground, among others, that she opposed the creation of a centralized Social Democratic party for the empire (and so collided with Lenin and the Bolsheviks). She held out for a federal party in the negotiations with the Russians (1902) to the point where the talks broke down.

The case evolved from Polish issues but, at its most general level, it became influential in many other countries, and particularly on the Left of the Russian party. There, a group of Bolsheviks, including Bukharin, Piatakov and Anovna Bosch, made several attempts to change the traditional position of the party which guaranteed the right of national self-determination to the subordinate peoples of the Russian empire. They argued that under imperialism there could be no separate 'national question'. 'It is impossible', Bukharin maintained, 'to struggle against the enslavement of nations otherwise than by struggling against imperialism, ergo . . . by struggling against finance capitalism, ergo, against capitalism in general'.[20] If a separate national question were raised, workers would be diverted from the pursuit of their own class interest to that of the petty bourgeoisie, spreading disunity between workers of different national origins. During the First World War, Radek of the Polish party and the Left abstained on national questions; 'Social Democracy does not advocate either an erection of new boundary posts in Europe nor the re-erection of those which have been torn down by imperialism'.[21] National independence could not be achieved under capitalism, and under socialism it would be unnecessary.

What was the reaction of the rest of the Social Democratic movement to this unequivocal internationalism? The leadership of the International were in general irritated by what seemed to be the sectarian squabbling of the émigré Poles and Russians, while generally defending the traditional interpretation of Marx's opinions. The famous Russian

Marxist, Plekhanov, was brought in to defend the traditional position of the Polish Socialist Party against this impertinent young woman, Rosa Luxemburg (in *Vorwärts*, 23 July 1896). Kautsky himself defended the orthodox case in *Neue Zeit* – namely, Polish national liberation, while not as strategically important as before, was still revolutionary and anti-Tsarist; any compromise on the issue would give aid and comfort to the Tsars.[22] Victor Adler and the Austro-Marxists were hostile, since Luxemburgism, with its unequivocal affirmation of class internationalism, threatened their precarious coalition. The German Social Democratic leaders, Wilhelm Liebknecht and August Bebel, were also in the first instance critical, since the Polish argument seemed to imply that the territorial expansionism of imperialism in general, and Prussia in particular, did not matter any longer beside the development of supranational class unity.

These purely doctrinal responses were, however, of lesser importance than one practical implication of Luxemburgism. Rosa Luxemburg spent much of her active political life in exile, working within the powerful German Social Democratic Party. It was natural that part of this work should be in the Prussian-held Polish territories of the eastern Reich. Here, the divisions among socialists in Russian-held Poland were reflected. A Polish Socialist Party of Prussia, formed in 1893, challenged the right of the German Social Democratic Party to represent Poles – even to the point of fielding election candidates against the German party (which then withdrew its fraternal subsidy to the Poles). It was Rosa Luxemburg, with the strong support of the German leadership, who defended the position of the German Social Democrats in the name of internationalism, urging the Polish worker in Prussia 'to give up national utopias and to accept that his national interests are best taken care of by Social Democracy, and not by taking up a separate position as a Pole in the wake of nationalist parties'.[23] 'In practical terms', Luxemburg's biographer, Peter Nettl, comments, 'Rosa Luxemburg's opposition to the PPS [Polish Socialist Party], and its policy of self-determination made her the most efficient ally of the SPD's [German Social Democratic Party's] policy of organizational integration for minorities in Germany'.[24] Luxemburg's internationalism made her insensitive to the possibility of German Social Democratic oppression – or at least, oppression by neglect or indifference – of Prussia's Poles. It was the blind spot of the internationalist Left. As we shall see in the Russian case, it was a common phenomenon, echoing Marx's description of Lafargue's internationalism as merely a mechanism for absorbing all in a model French nation.

If Rosa Luxemburg's internationalism might be used as a cover for German chauvinism in Prussia, in Russia it was its potential as a cover for Russian chauvinism which motivated Lenin. The Poles, under her leadership, broke off the 1902 unity talks partly because the Russians refused to give up their guarantee of the right of national self-determination for the subordinate peoples of the empire. Rosa Luxemburg was full of scorn – 'such a formula expresses either absolutely nothing, so that it is an empty non-committal phrase, or else it expresses the unconditional duty of socialists to support all national aspirations, in which case it is simply false'.[25] Lenin replied:[26]

> In her anxiety not to 'assist' the nationalistic bourgeoisie of Poland, Rosa Luxemburg, by her denial of the right of secession in the programme of the *Russian* Marxists is, *in fact*, assisting the Great Russian Black Hundreds [extreme Right]; she is in fact assisting . . . the nationalism of the Great Russians . . . the most formidable at the present time: it is precisely the one that is less bourgeois and more feudal, and it is precisely the one that acts as the principal brake on democracy and the proletarian struggle.

Rosa Luxemberg made no concessions. When the disputed questions were put to the practical test of revolution in 1917, she saw the 'doctrinaire obstinacy' of the Bolsheviks on the national question as one of the key factors in the disintegration of the Tsarist empire in 1918. The bourgeoisies of the Russian dependencies of Finland, Poland, Ukraine, Lithuania and the other Baltic States were able to exploit the Bolshevik promise of national independence to ally with Germany against Soviet Russia. 'The Finnish bourgeoisie, like the Ukrainian, were unanimous in preferring the violent rule of Germany to national freedom, if the latter should be bound up with Bolshevism.'[27] The Bolsheviks destroyed the unity of workers of different nationalities and laid the way open for national leaderships to capture 'their own' working class, when they should have defended the integrity of the former Russian empire 'tooth and nail'. As it was, quite shallow social forces – like the 'few university professors and students' who, she said, constituted Ukrainian nationalism – were allowed to rally counterrevolution and threaten Soviet power. The damage spread far more widely:[28]

> the phrases concerning self-determination and the entire nationalist movement, which at present constitute the greatest danger for international socialism, have experienced an extraordinary strengthening from the Russian revolution.

Rosa Luxemburg was right on the dangers of nationalism. But, as we shall see, it was not the Bolshevik position on the question which alone determined what happened in the Russian empire, nor is it clear that, in practice, the Bolsheviks had had any real alternative if the revolution was to be successful.

Lenin and the Bolsheviks

From different motives and perspectives, the political theorists of empire, the socialist defenders of colonialism, the Austro-Marxists and the 'ultra-Left' of the Polish and Russian socialist movements explicitly or in effect denied the right of national self-determination in defence of empire, large multinational economies or a world economy. All agreed that the national State was archaic in Europe. It was the peculiarity of the Bolsheviks that they unequivocally defended the right of national minorities to secede from the Tsarist empire, to create separate national States.

The position was uniquely associated with the name of Lenin. For those who regard ethnic origin as an important part of the explanation, this might have seemed odd, for Lenin was, despite recent disputes, solidly Russian, whereas much of the intellectual leadership of the rest of European Social Democracy was drawn from minorities – Rosa Luxemburg was Polish and Jewish, Piatakov was Ukrainian, Bauer and Karl Kautsky were Austrian and Jewish etc. Yet of all the leaders of European Social Democracy, Lenin came to show the greatest sensitivity to the issues associated with the oppression of national minorities, and to the need for dominant nationalities to demonstrate their rejection of this oppression. But the issue was still a *tactical* one, as it had been for Marx; national liberation was a means to support or obstruct the unity of the working class and the achievement of socialist revolution in Russia, not a matter of general principle.

There were several phases in the evolution of Bolshevik thinking. Up to 1913, the national question did not loom large in the preoccupations of the party. But from then until 1917 it became an issue of major importance. From 1917, it was a matter of practical politics, but one which, in the period of civil war, was subordinate to questions of immediate survival. In the first phase, the question related most importantly to the organization of the party; in the second, to the strategy for overthrowing Tsarism; and in the third, finally, to the overthrow of world capitalism. In the last two phases, the preoccupation was in creating 'alliances' – temporary unity in action for immediate purposes by forces which pursued ultimately incompatible aims. Thus, workers, with an interest in the collective ownership of land, might ally with peasants, dedicated to the break-up of large estates and the establishment of private land holdings, for the common but short-term purpose of overthrowing aristocratic control of land. In the same way, workers, committed to the abolition of national States and to internationalism, might ally, to overthrow the Tsar, with national movements dedicated to the creation of new national States.

Let us examine the first two phases.

1897–1913

The right to national self-determination was formally included in the first programme of the Russian Social Democratic Labour Party (RSDLP), but was accorded a relatively low priority. Like most of Europe's Social Democrats at that time, the party saw nationalism as a declining issue, characteristic only of the economically more backward areas. Lenin did not find it necessary to discuss the issue in his elaboration of the party programme in 1895–6.[29] Even in 1903, he could still observe that:[30]

> Class antagonism has undoubtedly relegated national questions far into the background, but, without the risk of lapsing into doctrinairism, it cannot be categorically asserted that some particular national question cannot temporarily appear in the foreground of the political drama.

However, the 1905 revolution included a number of significant national agitations, small previews of what were to come. They were important enough to prompt other parties to formulate national demands. The Kadets, at this time a middle-class reform party, promised cultural self-determination and equality for the peoples of the empire, but in a unitary State. At their 1905 Congress, the Social Revolutionaries, a peasant party, embraced the principle of national self-determination and a federal State.

On the question of Poland, Lenin accepted much of Rosa Luxemburg's case that circumstances had qualitatively changed since the time of Marx – 'the restoration of Poland, prior to the fall of capitalism, is highly improbable, but it cannot be asserted that it is absolutely impossible'.[31] However, this was not the key issue for Great Russians, those who historically had participated in the dismemberment of Poland and oppressed its people. Whatever else was said, it was vital for *Russian* socialists clearly to dissociate themselves from the Tsarist record:[32]

> The accursed history of autocracy has left us a legacy of tremendous *estrangement* between the working classes of the

various nationalities oppressed by that autocracy. This estrangement is a very great evil, and a very great obstacle in the struggle
against the autocracy, and we must not legitimize this evil or
sanctify this outrageous state of affairs by establishing any such
'principles' as separate parties or a 'federation' of parties.

Recognizing the right of Russia's minorities to self-determination
was the essence of repudiating the Tsarist inheritance and affirming
democracy and the principle that peoples should not be compelled to
co-operate by force.

However, acknowledging the right did not mean that the party
favoured people using it. For[33]

The Social Democratic Party considers it to be its positive and
principal task to further the self-determination of the proletariat
in each nationality rather than that of peoples or nations ...
it is only in isolated and exceptional cases that we can advance
and actively support demands conducive to the establishment of
a new class state.

It was on the issue of party organization that the national question
assumed most importance at this time. The Jewish Bund (the general
Jewish Labour League of Lithuania, Poland and Russia) was formed
in western Russia in 1897, and joined the RSDLP in 1898. At its fourth
congress in 1901, the Bund adopted the position taken by the southern
Slavs at the Brno congress of the Austrian Social Democrats (the Bauer
position). The RSDLP should be reorganized as a federal party, with
the Bund being recognized as the sole representative of Jewish workers
and the party programme promising 'personal cultural autonomy'
(that is, all Jewish workers, regardless of where they lived in the empire,
would be members of a national Jewish association, responsible for
all Jewish educational and cultural affairs). At its 1903 congress, the
RSDLP rejected these demands in the name of a single centralized party
(representing the unity of the working class, regardless of nationality)
and the Bund withdrew. On a compromise proposal, in 1906 at the
Stockholm RSDLP Congress, it rejoined the party.

The Bauer/southern Slav position on the national question, however,
spread much wider than the Bund. It was taken up by the Armenian
Dashnaktsutiun, the Byelorussian Socialist Hromada, and the Georgian
Socialist Federation Party (Sakartvelo). These organizations met in
1907. The split in the RSDLP (into the Bolshevik majority and
Menshevik minority) meant that some of the Mensheviks became
influential among these parties (particularly in the Georgian and Jewish
parties). In August 1912, the organizations, along with the Bund, the

Latvian Social Democrats and the Caucasian Regional League, held a meeting and in attendance were some important non-Bolshevik Marxists (Martov, Aleksandr, Martynov, Trotsky, Akselrod). There appeared to be growing agreement on the idea of 'personal cultural autonomy'.

Lenin was willing to make concessions, but not on the centralized unity of the party – 'we must not weaken the force of our offensive by breaking into numerous independent political parties; we must not introduce estrangement and isolation and then have to heal an artificially implanted disease with the aid of these notorious "federal" plasters'.[34] At this stage, he was firmly opposed to federation; 'Federation is harmful because it *sanctions* segregation and alienation, elevates them to a principle, to a law.'[35]

Furthermore, as Martov put it at the 1903 congress, all members of the party should be concerned with the disabilities of minorities, not just the minority itself. Anti-semitism was not a matter only of concern to Jews; all Social Democrats must campaign against it – or leave the party.[36] On the Jewish question, Lenin adopted Kautsky's position. A nationality must have a common language and territory. The Jews had neither. The remedy for their disabilities lay therefore in establishing complete equality between Jew and non-Jew, so allowing Jewish assimilation in the majority.

1912/13–1917

By 1912, the Bauer case had achieved some prominence among the politically aware socialists of Russia's minorities. So much so that Lenin commissioned a leading party organizer and Georgian, Josef Stalin, to write a counter-attack (published in 1913).

Meanwhile, events rather than debates intervened. The Balkans underwent successive crises of competing nationalisms, one of which finally brought down the pre-1914 structure of European power. In that collapse, the European Social Democratic parties, which had for so long bravely vowed to prevent war between their respective States, lined up with the belligerents; the second International collapsed, another casualty of the trenches of northern France. The war in turn stimulated an unprecedented number of new nationalisms. Nor was this simply on the eastern periphery. Even in the heart of supposedly the most advanced power, Britain, the issue of Irish national liberation re-emerged in the Easter Rising of 1916; for the British, this was as shocking an act of disloyalty in the midst of war as was the Bolshevik revolution for the Russian establishment.

Lenin became more and more preoccupied with the question of national liberation, and in a tireless stream of speeches, letters, articles and pamphlets, sought to clarify the right approach to the nationalism of Russia's minorities. Nationalism was still *bourgeois* nationalism (and so irreconcilable with proletarian internationalism), but it needed to be sharply divided between the nationalism of the dominant imperialist powers and of those who were oppressed.[37] There was at this stage no *general* right to self-determination.

The war suddenly incited the full force of Russian nationalism, and Lenin's emphasis changed to the struggle against what he called 'Great Russian Chauvinism'. The Armenian Bolshevik, Shahumyan, reproached him – as many were to do – with exaggerating the dangers here and was roundly chastised:[38]

> I exaggerate the danger of Great Russian chauvinism!!! Now that's really funny! Do the 160 million Russians suffer from *Armenian* or *Polish* nationalism? Is it not a shame for a *Russian* Marxist to adopt the point of view of an Armenian hen coop? Is it Great Russian nationalism that oppresses, and shapes the *policy* of Russia's ruling classes, or is it Armenian, Polish?

The public repudiation of Russian chauvinism was to offer the oppressed the right to self-determination, or as he now put it, so that there should be no ambiguity, the right to secede from Russia. It was this clarification which increased the degree of opposition to Clause 9 of the Party programme. In November 1915, a Bukharin–Piatakov platform argued that national liberation could not be achieved within capitalism in its current form of imperialism; to demand it was therefore to sow illusions and divert efforts away from the central task of worker revolution. The same opposition, but enlarged, emerged in April 1917. Piatakov, a Ukrainian, now argued that, following Lenin's April theses, prepared on his return to Russia, which rejected the existing party policy of supporting the provisional government and set the Party on the road to the seizure of power, socialism was on the immediate agenda, not the establishment of a bourgeois republic. Therefore, the right of national self-determination could have no place in the party programme. The programme's drafting commission voted 7 to 2 for the proposition that the national question could be solved only by socialist revolution and that the party slogan should not be new frontiers, but the abolition of all frontiers. At the Congress itself, there was a strong fight, and Lenin's resolution affirming the traditional position was opposed by 16 (with 18 abstaining) but with 56 in favour. Piatakov's resolution was defeated by 48 to 11, with 19 abstentions.[39] The size of the combined opposition and abstentions indicated how far Lenin's arguments had won the day, just before the Bolsheviks were to be put to the test of power. Over a third of the vote was not convinced that 'To deny the *right* to secede is to help Tsarism and to *indulge* the Russian muzhik's nationalism.'[40]

There were other grounds on which to support the right of self-determination. Democracy implied the equality of nations and languages and the prohibition of privileges attached to any one nation. It was the lack of democracy and equality which impelled the oppressed to fight for secession. Lenin reproved the luckless Shahumyan,[41]

Why will you not understand the *psychology* that is so important in the national question and which, if the slightest coercion is applied, besmirches, soils and nullifies the undoubtedly progressive importance of centralized large States and a uniform language? But the economy is still more important than psychology: in Russia, we *already* have a capitalist economy, which makes the *Russian* language essential. But you have no faith in the power of the economy and want to prop it up with the crutches of the rotten police regime.

However, once peoples had chosen not to exercise their right to secede, they should join a fully centralized State. For 'The great centralized State is a tremendous historical step forward from medieval disunity to the future socialist unity of the whole world, and only via such a State (*inseparably* connected with capitalism) can there be any road to socialism.'[42] This advantage would constrain the drive for secession:[43]

from their daily experience the masses know perfectly well the value of geographic and economic ties and the advantages of a big market and a big state. They will resort to secession only when national oppression and national friction make joint life absolutely intolerable.

After the coming of socialism,[44]

a great State will mean so many hours *less* work a day, and so much more pay a day. The mass of working people, as they liberate themselves from the bourgeois yoke, will *gravitate* irresistibly towards us ... provided yesterday's oppressions do not infringe the long oppressed nation's highly developed democratic feeling of self-respect and provided they are granted equality in everything.

Divisions must be eliminated for they would institutionalize estrangement. The most that could be offered would be autonomous areas within regional self-government 'towards which members of the respective nationalities, scattered all over the country or even all over the world, would gravitate and with which they could enter into relations and free associations'[45] – some measure of accommodation to Bauerism.

The future lay with full assimilation of all peoples into one and the emergence of an international culture. This would create 'a unity that is growing before our eyes with every mile of railway line that is built, with every international trust and every workers' association that is formed'.[46] Again, the key to assimilation was complete equality of peoples, and opposition to those who pretended there were separate national cultures operating above the two classes in each culture (as argued by Bauer).

Lenin's division of nationalism into that of the oppressed and that of the oppressor offered a special type of answer to Rosa Luxemburg, a dual policy:[47]

> the right to unite implies the right to secede. We Russians must emphasize the right to secede while the Poles emphasize the right to unite.

The Poles must oppose secession in the name of the unity of the working class of all the Russias, but they should not ask the Russians to compromise with Great Russian chauvinism by refusing the Poles the right to secede.

Rosa Luxemburg, Lenin argued, assumed that economic integration within empires rendered political separatism impossible. But this confused political and economic independence, as if politics were no more than a reflex of economics. The mass of politically independent States were economically dependent on the world economy, for parliaments could not tame capital:[48]

> The domination of finance capital and of capital in general is not to be abolished by *any* reforms in the sphere of political democracy; and self-determination belongs wholly to this sphere. This domination of finance capital, however, does not in the least nullify the significance of political democracy as a freer, wider and clearer *form* of class oppression and class struggle.

Up to 1917, Lenin's views on national liberation were in the main uniquely related to the situation in Russia and the need to create an alliance for the overthrow of Tsarism. But as the war progressed he became increasingly preoccupied with understanding the world order. Once the perspective extended to the world, the significance of national liberation became much greater and less conditional: for the national liberation of the colonies of the European empires could overthrow the imperialist world order. However, at this stage, some of the same qualifications occurred:[49]

> if we demand freedom of secession for the Mongolians, Persians, Egyptians and all other oppressed and unequal nations without exception, we do so not because *we favour secession*, but *only* because we stand for *free, voluntary* association and merging as distinct from forcible association.

Furthermore, national liberation could only be supported if it took place in a revolutionary way (as Marx had argued on Germany and therefore gone on to oppose Bismarck's route to German unity), not leaving 'intact the foundations of the power of the ruling class'.

On the eve of the October revolution, Lenin continued in the affirmation of the party's case:[50]

> the proletarian party must first of all advocate the proclamation and immediate realization of the complete freedom of secession from Russia of all the nations and peoples who were oppressed by Tsarism, or who were forcibly joined to or forcibly kept within the boundaries of the State.

The new State would seek to draw the minorities back into union with Russia but only as 'a free and fraternal union of workers and working people'. To those who expressed alarm at the fact that Finland and Poland were already separating from Russia:[51]

> Our attitude to the separatist movement is indifferent, neutral. If Finland, Poland or the Ukraine secede from Russia, there is nothing bad in that. What is wrong with it? Anyone who says that is a chauvinist.

If Finland were free, 'then there will be greater trust in Russian democracy and the Finns will not separate'.

Lenin used a number of different arguments to justify recognizing the right to secede, and it is worth summarizing them. First, it was required in order to establish the trust of Russia's oppressed minorities, as the basis for an alliance between workers and minority nationalists to overthrow Tsarist rule. Second, the affirmation of the right was to ensure that the unification of different peoples was voluntary, part of a well-founded democracy and ensuring the equality of nations at a particular stage in Russian history, the bourgeois revolution. Third, the right was needed to make a clear public rejection of the Tsarist record and to combat Great Russian chauvinism. Recognizing the right to secede was seen as the means of securing the unity of the peoples of the old empire in a new State, not of precipitating disintegration. The logic of a modern economy would encourage a voluntary assimilation of all, and recognizing the right would in no way impede this forward movement of society to integration. Finally, as the revolution approached, the issue assumed much wider significance. It moved from being a component in the domestic strategy for the conquest of power to the key element in the overthrow of world capitalism, founded now upon an alliance of European workers and the nationalist movements of Asia.

Postscript

In 1913, Lenin commissioned Stalin to draft a reply to the Austro-Marxists. The results were of little significance at the time. However, with Stalin's ascent to power after the revolution, his pamphlet came to define the orthodoxies of the world Communist movement.[52]

Despite its subsequent reputation, however, Stalin's account is a poor one. The line remained Lenin's, but the arguments had become something quite different. Stalin sought to lay down criteria for the identification of a 'nation' (the entity which possessed the right of national self-determination) as a means, a moral theory, to separate authentic and spurious claims. However, in doing so, he absorbed much from the Austro-Marxists. Thus, in his eyes, a nation was a community of people with a common language, territory, economic activity, and a particular psychological make-up as the result of a distinct historical experience, expressed in a common culture. If a group lacked one of the specified features, it could not be counted as a nation. Thus, the Jews lacked a common language and territory and so could not be counted as a nation. Switzerland, on the other hand, consisted of three nations.

Stalin was not to know that his criteria would exclude many nations that were subsequently to emerge (for example, Pakistan, without a common language or territory, but with a common religion), and force some groups into being nations (the most notorious example being the black American population). Nor was he apparently aware of Lenin's scorn for those who spoke of common culture, let alone psychology and community. This was pure Bauer.

Stalin's account also misrepresented the Austro-Marxist case, and he made a number of mistakes indicating his unfamiliarity with the subject. (Thus, he said that the Brno Congress had accepted the demand for 'personal cultural autonomy', when it had not; indeed, Lenin made the point that not even the Austrian party had accepted the southern Slav position.)

It is not surprising that Stalin's document played no role in the party until 1922 and his consolidation of power. It was a considerable retreat from the sophistication of the case as argued before 1917.

Part II

THE RUSSIAN
EXPERIENCE

5

THE TSAR'S NATIONAL MINORITIES

*I*N the second half of the nineteenth century, the pace of economic growth in the domains of the Tsar quickened, particularly affecting the western borderlands (and some of the more important ethnic minorities). Poland, the St Petersburg region and Baltic coast, and the eastern Ukraine were industrialized more intensively. Improvements in agriculture assisted the emergence of a relatively prosperous farmer stratum in the Ukraine; and the commercial unification of the empire created more significant merchant trading classes (for example, among the Tatars, particularly those of the Crimea). An intelligentsia was one of the byproducts, ranging from priests to teachers, journalists and writers.

It was the heyday of imperialism, and all the Great Powers were under pressure for competitive modernization. For the archaic empires, this entailed attempts to create modern States in the supposed image of those of Western Europe – a task that was made more difficult by the accelerating technical advance of the West Europeans. The rising costs of upgrading production and military forces became an increasing burden on the taxable capacity and military services of the sorely tried inhabitants. Furthermore, war is one of the most radical forces centralizing a country, and the First World War was, for the Russias, a massive influence in this respect. What was barely tolerable before 1914 became increasingly intolerable to the mass of the population, as the enemy forces pushed the Tsarist regime into more and more desperate expedients to raise the finance and manpower with which to conduct the war.

Part of the process of 'modernization' was seeking to achieve a measure of 'homogenization': that is, in the Russian context, Russification of the non-Russians. But for that to happen a Great Russian culture had to be identified and fostered. Thus, the government and the intelligentsia of the Great Russians themselves became increasingly nationally conscious, a change felt in the borderlands as outright hostility to the symbols and practices of the local peoples.

In the borderlands themselves, in Poland, for example – as Rosa Luxemburg so cogently argued – the interests of the aristocracy of the minority peoples (where it existed) had become interwoven with the Tsarist order. Thus, the traditional champions of a separate nation refused to seek to create and lead it. The new business groups were part of an imperial market and often this was far too important to them to risk the fragmentation of nationalism.

However, cultural Russification directly threatened those who claimed to carry the cultural traditions of the minority peoples, from the priesthood to what there was of a modern intelligentsia. Their very *raison d'être* was undermined by the extension of 'Russianism'. The intelligentsia were required to fill the role vacated by other classes, but, in the more advanced borderland principalities, their social significance was not large enough to advance national demands in isolation. They needed a vehicle of much greater weight in the society if national liberation was to be promoted. In Poland, the new working classes provided just such a vehicle.

The intellectuals often gave their version of national identity a cultural–linguistic stress. But, even with this emphasis, an emerging nationalism could provide the medium for many class conflicts – for example, between Ukrainian peasants and Russian or Polish landlords and Jewish land agents and tax collectors; between Tatar workers and Russian employers, between Baku Muslim oil workers and Christian oil magnates (Armenian, Russian, Swedish, Georgian). And far out on the perimeter of empire in the Russian Middle East, where – apart from the mullahs – there was no intelligentsia, Russian colonization of the nomadic grazing lands made class conflicts over land and revolutionary land reform vital national issues.

If they did not instigate it, the Tsars immensely exaggerated the process of 'nationalization' of the subordinate peoples of Russia. The attempts to rationalize the administration, to centralize power, collided directly with local liberties and the particularist and traditional privileges of the old supporters of the regime (for example, the Tatar nobility).

Furthermore, Russification intensified. Under Alexander III up to the 1905 revolution, particular efforts were made to Russify the European peoples of the empire, to stretch, in Seton-Watson's evocative phrase, 'the short, tight skin of the nation over the gigantic body of the empire'.[1] Finland was more closely incorporated into the central administration, losing the privilege of being a separate Grand Duchy. Restrictions were imposed on the use of the Polish language in culture and literature. Publications in Ukrainian were banned (so publishing activities moved over the border, to Austrian Galicia). Thus, it was the Russian Establishment which made language a key national issue. Furthermore, the properties of the Armenian Church were confiscated. Worst of all was the horrifying anti-semitism which was fashioned as a vital support for Great Russian chauvinism; the Jews, long discriminated against – to the tune of 650 legal restrictions on their activities – were used in the great pogroms of the late nineteenth century as the butt of national policy. Of course, the mass of the Russian people themselves were almost as hideously oppressed within the empire, but without the 'national' dimension.

The 1905 revolution brought many of these issues to a head, for it was[2]

> as much a revolution of the non-Russian against Russification as it was a revolution of workers, peasants and radical intellectuals against autocracy. The two revolts were, of course, connected: the social revolution was in fact most bitter in non-Russian regions, with Polish workers, Latvian peasants and Georgian peasants as protagonists.

For a period after 1905, there was a reversal of Russification as part of the programme of reforms. But it was short-lived and the State soon sought once again to enforce 'homogeneity'. To these oppressions, the First World War added unforeseen horrors, particularly where, in the western borderlands, actual fighting took place. The promise of peace and order which was the supposed vindication of the Tsarist empire was completely betrayed.

As a result of this history, the collapse of the Tsarist regime in the February revolution of 1917 raised great hopes of a new and just order in the borderlands. The Provisional Government committed itself to recognizing the right of national self-determination and, in place of the old Tsarist governors, installed in the minority areas governing committees of local dignitaries and deputies of the relevant nationality to the national parliament, the Duma. However, the Provisional Government interpreted the right of national self-determination as meaning no more than the abolition of discrimination and the establishment of legal equality among the peoples of the former empire. Even with this limited aim, the strains of war severely inhibited its capacity to pursue any serious reforms.

In any case, the continuation of the war was forcing the revolution to dig much deeper than the topsoil of reforms. The representatives of national groups increasingly demanded the right of autonomy, of self-government, if not outright secession. Furthermore, mutinies and desertions in the forces led to soldiers of the different nationalities returning home to offer their armed support for national administrations. The army became a forcing house for national liberation.

At each stage the beleaguered national government urged self-restraint, for the continuation of the war necessitated a postponement of all subsidiary issues. Ultimately, it was said, a Constituent Assembly would have to decide the form of a new State. Through the summer of 1917, impatience grew at the temporizing of the government. An Estonian delegate to an August conference summed up the sense of frustration:[3]

> We consider it necessary ... to proceed to the resolution of the nationality question. There can be no delays. No people can live by promises alone ... preliminary work must be started for the reorganisation of the State on principles providing the highest guarantee of freedom and national self-determination in a democratic Russian Republic, based on the federal principle of a friendly family of Russian peoples where autonomous regions – Estonia among them – would constitute equal members.

On the other side, the army high command – and the political party, the Kadets – were horrified at the Provisional Government's flirtation with the disintegration of Russia. As General Kaledin put it:[4]

> Russia must be indivisibly whole. All separatist tendencies must be nipped in the bud.

The Bolsheviks were merciless in their attack on the government for frustrating the movement for self-determination, which they interpreted as the right to secede, to create a new State, and to do it through the direct action of the peoples concerned without awaiting the approval of the central Government. For Lenin, the growing conflict between Finland and the Provisional Government demonstrated 'that denial of the right of secession leads to a direct continuation of the policy of Tsarism.'[5]

The nationalities

In 1917, *Poland* was under German occupation. The occupying forces set up a puppet government and proclaimed it independent of Russia.

The Russian Provisional Government could hardly do less, a position the Bolsheviks also accepted after the October revolution. Thus Poland, which had played so important a role in the debates on the national question, slipped into independence by courtesy of German arms without playing any role in a revolution in Germany or in Russia.

Finland was not an obvious candidate for the status of an oppressed nationality. Under a constitutional monarchy, the Tsar was Grand Duke, with a bicameral legislature. In 1917, the lower house, the Sejm, had an elected majority of Social Democrats (103 out of 200). On 5 June, it declared Finland to be self-governing in all matters except defence and foreign policy.

From there the Sejm moved to call for independence, appealing directly to the All-Russian Congress of Soviets. The Congress, at this time under the control of the Social Revolutionaries and Mensheviks, rejected the demand, and Kerensky, on behalf of the Provisional Government, affirmed the right of the central government to veto any secessionist proposals.

He promised that the government would fight to keep Finland. He announced the dissolution of the Sejm and sealed off the building. He began to move troops northwards. The Social Democrats called a general strike in protest (denounced by the leadership of the Petrograd Soviet as mob rule), which the Russian Governor General banned, promising to put down all disorders by force.

However, despite the bluster, the Provisional Government – in the midst of a World War – was unable to sustain a serious punitive expedition. The Social Democrats broke into the sealed Sejm building and declared Finland to be self-governing. On the eve of the October revolution, the Provisional Government accepted this as a temporary expedient.

The *Ukraine* posed particularly intractable problems for Petrograd. Advanced in certain respects, it was also divided between an industrialized and Russian-dominated east (with Kharkov as the chief city) and the rural west (with the ancient capital of Kiev), between the cities inhabited by Russians, Poles and Jews (the historic instruments for the Russification of the Ukraine) and the Ukrainian peasants of the countryside (with Polish and Russian landowners). On the other hand, economic interdependence was great – the Ukraine depended upon the Russian market, and Russia depended upon Ukrainian raw materials (especially grain, but also coal and iron) and manufactured goods. The hunger of Russia during the civil war added a sharp edge to the demand for Ukrainian independence, the right to dispose of the grain surplus.

The Ukrainian national leadership was fatally weakened by being restricted to the intelligentsia and without the dedication to escape from this. For the tiny group of declared nationalists, cultural and linguistic oppression loomed large, far larger than it could for an illiterate peasantry (although the use of the Ukrainian language had considerable popular support). Insofar as Ukrainian nationalism existed as a popular force, it was hostile to Russian and Polish landlords and anti-semitic. However, even with this unpromising start, more could possibly have been achieved with a leadership less trapped in its own class origins.

Following the February revolution, a Central Ukrainian Council (the 'Rada') was formed in Kiev from the small circle of nationalists. They formulated a programme of demands, but these fell on deaf ears in Petrograd. The frustration of mild proposals promoted more radical ones: the right to self-government, backed by Ukrainian military forces.

In the eastern Ukraine, many rejected the pretensions of the Rada to speak for the province and sought to promote a workers' revolutionary movement as an alternative focus. Some rejected entirely any talk of self-government or treating the Ukrainians as an oppressed people. Nonetheless, the Rada persisted, producing a manifesto that proclaimed self-government. In Petrograd, the Kadets accused the Rada of being agents of the Germans, and the newspaper of the Soviet, *Izvestia*, proclaimed:[6]

> The revolutionary democracy of Russia stands for the indivisibility of the State. To split up a great State, created by a thousand years of historical development, means taking a big step backwards.

Negotiations between Kerensky and the Rada were fruitless, and the Rada began to speak of the 'imperialist tendencies of the Russian bourgeoisie towards the Ukraine'. Meanwhile, the cities experienced growing disorder; in the countryside, a diversity of agitations was beginning.

The Ukrainian Bolsheviks tended to be restricted to the eastern Ukraine; they were therefore limited in their capacity to combat the Rada's position by, for example, raising revolutionary peasant demands. Opposition to the Rada did not mean opposition to Ukrainian nationalism (although the Rada was happy to make this deduction). However, the party leader of the southwestern region was Piatakov, the Ukrainian-born collaborator of Bukharin who had consistently opposed the Party position on national self-determination. He bluntly rejected not only the demands of the Rada but also the claims of Ukrainian nationalism (and so contradicted Party policy:[7])

> we must not support the Ukrainians, because their movement is not convenient for the proletariat. Russia cannot exist without

the Ukrainian sugar industry, and the same can be said in regard to coal (the Donbas), cereals (the black earth belt), etc.

Given Piatakov's views and his official position, the Bolsheviks of the Ukraine seemed to the Rada indistinguishable from both the Kadets and the Petrograd Soviet.

There were numerous other stirrings of national opinion, from the Baltic States to the Transcaucasus. In the latter case, two ancient Christian principalities, Georgia and Armenia, had claims to distinct national identities, along with a Muslim and Shi-ite people in Azerbaijan (which contained the economically vital oil city of Baku). *Georgia* had long provided a cadre for the Social Democratic movement, and the Tiflis Soviet was of more substance than many in the region. *Armenia*, shattered by the Turkish persecutions, was wholly dependent upon the protection of Russia (whatever its regime), against the Turks. The people of *Azerbaijan* sympathized with Turkey, so that domestic collisions were closely related to external threats.

The Azerbaijanis were part of a broader movement of reform among Muslims, led by the more advanced Tatar peoples of the Volga and Crimea. The spread of secular schools and Turkish-language newspapers (there were 16 by 1913, all except three in the dialect of the Volga Tatars) began to create some sense of identity among the Muslims of the west, or at least among those who were literate.

A key material issue in Central Asia was opposition to the Russian seizure of the historic lands of minority peoples. Russian colonization, cities and railways cut up the great grazing lands of the nomadic peoples as violently as American settlers had done to the Amerindians in the United States. There were increasing clashes between the Russians and the minority peoples on the issue in the run-up to the First World War. By 1916, there were some 144,000 Russian colonists in the Kazakh-Kirghiz steppes.

At that time, the central government, desperate to find new conscripts for the war, for the first time introduced military service for the minority peoples. This set off a major rebellion in which Russian settlements were sacked with a death toll of over 2,500. The government reacted with even greater violence, driving out some 300,000 of the indigenous peoples (some fleeing to the mountains and beyond, to Chinese Xinjiang or Eastern Turkestan). The grateful colonists used the opportunity to expropriate the cattle and other assets of the fugitives.

The February and October revolutions seem to have had the same effect on the Russian colonists as the expulsion of the British had on the American colonists in the eighteenth century – a removal of all restraint on the ambitions to despoil native lands and assets. In July

1917, at Semirechensk in Turkestan, Russian peasant representatives met to deliberate the subduing of the natives, and resolved to create vigilante groups to keep at bay those fugitives who were now returning (Muslim sources claim 83,000 were killed).

By 1917, there were three trends among the emerging political leadership of the more significant Muslim peoples – a religious right (with the mullahs and a landowning interest), a liberal centre (westernized, sometimes associated with merchant or business groups, and aligned with the Kadets in Petrograd), and a socialist group (among the Russian-educated young, often aligned with the Social Revolutionaries). The February revolution gave some of these forces the opportunity to enter the administration, but often only temporarily, until the Russian colonists could re-establish their power. Thus, the Turkestan Committee (5 Russians and 4 Muslims) that was recognized by the Provisional Government was superseded by the Tashkent Soviet from which Muslims were excluded.

The complexity of social forces – from the quasi-independent states of the western borderlands, to the anti-colonial ferment of Central Asia – belied the simplicity of the slogans. Abstract internationalism had a strong role to play in rationalizing much more sinister forces than appeared in the rhetoric of Petrograd.

6

NATIONAL LIBERATION IN PRACTICE: THE FIRST PHASE

*H*ISTORY, as Marx once said, is not made in conditions of our own choosing. The Bolsheviks came to power not in the relatively peaceful conditions in which policy had been framed, but in conditions of social collapse. The chaos on the military front, the continued threat of German invasion, the disintegration of the domestic economy with the prospects of both famine and civil anarchy: all these established the first emergencies facing the regime, the imperatives which cried out for response. Beyond these factors were the numerical weakness and cultural backwardness of the working class, the low average productivity of labour (even if the factories could be put back to work), the vastness of the land area and the isolation of its rural inhabitants, the barbaric inheritance of Tsarism – all in comparison with the exiguous forces of the Bolshevik party.

To come to power in conditions of war was to expose the new regime to the maximum pressures of the world system. For in war national loyalty is an unequivocal issue, and war and the subsequent Civil War reshaped the Bolsheviks more radically than anything else could. In selecting only one thread of policy – on the national issue – we are in danger of misconstruing its significance relative to the overall context. For the Bolsheviks were obliged to be obsessed with one issue and one issue only: the survival of their regime. All other considerations, to a greater or lesser degree, had to become secondary if that survival was to be ensured. Once distant from the history, it is difficult to envisage just how powerful that central imperative was and how often the options available were so narrowly restricted as to exclude most of what the party was supposed to stand for. After the Civil War, the Bolshevik party had recreated itself in response to events; it was virtually a new organization.

However, despite all the emergencies, in the first instance, the Declaration of the Rights of the Peoples of Russia (of 18 November 1917) boldly committed the new Bolshevik Government to support the national self-determination of Russia's peoples 'even to the point of separation and the formation of an independent State'. And when the regime finally came to reverse its former position and accept the principle of federation embodied in the new Russian Soviet Federation of Socialist Republics (RSFSR), the same promise was embodied in the new constitution.

Lenin argued tirelessly that, for the majority of the inhabitants, who were not workers, capitalists or landowners, the national question – like the questions of land and peace – was fundamental. In immediate terms this meant that[1]

> we must immediately satisfy the demands of the Ukrainians and the Finns, ensure them, as well as all other non-Russian nationalities in Russia, full freedom, including freedom of secession, applying the same to Armenia, undertaking to evacuate that country as well as the Turkish lands occupied by us.

There was still opposition within the Party, but the immediate confidence of the revolution swept the leadership along on a tide of optimism:[2]

> We are told that Russia will disintegrate, or split up into separate republics, but we have no reason to fear this. We have nothing to fear, whatever the number of independent republics. The important thing for us is not where the state border runs, but whether or not the working people of all nations remain allied in their struggle against the bourgeoisie . . .
>
> We are going to tell the Ukrainians that, as Ukrainians, they can go ahead and arrange their life as they see fit. But we are going to stretch out a fraternal hand to the Ukrainian workers and tell them that, together with them, we are going to fight against our bourgeoisie and theirs.

However, the immediate issues of the war intervened at every stage. The treaty of Brest-Litovsk, which the military superiority of Germany forced upon the young Soviet State at the end of the year, revealed the limits of its power: 'The past keeps fast hold of us,' Lenin observed gloomily at the 8th Party Congress, 'grasps us with a thousand tentacles, and does not allow us to take a single forward step, or compels us to take these steps badly.'[3]

By January 1919, qualifications were emerging. For if the right of self-determination for the Finns, the Ukrainians and the rest could in practice threaten the very existence of the Soviet State, 'naturally the preservation of the Socialist Republic has a higher claim'.[4] It was no more than a change of emphasis, but it emboldened the opposition. This time, a theoretical revision was created by Josef Stalin, the Bolshevik responsible for the execution of policy on the national question: in effect, the right could be reversed. Only five weeks after the October revolution, he had narrowed the group that could exercise the right to the labouring masses.[5] Without this restriction, he said, those opposed to the Soviet regime would be able to invoke the principle to subvert the new order.[6] A month later, he broadened the case: the October revolution had qualitatively changed the context; now the task was not to complete the bourgeois, but to establish the proletarian, revolution. This rendered the old national movement, led by the bourgeoisie, reactionary. Now only workers and peasants should enjoy the right to self-determination.[7]

A year later, perhaps to justify his rough treatment in suppressing the national movement among the Tatars and Bashkirs, he affirmed: 'the slogan "all power to the national bourgeoisie" is being replaced by the slogan of proletarian socialism, "all power to the working masses of the oppressed nationalities"'. Bukharin, one of the leaders of the Left opposition to Lenin on the national question, embraced the idea and brought to its exposition his formidable talents. At this point, as Carr observes, 'the dividing line between Bukharin's thesis of "self-determination for the workers" and the Polish thesis [of Rosa Luxemburg] of "no self-determination for nations" was tenuous and tended to vanish'.[8]

Stalin's argument was part of a broader one that he derived from Lenin: the right of national self-determination was valid only where countries were passing from feudalism to capitalism. Now, when the transition to socialism was on the agenda, the issues of the national question were no longer relevant. However, the party did not follow this line; otherwise they would have opposed independence for the more advanced Poland, Finland, the Baltic States and the Ukraine, and supported it only for the more backward minorities. In any case, the argument was quite remote from Lenin's preoccupation with binding up the wounds of national estrangement. However, at one stage, different conditions were laid down for different nationalities: a national plebiscite was demanded in order to ratify independence for Poland, Courland and Lithuania, whereas a vote of workers alone was required for the Ukraine, the Caucasus republics and Latvia. There was no practical validity in this discrimination, nor was it implemented.

Narkomnats

As earnest of its intentions, the new Soviet government established a People's Commissariat of Nationalities (Narkomnats) under Stalin's direction, and this set up commissions for the main nationalities. During the Civil War these became important agencies in stimulating and co-ordinating resistance to the German occupation and the activity of the White armies. By November 1918, there were some 18 commissions or sections.

These were used to draw young nationalists into the work of the Party. The chiefs of the commissions were often older Bolsheviks of the nationality concerned and often on the Left – that is, opposed to the Party line on the national question. They criticized the approach of bringing young nationalists with no Bolshevik credentials into the Party as a dilution of Party policy. Trotsky later noted 'these russified non-Russians who opposed their abstract internationalism to the real needs of the oppressed nationalities. Actually, this policy supported the old tradition of russification and was a special danger in the conditions of the civil war.'[9]

Nonetheless, the Narkomnats journal, *Zhizn' Natsional' nostei* (Life of the Nationalities) demonstrated the relative liberalism of Party control on the issue. Most striking was the case of the young Tatar Muslim, Mir Sajit Sultan Galiev, who was drawn into the work of the commissions, becoming one of Stalin's assistants. His contributions to the Narkomnats journal showed how far he was from accepting the Party line on nationalities or even understanding some of the basic Marxist concepts. The journal also allowed him to display his growing alienation from the Bolsheviks. In the first instance, he did not accept that there were classes among the Muslims, so there could be no class struggle. Furthermore:[10]

> as almost all classes in Muslim society have been oppressed by the colonialists, all classes have the right to be called 'proletarians' . . . Muslim peoples are proletarian nations. From an economic standpoint, there is an enormous difference between the English and French proletariat and the proletariat of Morocco and Afghanistan. It is therefore legitimate to state that the national movement in the Muslim countries has the character of a socialist movement.

He also began to assert that capitalism would be able to survive class struggles in Europe while it retained its powerful economic base in the colonies. Decolonization was thus the decisive route to proletarian revolution in Europe.[11] The most important struggle was not in Europe but in the colonized east.

As the ravages of the Civil War continued – and the Red armies, under the fierce exigencies of immediate action, were remote from the scrupulousness Lenin required – the mood changed to gloom. Once a people had been colonialist, the working class would continue to be colonialist even after they had carried out a revolution. A Communist International would not help, for it would be dominated by the working classes of the colonial countries, who would continue to be colonialist. The east could only overthrow colonialism if it formed a separate Colonial International to fight against it (and, by implication, the working-class form of colonialism in the Communist Party).

For Sultan Galiev, the picture was dominated by the need of the Islamic peoples of the Russias to secure their own liberation, not by the self-emancipation of the industrial working class of Europe. Operating within a particular tradition, he endeavoured to draw its language and concepts into the tasks of Muslim anti-colonialism, with an inevitable change of meaning. What is remarkable is that he was able to do this as a Party member and an official. As we shall see, the attempt to employ the same concepts to describe quite different tasks was a common phenomenon among young nationalists.

Eighth Congress of the Russian Communist Party (Bolshevik)

The Left, as we have seen, believed that the October revolution had once and for all buried the national issue. Proletarian power now superseded the unfinished business of the bourgeois period of history. The next target was a single unified world, an international workers' republic, where – in Europe, at least – there would be no room for separate national political entities.

At the 8th Party Congress in March 1919, the Left now made yet another attempt to revise the Party programme on the national question. Bukharin advanced the case that the right of self-determination be restricted to the 'toiling masses', buttressing his argument with quotations from Lenin's writings that affirmed that the Party's task was to secure the 'self-determination of the working class' rather than that of peoples. The issue now facing the Party had become the defeat of global finance capital, and in that struggle the Party could choose to support the rights of national independence or of world proletarian unity, but not both. Piatakov also spoke, arguing that national rights were now the weapon of a counter-revolutionary bourgeoisie. 'Once we unite the economy and build one apparatus ... all this notorious self-determination is not worth one rotten egg.'[12]

Lenin's reply reiterated his argument that world and social development was 'uneven', so that, even in the most economically advanced countries, the social differentiation between classes and awareness of this differentiation were not yet sufficient to take for granted the primacy of class, as opposed to national, identity. Thus, one could not afford to ignore or deny the right of national self-determination. In Russia, any attempt to refuse this right would immediately aid the bourgeoisie of each nationality and tend to push the local working class into its arms. 'In my opinion, this kind of Communist [who denies the right to secede]', he repeated, 'is a Great Russian chauvinist; he lives inside many of us and must be fought.'

Then, turning to the Bukharin–Stalin argument, he agreed that recognizing the right to secede would vary according to the social transition involved. But, even so, it was still true that the bourgeoisie was the rightful champion of nationalism. The working class must therefore support the bourgeoisie in this respect – 'A nation means the bourgeoisie together with the proletariat.' There could be no sense in restricting the exercise of the right to the labouring class alone.

In passing, Lenin extended the general argument to a much wider audience, and without the earlier reservations:[13]

> All nations have the right to self-determination ... The vast majority, most likely nine-tenths of the population of the earth, perhaps 95 per cent, come ,under this description ... To reject the self-determination of nations and insert the self-determination of the working people would be absolutely wrong, because this manner of settling the question does not reckon with the difficulties, with the zigzag course taken by differentiation within nations.

For those not already convinced, it is unlikely that Lenin's argument persuaded them. Particularly since the discipline of administering State power in peculiarly obdurate circumstances inclined all in the reverse direction, and obliged them to limit their preoccupations to ensuring the survival of the State and its domains. For the old Bolsheviks, imperceptibly, the political terrain was shifting.

The nationalities

The history of the nationalities of the former Russian empire is complex, and here only a few details can be given to illustrate how doctrine was radically reshaped by events until in content, if not in form, it became its opposite.

Poland and *Finland* established independent regimes most swiftly. As we have seen, German arms achieved a separate Polish State which remained after the end of the war and the evacuation of the German armies. The Soviet Republic respected Polish independence until the Poles invaded the Ukraine. In turning the Polish armies back, the Red Army crossed the border and advanced on Warsaw, vainly expecting a Polish rising to support its advance. There was none, and the Red Army was defeated at the gates of Warsaw. It had been a major error of judgement on the part of Lenin and the Bolshevik leadership, disregarding Lenin's earlier warnings that it could not be assumed in any country that class issues would automatically supersede national ones.

In *Finland*, the Bolsheviks expected a workers' revolution but in the short term recognized the independent bourgeois republic. As Stalin scornfully put it, 'the bourgeoisie of Finland . . . by a strange confluence of circumstances has received its independence from the hands of a socialist Russia'.[14] In January 1918, the Finnish Social Democrats, with help from the Russian troops still in the country, attempted to seize power. In March, the RSFSR recognized the Finnish Socialist Workers' Republic. But the move was premature, for a bitter war ensued that was settled only when the Finnish government called in the aid of German troops, supported by Swedish volunteers. The defeat was severe, for the internationalist Left had been as strong in Finland as in Great Russia.

A not dissimilar sequence of events occurred in the Baltic States. *Latvia* alone, without much national tradition before 1917, gave the Bolsheviks an absolute majority of votes in the elections to the Constituent Assembly. The regimes which emerged in *Lithuania* and *Estonia* had considerable popular support (both implemented quite radical land-reform programmes), and might have been able to sustain independent national States without foreign intervention. However, in the event, Soviet regimes were set up in Estonia and Latvia in October 1917, but were overthrown by German occupation. Soviet governments returned in late 1918 with the end of the war, but fled early in 1919, when British naval forces in the Baltic landed to establish a base in Estonia, providing the White forces with an opportunity to attack Petrograd. In 1920, Moscow recognized the independent governments set up after the defeat of the White forces.

In Lithuania, a similar sequence of events occurred, except that it was not the British who eliminated the independent Soviet government but a Polish invasion (in April 1919). When the Poles finally repulsed the Russian counter-attack, they sponsored an independent bourgeois republic, which in due course was recognized by Moscow. Thus, again, the simple expression of the principles of national self-determination or workers' international unity was vastly complicated by the context of competing Great Powers and Russian exhaustion.

In the *Ukraine*, the already strained relations between the Rada and the Provisional Government could only be exaggerated under the Bolsheviks as the Civil War developed. One of the main initial bases of the White armies under General Kornilov was on the lower Don river with Kaledin, Ataman of the Don Cossacks. From the Russian perspective, it seemed that the Rada increasingly favoured the Whites; Cossacks deserting from the Russian armies were allowed to cross the Ukraine to join Kaledin, whereas the Red Army was refused permission to pursue them and confront the Whites.

A new focus of power was also created by the initiation of Ukrainian Soviets, the strongest being in the industrialized east, led by Kharkhov. In the All-Ukrainian Soviet, the Bolsheviks constituted an important political alternative to the Rada in Kiev. However, when Moscow threatened war on the Rada if it continued to collaborate with Kaledin and to refuse to allow the Red Army to cross Ukrainian territory to attack the White forces, the anti-Bolsheviks read out the ultimatum to the shocked delegates. One of their number said, as if consciously echoing Lenin, that the ultimatum 'destroys the brotherhood of the labouring classes of all nations, awakens manifestations of national animosity and obscures the class consciousness of the masses, in this manner favouring counter-revolution'.[15] The Bolshevik delegates were obliged to withdraw from the Soviet.

Piatakov and his faction made a virtue of necessity. It was now no longer necessary to make even token gestures towards Ukrainian opinion. Piatakov rejected any idea of an independent Ukraine and urged military invasion to re-establish Russian control. In the interim, the Kharkov Soviet declared a Soviet Republic and the end of the Rada. In turn, the Rada declared the Ukraine independent.

Simultaneously, Red Army units crossed the border en route for the campaign against Kaledin. Lenin, watching the military advance closely, was particularly concerned to reassure Ukrainian opinion that this was not the beginning of the end of the right to secede. His telegrams to the army reiterated the need at all times to respect Ukrainian sovereignty.[16]

The reality, however, was quite different. Lenin once argued that a political leader is responsible not only for policy but for the action of those who execute it. In the Ukraine, it was impossible to adhere to this principle. The Red Army units had their own dynamic and their own imperative – to reach Kaledin as swiftly as possible, regardless of peasant opinion. While he was not typical, the notorious sadist, Lieutenant Colonel Muraviev, one of the former Tsarist officers on whom the Red Army was obliged to rely, vowed to hold the Ukraine by fire and the sword. There were stories of Red Guards who shot those who dared to speak Ukrainian in public or to affirm the rights of Ukrainian nationality. The military rode roughshod even over the Ukrainian Bolsheviks.

Even if the Russians had wanted to use the pretext to reconquer the Ukraine, however, they could not have done so. The Kiev Rada, panic-stricken at what they saw as a Russian invasion, summoned the German army to defend their power by taking over the western Ukraine and its grain resources. The Germans obliged but, once installed as an occupying force, dismissed the Rada and created their own puppet government. With the end of the First World War, the Germans left, but did not remove their client State. The Rada now summoned the Red Army to restore its power.

Simultaneously, Piatakov became the head of a new secret Soviet Government of the Ukraine at Kursk. Lenin was furious when he learned about it. The Russian Government denied that it was supporting the 'Kursk clique' but, for Ukrainian opinion, it must have seemed inconceivable that this were true.

With some armed detachments, Piatakov now seized Kharkov. Again Moscow denied any involvement. However, this time the Central Committee intervened to remove Piatakov from his official position. Party leadership was put in the hands of Rakovskii (a Roumanian), who was instructed to make every effort to win over the support of the Ukrainian Left and make all concessions required to conciliate the Ukrainian peasantry. At the same time, however, the armed forces advanced on Kiev.

The country was in turmoil. Bands of predatory freebooters, ex-soldiers turned bandits, preyed on a severely impoverished peasantry which had only the lowly Jewish traders as a target for its hatred. Warlords operated in the west, and the east was dominated by an independent anarchist force, the green armies of Makhno.

In practice, the Red Army units did nothing to conciliate the Ukrainian Left or the peasants. Agriculture was brutally collectivized and no concessions were made in the use of the Ukrainian language and culture. However, Denikin's White armies counter-attacked and after seven months the Red Army was obliged to withdraw. In Kiev, the military secretary of the Rada, the notorious Petlyura, seized power and instituted a new wave of repression, marked by savage anti-semitism. Famine and a typhus epidemic struck in the winter of 1919–20.

In October 1919, at long last the Russian Party recognized the seriousness of the role of the Bolshevik Left in reversing Party policy. The central committee of the Ukrainian section of the Party and the supposed Ukrainian Soviet Government were dissolved. Manuilski, on behalf of the Party, indicted the Ukrainian Bolsheviks for excluding Ukrainian participation from the government, for behaving like a typically colonial regime (at the 8th Party Congress Lenin had launched a scathing attack on Great Russian chauvinism in the Ukrainian regional section). The Party resolved to recognize Ukrainian independence, but to work towards a federal relationship. It was vital, the Central Committee in Moscow decided, that all Party members support the free development of the Ukrainian language and culture, and defend them against Russification. All institutions in the Ukraine must move towards the use of the local language. In order to conciliate the Ukrainian peasants, the agrarian policy of the Party should not be implemented.[17]

The saga of horrors had not yet run its full course. Petlyura, the military dictator of Kiev and parts of the western Ukraine, had grown desperate at his inability to establish his power. He now appealed to the ancient enemy of the Ukraine, Poland, to clear the land of all Russian forces – and offered as reward the concession of eastern Galicia to Poland. In the spring of 1920, Polish armies swept through the western Ukraine to Kiev. It took a year for the Red Army to prize them loose.

Three years of horrifying anarchy and nine governments destroyed what there had been of Ukrainian nationalism. In the end, sheer exhaustion and hunger made political questions remote for the majority. Whatever their errors – and they had been considerable – the Bolsheviks did at last establish some measure of order that allowed some recovery from the attrition of the years. However, it did not prevent, in the winter of 1921–2, an appalling famine afflicting the southern districts of the Ukraine, 'the worst', a League of Nations report declared, 'both as regards the numbers affected and as regards the mortality from starvation and disease which has occurred in Europe in modern times'.[18] The price of national freedom might well have seemed impossibly high.

In the Transcaucasus a similar mixture of the threat of external intervention and 'Great Russian chauvinism' produced not dissimilar effects. Following the October revolution, the three countries of the region – *Georgia, Armenia and Azerbaijan* (with the vital oil centre of Baku) – established a common assembly which declared the region independent (simultaneously, a Baku Soviet was set up). However, frictions between the three grew, exacerbated by Georgia's increasing involvement with Germany and Azerbaijan's relationship with Germany's ally in the World War, Turkey. Georgia announced its independence and alliance with Germany. Shortly afterwards, Turkish military forces invaded the other two countries, and finally took Baku – with great slaughter.

The defeat of the Central Powers in the autumn of 1918 removed German forces from the scene, and the Turkish military evacuated the region. However, British forces from Persia temporarily intervened to offer support for Armenia and Azerbaijan against the advance of the Red Army (and to crush the Baku Soviet). After their withdrawal, the Azerbaijan government was overthrown by a rising in Baku and a Soviet Socialist Republic was established.

Armenia, the scene of fearful destruction with half its population refugees from Turkish persecution, continued to press claims for the return of its homelands in Turkey. The Turks invaded, but the Red Army was now beginning to re-establish order and a Turkish withdrawal was negotiated. The Red Army was the sole force available to prevent a complete liquidation of Armenia by Turkey.

The Georgian independent republic was the most solidly based of the three. It survived for two and a half years under the Georgian Social Democrats (mainly Menshevik), and instituted important reforms. However, the Georgian Communists, encouraged by the regional Party directorate, were eager to precipitate a military intervention by the Red Army. Like Piatakov in the Ukraine, the Transcaucasian Party chief, a Georgian, Orjonikidze, was impatient to resolve the question, and establish co-ordinated economic communications with Baku through Georgia. He tried to force the military issue but was checked; a telegram in the names of Lenin and Stalin forbade him 'to "self-determine" Georgia'.

However, he continued to press the need for military intervention to support, he said, worker risings in the country. When he finally launched the attack, he did not inform the Central Committee in Moscow. The Georgian forces manfully defended the capital, Tiflis, but were finally obliged to concede. Simultaneously, Turkish forces seized the port of Batum, but were subsequently expelled by Red Army detachments.

The Georgian case was as close as could be to straight annexation, without the pretext of disorder (although the Turkish army remained an important threat). By default, Lenin accepted the *fait accompli*. Perhaps a certain sensitivity on this question inspired his particularly detailed instructions to Orjonikidze on how the Georgians were to be treated; the intelligentsia were to be offered particular concessions, and the Mensheviks to be invited to participate – 'avoid any mechanism copying the Russian pattern . . . bigger concessions to all the petty bourgeois elements'.[19] But the instructions were no more effective here than in the Ukraine, and, as we shall see, it was Georgia that came to sum up Lenin's revulsion not only at the implementation of Party policy in the national field, but also at the general evolution of the Party.

For the *Muslims* of Central Asia the October revolution was in important respects a retreat. For 'All Power to the Working Class' in a colonial context meant all power to Russian colonists, the only workers available. As one Central Asian observed:[20]

> Under Tsarist colonialism, it was the privilege of the Russians to belong to the industrial proletariat. For this reason, the dictatorship of the proletariat took on a typically colonialist aspect.

To the victims, the abstract Leftism of some of the Bolsheviks seemed in practice much the same as colonial domination. Particularly since, almost invariably, the colonists used socialist slogans to reject any nationalist demands and justify the elimination of nationalists.

Thus, the early Bashkir Soviet Republic excluded all Bashkir participation. By means of an appeal to Lenin, Bashkirs were able to secure some positions in the government, only to have their agreement with Moscow cancelled a year later when Bashkiria was forcibly incorporated in the RSFSR. The Bashkir Revolutionary Commission resigned in protest at this 'Russian chauvinism' and the 'imperialistic tendencies of the Russians which hinder in every manner the development of national minorities'.[21] Zeki Validov, one of the most famous Bashkir military leaders, fled to the Urals – to the shock of Moscow – and thence to the armed revolt of the Basmachi in eastern Turkestan. Behind him, the Russian colonists created vigilante groups to seize Bashkir land.

In Turkestan, the issues were at their most stark, for the province was cut off from Moscow during the Civil War. The Tashkent Soviet was created from Russian workers. It excluded Muslims; 'one cannot permit the admission of Muslims into the higher organs of the regional revolutionary authority', the Soviet resolved, 'because the attitude of the local population towards the Soviet of Soldiers, Workers and Peasants is quite uncertain, and because the native population lacks proletarian organizations'.[22] When a Muslim group in Kokand declared an Autonomous Republic, the Soviet resolved to 'subordinate entirely the principle of national self-determination to socialism' and crush it. The Soviet's military forces instituted a three-day orgy of slaughter and looting in Kokand.

Kokand was by no means an isolated incident, and drove those initially favourable to the Bolsheviks into opposition. As Ahmed

Bayturson, commander of the Kirghiz-Kazakh military forces, put it later:[23]

> They [the Kirghiz-Kazakh people] received the first revolution with joy and the second with consternation and terror ... The first revolution had liberated them from the oppression of the Tsarist regime and reinforced their perennial dream of autonomy ... The second revolution was accompanied in the borderlands by violence, plundering, exactions and the establishment of a dictatorial regime ... in the past, a small group of Tsarist bureaucrats oppressed them; today, the same group of people or others who cloak themselves in the name of the Bolsheviks perpetuate in the borderlands the same regime.

It was only the proclamation, in the words of the head of the White armies, Denikin, of 'Great Russia, One and Indivisible',[24] as well as later Bolshevik efforts to rectify the situation, that persuaded Muslim nationalists to opt for Moscow. But there were still plenty of forces in the Party that remained ambiguous or hostile. When the Bashkirs, supported by Lenin and a minority of the leadership, complained at being deprived of the autonomous republic, the secretary of the central executive told them, 'That whole autonomous republic which you take so seriously is only a game to keep you people busy.'[25]

Successive efforts to force the Tashkent Soviet to open its ranks were unsuccessful. Moscow's real forces on the ground were too thin and too preoccupied with the Civil War. Finally, in 1919, a special commission reported that the thin layer of workers had fallen under the influence of 'colonially nationalistic hangers-on'. The Politbureau was horrified. It resolved to equalize landholdings between Russians and non-Russians, and to 'overcome, oust and subordinate the Russian *kulaks* in the most energetic manner'. Errors must be publicly acknowledged, natives recruited at all levels of the administration, and negotiations begun with the Basmachi rebels. Dismal though it might seem relative to the great hopes earlier, this was perhaps the high point for the accommodation of the nationalists. Muslim nationalists were encouraged to see themselves as the spearhead of the anti-colonial movement, and Lenin himself addressed their congress (in November 1919).

The end of the Civil War

By 1920, there could be a pause for breath, an attempt to remember what the meaning of the revolution was supposed to be. The regime had been entirely obsessed with the immediate issues of survival and had on occasions mistaken the exigencies of the present for long-term principle. But now the medium-term future of the new federation was becoming more clear, the precedents and balance of powers were clarified. The more important enemies had, at least for the moment, been defeated.

The Civil War had been fought in the main in the borderlands, precisely where the national question was at its most urgent. Despite the Party programme and frequent reiteration of the line, the record in practice seemed appalling – ranging from the Russian colonists, operating under the banners of Soviet power and universal freedom; the arbitrary and cruel behaviour of raw troops operating in alien lands and in danger, far from the watching eyes of Moscow; the role of former Tsarist officers whose instincts were for the patriotic defence of all the territories of the former empire, without concession to local nationalism; to the contempt of the Bolshevik ultra-Left for all forms of nationalism. There hardly seemed room for the Party's official policy.

Yet, despite everything, it did work. Part of its working was the recognition of sheer necessity; as the old empire disintegrated, the tiny forces of the embattled Soviet republic could not hold it together. Yet whereas the old political order, including much of the Left, denied the principle of secession, the Bolsheviks were officially proud to embrace it. The Western peoples – with the exception of the Ukraine – did attain independence.

Elsewhere, the White armies offered the subordinate peoples of the old empire only the same as before, and this made even the Bolsheviks seem acceptable. While it may not be reasonable to go as far as official opinion, there was some truth in Stalin's retrospective judgement at the 12th Party Congress:[26]

> the Party, in its work, never tired of advancing this programme of national emancipation, in opposition to both the frankly coercive policy of Tsarism and the half-hearted semi-imperialist policy of the Menshevik and Social Revolutionaries . . . There can be little doubt that this sympathy and support [of masses of nationalities for the Party] was one of the decisive factors that determined the triumph of our Party.

Clause 9 of the Party programme could not be blamed, as Rosa Luxemburg argued, for the disintegration of the old Russia; it had been one of the resources for saving what had been saved.

Yet in one respect Rosa Luxemburg, Bukharin and Piatakov were right. In an imperialist world, the Great Powers, a world system of States, dominated and shaped all lesser national demands. The Bolsheviks might wish to prove their democratic credentials to the subject peoples, but the Great Powers would inevitably see this as an opportunity to advance their own interests or eliminate a threat to them. History was indeed not made in conditions of the Bolsheviks' choosing.

The native intelligentsia provided the opportunity for outside intervention. They seized the opportunity for independence or at least a new bargain with Moscow – regardless of whatever views might be held by the silent masses. But the leaders needed to support their bid with sufficient military backing, and that was usually available only through collaboration with foreign powers. The Great Powers who wished to intervene were primarily interested in the destruction of Bolshevism rather than in national independence *per se*. Thus the immediate issue at stake was not between Moscow and a former Tsarist dependency, but between the Soviet Republic and a hostile Great Power. As Carr puts it:[27]

> What was depicted as a struggle between a national proletariat and peasantry, and a national bourgeoisie, was in fact a struggle between the Russian Bolsheviks on the one hand, and Russian and foreign anti-Bolsheviks on the other hand, for the controlling influence over the territory concerned. The choice was not between dependence and independence, but between dependence on Moscow or dependence on the bourgeois governments of the capitalist world.

In practice, as the Party learned, so its patience diminished: it shifted to incorporating territories by force, while conceding the forms of federation and a measure of cultural autonomy (those things formerly ruled out as institutionalizing division). The real Soviet nationalities policy was fashioned in conditions of extreme struggle and desperate material need (for the wheat, coal and iron of the Ukraine, the oil of the Caucasus, the cotton of Turkestan). The priority was to neutralize the borderlands against the Whites and foreign intervention, to ensure the military security of the Republic.

Furthermore, the cadres believed they were about to ignite the European socialist revolution. So policy compromises, even reversals, were only temporary. Provided the Soviet regime could ensure its short-term survival, there would be time for the German revolution to bring political and material relief to the Soviet federation. Then it would be possible to set matters right and return to the correct position of Clause 9.

However, the legacy was different. For outside Europe, among that still tiny minority of nationalists in the colonial possessions of the European powers, it was the official position of the Soviet Republic, not the contradictory practice, that was noted. The Bolshevik reputation stood high, and rightly so, for at least they acknowledged the question and officially embraced national independence. The European powers flatly – and brutally – rejected the right of national self-determination for their colonies both in the immediate and the long term.

Once peace returned, the government made genuine efforts to be respectful and protective of national cultures, languages and traditions, to be conciliatory towards peasant and middle-class interests, and to create regimes composed of members of the nationality concerned. This did not, as we shall see, amount to tolerating real nationalists, those who demanded secession. But, in the policy on nationalities, hypocrisy was no more extreme than in other sectors of policy. For already domestic class forces were being invented and manipulated at will to validate policy decisions. Lenin, with his characteristic bluntness, might affirm that[28]

> owing to the war and to the desperate poverty and ruin, [the proletariat] has been declassed, i.e. dislodged from its class groove, and has ceased to exist as a proletariat . . . Since large-scale capitalist industry has been destroyed, since the factories are at a standstill, the proletariat has disappeared. It has sometimes figured in the statistics, but it has not held together economically.

The mythology continued: the Party spoke on behalf of a working class. And the subordinate nationalities freely embraced federation within the RSFSR.

How far were Lenin and those who seriously supported Clause 9 aware of the real logic of events? The evidence would seem overwhelming that Lenin was not devious in defending Clause 9. The defence is too frequent, passionate and uncompromising to suggest that it was all a short-term tactic to confuse. Yet he accepted the military conquest of the Ukraine, the forcible absorption of Bashkiria and the annexation of Georgia. It would have been impossible to predict the way events developed after October 1917, and the policy of the Party seemed on numerous grounds to be the most sensible, the only one which went some way to reconciling the need for large economic units (which, rightly or wrongly, was assumed to be decisive for material progress) and for democracy, understood as the right of peoples to choose their own State.

Lenin was not a nationalist, and his central political aim was to preserve the Republic as a springboard for world revolution. All other questions were secondary, so it is not reasonable to reproach him for not being a nationalist. His strength was his obsessive single-mindedness, his refusal to be diverted by what at that moment were secondary issues (even though they might be issues of far greater importance in the medium or long term). Winning the Civil War was just such an overriding priority, and all other issues were in part subsidiary to this. The troops might be raw, Piatakov might be an ultra-Leftist, but the ship had to be built with the timbers that were available, not some hypothetical timbers that might one day become available.

Of course, he was to some extent screened from the uncomfortable reality. Friends of Piatakov restrained him from time to time lest Lenin discover the truth. Stalin kept his friend Orjonikidze warned of the moments when he might or might not move against Georgia. Even so, it is impossible that he could have evaded knowledge of the reality. We must presume that, for much of the time, he suspended judgement in order to support the main sweep of the Red Army. People were changed – as Piatakov was dismissed, or the Ukrainian section purged – or checked, but only in extreme circumstances. Winning the war took priority over all else. With victory, other things would become possible, especially if the German revolution took place.

The Civil War and the intervention of the Great Powers were a baptism of fire for the Bolsheviks. It was so scarring that it dominated perceptions in Moscow for years to come. For those who survived, the heady talk and dreams, the vision of a global system and of revolutionaries without national allegiances, all that had inspired them before 1917, must have seemed as remote and irrelevant as childhood. They had been driven by brute necessity to defend one country. The Bolsheviks had suddenly become exposed to the full blast of inter-State competition. It was 1914 all over again. Then the sections of the Second International had divided up between the different belligerent powers. The rhetoric of internationalism faded like morning mist before the sun of reality. War allowed no equivocation. The instrument of war was the national State and it mattered little whether that State was called the beachhead of a world working class or simply an ordinary republic: the disciplines remained the same.

Thus, in the absence of revolutions in other countries bringing a genuine international dimension to the events in Russia, the material basis of the Soviet State, locked in military contest, inevitably generated what Lenin called 'Great Russian chauvinism'. It was not a peculiar psychological deviation, nor yet a hangover from the old order (although it might be that as well). It was precisely the ideological companion of the *national* struggle for survival of the Soviet State. Bolshevism, for the more sophisticated Party cadres, was battered by events into a defensive, half-shamefaced, opaque Russian patriotism. For the less sophisticated, it was chauvinism. What is so remarkable is that, given the force of the currents in which the Bolsheviks were swimming, Lenin retained such an obstinate consistency in resisting them.

7

GREAT
RUSSIAN
CHAUVINISM

*T*HE period 1920–21 was a turning point in the history of the
new regime. The Civil War had been won, but at enormous cost.
The country was exhausted, large parts of it devastated by war
and continued banditry. Famine crippled most of southern Russia and
affected much of the rest of the country. The European revolution that
was supposed to bring relief to besieged Moscow had failed to occur; the
Reichswehr crushed the March Action of the German Communist
Party in 1921. The Great Powers had successfully isolated the Soviet
regime and prevented it from spreading the revolution. And the
isolation was not just political, for it disastrously affected the basic
means of recuperation: capital and imported commodities.

On all issues, the orders of the day were retreat and recuperation,
consolidation and reconstruction. At the 10th Party Congress (in March
1921), a New Economic Policy was launched to restore the incentives
to peasant household production through an end to the requisition
of agricultural products, the return of confiscated land, a revival of
private commercial life (and the right of peasants to sell their crops
freely), and the reopening of schools. This presupposed a reassertion
of administrative control of the whole country rather than the local
autonomy that had characterized much of the Civil War. Abroad,
emphasis shifted to a re-establishment of orthodox diplomacy in
order to create stable political and economic relationships with foreign
governments and so ensure the security of the Soviet Union. In the same
year, Josef Stalin was made General Secretary of the Communist Party.

In terms of the national question, consolidation meant an increase in
efforts to reunify the country, to focus its disconnected economic efforts

on immediate priorities. Out of what remained of the old empire of the Tsars had emerged the RSFSR (including 20 autonomous non-Russian areas) with 70 per cent of the total population, and eight Republics (White Russia, Azerbaijan, Armenia, Georgia, the Ukraine, the Far Eastern Republic, and two Central Asian republics Khorezm and Bukhara). The formal existence of federal relationships during the Civil War could not, of course, be allowed to obstruct a unified military organization. Within the RSFSR, there were single Commissariats for War, National Economy, Railways, Finance and Labour. The State Planning Commissariat divided European Russia into twelve economic regions and Asia into nine, without regard to the boundaries of the republics. In practice, republics were tacked on to the RSFSR in order to operate a unified military, railway and communication system.

The model for incorporation was seen as the treaty between the RSFSR and the Azerbaijan Soviet Socialist Republic (SSR) of September 1920. This unified the military formations, the economic and foreign trade agencies, supply organizations, railways, water supply, posts and telegraph, administration and finance. The representative of the RSFSR had a casting vote on the Azerbaijan Sovnarkom. As Carr comments:[1]

> the result of the union could hardly be other than the dependence of Azerbaijan on the RSFSR. No great care was thought necessary in the text [of the treaty] to mask this reality.

The Party had always been centralized. Now the extension of Moscow's power over all the territories led to the despatch of cadres throughout the land. Many were raw recruits; by 1922, the overwhelming majority of active Party members had joined since 1917 (and 72 per cent were Russians). Often they were heroes of the Civil War, tough, energetic, dynamic, but with little knowledge of the detail of the Party programme, a great drive to work, and great irritation at petty obstacles, such as the separation of new 'Republics', let alone the more fictional 'autonomous areas'. It was hardly surprising that, as Richard Pipes puts it:[2]

> To the overwhelming majority of Communists and Communist sympathisers, the goals of the movement – the 'dictatorship of the proletariat', the 'unity of the anti-capitalist front', or the 'destruction of counterrevolutionary forces' – were synonymous with the establishment of Great Russian hegemony.

Soviet military power had in many cases made possible the survival of the borderlands in the face of threats of foreign occupation. This brute fact of inequality in power belied the formal equality enshrined in declarations and treaties. After the war, the inequality continued. It underlay Stalin's emphasis that there was now no third choice for the Republics – either they were with Soviet power or with the Great Powers, the Entente: 'the interests of the masses of the people', he declared loftily, 'render the demand for secession of the border regions at the present stage of the revolution a profoundly counterrevolutionary one'.[3] The second period of the revolution, he said, was now giving way to the third, from military co-operation to 'military–economic and political union of the people'. Now, in what seemed a Luxemburgist point, he stated that the class struggle and the interests of the world proletariat had become incompatible with national self-determination.

At the 8th Party Congress (in March 1919), Lenin had found it necessary once again to beat off the attack with the stinging rebuke – 'Scratch some communists and you will find Great Russian chauvinists.'[4] For the Bashkirs, he went on, 'the term Great Russian is synonymous with the term "oppressor", "rogue"'. 'Exceptional caution must be displayed by a nation like the Great Russian who has earned the bitter hatred of all other nations.' And he condemned the Commissariat of Education for insisting on a uniform medium of education, Russian; *that* was Great Russian chauvinism.

At the two following Party congresses, Great Russian chauvinism was again duly condemned. At the 1921 Congress, Stalin himself identified the same target 'as the fundamental force which is putting the brake on the union of the republics', 'seeking to sweep away everything non-Russian, to concentrate all the threads of the administration round the Russian element and to squeeze out the non-Russian'.[5] However, when a Turkestan delegate took this seriously and demanded greater efforts to control Russian chauvinism, the congress decided that[6]

> Native Communists . . . not entirely liberated from the ghosts of the past, tend to overestimate the importance of national particularism . . . They tend to neglect the class interests of the toilers and to confuse them with so-called national interests.

Another delegate put the other side rather more boldly:[7]

> The fact that Russia had first entered on the road to revolution, that Russia transformed itself from a colony – an actual colony of Western Europe – into the centre of the movement, this fact has filled with pride the hearts of those who have been connected with the Russian revolution and engendered a peculiar Red Russian patriotism. And now we see how our comrades consider themselves with pride, and not without reason, as Russians; at times, even look upon themselves above all as Russian.

The war to repel the Polish invasion of the Ukraine played a peculiar role in the re-establishment of patriotism as a legitimate Communist attitude. Zinoviev, with a certain exultation, reflected this spirit when he wrote in *Pravda* (18 May 1920) that:[8]

> The war is becoming national . . . We Communists must be at the head of this national movement which will gain the support of the entire population and daily grows stronger.

The war had an even greater effect on the 30,000 ex-Tsarist officers serving in the Red Army and the ex-Tsarist officials working in the government. Many might detest much of the domestic policy of the Soviet government but still respect the role of the Soviet State as embodying the unity of the old Russias. In the event, the war led to the invasion of Poland and Russian defeat; the advance on Warsaw seemed to cast doubt upon Moscow's claims to respect the national independence of the Tsar's Polish possessions.

After the Polish war, many more skilled and professional staff rallied to the task of reconstruction. And abroad, even a section of émigré opinion argued the case for the new regime on patriotic, not Bolshevik, grounds. A group of Russians in exile published a collection of articles, *Smena Vekh*, and later a weekly journal, that urged reconciliation with the Soviet regime. One of the contributors argued that:[9]

> The Soviet Government will strive with all means to re-unite the outlying lands with the centre – in the name of world revolution. Russian patriots will fight to achieve the same objective – in the name of great indivisible Russia. For all the ideological differences, they practically take the same road.

It was a sign of the times that some of the Bolsheviks could take pride in this testimony of support. As Stalin put it:[10]

> it is no accident that these gentlemen, the *smenovekhovtsy*, praise the Communist–Bolsheviks, as if to say: 'Talk as much as you like of your international tendencies, but we know that you will achieve what Denikin did not succeed in achieving, that you Bolsheviks have restored the idea of Great Russia, or at any rate, will restore it.'

In the new Bolshevik role as the national government, the great separation between the Tsarist and Soviet periods became less clear-cut. Commanding a territory in a competitive world order imposed its own disciplines, independently of the wishes or aspirations of the people concerned.

The nationalities

Among the first tasks of the postwar order was the recentralization of civil affairs (military affairs, like those of the Party, had not, in principle, been decentralized, though, in practice, the autonomy of local military commanders and Party units had been vital for victory). The most radical effects of this change were seen in the Republics that had so recently had some degree of separation. The accidental privileges of self-determination that the exigencies of war had allowed had become rights, and there was much resistance to their loss. The trend forced many of the old Bolsheviks, active in the governments of the Republics, into defence of their rights against the centre – Mykola, Skrypnik, Rakovskii, Mdivani, Makharadze. For the newer nationalists of Central Asia, it led to a purge.

In the *Ukraine*, the prospects seemed most favourable. Despite the horror of the Civil War, the Ukraine appeared to have established its right to sovereignty and equality with the RSFSR, embodied in the treaty signed in December 1920. Kiev ceded to Moscow control of military affairs, foreign trade, finance, labour, communications and higher education. Among what it retained was foreign affairs (it was therefore a separate signatory to the treaty of Rapallo, the last occasion when this right was exercised). Moscow affirmed that it had no power to issue directives to the Ukraine except with the prior agreement of the Ukrainian Council of People's Commissars.

However, from the end of 1921, no attempt was made to keep to this treaty. Moscow administered the Ukraine as if it were part of the RSFSR, and did not restrict its directives to the items reserved to it under the treaty. The Ukrainian Council was not consulted, still les was its permission sought. Protests proved in the main ineffective. However, a commission of enquiry under Frunze was finally set up, and its report strongly condemned the Russian Foreign Affairs Commissariat for violating Ukrainian sovereignty.

The Frunze report made no difference. Moscow continued to treat the Ukraine as its province. At the 11th Party Congress, the old Bolshevik, N.A. Skrypnik (who had joined the Party in 1897 and been a member of the committee that had planned the seizure of power), attacked the Party's approach to the Ukraine as Great Russian chauvinism. He complained that once again the Ukrainian section of the Party had been infiltrated by those who opposed the Ukrainian right of national self-determination. He ended his speech with the cry: 'The one and indivisible Russia is not our slogan.' A voice from the audience countered with: 'The one and indivisible Communist Party.'[11] The protests made no difference. The government of the RSFSR continued as before.

From the autumn of 1920, the minority of political activists among the *Muslim* peoples came under generally increased pressure to conform to the central power and eliminate 'nationalist deviations'. As we have seen, in some places, the process, hurried on by the interests of Russian colonists, started earlier. A by-product of the campaign to centralize was a major purge. In 1922, it is said, some 14,000 members of the Bukhara Communist Party were expelled (leaving some 1,560 members), and between 60 and 90 per cent of the membership of other Central Asian parties were removed. Probably the majority of those expelled had been less Bolsheviks than representatives of local interests seeking to ensure survival in the new order (and admitted to the Party in the heat of the Civil War with precious little discrimination). But there were also genuine nationalists misled by their interpretation of the Party's line.

By 1923, Moscow was ready for a decisive turn in its general political stance, for it was now clear that no revolution was likely in the short term in the rest of Europe. The Soviet Republic must stand alone, dependent solely on its own resources. It was perhaps symbolic that in May of that year the most famous of the Muslim Communists, Sultan Galiev, was publicly attacked and then arrested, a warning to the rest. In June 1923, at an enlarged conference of the Central Committee (with members from the national republics), he was condemned for nationalism, for creating an illegal anti-Party organization in the north Caucasus, for planning an anti-Party International of Turkish peoples, and for conspiring with Validov and so the Basmachi rebellion. Unlike the charges that were to be fabricated in the future, these were not implausible. However, the conference was not entirely convinced of Stalin's case. He finally won the vote, but in his reply to the discussion indicated at least two Central Asian critics who had argued, he said,[12]

'there is no difference between present-day Turkestan and Tsarist Turkestan, that only the signboard had been changed, that Turkestan remained what it had been under the Tsar'.

He concluded, correctly, that

In that case, the Basmachi are right and we are wrong. If Turkestan is in fact a colony, as it was under Tsarism, then the Basmachi are right, and it is not we who should be trying Sultan Galiev, but Sultan Galiev who should be trying us for tolerating the existence of a colony in the framework of the Soviet regime.

Stalin would not in the future allow himself such a dangerous hypothetical interpretation. Skrypnik of the Ukraine summed up a different assessment: Sultan Galiev was just a scapegoat. Nationalist deviations were not the result of Sultan Galiev, but of the 'the incapacity of the RCP(B) to apply correctly the national programme'.[13] Only the establishment of the equality of the nationalities, of justice, would overcome the central problem.

Sultan Galiev was ultimately released. Stalin's power was not yet secure; that required his triumph over the opposition in 1927. In 1928, Sultan Galiev was rearrested in a much more massive purge of the Central Asian republics, affecting in particular the commissariats of education, culture, arts and science, and the ranks of the Muslim priesthood and the number of mosques. Physical liquidation rather than criticism was now the threat. Sultan Galiev was accused of conspiring both with the old Muslim nationalists and – now the standard prelude to the death sentence – with fascists.

If Sultan Galiev were indeed a member of the clandestine Socialist Party of Turkestan, then the degree of what Lenin had called 'estrangement' was extreme. The events of the years since 1917 had disastrously affected at least some of the thin stratum of educated and politically committed Muslims, as can be seen from the documents of the organization:[14]

> Turkestan, dominated at present by an imperialistic power, cannot develop economically as it should ... native workers consider the socialists of the metropolis as hypocritical oppressors, of even a worse kind than the bourgeoisie, utilizing the slogan of the liberation of the colonies as a means of propaganda for their own profit in the colonies of their competitors.

The crisis of Georgia and the USSR

The national question proved to be the issue which finally invoked Lenin's intervention and symbolized for him the degeneration of the ideals of the October revolution.

Economic reconstruction required the integration of the economies, and particularly the transport systems, of the three Transcaucasian republics. Lenin himself urged this on the regional Party chief, G.K. Orjonikidze. Initially, both Azerbaijan and Georgia resisted it. The Georgian Communists argued that, since the former Menshevik government had been overthrown by force, no changes should be introduced which might imply disrespect for Georgian rights of self-determination. The old Georgian Bolshevik, Makharadze, who had been part of the Bukharin–Piatakov Left opposition to Clause 9 and could not therefore be accused of nationalist sympathies, indicated his support for the Georgian Party's position. In late 1921, with some reluctance, Lenin admitted that the project for economic integration had been premature and that Moscow must retreat.[15]

Orjonikidze was furious at the obstruction presented by the Georgians. He took steps to change the attitude of Azerbaijan, and then to integrate the transport system, post and telegraph and foreign trade relationships of the three Republics – without consulting the Georgians. In response to the attempt to force traffic through Georgia, the Georgians posted military guards on their borders and instituted residence permits for non-Georgians. Orjonikidze responded by ordering 'political integration'; in March 1922, he proclaimed a Transcaucasian Federation, with a Congress to elect a Federal Council.

Quite separately, the Party Central Committee in Moscow was seeking to define a proper constitutional relationship between the RSFSR and the Republics. In early August 1922, a commission was set up under Stalin to draft the format. The commission had a majority of Stalin's associates. In the third week of September, it accepted Stalin's draft (with one abstention, the Georgian Mdivani), which in essence proposed that the Republics be absorbed as additional components in the RSFSR. Indeed, steps were taken to implement this formula before it had been approved by the Central Committee; Mdivani was told in late August that henceforth the instructions issued by the RSFSR were binding in the Republics.

However, when consulted, only two Republics (Armenia and Azerbaijan) agreed without qualification to the proposal. Byelorussia and ultimately the Ukraine favoured the existing arrangements. Georgia opposed the proposal. The Transcaucasian Federal Council approved – and ordered the Georgian Communist Party to do likewise.

Lenin's health was now proving an increasing problem. He had never fully recovered from the attempted assassination of August 1918, and recurrent illness, and operations, dogged his life. In May 1922 he was partially paralysed and temporarily lost the power of speech. Nonetheless, despite these difficulties, he was beginning to reconsider what had been achieved. In late September, he asked to see the file of the work of Stalin's constitutional commission. On the basis of this, he prepared for the Politbureau a rejection of Stalin's proposals and an alternative – a separate government of the union (the Union of Soviet Socialist Republics, USSR) into which all federating elements (including the RSFSR) would enter as equals. Once again he proclaimed:[16]

War to the death on dominant nation chauvinism . . . It must be *absolutely* insisted that the Union Central Executive should be *presided over* in turn by a
Russian
Ukrainian
Georgian, etc.   *Absolutely.*

Severe toothache kept Lenin from attending the relevant Politbureau meeting and Stalin hurried to circulate his proposals in the hope of forcing the issue. When he came to circulate Lenin's statement, he included his own comments, which were, in Pipes' words, 'surprisingly insolent in tone'.[17] He accused Lenin of 'national liberalism' and encouraging separatism; a new 'USSR', he said, would merely duplicate the governmental bureaucracy.[18] Stalin was initially confident that he would win, but the discussions ultimately favoured Lenin's proposal. Stalin accepted, saying that the changes were merely verbal. Mdivani also accepted the amended proposal, but stipulated that Georgia would enter the new USSR as an independent Republic, not part of a Transcaucasian Federation. (Stalin subsequently informed the Georgians that their request had been refused.)

Meanwhile, the Georgian affair matured. In late September, Orjonikidze reported to Lenin in Gorky on the progress in consolidating the Transcaucasian Federation. Later, three members of the Georgian Central Committee called on him. At this stage, Lenin's sympathies were entirely with Orjonikidze and he was irritated with what he saw as Georgian obstructionism over the urgent need for the integration of the Transcaucasus. Perhaps it was this sympathy which emboldened Orjonikidze to dismiss the Georgian Central Committee and order its members to report in Moscow. Lenin backed him up:

I firmly condemn the invectives addressed to Orjonikidze and insist that your conflict, conducted in a more seemly and loyal tone, should be settled by the Secretary of the Central Committee of the RCP.

Nine of the eleven members of the Georgian Central Committee resigned. Orjonikidze and the Federal Council then appointed a new Central Committee which voted to accept the Transcaucasian Federation. However, resistance and criticism did not stop. Then, in late November, Orjonikidze's frustrations so enraged him that he went so far as to punch one of the Georgian leaders. Rykov, one of Lenin's deputies, was by chance a witness to this assault.

It was this seemingly trivial event which suddenly began to unwind the affair in the opposite direction. The Russian Secretariat appointed Dzerzhinsky and two others to report on the incident (Rykov also accompanied them). They returned to Moscow to exonerate Orjonikidze; the blame was attributed entirely to the Georgians.

Orjonikidze's behaviour shocked and alarmed Lenin. Dzerzhinsky's report did so even more, for it now appeared that there was a conspiracy. However, before he could pursue his suspicions, he was struck by a serious heart attack (on the day following a visit by Dzerzhinsky). Three days later (16 December) a second one followed. His doctors ordered a complete rest with no involvement in Party affairs or communication with his colleagues (Stalin was put in charge of these arrangements).

A race now began between Lenin's efforts to get the information he required and draft his final thoughts (in preparation for the 12th Party Congress) and his declining health. He used his wife, Krupskaya, and his secretaries as his ears. When Stalin discovered Krupskaya had written a letter for Lenin, he reprimanded her with, in Lenin's words, 'a storm of the coarsest abuse' and a threat of prosecution. Lenin was permitted to dictate for only five minutes a day, and on that basis he drafted his final thoughts on the leadership of the Party (his 'testament'), its organization and the key agencies of the State (in particular Stalin's Workers' and Peasants' Inspectorate). The last three notes concerned the national question.[19]

He began with an apology for not having intervened more energetically on the question of the USSR, and went on to express the growing pessimism of his declining months:

> we must, in all conscience, admit . . . the apparatus we call ours is, in fact, still quite alien to us; it is a bourgeois and Tsarist hotch-potch and there has been no possibility of getting rid of it in the course of the past five years without the help of other countries and because we have been 'busy' most of the time.

The issues of Georgia and the USSR had suddenly exposed the reality of a *Russian* apparatus which 'we took over from Tsarism and slightly anointed with Soviet oil'. With such an apparatus,[20]

> the 'freedom to secede from the union', by which we justify ourselves, will be a mere scrap of paper, unable to defend the non-Russians from the onslaught of the really Russian man, the Great Russian chauvinist, in substance a rascal and a tyrant . . . There is no doubt that the infinitesimal percentage of Soviet and sovietized workers will drown in

that tide of chauvinistic Great Russian riffraff like a fly in milk.

On the Georgian issue, 'Stalin's haste and his infatuation with pure administration, together with his spite against the notorious "national socialism", played a fatal role'. And Dzerzhinsky (by origin, a Pole) 'distinguished himself by his truly Russian frame of mind (it is common knowledge that people of other nationalities who have become Russified overdo this Russian frame of mind) ... [and is] inexcusably guilty in adopting a light-hearted attitude' towards the violence of Orjonikidze. Lenin repeated the special obligation of Russians 'to compensate the non-Russians for the lack of trust, for the suspicion and the insults to which the government of the "dominant" nation subjected them in the past'. This required[21]

profound caution, thoughtfulness and a readiness to compromise. The Georgian [that is, Orjonikidze] who is neglectful of this aspect of the question, or who carelessly flings about accusations of 'nationalist socialism' (where he himself is a real true 'nationalist socialist', and even a vulgar Great Russian bully) violates in substance the interests of proletarian class solidarity ... it is better to overdo rather than underdo the concessions and leniency towards the national minorities.

He then made a series of proposals to try to right the balance, which included exemplary punishment for Orjonikidze, new rules to protect national languages and the relative autonomy of national administrations. It was vital, he said, that this be seen to be done since what was at stake was the reputation of the Soviet Union among the rising movements for colonial independence in the empires of the Western European powers.

It was too late. The shadows lengthened, darkening his last days. Despite his rage, Lenin was now trapped in the bureaucratic web, and fighting required far greater resources than his failing powers. Nonetheless, he set up a three-man enquiry which Stalin refused to supply with materials until overruled by the Politbureau. But by the time the Report was complete (3 March), Lenin was very ill. He had time only to ask Trotsky to assume responsibility for the defence of the Georgians at the 12th Party Congress. The last item in the last volume of his collected works is a top-secret telegram to the Georgians:[22]

I am outraged at the rudeness of Orjonikdze and the connivance of Stalin and Dzerzhinsky. I am preparing for you notes and a speech.

On 10 March, paralysis struck again. Lenin did not recover the power of speech before his death on 21 January 1924.

The 12th Party Congress (April 1923)

By 1923, the new Soviet bureaucracy had become consolidated, confident in its power and, if the truth were known, in its capacity to control those in the Party who might still think that world revolution was on the immediate agenda and ought to be a key policy directive. Thus, the changes that followed did not concern simply the national issue, which was of relatively low priority. What happened on the nationality question was only a detail in a much broader picture of the consolidation of a much more authoritarian regime: not as sure as it was to become in 1927, but with growing confidence.

However, given Lenin's last words, the 1923 Congress could still have been peculiarly crucial for the future of the national question, as well as for the personal future of Stalin as General Secretary of the Party and of Trotsky as Lenin's supposed heir. In fact, the Congress did settle these issues for the foreseeable future, but not at all in the way Lenin had suggested. Stalin, the organizer of the Congress, had done his work well, and his supporters were everywhere in evidence. There were rumours about Lenin's notes, but when a Georgian delegate requested that they be read out, it was refused on the grounds that they were for restricted circulation and only rough and provisional; Lenin would recover and finalize what he wanted to say. Above all, however, it was the refusal of Trotsky to provide a lead, to shoulder the responsibility Lenin had thrust upon him, which gave Stalin a clear run. During the session on the national question, Trotsky was absent, preparing his speech for another session.

Stalin presented his report. He was sufficiently sure of his audience to attack directly the Georgian opposition to federation. The Mdivani clique, he said, demanded privileged status over the other two members of the Transcaucasian federation, flouting the principle of equality of peoples and making harmonious federal relationships impossible. 'I think', he said, with what was to become a characteristic mixture of archness and crudity, 'that some of the comrades working on a certain piece of Soviet territory, called Georgia, have apparently something wrong with their marbles.'[23]

The Georgians did not give up. Mdivani made a bitter attack on the behaviour of the Russian Central Committee and the Transcaucasian Regional Committee, and on Orjonikidze in particular. In turn, Orjonikidze accused the Georgians of nationalist deviations. Makharadze pointed out that, with a single centralized party controlling the governments of all the Republics, there could be no serious independent sovereignty. He might have gone further to remind his audience that, in any case, while the multinational unity of the Party was supposed to represent the unity of the working class, in the majority of the Republics there was no politically significant working class (and indeed, as we noted earlier, in Russia during the Civil War, Lenin himself had said that the working class, as a class, had virtually disappeared). The Party, the supposed instrument of the working class, had completely displaced it.

Bukharin intervened to stress once again the dangers of Russian chauvinism. Rakovskii went further, saying – perhaps with a secret reference to Lenin's notes – that civil war was threatened by the divergence 'between our Party, our programme on the one hand, and our political apparatus on the other', an apparatus which mixed the aristocratic and the bourgeois. The rights of the Republics against the Union must be strengthened; for example, the RSFSR had three times as many representatives on the Council of Nationalities as all the rest; it should be limited to two-fifths (a proposal which Stalin, no doubt still smarting from Lenin's accusation of his 'infatuation with pure administration', dismissed as 'administrative fetishism').

The 12th Congress as a whole had few fears that Communists lacked sensitivity on the national question. Lukashin defined the proper distribution of responsibility for national problems – 'One fourth of the problem is caused by Great Russian chauvinism, and three quarters by local chauvinism.'[24] Stalin underlined the theoretical vindication of Russian dominance:[25]

> the basis of all our work is our effort to strengthen the power of the workers, and only then do we face that other question . . . the national question . . . We are told one must not offend the other nationalities. This is perfectly correct . . . But to deduce from this a new theory that the Great Russian proletariat must be put in an inferior position vis-à-vis the formerly oppressed nations is absurd . . . the political basis of proletarian dictatorship lies primarily and chiefly in the central industrial regions and not the border regions which are peasant countries . . . the right of self-determination cannot and must not be a barrier to preventing the working class from expressing its right to dictatorship.

The transition had been accomplished. The Party and the State bureaucracy had assumed the right to define who was and who was not oppressed on the national question. The historic position of the Bolshevik Party had thus, without any change of programme, been completely reversed.

*

With the benefit of hindsight, the right of national self-determination had little chance in a revolutionary Russia that was forced to accept its beleaguered and impoverished national existence. Those who inherited the Tsarist State found the right inconsistent with their exercise of national power. Those who followed the Luxemburgist tradition of opposition to all nationalisms opposed it. But, above all, the practical men and women, in the main innocent of the Party's position on the national question, who fought the Civil War and then fought again to get the trains running across the enormous length of all the Russias, to ship the wheat and the iron, to build and to feed, also opposed the petty restrictions that the rights of minorities implied. Should the Georgians, a tiny minority, have the right to interdict the flow of oil from Baku to Leningrad, centre of the overwhelming majority? It was this last group, rather than the first two, who were decisive by 1923 and for whom Stalin represented practical good sense; for them, the world proletariat and Soviet Russia were imperfectly distinguished. The petty bourgeoisie of the borderlands were known to have intrigued with capitalist foreigners in order to obstruct the great chariot of history that was already rolling forward. Had not Lenin himself opposed federation for most of his political life because it obstructed that unification of economic forces which could transform the country?

By 1923, the nationalists proper of the borderlands had been silenced or exiled. The Muslim radicals that the revolution had raised were in decline. The Communists of the Republics inherited the role of defending the nationalities. This was ironic, for many of them had opposed Lenin on the national question from the ultra-Left Luxemburgist position. But the logic of running a Republic now forced them to defend their nationality against Moscow, just as those who ran the apparatus of the RSFSR, defending Soviet Russia against its enemies abroad, were obliged to embrace Russian nationalism. The Leninist group dwindled with its inspiration. But it is remarkable that Lenin, even as he was dying, chose to fight his last battle on the issue and came within an ace of toppling Stalin.

It was not, of course, a simple matter of individuals. The Soviet Union was creating a new ruling order that, by its position in the world, inevitably re-created elements of national continuity with Tsarism. It was done in an ideological context that disarmed them, that seemed to disallow any accommodation of the notorious Tsarist oppression of peoples. The more far-sighted, however, felt the contradiction between theory and practice, that, as they intended to do one thing, they were forced to do something quite different. Lenin felt it vividly:[26]

The machine [the State] refused to obey the hand that guided it. It was like a car that was not going in the direction the driver desired, but in the direction someone else desired; as if it were driven by some mysterious, lawless hand, God knows whose, perhaps of a profiteer, or of a private capitalist, or both.

Short of a transformation of the context from which the competitive necessities derived, the process of national centralization had to continue.

One casualty of the divergence between theory and practice was the theory itself. The Bolshevik combination of programmatic aims and tactical flexibility could no longer encompass the hypocrisy. Theory had to be transformed into rationalization; the Party's inheritance had to be converted into a body of unchanging principles, abstract general propositions which were not the basis for current practice but which reconciled current practice to a scholastic tradition, a set of precedents. Marxist terminology now became the language of a kind of religious dogmatism, a mystification of reality.

8

RUSSIA AND THE NATIONAL QUESTION AT LARGE

THE revolutionaries of October 1917 assumed that, in a relatively backward Russia where the peasantry were the overwhelming majority, it would be impossible for a regime founded upon the minority of urban workers to survive for long without the support of a proletarian revolution in an advanced country (where workers were the majority). Thus, it was vital for the Soviet Union to seek by all means to spread its revolution to Western Europe. However, by the time the internal situation had stabilized after the Civil War, the short-term prospects of another revolution appeared unpromising, and the Soviet Republic was obliged to accommodate itself in an arena dominated by the existing Great Powers. Supporting Communist parties in Europe in fomenting agitations, strikes and ultimately revolutionary actions had now to go with seeking to influence other governments through orthodox diplomacy.

At the same time, however, there was another shift of attention: from worker revolutions in Europe to nationalist revolutions in Asia. The Bolsheviks were among the first to recognize the increasing vulnerability of the European empires to anti-colonial movements. In this development, it seemed the Soviet Union could play a crucial role as the link between the worker revolution in Europe and the nationalist revolution in Asia. The October revolution, as Stalin proclaimed, 'built a bridge between the socialist west and the enslaved east, creating a new revolutionary front, which runs from the proletarians of the west through the Russian revolution to the oppressed peoples of the east'.[1]

This emphasis changed the significance of Russia: formerly, it had been among the most backward countries of Europe, 'the weakest link in the capitalist chain', but now it became one of the more advanced of the backward countries outside Europe, even, it was said, a former European colony that had now become a model of national independence.

Initially, however, little could be done abroad until the Soviet Republic had secured its right to survive. By then, the prospects of European revolution were dimming. Lenin drew the conclusion: 'we have won something more than a breathing space: we have entered a new period in which we have won the right to our fundamental international existence in the network of capitalist States'.[2] The Treaty of Rapallo with Germany in 1922 and the Anglo-Soviet Agreement of 1921 were the symbols of this new phase. *Izvestia* (7 December 1922), on the occasion of Soviet participation in the Lausanne international conference, drew an appropriate conclusion:

> As a result of the imperialist and civil wars, Russia temporarily disappeared from the horizon as a Great Power. Russia is coming back to the international stage. Let us hope that the day is at hand when the reappearance will be felt so strongly that no one will dare to contradict her voice.

Diplomatic relationships entailed compromises. The British required that the Soviet Government refrain from any action to foment rebellion in the British Empire, and listed past actions which were henceforth disallowed. The Communist International (Comintern) established in 1919 was thereafter to propagate revolution on its own responsibility, while the Soviet Foreign Office dissociated itself from any involvement in this.

The defeat of the attempted German revolution of 1923 put paid to the last hopes of the relief of Russia through the spread of revolution in Europe. Feelings of defeat and frustration swept through the Party, ultimately producing a new resolve that Russia – rather than the world proletariat – now had to stand and triumph alone. It would be Russia which would demonstrate the achievements of socialism. Stalin's most important theoretical innovation, that socialism could be achieved in one country (it did not depend upon a world movement), fitted exactly the feelings of the Soviet ruling order in this new phase. The Russian national framework, rather than a global class one, was the decisive element now.

The Middle East

The Bolshevik leadership might claim that Russia was the keystone in the arch linking proletarian Europe and peasant Asia, but, in practice, it proved very difficult to put this in place. In the Middle East, alongside Soviet Central Asia (and controlling access to the Russian ports of the Black Sea) the early lessons were not promising.

a) *Turkey*. In August 1919, Kemal Pasha (Atatürk) led a rebellion against the government in Constantinople and its subordination to western interests. From the perspective of Moscow, this seemed a classic case of national liberation, with, for some observers, resemblances to pre-revolutionary Russia – a defeated monarchy and empire, foreign occupation (the British occupied Constantinople in March 1920), economic ruin with high unemployment among a significant working class, peasant risings in Anatolia, a clandestine Communist party in Ankara, and a bourgeois national liberation movement. When Kemal turned to Moscow for support in the spring of 1920, it was welcomed as the natural alliance of a workers' revolution and revolutionary nationalism.

Kemal Atatürk was happy to accept Russian military and diplomatic assistance when it was needed, but this did not include permitting a role for the Turkish Communist Party. In January 1921, his forces seized Mustafa Subhi and 16 other leading members of the Party and drowned them in the Sea of Trebizond.

The shock of this, however, was tempered by Moscow's nervousness about the possibility of losing its narrow foothold in the loyalties of the new Turkish order. On the other hand, given the fragility of the Anglo-Soviet Agreement, there was no less nervousness about inciting British hostility by interference in Turkish affairs. There was therefore no protest at the destruction of the Turkish Communist leadership, and only two months later the two governments signed a treaty of mutual support. However, when a Greek army, with British financial backing, advanced into Anatolia, and Ankara appealed for Russian help, only a few token military advisers were sent. The 15-month repression of the Communists was eased; after Atatürk had routed the Greek forces, he resumed the repression.

At the fourth Congress of the Comintern, Radek reassured the Turkish Communists that it was objectively necessary for them to continue to support the 'bourgeois nationalism' of Atatürk:[3]

> Even now, with the persecutions, we say to our Turkish comrades, do not let the present moment blind you to the near future ... historically the time has not yet come to take up the decisive battle ... you still have a long road

to travel, side by side, with the revolutionary bourgeois elements.

On the same occasion, Varga presented what was to become orthodoxy – first, national liberation, then, at some later date, social revolution. In Turkey, where it was Comintern orthodoxy that landowners led the national liberation movement, it was necessary for the peasants to resist the temptation to seize the land until later 'after the victory in the struggle for liberation'. The peasants must support the landowners in the national struggle. The Comintern generals had already become remote from what it was realistic to assume about the feelings of the peasant troops.

A postponement of issues, satisfying neither imprisoned Communists nor peasant rebels, could be justified only if there were solid gains in terms of Russo-Turkish relations. There were none. At the Lausanne conference, the USSR, thinking itself in alliance with the Turks, opposed the British demand for free international rights of navigation through the Dardanelles. The Turks, suddenly alarmed at facing alone the Russian fleet in the Black Sea, abandoned the Russians to side with the British.

Thus, in this initial foray, Moscow had supported Atatürk and thereby assisted in the repression of the Turkish Communists, without gaining anything politically or diplomatically. Nonetheless, the policy continued. The Comintern continued to praise 'Turkish democracy' and, insofar as it was necessary, curb the Turkish Communists. When a Kurdish revolt broke out, the Comintern, out of deference to Atatürk, condemned it. But Atatürk did not need Moscow: condemning the Kurds only indicated Russian impotence. The leadership of the anti-colonial struggle by the world proletariat was on terms laid down by the Turkish bourgeoisie.

b) *Persia.* In May 1920, a Red Army force under Commander Raskolnikov crossed the Caspian Sea and landed in Persia in pursuit of the Russian Caspian fleet, abandoned by General Denikin. It was a timely move for it allowed Russian support to be given to a rebellion by Kuchik Khan against the old order in Teheran. With Russian help, Kuchik Khan set up the Soviet Socialist Republic of Gilan and an Iranian Communist Party. Russian help went also to two other rebellions and, at one stage, it seemed that the whole of Persia might undergo revolution, expel both the old order and the British military occupation, and ally with or join the Soviet Union.

However, in October 1920, the old order in Teheran itself officially approached Moscow for an alliance. The Soviet Foreign Office did not demur, and an agreement was accomplished the following year with a Russian promise of military support in the event of foreign intervention.

After this, as Carr comments, 'Soviet policy was quickly emptied of any revolutionary content.'[4] The Iranian Communists were reminded that social revolution in Persia was possible only after the bourgeois democratic revolution and full development had taken place.

In February 1921, the Shah's leading general, Reza Khan, seized power on a programme simultaneously opposed to both the aristocracy and the Communists. Two months later, the Soviet ambassador arrived in Teheran. The British occupying forces left, and shortly afterwards Kuchik Khan launched a march on Teheran. The Russian Foreign Minister, Chicherin, and the Soviet ambassador in Teheran immediately condemned the march and dissociated the Soviet Union from Kuchik Khan. Soviet forces abandoned Gilan. After their departure, Reza Khan's troops seized and executed the former ally of the world proletariat.

In the autumn of 1925, Reza Khan removed the Shah and took the Crown. The Comintern gave a cautious welcome to this arrival of 'bourgeois democracy' – while Reza Khan liquidated the Iranian Communist Party. Simultaneously, the Soviet ambassador presented his credentials.

As in Turkey, the Soviet Union had little power to achieve its purposes, and was severely constrained by its fear of provoking Great Power retaliation. Caught in a cleft stick, it chose to seek to maximize the benefits of orthodox diplomacy rather than gambling on revolution. It achieved little but the destruction of its cadres in return for flimsy diplomatic recognition. Reza Khan remained in control.

c) *'Objectively revolutionary'*. Moscow's lack of power was reflected in the fact both that it could not afford to discriminate between nationalist movements, and that its only instrument to induce loyalty was a supply of arms. In *Arabia*, the Russians supported the fanatical Wahhabite movement under Abd El Aziz Ibn Sa'ud (against British support for the Hashemites). The Comintern commented that 'Ibn Sa'ud is becoming the chief of a great national movement.'[5] Ibn Sa'ud thanked the Soviet Government for its support – and opened negotiations with the British.

In *Egypt*, Moscow identified a leader of the Wafd, Zagul, as a potential Kemal. As Prime Minister in 1924, however, during a wave of strikes, he arrested the Communist leadership. Stalin himself produced the notable formula:[6]

> The struggle of the Egyptian merchants and bourgeois intelligentsia for the independence of Egypt is ... an objectively *revolutionary* struggle in spite of the bourgeois origin and bourgeois status of the leaders.

For those trained in a methodology which so well identified forces of history that shaped events without regard to the subjective intentions of the participants, Stalin's formula was seductive. But it could not hide the uncomfortable failure of the predictions. No ideological commitment to nationalism led the bourgeois leaders to Moscow, let alone induced them to exchange the oppression of the Great Powers for dependence on the Soviet Union.

By 1927, little remained in the Middle East of the movements which had seemed so promising in the early 1920s. The sum of Soviet influence lay in Soviet embassies, at arm's length from those to whom they were accredited.

The Communist International

These preliminary forays in Soviet foreign policy, relative to national liberation, highlighted some of the problems that perpetually dogged Communist action in what were known as the backward and colonial countries. The Bolshevik strategy for Tsarist Russia – a worker-led alliance of workers, peasants and national liberation movements – was not easily translated to the world stage. The workers had become a Great Power in Russia. The forces of national liberation were led by national bourgeoisies which were not at all prone to accept Soviet claims at face value and had their own purposes. Without a peasant rebellion – which the Comintern in practice ruled out since this would alienate the national bourgeoisie – there was no way of changing this in Moscow's favour.

At the second Congress of the Comintern, it had been hoped that some of these questions could be anticipated. So important was it felt to be, that Lenin himself drafted the initial theses on the 'National and Colonial Question'. The centre-piece was the alliance between proletarian and peasant, but the statement was not clear about whether this was between Moscow or local Communist parties and the peasant-nationalists of Asia. This was understandable, given how little experience there had been and how few Communists there were in the colonies. Indeed, at one stage, Lenin expressed doubts about how far Communist parties could be created in peasant societies; certainly such parties could only operate in alliance with peasant movements. But that alliance would have to be 'only for the purpose of gathering the components of the future proletarian parties'.[7]

Communist parties, the theses proposed, both in the imperial centres and their colonial dependencies, must bend all efforts to assist the bourgeois democratic forces in the colonies to come to power and defeat the old social order, particularly the landed interests that were so often allied to the imperial order. But this support was to be temporary; the Communists should never merge with the bourgeois forces, always upholding the independence of the proletarian movement. The Communists should also strive to give the peasant movements a revolutionary character (contrary to Varga's recommendation to the Turkish peasantry at the Fourth Congress).

A remarkable young Indian, M.N. Roy, was a member of the commission which accepted the theses, and he presented a set of counter-theses. In these he argued that working-class and peasant movements already existed in the more advanced backward countries, and they ought not to be directed at seeking to support the local bourgeoisie: merely replacing foreign with native employers. These worker movements were likely to increase, he said, because the imperial powers were no longer devoted to preventing industrialization in their colonies (as a means of protecting colonial markets for goods manufactured in the metropolitan centres). Now, the imperialists required secure manufacturing centres in the colonies as their reserve against the possibility of European revolution. The growth of native capitalism in the colonies would increase the links between native and imperial ruling orders, and simultaneously give the imperialists more room to manoeuvre. This would end any revolutionary ambitions on the part of the native bourgeoisie. By now, Roy concluded, Asia had replaced Europe as the 'fountainhead' of capitalism.[8]

> European capitalism draws its strength in the main not so much from the industrial countries as from its colonial possessions . . . without the extensive colonial possessions that are essential for the sale of her goods and at the same time form the source of her raw materials, the capitalist order in England would long since have collapsed under its own weight

Thus, on all counts, Communist parties must develop an explicit class line, rather than a national one, to *defeat* bourgeois democracy and assume the leadership of the nationalist movement. This would bring a swift transition to Soviet power in the colonies and thus unlock the European revolution, which in turn would bring closer the ultimate aim of 'a world socialist federation, based on a unified world economy with a common plan regulated by the proletariat of all nations'.[9]

It was a remarkable *tour de force*, with parallels to the writings of Sultan Galiev and foreshadowing other attempts to reconcile the struggle for national liberation and Marxism. It had little significance at the time (indeed, it was not discovered until 1934 that the version circulating in German and Russian was the unrevised one), except that Lenin took it very seriously and made amendments to his own draft:

to support revolutionary bourgeois democracy, rather than bourgeois democracy in general, and to acknowledge that 'Extra profit gained in the colonies is the mainstay of modern capitalism.' He also skilfully edited Roy's theses so that they could be published along with the official draft.

Despite the importance attached to the issue by the Russian leadership at the time, the debate added little to the theses. The document itself was tentative for there was too little experience to test the arguments against reality. With the benefit of hindsight it is easy to see the problems, particularly when a provisional draft was turned into a sacred text, its ambiguities becoming easy routes to rationalize whatever occurred. Some signal features were not confronted: how could bourgeois democracy be so blind or so foolish as to allow Communist parties to direct independent mass class-based movements under the banner of a united nationalist struggle; how were Communists to tell who were revolutionary and who not in an atmosphere where even feudal landlords could speak of the violent overthrow of foreign rule, let alone ambitious army officers like Chiang Kai-shek in China? When Stalin could so lightly accord the accolade of 'objectively revolutionary', the picture became only more confused. In an organization which retained a capacity to learn, the theses would have provided a basis for amendment, but the Comintern became an outlying satrapy of the Russian government, and that made any learning process independent of Russian foreign policy impossible.

The second Congress also laid down the conditions for a centralized world party, centralized so that it would not repeat the failure of the Second International in 1914. The centralized Party in Russia was a powerful instrument for cutting across separatist tendencies, but it presumed a unified interest, based supposedly on a working class that had itself been unified by the operation of modern capitalism. The Comintern in Asia was supposedly oriented on the peasantry and nationalism, however, since scarcely any working class existed. It could only operate as an outside force, embodying a world, not a local, working class. Furthermore, a centralized world party would always tend to lag behind local events, becoming a serious obstacle to revolutionary action. On the other hand, it was an efficient means of exercising the authority, not of a world working class, but of the Soviet government.

Nonetheless, in the conditions of 1920, the theses served to support new efforts to spread the revolution to the colonies. At Baku, in September, nearly 2,000 people met for a 'Congress of the Peoples of the East', two-thirds of them members of the Party and drawn from the territories of the old Tsarist empire. The line taken, reflecting the innocent enthusiasm of the time, was bluntly Royist – not for an alliance with bourgeois democracy, but for its destruction. The Teheran regime was denounced and a warm welcome given to the peasant risings against Kemal Atatürk. Zinoviev, the Comintern President, proclaimed that world revolution was now the order of the day, and that 'in China, India, Persia and Armenia, it is possible and necessary to begin fighting directly for a Soviet system . . . to create a state of the working people and conclude a close alliance with the organized workers of the whole world'.[10]

The moment of heroism was brief. By the time of the third Comintern Congress nine months later, the political geography had come to look very different. Neither Asia nor revolution now occupied the centre of the stage, but retreat and consolidation. Zinoviev's report scarcely mentioned the anti-colonial movement. The commission on the backward countries was poorly attended; there were no delegates from Europe and North America. Roy's report to the Congress was cut by the chairman to five minutes, provoking his strong protest at this 'method of liquidating the Eastern question'.

Sixteen months later, at the fourth Congress, there was a more substantial discussion, but the proceedings were entirely overshadowed by the New Economic Policy in the Soviet Union (Lenin's address was preoccupied with domestic Russian affairs). Roy argued his by now familiar case, but the platform explicitly rejected it. Others from backward countries contributed more than before, but Radek grumbled, 'Interest is aroused by deeds. When we hear for the twentieth time that Persia has plenty of workers, these are things which one doesn't learn at a Congress but from a geography primer.' The final resolution threaded its way through the issues while avoiding clarity on any of the difficulties.

National Bolshevism in Germany

Marxist discussion of the national question had always assumed that it was relevant only to the more backward parts of Europe. In Western Europe, advanced capitalism had long since superseded such issues; only reactionaries would now raise them in order to justify imperialist war. In Germany, however, the Comintern encouraged the question to be raised again. At the time, it was not important and would have been forgotten if events had turned out differently. But in retrospect it seemed to show a particular drift emerging in Comintern politics.

Under the impact of the French occupation of the Ruhr and hyperinflation, the nationalist Right in Germany had grown significantly. It was in this context that the Comintern prompted its German section (the KPD) to identify Germany as a *nationally* oppressed country. There had been an earlier dispute in the KPD on the issue. In 1919, a certain H. Laufenberg led a split from the Party with the slogan of a 'revolutionary people's war' against the Treaty of Versailles (which had embodied the postwar settlement of Europe after the First World War). The deviation, 'national Bolshevism', had been condemned as an accommodation to the German bourgeoisie.

Early in 1923, the KPD leader, Thalheimer, published an article in *The International*[11] in which he argued that, as a result of the war and the French occupation, the German bourgeoisie had acquired 'an objectively revolutionary role'. German nationalism was potentially revolutionary, and not, as hitherto assumed, necessarily imperialist. He concluded that 'the defeat of French imperialism in the world war was not a Communist aim; its defeat in the war in the Ruhr is a Communist aim'.

Later, Radek, the Comintern official responsible for Germany, elaborated the case in an article on the killing of a Right-wing activist, Schlageter, by the French. He observed that the KPD no longer rejected the label 'nationalist' or 'national Bolshevik'[12] –

> Today, national Bolshevism means that everyone is penetrated with the feeling that salvation can be found only with the Communists . . . The strong emphasis on the nation in Germany is a revolutionary act, like the emphasis on the nation in the colonies.

Schlageter, Radek observed to the Executive Committee of the Comintern (ECCI), was 'a brave soldier of the counterrevolution'.

There were talks between the KPD and the Nazis on the issue, and a joint pamphlet on Schlageter. Germany had become a 'semi-colony', and anti-imperialist tactics were therefore appropriate – the creation of a broad coalition of forces to win national independence. In fact, Radek only flirted with such opportunism at this stage, and the idea was forgotten; but it was an interesting suggestion of a radical change in relating Bolshevism to nationalism.

The fifth Congress

The defeat of the KPD in October 1923 closed the issue of revolution in Europe for the foreseeable future. It also closed the door on the original strategy for revolution in October 1917. Russia had been the only success. Europe had failed. But, even as this failure was acknowledged, it seemed there were new movements afoot in the east. However, whereas the German revolution had been seen as fundamental to the survival of Soviet Russia, whatever happened in

Asia could not be so. It could be, as it were, exciting, decorative, vindicating the correctness of the Party, but it was now marginal to the central task of 'building socialism' in the USSR. It also changed the emphasis from the struggle for international class power to that for national independence.

Nonetheless, Asia gave comfort in the darkness. At the 14th Russian Party Congress, Zinoviev hailed the great strikes in Shanghai as the beginning of a new wave of rebellion within the empires. Clashes in Egypt and Morocco seemed to confirm this prognosis. At the Comintern's fifth Congress, Manuilsky emphasized the shift of attention. Just as Marx had seen the national independence of Ireland as the means to promote a working-class revolution in England, so now the backward and colonial peoples would provide the means to revolution in Europe: 'The liberation of the workers of England depends on the liberation of the colonies.'[13] One of the points argued by M.N. Roy and Sultan Galiev, it seemed, had been accepted.

The Congress acknowledged the importance of the issues by, for the first time, creating a permanent commission on National and Colonial Questions, with both Stalin and Manuilsky as members. However, some felt that the change of direction was merely a token, for the Congress discussions were desultory and the main interest was in Asia's effect on Europe rather than in Asia itself. Ho Chih-minh (Nguyen Ai Quoc) was one of the sceptical participants:[14]

> The colonies provide raw materials for its [Europe's] factories. The colonies supply soldiers for its armies. The colonies will serve it as a mainstay of counterrevolution. And yet, you, in speaking of the revolution, neglect the colonies.

The desultory character of the discussion might have had other explanations. For the Comintern was simultaneously seeking to impose 'iron discipline' upon its constituent parties as a means of preventing the fierce faction fight in the Russian Party from infecting the rest of the organization. Part of the discipline was an extraordinary religious cult of Lenin, and a completion of the subordination of the Comintern – and its parties – to the priorities of the Politbureau of the Russian Party. The purge was increasingly to become the means to ensure this discipline and prevent foreign Communists from giving priority to the class struggle in their own countries rather than the directives from Moscow.

Alliance with bourgeois nationalism

By 1925, Soviet Russia as a national territorial power had come to displace completely the idea of world proletarian revolution. In E.H. Carr's words:[15]

> It was no longer, as the Bolsheviks had at first believed, the Russian revolution which depended for its survival on world revolution; the prospects of world revolution were now seen to depend on the triumph of the Russian revolution and on its successful advance towards socialism in the Soviet Union.

Socialism itself changed its meaning, from the self-emancipation of the proletariat to national economic development. Zinoviev made the point in a resolution to the ECCI in early 1926:[16]

> The successes in the field of socialist construction in the USSR are becoming more and more the test for the success of international socialism in general.

Socialism was becoming a kind of technology to speed the construction of a modern economy, not an issue of popular liberation. In an analogous way, as we have seen, organizational structures displaced classes; the proletariat had become the Soviet State, the administrative effectiveness of which demonstrated the superiority of socialism. Soviets, detached from their origin in Petrograd, became universal organizational panaceas.

For Communists, internationalism had become almost at one with Soviet nationalism (which was itself imperfectly distinguished from Russian nationalism). The criterion of good Party members was their dedication to the preservation of the Soviet Union. Stalin described the tasks of Communist parties to the ECCI in March 1925:[17]

> To support the Soviet power and defeat the machinations of imperialism against the Soviet Union, remembering that the Soviet Union is the bulwark of the revolutionary movements of all countries, and that the preservation and strength of the Soviet Union means the hastening of the victory of the working class over the world bourgeoisie.

In the Comintern, 'national deviations' were deviations on the part of foreign Communists from Russian nationalism (which was internationalism). It followed that, if Communists were to rebel against Russian domination, it would in the first instance almost certainly take a national form, a reassertion of the importance of their own country.

It also followed that, if a capitalist government, for whatever reasons, was favourably disposed towards the Soviet Union, the workers in that country might have to restrain their opposition in the interests of Soviet foreign policy. Foreign Communists were obliged to accept the compromises this entailed. Thus, the Italian Communist Party, savagely persecuted by the new Fascist regime, was reproved by the Comintern for its indignant protests at the Soviet ambassador in Rome giving a banquet in honour of Mussolini (and inviting him to a reception to commemorate the anniversary of the October revolution). The interests of Russian foreign policy took priority over the Italian class struggle. As we have seen, the tortuous concept of 'objective' did good service in translating the apparently reactionary into the objectively revolutionary:[18]

> The struggle of the Emir of Afghanistan for the independence of Afghanistan is objectively a *revolutionary* struggle in spite of the monarchistic caste of the views of the Emir and his associates, since it weakens, disunites and undermines imperialism.

If reactionary forces could be 'objectively revolutionary', then the insistence of the 1920 theses on the need for Communists to support only the revolutionary bourgeoisie restricted no one. Henceforth, it seemed, any nationalist forces, provided they were opposed to imperialism, were acceptable as allies. The nationalist forces, on the other hand, would accept Communist support only on their terms, and these did not include allowing the Communists to retain their independence. If defence of the Soviet Union demanded that foreign Communists support bourgeois nationalism, the Communists became hostages. Furthermore, the theory opened up an appalling gap, for regimes could be 'progressive' abroad (favouring the Soviet Union) and thoroughly 'reactionary' at home (that is, destroying the Communist Party).

On the other side, the bourgeois nationalists lost little. In exchange for arms, they traded anti-imperialist rhetoric. Communist parties were usually too weak to bargain, and Moscow had too little power on the ground to influence events: the alliance was very one-sided, in favour of bourgeois nationalism.

9

POSTSCRIPT

WITH the benefit of hindsight, it is apparent that a new order of regime had emerged in the Soviet Union by 1927. There were many vicissitudes, trials and crises yet to come, but the basic transition from the aspirations of October 1917 to the USSR as a Great Power had been accomplished. The decisive defeat of the inner Party opposition thus marked a fundamental change. The fact that the language of the regime preserved elements of continuity – which misled both friends and enemies – should not surprise us. There were many precedents for transforming the language of rebellion into that of conservative iconography, not least in the motto that appears on the coat of arms of the French Republic: Liberty, Equality, Fraternity.

The turbulence of the times, the long-running faction fight and the severe difficulties over grain supply (with strikes and mutinies) might have misled the observer into thinking the regime less stable than it was. Still to come were the great shocks of the collectivization of agriculture and the social liquidation of the peasantry, breakneck industrialization and the great purges. In fact, the signs of instability were precisely those that indicated the power of the regime: it could weather such gigantic storms and survive. Stalin's order represented a genuine *status quo*.

So far as the national question was concerned, it was somewhat marginal to the great events of the time. The establishment of the new order – Party, State and a bureaucratic class – was not a victory of Russians, although a majority of those concerned were in fact Russians. But then a majority of those who were to be most oppressed by the new order were also Russians. That the members of national minorities should attribute their hardships to *Russian* oppression was a displacement. The oppressor was, as with the Tsars, the State and it was the State which employed 'Russianness' as an instrument of its purposes. But the General Secretary of the Party was a Georgian, and scattered throughout the top leadership were members of other national minorities. The explanation of national oppression as flowing simply from the dominant majority was far too simplistic to fit the complicated reality, but it provided a spurious cover for the State.

The Soviet Union abroad

These domestic events seem to have been the source of an increasingly wild perspective abroad. The hopes of advance in Europe had long since faded. With an appalling defeat in China (see Chapter 10), the brief aspirations attached to the anti-colonial revolution also died. The Soviet Union seemed more isolated and vulnerable than at any time since the Civil War.

This was the background to a neurosis of fear in the Soviet leadership that the Great Powers were moving once again towards war. They began to give insistent warnings to this effect. Thus, Voroshilov observed that[1]

> a war this year is improbable [but] events develop so rapidly that we cannot predict with certainty what awaits us in the immediate future ... It can come in two years or in one year, but it is possible, though not probable, that the delay may be only a few months.

For the Comintern, fears of war took the form of a sharp turn to sectarianism. The prospect of world war raised, it was said, the immediate possibility of revolution – provided Communists relied only on their own resources. As the prospect of revolution approached, the true colours of all other political forces on the Left were revealed: they became counterrevolutionary. Thus, the largest body of socialists in many European countries, the Social Democrats, were now described as 'social fascists', and must be fought; indeed, because they led workers to betrayal and defeat, they were more dangerous than the Right itself. This, Bukharin said, marked the 'Third Period' since 1917.

At the sixth Congress of the Comintern (July–September 1928), the new direction was presented to a completely compliant audience. All the defeats that had recently been experienced, it was now said, were only so many indications of the sharpening of class conflict, the vulnerability of capitalism and the vital role of Communists. Now the old ultra-left line of M.N. Roy became the orthodoxy. In the colonies, the national bourgeoisie had already become counter-revolutionary, symbolized, as Kuusinen put it in his report on the colonial question, by the 'reactionary role of Sun Yatsenism and Gandhianism'.

As the rulers of a national power, the Soviet leadership were increasingly more comfortable with a nationalist orientation on the world (albeit with a sectarian view of the nationalist leaderships). While the Comintern's tactics became increasingly schematic and remote from reality, it was the national question which was now generalized to all countries (rather than being restricted to the backward and colonial countries). One of the most extreme examples of this combination of schematism and nationalism occurred in the United States.

The Black Belt issue was, in the words of the historian of the Communist Party of the United States, 'the most obscure and puzzling chapter in the story of American Communism'.[2] At the second Congress of the Comintern, Lenin's theses had urged Communists to give aid to revolutionary movements among 'the dependent and underprivileged nations (for example, Ireland, the American negroes etc.)'.[3] At the time, no one paid much attention, and when the American delegate, John Reed, spoke, he treated the question of the American black population as solely a class issue; they were racially distinct but fundamentally part of the American working class.

This remained the position up to the sixth Congress. There Stalin promoted an informal commission in which a Russian professor argued the case for treating the American black population as a separate nation. Given Stalin's interest, it became a serious issue and a Negro Commission was created. The ECCI then moved that black Americans were indeed a separate nation, and therefore had the right to national self-determination and to secede from the United States. The Comintern even went so far as to publish maps giving the boundaries of the proposed new independent State located in the 'Black Belt' in the south of the United States. This was an astonishing piece of audacity, given the lack of any consultations with any of the inhabitants as well as the known opposition of the American Communist Party.

It took some time to get the Communist Party of the United States to adopt the demand, particularly since none of its black membership, recruited overwhelmingly in the north, accepted the proposal. By 1930, the Party was pressing the case for a national rebellion in the south. In 1936, in order to try to form a popular alliance of political forces (the new line of the Comintern at the time), the Party dissolved its main instrument for pressing the case for a black State, the League of Struggle for Negro Rights. But the line remained officially intact up to 1958, when at long last it was agreed that the negro should be repatriated and accepted as an American.

The American Communist Party was of limited significance in the United States, and its line on the black question of even less importance. Nonetheless, the attitude of the Comintern appeared quite irresponsible. The right of national self-determination for oppressed peoples within the Tsarist empire, which Russian Bolsheviks had been required to support (but certainly not to initiate), was now to be imposed upon an indifferent minority. The right of the black minority had been expropriated by Moscow, which insisted not only on affirming the principle, but also on defining the appropriate territory.

The issue of the Black Belt had only symbolic significance. But in Europe, the growth of nationalist politics in Communist parties had more serious consequences. The growth of nationalism spanned both the Third Period sectarianism and what came after it, Moscow's search for allies to defend the Soviet Union against Nazi Germany. There were two important cases here, the German Communists (KPD) and the French (PCF).

(i) *The KPD*. In the late 1920s, the Weimar Republic moved, apparently inexorably, to crisis. The country had scarcely recovered from the French occupation of the Ruhr and the ensuing hyperinflation when the economic collapse that flowed from the financial disaster of 1929 fell upon it. It was the most extreme testing time for all political forces. Yet the Communists were snared in the absurdities of the Comintern's Third Period. Competing with extreme right-wing politics, the KPD and the Comintern embraced National Bolshevism. The ECCI now came to describe Germany as an oppressed colony of British and French imperialism, and the KPD Manifesto for the 1930 Reichstag elections spoke of the need for its 'national liberation'. Indeed, the KPD's main attack on the Nazis was that they *failed* to fight for German national liberation, for the recovery of the territories lost under the terms of the Versailles Treaty. The Germans of Austria, Danzig, the Saar and Silesia had, the KPD said, been betrayed by the Nazis; only the KPD championed their right to rejoin Germany.

However, events were reshaping the line in Moscow. Quite abruptly, the Soviet government, in sudden alarm at the possibility of a Nazi triumph in Germany, decided that, instead of attacking the Versailles Treaty on behalf of German nationalism, the KPD must seek to defend it in the name of protecting the existing settlement of Europe against change. This line was not effective, however, since another element of the Third Period position was not changed: the KPD was forbidden to collaborate with other parties to block the Nazi rise to power. Thälmann might, in the earlier phase, formulate the strategy of a 'people's revolution' (including all classes in Germany) against the Versailles Treaty, but the KPD could not collaborate even with the Social Democrats to achieve this end.

The failure to collaborate had catastrophic consequences. At the moment of supreme challenge in the Nazi advance, Hitler's temporary toehold on power was transformed into the Third Reich: the Left could do nothing to stop it. The burning of the Reichstag and the devastating purge which followed put an end to the issue; 'A single blow had felled the once powerful KPD, the beacon of hope of proletarian revolution in Europe.'[4] The politics Moscow had imposed upon the Comintern had led to one of the most shattering defeats of any Communist Party. Germany now began that march through the 1930s which was to lead to world war and the devastation of Europe.

However, even this historic catastrophe failed to check Moscow, now increasingly stalwart in its defeats. The German Foreign Minister hastened to reassure Litvinov, Soviet Commissar for Foreign Relations, that the destruction of the KPD need not affect German–Soviet relations. And indeed it did not.

The ECCI blamed the Social Democrats for Hitler's assumption of power. It boldly assured the world that the victory of fascism would only hasten the advent of the proletarian revolution. Later, after the line had changed, it attributed the KPD's error to its refusal to embrace German nationalism wholeheartedly enough. At the seventh Congress of the Comintern in 1935, the KPD was reproached because it had 'underestimated the feeling of national humiliation and the indignation of the masses against Versailles'.

(ii) *The PCF*. Moscow's diplomatic isolation and the need for allies among the European Great Powers were only emphasized by Hitler's ascent to power in Germany on an aggressively anti-Bolshevik platform. Officially, however, Third Period politics continued up until June 1934 when the ECCI instructed the PCF that demands for the abolition of French bourgeois democracy should cease and that the Social Democrats were no longer to be regarded as 'social fascists'. There was real fear in both Moscow and Paris at the growth of the extreme Right, not only in Germany but also in France. If the Nazis could come to power in Berlin, they could, it seemed, also do so in Paris. National unity now became the precondition for firm resistance. Thus, once released from the constraints of the Third Period, the PCF changed swiftly. One month later, it reached agreement with the Social Democrats to defend French democratic liberties, and to oppose war preparations and the fascist terror in Germany and Austria.

With this base, the PCF leader, Thorez, set out to construct a national coalition. By October, he was appealing to the middle classes and the Radical Party – all those who were opposed to the Nazis, regardless of what other issues might divide them. Thus, the social question – the class struggle – now became subordinate to the threat to France itself, where all the French ought to be united. For Lenin, 'France' would have meant the French ruling class, and there should never be circumstances in which French workers would give up their challenge to power in a common defence; that is what had occurred in 1914. At the Radical

Party Congress in the autumn, the name, the Popular Front, was unveiled.[5]

There were problems. The PCF was proud of its record in opposing French defence spending. But the Soviet Union wanted an ally with strong military forces. The logic of the PCF's politics – forming a national coalition to oppose Nazi Germany – called for the same outcome. Patriotism necessitated arms and the PCF dutifully conformed.

At the seventh Comintern Congress there was great excitement for the Thorez initiative was becoming the model for all, the model of how Communists could indeed 'defend the Soviet Union' and simultaneously re-enter the mainstream of national political life after the demoralizing isolation of the Third Period. The Popular Front would simultaneously free them of the stigma of treason, of being agents of a foreign power. Thorez now turned what might initially have been a somewhat disasteful political necessity into a positive virtue:[6]

> We will not abandon to our enemies the tricolour, the flag of the great French revolution, or the Marseillaise, the song of the soldiers of the Convention.

The Communists now claimed even the symbols of bourgeois power.

There were other implications. National unity required that no unpleasant class conflicts should jeopardize co-operation between the collaborating classes, that no social upheavals should weaken France in the face of fascist threats. Nor should the French colonies persist in anti-imperialist struggles. Thorez observed in 1937:[7]

> If the decisive issue at the moment is the struggle against fascism, the interest of the colonial people lies in their union with the people of France, and not in an attitude which could facilitate the enterprise of fascism and put, for example, Algeria, Tunisia and Morocco under the yoke of Mussolini and Hitler.

In April 1936, the Socialist leader, Léon Blum, was able to form a Popular Front government. It was thought discreet that no PCF Ministers were appointed. However, the heady mixture of class rhetoric and patriotic politics was part of the source of the great expectations raised by the new government. A wave of strikes and sit-ins broke out, threatening to undermine all talk of national unity. Blum appealed to Thorez who negotiated a package of reforms to get workers to return to work.

By the end of the year, the PCF was calling for an even broader alliance, a 'French Front' that would include the conservative party.

However, in the following year, the Blum government fell. Nonetheless, the PCF continued to support the next government under a Radical Prime Minister. Indeed, the supposed Popular Front continued to hold a majority in the Chamber of Deputies up to September 1939 and the outbreak of war, when the PCF was outlawed. The patriotism of the Communists down the years failed to save them.

The seventh Congress of the Comintern

The last Congress of the Communist International in 1935 was long delayed (the sixth had occurred in 1928). The delay suggested that the International was no longer of much importance to Moscow. The function of the seventh Congress was to spread the idea of Communists leading national coalitions for alliance with the Soviet Union and for opposition to fascism. The Communists, so long vilified for lacking patriotism, embraced nationalism with relief, and without shame or qualification.

For colonial Communist parties there might have been more difficulties, for the creation of broad anti-fascist fronts implied a suspension, or at least downgrading, of the struggle against imperial authority. In the case of China, the fascist was fortunately the same as the imperialist, Japan, so there was less difficulty. But for India, Vietnam and Indonesia, the imperial powers, Britain, France and Holland, were prime candidates as allies of the Soviet Union. Fortunately, there were no Indian, Vietnamese or Indonesian delegates at the Congress to raise these divisive issues. From his bunker in Mexico City, Trotsky sardonically observed that 'India is now being defended by Stalin, Dimitrov and Manuilsky against Japan, but not against the English.'[8]

The policy prevailed from 1935, but with one break between 1939 and 1941. In the 1930s, the Soviet government pursued two strategies to secure allies – a restoration of the Triple Entente of the First World War (Britain, France and Russia) and a neutralization of the threat of Nazi Germany by allying with it. In 1939, to the shock of all onlookers, the second came to fruition in what was known as the Molotov–Ribbentrop pact. In an instant, the war to defend democracy against fascism turned into a war between imperialists, in which workers should resist their ruling classes who had used patriotism to mislead them into war. The organs of the Comintern dusted off the old documents:[9]

> Workers! Do not believe those who wave the flag of national unity. What can there be in common between you and those who profit by war? What unity can there be between exploited and exploiters?

The German invasion of Russia two years later abruptly and brutally closed this period of embarrassing 'anti-nationalism'. The old slogans were once more brought out. The PCF was once again able to proclaim:[10]

> For us, there is no division into communists, socialists, radicals, catholics or followers of De Gaulle. For us there are only Frenchmen, fighting Hitler and his agents.

During the war, the Soviet Union finally attained its place in the councils of the Big Four (the United States, Britain, China and the Soviet Union). The Comintern had been of declining value; its role as a purely subsidiary element in Russian foreign policy became increasingly marginal. Indeed, the distant memory of what it had been was an embarrassment. Britain and France with their vast restless empires still feared Communist subversion, and this jeopardized the trust required between the allies. Moscow decreed the dissolution of the Comintern, a proposal, as usual, ratified unanimously by all member parties.

The Comintern record was inglorious. It had no victories to its name. Indeed, it had had an almost unbroken record of defeats – from the Hungarian Soviet Republic, the beheading of the Chinese revolution of 1927, the destruction of the KPD and the triumph of Hitler, finally to the defeat of the Spanish Republic. Only flamboyant rhetoric and the fantasies of anti-Communists could give it a semblance of achievement. Yet, for all that, the stubborn loyalty of generations of Communist workers was remarkable.

The achievement of the seventh Congress was to insist that the defence of Russia required all Communists in non-fascist countries to be loyal to their own country – and, which this entailed, to the classes that ruled them. Only after the defeat of fascism could Communist parties return to the lower priority of the class struggle.

In the dissolution of the Comintern, Moscow formally recognized that far greater gains could now be made through orthodox diplomatic and military means. The Molotov–Ribbentrop pact led to the partition of Poland, the Soviet expropriation of the Baltic States and, later, the conquest of Finland. Stalin had restored the entirety of the domains of the Tsars. And after the war he went far beyond their imperial ambitions when, following the decisions of the Big Four at Teheran in 1943, he took most of eastern Europe into the Soviet sphere of influence.

A prison of peoples

The national issue in the Soviet Union in the 1930s was interwoven with appalling conditions for almost all. The enormous efforts required for the development of the Soviet Union were laced with the great purges and the preparations and crises that led to war. Only a few elements relating to the detailed history of the national question can be described here without burdening the text with tedious detail.

a) *The Ukraine*. Much the worst experience for the Ukrainians was the famine of 1932–3. In essence, Moscow kept up the Soviet export of grain (to sustain the imports of industrial machinery required for the industrialization of the First Five Year Plan) whatever the harvest out-turn. The total grain harvest in the Ukraine in successive years from 1930 was (in million tons): 23; 18; 15; 22; 12. Yet, regardless of the variation in the crop or in world selling prices, exports were sustained to keep revenue stable. In 1932, grain prices were a quarter of their 1928 level (and 1928 had been two-thirds of the 1914 level). In 1928, 0.14 per cent of the crop was exported; in 1931, 7.3 per cent. In 1931, procurements were held constant when the crop declined by a fifth. In 1934, there was no famine despite the decline in output because procurement policies were changed.

The appropriations were enforced by terror. The richer farmers were already severely weakened by the procurements of the late 1920s (particularly in 1929), and 1931 pushed them into catastrophe. On some estimates, 5 million people died, 1–2 million were liquidated, and an unknown number exiled for resisting.[11] Very little information leaked out, but it is not surprising to learn that, when the Germans invaded in 1941, the Ukrainian peasants welcomed them as liberators.

b) *The Muslims*. By 1925, the constituent Republics of Soviet Central Asia had been established. The Moscow government followed consistent policies of eliminating nationalists while accelerating the process of promoting a loyal indigenous cadre, the *korenizatsiio*. For example, despite purges, the Kazakh proportion of the membership of the Kazakh Communist Party increased from 4.4 to 48.8 per cent between 1922 and 1937. In time, the Republican administration operated, at least in theory, in the local languages and biased recruitment in favour of local people. In practice, Russians tended to participate in all the important committees, and since they usually did not know the local language, it is likely that the Russian language was more commonly used.

On the other hand, measures were taken to force the nomads to settle. This campaign included at one stage the slaughter of nomadic livestock, which led to a severe loss of life. Reform measures were directed to ending the seclusion of women, polygamy and marriage.

Clerical property was expropriated to undermine the priesthood, the mosques and the operation of Koranic law. There were said to be 8,000 Islamic schools before 1917, and none after 1928. In 1928, there were 26,000 mosques and 45,000 mullahs; by 1942, only 1,312 mosques had survived. Of course, the suppression of Islam was no greater than that of Christianity; the regime was not directed against Muslims *per se* but against religion. During the war, following a concordat between the Orthodox Church and the State (to intensify patriotic unity in war), a similar agreement was reached with the Mufti of Ufa (and the number of mosques was allowed to increase to 1,500 by 1954).

Simultaneously, major economic changes were transforming the lives of many of the Central Asian inhabitants, marking out the Republics from the way of life south of the Soviet border in the Middle East.

c) *Russification*. Much effort went into stimulating the development of local cultures and languages. But economic centralization inevitably spread the use of the Russian language and a predominant Russian culture. Stalin, a Georgian, made the Great Russians the leading group of the USSR, the standard of power and prestige for all others. But the patriotism was officially Soviet, even though for most Russians this was identical to Russian nationalism.

In 1937, the government officially rejected the view that Tsarist colonialism had been an absolute evil. The Tsarist conquests, it was said, were less calamitous than the Turkish, Iranian or British. Later, in the 1950s, Tsarist colonialism was reclassified as progressive since it introduced a more advanced Russian culture into backward areas. Formerly, Muslim opposition to Tsarist conquest had been seen as patriotic resistance to oppression; now it was redefined as reactionary.

The Second World War was inevitably the time of greatest patriotic feeling and a conscious rehabilitation of older continuities. This was symbolized in 1945 by Stalin's call to non-Russians of the USSR to pay tribute to the victory of the Great Russians in the war. However, Russian nationalism was an official ideology – a response to the competition with the countries of Western Europe and the United States.

But its pressure had its own knock-on effects. It led to some of the intelligentsia of the Muslim Republics reacting by inventing native traditions to match the Russian – Timur for the Turkic peoples, Genghis Khan for the Mongolians. The Tatar reaction to Russian praise of Prince Dimitri Donskoy (whose armies defeated the Tatars at Kulikova) was to rehabilitate Khan Edighe who sacked Moscow. Imam Shamil, leader of the Caucasus mountain people in the second quarter of the nineteenth century, was rediscovered because he had fought off Tsarist encroachment (officially he was condemned as an Ottoman and British agent).

The Russian interpretations of history were irritations rather than issues of major oppression. But welcome of the advancing German armies in the borderlands suggests greater alienation from the Soviet Union. Many inhabitants of the border Republics are said to have fought for the Germans – up to one million by late 1941 (of course, even larger numbers of Russians fought on the German side). Young men in the Baltic Republics, so recently and bloodily expropriated by Russian arms, volunteered for German war service, supplying three Baltic divisions in the Waffen SS.[12]

Fortunately for the Soviet Union, the Germans failed to capitalize on local nationalism. The policies of heavy exactions, particularly in the Ukraine, stripped the Republics of resources. Education in Ukrainian was banned. The Germans failed even to reverse the collectivization of agriculture. The overt racialism underlying the stated policy of deporting 50 million people and resettling the vacated lands with Germanic peoples must also have revised the perceptions of the liberated.

Thus, Moscow was saved, as it had been in the different circumstances of the Civil War, by the failures of Russia's enemies rather than its own merits.

d) *Deportations*. One of the most notorious demonstrations of the real Soviet attitude to nationalities came with Stalin's deportation of whole peoples, supposedly in reprisal for their alleged collaboration with the German occupation. In August 1941, the Volga Germans – some 300,000 of them – were banished to Siberia and Kazakhstan. The official explanation is worthy of repetition:[13]

> According to reliable information, there are thousands and tens of thousands of diversionists and spies among the German population of the Volga region who are prepared to cause explosions in these regions at a signal from Germany. No Germans (living in the Volga districts) ever reported to the Soviet authorities the presence of such great numbers of diversionists and spies. Therefore the German population of the Volga region are covering up the enemies of the Soviet people.

Russians and Ukrainians took over the vacated land.

Other 'Autonomous Regions' (ASSR) were simply abolished by administrative fiat. For example, the Kalmyk ASSR was dissolved in December 1943, and its quarter of a million inhabitants exiled to Siberia. After the war, the Chechen-Ingush, Karachay and Balkhars ASSRs were abolished, and their peoples banished. Some 100,000

Meskhetians were deported from Georgia to Central Asia in the autumn of 1944 (many thousands were said to have died in transit). The Cherkers, Muslim Ossetians and some Dhagestanis suffered a similar fate. Some 200,000 Poles and a quarter of a million inhabitants of the Baltic Republics were also deported.

After Stalin's death, many were rehabilitated but few were allowed to return to their former homelands (now occupied by others). The Tatars continue a very long-drawn-out campaign to return to the Crimea.

These were extraordinary crimes, 'monstrous acts', as Khrushchev put it in his secret speech to the 20th Party Congress,[14]

> whose initiator was Stalin and which are crude violations of the basic Leninist principles of the nationality policy of the Soviet State . . . Ukrainians avoided meeting this fate only because there were too many of them and there was no place to which to deport them.

e) *After Stalin.* Up to the 1980s, nationalism in the Republics was a recurrent problem but one of marginal importance. Its marginality allowed the Russian leadership to speak of moving on from Stalin's policy of a flowering of national cultures, to a growing together of nationalities, and finally assimilation in a Soviet nationality (Khrushchev's proposal to the 22nd Party Congress in 1959). For Brezhnev in 1972, 'the national question, as it came down to us from the past, has been settled completely, finally and for good'.[15]

With the benefit of hindsight, we can see that these judgements were premature. With the first elements of democratization under Gorbachev's *perestroika,* it was the national question which provided the first form for opposition both in the Soviet Union and its allies in Eastern Europe – once again, in the Transcaucasus (in the conflict between Armenia and Azerbaijan, and in Georgia) and the Baltic Republics. The Republics might have little enough power, but what they had they defended and sought to extend, against decisions to locate nuclear plants inside their territory, to allow Russian inmigration, and in efforts to re-establish the predominant official use of the local language etc. The Republican form organized the presentation of statistics and highlighted certain territorial conclusions – a higher standard of living in the Baltic Republics, or higher infant mortality rates in Central Asia (Turkmenistan's rate is nearly three times the Soviet average). All could be occasions for resentment, for Lenin's 'estrangement'.

Furthermore, the Gorbachev reforms threatened increased centralization of the Soviet Union, which in Central Asia included a purge of indigenous leaders as corrupt. This in turn provoked demonstrations of protest, and influenced the willingness of the authorities in Armenia and Azerbaijan to tolerate mass agitations. Democratization, reform and centralization were the key to the revival of nationalist resistance and the sudden resuscitation of ancient oppressions and current furies. The years had not washed away the scars. And when the regime reacted with violence – with poison gas and sharpened spades in Tbilisi and slaughter in Baku – the scars swiftly became wounds once again.

Yet, fierce though these sudden revivals of nationalism were, they were harbingers of much more complex forces. For overlapping and overshadowing the disturbances in Georgia was the re-emergence of a Soviet working class as a crucial political force in the extraordinary miners' strikes. It now appeared that Solidarity's challenge to the Polish Communist Party had not gone unnoticed in the Soviet Union. Perhaps the nationalist movement had served the role of modest introduction to rebellion. Once confidence rose, then an astonishing manifestation of all-Soviet class struggle became possible.

Elsewhere, outside the immediate perimeter of Soviet power, however, the nationalist forces burst out. The fear of Serbian domination – and the intimidation of an Albanian minority – once more symbolized a severe economic crisis in Yugoslavia. Hungary and Roumania nearly came to war over the Roumanian treatment of its Hungarian minority. The Bulgarians sought to force the Turkish minority to adopt Slavic names. The Germans of East and West rushed towards national reunification. It was as though the passage of the years had achieved nothing, and the internecine warfare of the Balkans, the lead in to the First World War, was beginning all over again.

Proletarian nationalism

The Russian experience had an extraordinary effect on what was called Marxism in both East and West. For what had been presented by Marx as an uncompromisingly internationalist perspective had become, through the alchemy of political practice, Russian nationalism. Outside the Soviet Union, it was to become – as 'Marxism-Leninism' – ultra-nationalism. The term also implied a commitment to State ownership (so Marx's objective of the abolition of the State was no less contradicted). There is probably no more vivid demonstration of the ideological domination of nationalism in our times than this power to subvert its opposite. The wilder shores of 'Marxism-Leninism' – from Kim-Il-Sungism, Pol Pot and the Khmer Rouge, to the Sendero Luminoso (of Peru) – are only the most dramatic heirs to that process of transformation that took place in the Soviet Union. Real social forces built an ideology from the materials they inherited, regardless of the original purpose for which those materials had been designed.

The pressures produced other configurations. The Soviet Union's official ideology was internationalism; Russian – or Soviet – nationalism therefore appeared to the subject peoples of the Soviet Union and their international equivalent, the Communist Parties abroad, as its oppression. It was inevitable that this oppression should provoke revolts against it in the form of nationalism, whether in the case of the children of *perestroika* in the Soviet Union, or the rebellions abroad on the part of Tito's Yugoslavia, Mao's China or Enver Hoxha's Albania.

Those subject to the peculiar rigidities of Stalinism often tried to adjust the ideological framework to reflect their need for a defensive nationalism. Sultan Galiev's attempts to create a 'Third World Marxist nationalism' were not the only case. The Indonesian Communist, Tan Malaka, after he left the Comintern, tried to fashion a blend of Marxism and pan-Asian nationalism. José Carlos Mariátegui sought to formulate a 'Peruvian way' to communism, finding a most unlikely 'perfect socialist and collectivist structure' in the Inca Empire.[16]

Li Ta-chao, a founder member of the Chinese Communist Party, identified a new non-white proletariat:[17]

Inasmuch as white men are the pioneers of culture, they consider the coloured people belong to the lower classes, and they themselves hold the higher positions. Consequently, on an international scale, the racial problem becomes a class problem. That is to say, antagonistic classes have taken form in the world ... in the future, racial struggles will inevitably break out and these struggles will take the form of wars between white and coloured men and will merge with the 'class struggle'!

The idea that classes – proletariat and bourgeoisie – coincided with peoples and that the bourgeoisie was invariably foreign, had appeal outside the ranks of Communists. Right-wing thinkers found it useful to describe their oppressed nation as a proletariat, thus merging all the natives into one class and ranking them against the foreign bourgeoisie. Both d'Annunzio in Italy and the Kuomintang ideologist, Tai Chi-t'ao, employed the idea.[18] Consider one of the creators of Italian fascism, Enrico Corradini:[19]

there are proletarian nations as well as bourgeois nations; that is to say, there are nations whose living conditions are subject, to their great disadvantage, to the way of life of other nations, just as classes are. Once this is realized, nationalism must, above all, insist firmly on this truth: Italy is materially and morally a proletarian nation . . . being subject to other nations; she is weak not in the strength of her people but in her strength as a nation. Exactly like the proletariat before socialism came to its aid.

A not dissimilar thought occurred to an important Japanese nationalist:[20]

The British Empire is a millionaire, possessing wealth all over the world; and Russia is a great landowner in occupation of the northern half of the globe. Japan with her scattered fringe of islands is one of the proletariat . . . The socialists of the West contradict themselves when they admit the right of class struggle to the proletariat at home and at the same time condemn war waged by a proletariat among nations as militarism and aggression . . . If it is permissible for the working class to unite to overthrow unjust authority by bloodshed, then unconditional approval must be given to Japan to perfect her army and navy and make war for the rectification of unjust international frontiers. In the name of rational social democracy, Japan claims possession of Australia and Eastern Siberia.

Once nationalism came to replace Marxism, then the concepts became similar on Right and Left. Of course, Stalin came from a more rigorous tradition and never allowed himself to turn the concepts 'proletariat' and 'bourgeoisie' into geographical entities, countries, but he came precious close to doing so:[21]

The world is divided into two camps: the camp of a handful of civilized nations, which possess finance capital and exploit the vast majority of the population of the globe; and the camp of the oppressed and exploited peoples in the colonies and dependent countries who comprise the majority.

Thus, there were many routes from Marxism to nationalism – from the high road, the transformation of a minority of the Bolsheviks into the new ruling order of a Great Power, to the diversity of low roads, those oppressed by the Russian nationalism which presented itself as internationalism. The fury of rebellion drew on the same concepts, but for quite different purposes. Once, within Stalinism, the proletariat became detached from real working men and women and was entirely encompassed by the Party, then anyone could appoint themselves the proletariat and thereby draw on the tradition. Turning class concepts into geographical ones was a prime method of nationalizing the terms.

Russian–Soviet nationalism

Russian nationalism was created and sustained by Moscow's perception of external threat, which forced industrialization and centralization upon the USSR. This obliged Moscow to invent and enforce a single culture. Despite the claims – and constitutional provisions – to protect other cultures, the enforcement of a single culture meant a return to the Tsarist policy of Russification. Elements of the process were already apparent during the period of foreign intervention and Civil War, but they were, at least at the centre, held in check by the known hostility of the national leadership. For the basic cadres in the field, however, for the Red Army soldiers, and the patriotic ex-Tsarist officers and experts, there were no such checks. But these spontaneous adjustments to the new role of being a national ruling order were slight in comparison to what came later when the State bureaucracy had secured its power.

By 1927, whatever constraints had existed had disappeared – without any large-scale attempt to adjust the inherited ideology or the legal framework. Hysteria about the possibility of a renewal of war produced the first sustained restoration of Russian nationalism which the 1930s could only enhance. The Second World War provided a fitting crescendo to this re-establishment of the Russias, now as an industrial Great Power. The State thus imposed upon the majority of non-Russians to different degrees the need to defend themselves against the Russian appropriation of the concept of Soviet nationality – itself presented as true internationalism. A set of reactive identifications emerged – national versus Russian international, Christian and Muslim against atheist, the home tongue versus Russian, one slice of history against another – with different victims and victors.

That is the unconscious side of the story, the shaping of psychologies by the material exigencies of the operation of an independent State. The other side is overtly political. Moscow conquered the meaning of the October revolution and turned it into its opposite. The most striking sign of this process was the reduction of Communist parties from their role as aspirant leaders of the working classes of different countries to extra-mural sections of the Soviet Foreign Office. The drive reflected the subordination of all elements to the defence of the Soviet Union. Simultaneously, within the USSR itself, alone and unaided, socialism was supposedly being built. World revolution – and Communist parties – were no longer required in this endeavour. The Soviet Union thus came to embody a triumph of nationalism and national will, not of class power or internationalism.

The shift entailed, for Communist parties abroad, a continual downgrading of domestic social or class issues in favour of foreign affairs. For the colonies, a similar separation took place. First, supposedly, came national liberation. That struggle was undertaken in alliance with the national bourgeoisie, so no serious social issues could be raised lest these undermine the national alliance required to achieve national liberation. After national power had been won, then the State would undertake social transformation. The national class coalition, the submerging of conflictive interests, would earn the Communists the trust of the bourgeoisie, and thereby make alliance with the Soviet Union more feasible. The Communists had become patriots and, in ordinary circumstances, wedded to national institutions, including parliaments.

For the advanced countries, the route to foreign policy was similar. The popular front was now the means to oppose fascism and prepare for a national alliance with the Soviet Union. Thus Communists within advanced capitalism were pushed back into the tasks of the bourgeois revolution, winning national independence.

In the colonies, if social issues could not be invoked to mobilize a mass revolutionary force, then the only alternative means to achieve change were independent military forces. Thus, it was inevitable that, when radical Communists broke away from the stifling and conservative 'internationalism' of Moscow, they opted not only for national Communist alternatives but for an obsession with military means. The guerrilla became the symbol of the revolutionary, and a willingness to use violence was the mark of his or her revolutionary consciousness. Thus, the military coup or guerrilla warfare became the revolutionary answer to the parliamentary politics of mainstream Communist parties.

There were other descendants of the final drama of the Comintern at the seventh Congress. The Bolsheviks had disagreed with the Austro-Marxists about the nature of imperialism. Lenin argued that imperialism was a new system of necessities which could not be avoided by the Great Powers; they were driven to expand and to war. The Austro-Marxists argued that the Great Powers could choose to be imperialist or not. Now it seemed, imperialism – advanced capitalism – had become divided into a democratic, peaceful non-fascist majority (which ought to be allied to the Soviet Union) and a dictatorial, warlike and fascist minority. War was not the automatic product of the system but the special character of German Nazism and Italian Fascism.

The seventh Congress did not end the fluctuations in attitude. There was another 'Left' sectarian phase in the late 1940s as the hysteria of Cold War afflicted both sides. But, in retrospect, it was no more than a reiteration of earlier themes, a girding up of loins for a new combat. Ultimately, the politics of the seventh Congress returned.

However, in the modern period, it is no longer necessary to force domestic subordination in order to prepare for war. *Glasnost* has brought a striking amelioration in the ideological controls, if not the material disabilities, of the Soviet people. It is most striking that this has led to a recrudescence of national feelings. Assimilation – the declared purpose of the modern Soviet State – has been the historical norm for most peoples. The United States, composed of people of virtually every national origin in the world, is a striking demonstration of this continued process of assimilation (despite the notorious resistance of some of the majority to accepting all minorities). By most indices of assimilation – intermarriage between individuals of different nationalities, religions and colours, the fading of different cultures, rituals and languages – the United States has been very much more successful than the Soviet Union. There are no *national* movements of significance in the United States. Even though the militants of the black population called themselves black nationalists, this was an identification with Africa not a claim on the Black Belt. The American economy grew faster and for longer than the Soviet Union. Its labour market required extraordinary levels of mobility, and generated incomes that accommodated most of the modest claims that people had. The United States did not inherit ancient territorial enclaves associated with national groups; the ruthlessness of the colonists ensured that the Indians could not constitute a significant claim. The immigrants did not reconstitute such territorial claims. And the constitutional order did not enshrine any such claims.

In the Soviet Union, however, the issue of assimilation is clouded by the fact that Lenin's promise was never put to the test. It did not fail, for in practice Soviet nationality policy was scarcely different from that of the Tsars. The secret legacy of Stalin and his successors was quite unknown until the late 1980s. Even as late as 1987, Mikhail Gorbachev could repeat Brezhnev's boast:[22]

> Against the background of national strife which has not spared even the world's most advanced countries, the USSR represents a truly unique example in the history of human civilization. The Russian nation played an outstanding role in the solution of the nationality question.

But, even as he was making the claim, the storms were about to break over his head. The anger at appalling social conditions, unemployment, bad housing, environmental contamination, and, above all, a dictatorial State, flowed into the form of national opposition to Moscow. In February 1988, Armenia was convulsed with the largest demonstration since the 1920s. Sections of the local Party tried to escape blame by themselves championing the argument that responsibility for all disasters lay with Moscow. But, try as they might, they were constantly outflanked by the new Popular Fronts. The process might have been manageable if history had occurred in conditions of Gorbachev's choosing.

Part III

Asia and National Liberation: Fragments

10

THE WIDER WORLD: CHINA

*T*HE struggle for national liberation in China provides us with both a final working out of the Stalinist strategy for revolution and its radical supersession by Chinese nationalism. The language of Mao and of Stalin retained surface similarities, but the content had become transformed. This chapter thus constitutes a shift of focus from the preoccupation with the Soviet universe of discourse, and provides a bridge to the concerns which follow – an account of struggles for national liberation in South Asia outside the Marxist tradition. The Chinese case has important similarities, as well as the better-known differences, with the South Asian ones, particularly in the continuing preoccupation with creating a single national people out of the heterogeneous mass.

The tormented and narrow tradition that Moscow had created shared some continuities of language with the writings of Marx but its main sources were the realities of Russia and the struggle of the dominant faction of the Communist Party to establish and maintain its rule. Stalinism arrived at just the moment when there began the most remarkable explosion of worldwide nationalism that had ever been seen: the colonial revolution. Out of the handful of multinational empires that dominated the globe outside Europe, North America and Japan, a mass of new States were created in barely thirty years. There were no representative cases in this process, and faced with the diversity of examples, one can select only a few to illustrate particular themes (hence the title of this part of the book: Fragments).

China provides the connecting link from the world of Moscow to that of colonial empire. The formal internationalism of Moscow makes it possible to see more clearly how this evoked subordinate nationalisms among the parties of the Communist International. The process forced a partial separation of theory and practice which at times became systematic hypocrisy. Marxism was the false consciousness of those radical nationalists who operated through Communist parties, but it was a Marxism of a peculiar kind with subtle redefinitions of concepts that rivalled the history of sectarian Christian theology.

The transformation of the Chinese Communist Party

The story of Comintern policy in China and the route to the appalling defeat of 1926–7 has often been told.[1] It became an important issue in the faction fights within the Russian Party which reached a climax at the same time. However, while the defeat provided lessons for the post-1927 Chinese Communist Party, in an important sense the Party that came to power in China in 1949 had been fashioned in the 1930s and owed little to the 1920s. Nonetheless, it is important to remind ourselves of some of the elements that went to make up the disaster of 1926–7.

In 1911 the Ch'ing dynasty collapsed. The First World War imposed on China a curtailment of imports which enormously stimulated the pace of industrialization in the big cities. Almost unnoticed at the time, by 1920 there already existed a significant urban middle-class student body, the champions of a new Chinese nationalism, and a significant urban working class. Politically, China was dominated by territorial warlords, by local gangsters, and by the foreign enclaves in the great trading cities of the seaboard. The Chinese nationalists proper, the Kuomintang (KMT), were a loose group of associates of the best-known nationalist, Sun Yat-sen. However, they lacked military power and were located in the south, far from the main centre of European power, Shanghai. They were initially of little account.

Moscow had little time to pay much attention to its eastern borders until after the period of Civil War. Eastern Affairs were left in the hands of the Irkutsk Bureau of the Comintern whose main concern was to identify friendly warlords who, it was thought, might protect the Soviet Union's Asian frontier. In mid-1921, the Comintern sent one of its more experienced leaders from Moscow to assess the situation. Maring was impressed with the potential of the KMT, and the tiny size and ineffectual character of the Communist Party. The KMT was not yet the party of a class, he said, and its loose organization would allow Communists to operate within it. In Moscow, no one was much interested; as Maring later noted, 'From my talks with Radek, it became clear to me that they were more interested in military affairs than propaganda.'[2]

What changed this was the growing militancy of the new Chinese working-class movement and the scale of student nationalism as well as the opportunity to assist the KMT. By early 1922, the Comintern had come to identify the KMT as a 'national revolutionary' organization. Shortly afterwards, Sun and his group were ignominiously driven out of Canton by an erstwhile KMT military commander, exposing to the KMT leadership their great military vulnerability. Sun's military weakness provided the opportunity for the intervention of Moscow.

The latter offered military aid and advice to create a KMT army and political expertise to turn the KMT into an effective party. Furthermore, it proposed that the Chinese Communists should 'ally' with the KMT. Since the Communists were so few, Sun regarded this proposal as of little moment and suggested they join the KMT as individual members (an idea which Moscow accepted, while continuing to pretend that the Communists were independent). At the fourth Comintern Congress (in November 1922), Radek defined the objective of the Communists as to 'bring the workers into a rational relationship with the objectively revolutionary elements of the bourgeoisie . . . [for] neither the question of socialism nor that of the Soviet Republic are now on the order of the day'.[3]

For the Chinese Party, however, its declared purpose – to create a workers' party – was powerfully affected by a brutal warlord assault on a railway strike in which the Communists were active. The Party derived a conclusion much the same as Sun Yat-sen's had been when he was driven from Canton: that military power is the first requirement of a political movement. The leadership concluded that military protection was required *before* it would be possible to undertake basic trade union work – in effect, a doctrine that became ultimately: first conquer the State, then undertake class struggle. In terms of the Communist tradition, the end was to be achieved prior to the means of achieving it.

Moscow's analysis of China's situation placed the main stress on the need for a peasant revolution, a position Marx would have recognized. The Communists were to press the KMT to lead a rural revolution by confiscating the land of the landlords and distributing it to the peasants. The class composition of the KMT had by now been defined as based 'partly on the liberal democratic bourgeoisie and petty bourgeoisie, partly on the intelligentsia and workers';[4] it was therefore presumed it had little following among the landlord classes and so was capable of leading such a rural revolution. The Chinese Communists were not so sure – a significant number of KMT officers were drawn from landlord families. The Party discreetly restricted its rural programme to demanding reductions in rent and interest and other improvements, well short of peasant seizures of the land.

Meanwhile, the Russian advisers set about reorganizing both military and civil KMT formations. The KMT had hithero had no proper organization, programme or regular congresses. Sun's 'Three People's Principles' (Nationalism, People's Rights and People's Livelihood) were slogans rather than principles with derived practical proposals. His main preoccupation was with securing military power with which to reconquer China rather than with creating a social movement sustained by a programme. The leading Russian adviser on the civil side, Borodin, adopted the model of the CPSU, and turned the KMT into a centralized organization with a membership under central discipline. Thus Maring's justification for Communists working within the KMT – that it was a loose organization which would not compromise the independence of the Communist Party – was invalidated.

At the same time, an astonishingly large and energetic mass movement emerged in the big cities. Thus, in 1925 the KMT and the CCP suddenly found the sails of the tiny nationalist craft filled with the winds of mass support. The contradictions in the Communist position, tolerable, if intellectually irritating, in times of peace, became insupportable when the Party was required to act.

The May 30th Movement, which began as a protest against the killing of a worker by a Japanese manager, swept through urban China. As the strikes spread, the issues broadened to include many worker grievances. When this happened, the movement could no longer be directed solely at foreign capitalists, as the KMT wished. However, the more workers raised issues in Chinese-owned factories, the more business supporters of the Kuomintang began to protest at the role of the Chinese Communists in championing worker interests. The alliance was under threat. Moscow urged restraint on the 'excesses' of the trade unions, but the strain was sufficiently severe for the Party leadership to favour ending the 'alliance'. The Comintern firmly forbade this, for now, it thought, the Soviet Union had, in the KMT, an important ally to protect the eastern frontier.

The increased activity within the new working-class movement was simultaneously reflected in the growth of CCP – from 994 members in January 1925 (with 2,365 in the Communist Youth), to 3,000 in May, 12.000 a year later, and 50,000 by March 1927. The composition or tne membership also changed as it increasingly became the most influential force in the working-class movement.

Meanwhile, the armed forces of the KMT were built up with great speed – and Russian support – to the point where the first steps towards the reconquest of China could be considered: a Northern Expedition. The KMT leadership were impatient to begin, but the Communists were reluctant to subordinate the issues of the class struggle, in field and factory, to military imperatives. The choice between military *or* social power could not long be postponed.

On 20 March 1926, Chiang Kai-shek, now the leading military figure in the KMT, made the first effort to determine the choice. On the pretext of an alleged coup to overthrow the KMT leadership, he introduced martial law and arrested the Russian and Chinese Communist advisers. At one blow, he removed all opposition to the Northern Expedition, and simultaneously demonstrated to the business classes of Shanghai (including the foreigners) who was in control of the KMT.

The Communists were caught completely off guard. Trapped by the injunction to keep the 'alliance' alive at all costs, they made no countermoves. The only card the Russians had to play was to break off military support, but that almost certainly would have ended the relationship altogether. As in the case of Kemal Atatürk, but with much more fearful consequences, Moscow was impotent. The faction fight within the CPSU also severely constrained Stalin and his followers from admitting any mistakes. The KMT now formulated new regulations to control the role of Communists and advisers and released them, on condition that they bend all their energies to the support of the Northern Expedition. Moscow denied that anything of substance had occurred. And the Comintern, in order to confirm this impression, formally accepted the KMT as a sympathizing associate.

Even as the military option seemed to have triumphed over the class struggle and the KMT armies marched northwards out of Canton, the revolutionary movement was galvanized by the prospect of the reunification of China. A vast movement of rebellion seemed to sweep the countryside, opening the way for the armies. The British were expelled from Hankow and Kiukiang. There were peasant risings in Hunan, Hupei and Fukien. The Communist cadres were carried helplessly along on a tide which advanced without pause from the national question to the agrarian, to the confiscation of land and the punishment or execution of landlords.

Matters were not static on the side of the KMT either, for Chiang Kai-shek was emerging as the only serious contender for national power, and the warlords, recognizing the value of discretion rather than valour, rallied to his cause. The seven army corps which set out from Canton became forty en route. Now, however, their social composition was less and less equivocal. For the sons of landlords who constituted the most important component of the officer corps, the peasant revolt was dynamite.

The Communist leadership were rightly alarmed at the 'excesses' of the peasants, and at the impossibility of containing the movement within the modest terms of the KMT programme. Moscow was no less fearful, particularly because of the intensity of the argument within the Russian Party. However, one concession was granted by the Comintern: while the agrarian revolution was to be intensified, land confiscation should apply only to the land of landlords who had no relative in the KMT armies. Just as Chinese workers had been required to fight only foreign employers, so now peasants had to distinguish between vicious and virtuous landlords by the activity of their relatives. A resolution of the Chinese Party bore witness to the melancholy situation in which it now found itself:[5]

> The movement of the masses advances towards the Left, while the political and military authorities, seeing the rapid growth of the mass movement, are seized with fear and begin to lean to the Right. If these extreme tendencies continue to develop in the future, an ever wider abyss will be dug between the masses and the Government, the united front will end by being broken, and the whole national movement will appear to be in danger.

In Shanghai, Chiang Kai-shek settled the dilemma swiftly. After awaiting the efforts of his warlord allies to liquidate the trade unions and the Communists, Chiang then allowed his armies to enter the city and finish off the task. While *Pravda* (22 March 1927) exulted that 'the keys of Shanghai have been handed to the Canton army by the victorious workers',[6] and the Comintern prepared a portrait of Chiang, signed by the leaders of all the Comintern parties, to present to the victor, Chiang decimated the Communist Party. Some estimates of those killed range as high as 5,000.

The CCP was perhaps not as appalled as it might have been. By then Chiang's real role would have been apparent in many of the incidents en route from Canton. But in Moscow the shock was breathtaking. Rarely has a policy – and the analysis upon which it was based – been publicly exposed as such a fiasco.

For the moment, the Comintern leadership sought to deny that anything had happened. However, within the Party, the 'objectively revolutionary' came into its own. The records of the April 1927 Central Committee meeting have not been published, but one notorious comment by Stalin has survived:[7]

> Chiang Kai-shek is submitting to discipline. The KMT is a bloc, a sort of revolutionary parliament, with the Right, the Left and the Communists. Why drive away the Right when we have the majority and when the Right listens to us? The peasant needs an old worn-out jade as long as she is necessary. He does not drive her away ... Chiang Kai-shek has perhaps no sympathy

for the revolution, but he is leading the army and cannot do otherwise than lead it against the imperialists ... [the Right] have to be utilized to the end, squeezed out like a lemon and then flung away.

Chiang took most of the KMT to his new capital in Nanking. A left-wing remnant, which retained the Russian advisers, set up an alternative government in Wuhan, and it was here the Communists sought to regroup. A new Comintern delegate, the luckless M.N. Roy, urged the Wuhan KMT leader, Wang Ching-wei, to unleash a peasant revolution that would defeat the warlords and undermine Chiang's position. 'To go with the masses', Wang is said to have replied, 'means to go against the army. No, we had better go without the masses but together with the army.'[8] By July, the Wuhan KMT had abandoned the CCP and the Russian advisers and joined the Nanking forces.

The CCP's loyalty to the international line had brought it to a terrible defeat. The Party was scattered, demoralized and broken. In April 1927, it had claimed 58,000 members (over half of whom were said to be workers), with 35,000 members of the Communist Youth, 2.8 million organized in trade unions, and 9.3 million in peasant associations. A year later the membership was put at 10,000. In the same year, some 230,000 people were said to have lost their lives in the course of the establishment of Chiang's power; the figure included 38,000 Communists and trade unionists.[9] Chinese workers were never again to play a significant role in the Party's advance to power.

The Third Period

The Party had still not reached its lowest point. Now Moscow's Third Period politics seemed designed to destroy what was left of it. The loss of Wuhan, it was now said, only showed the scale of China's revolutionary crisis. The Party must now abandon all reform activity and spearhead revolution by armed insurrection.

In fact, the popular rebellion was ebbing even faster than it had formerly flowed. As a result, the Autumn Harvest risings were a further débâcle. The Shanghai 'Commune' led to 2,000 being killed. The Canton 'Commune', a victory said to have been timed for the 15th Congress of the CPSU in order to vindicate Stalin's perspectives, lasted three days, after which the Communists were butchered.

Defeat did not deflect Moscow. At the 6th Congress of the CCP, held in Moscow, it was the Chinese leadership who were held responsible for the failures. They had not prosecuted the agrarian revolution with sufficient zeal. For the Chinese leadership, a different conclusion seemed appropriate: military power was the precondition for waging class struggle; Chiang Kai-shek's argument on the Northern Expedition had won the day. The CCP leader Chü Chiu-p'ai expressed the pessimistic conclusion: 'Protection of the masses' class struggle might be possible after a *coup d'état*, but the masses must await the *coup*.'[10] Two years later, Mao advanced the same conclusion on the primacy of armed power:[11]

> Only after wiping out comparatively large enemy units and occupying the cities can we arouse on a large scale and build up a unified political power over a number of adjoining counties. Only then can we arouse the attention of the people far and wide.

Mao, defeated in the most promising military situation in Hunan, retreated with Chuh Teh and their tattered forces into the Chinkang mountains. Although neither was probably aware of it, the creation of a quite new party had begun. This one was primarily guided by the need to survive in peculiarly harsh conditions, remote from the fantasies and interference of the Comintern.

In fact, Moscow was now much less interested. Its concern with China had been less in advancing revolution and rather more in seeking means of safeguarding the eastern borders of the Soviet Union by finding an established ally. It had also had the subsidiary purpose of avoiding the appearance of mistakes, lest this arm the opposition in the Russian Party to discredit Stalin and his followers. Now the eastern ally was gone and the opposition had been completely destroyed. Once that was accomplished, events in China became of marginal significance, and attention shifted back to the much more threatening situation in Europe.

Within the traditions of the Communist movement, military forces had always to be the instrument of the Party's political purposes. Thus, the Red Partisans, Mao's guerrillas, were the supposed weapon of a mass urban working-class party. But the Party hardly existed and, far away in Shanghai, was in no position to direct the partisans. On the other hand, the guerrillas had to accommodate to the material circumstances in which they found themselves. There were precious few 'masses' and little role for mass participation. The partisans were necessarily rootless; the essence of survival was mobility, not relating to a settled and, in the areas where the partisans could ensure their military survival, an obdurately poor peasantry. Mao was proud of the accusation that his troops were not much more than bandits, that he recruited vagrants.[12]

The peasants were understandably unsympathetic; 'Wherever the Red Army goes, it finds the masses cold and reserved; only after propaganda and agitation do they rouse themselves.'[13] For the peasants, the partisans were extra mouths to be fed, backs to be clothed and feet to be shod in extremely poor conditions. The partisans even tried to steal their sons for soldiering. And their mere presence invited military retribution from the KMT or the local warlords.

For the Communists, there was little opportunity for political work. Nonetheless, the partisan leaders dutifully claimed to have set up peasants' associations, confiscated and redistributed land etc. The Party's official Third Period programme could be implemented only on paper – when paper was available.

Even when the partisans settled in the border mountains of Kiangsi, conditions did not change. Thus, for example, their boots were imported into the area, paid for from the surplus produce exported by the richer peasants and small landlords. To seize their land might improve the condition of the poor, but it eliminated the exports – and so the boots. Yu'n Tai-ying gave a different account with the same result:[14]

> When we say that we must distribute the land among the poor peasants and soldiers, this sounds good. But all the available land is already being worked, and after it has been distributed, it will, as before, be worked by the same tenants. In such a case, from where can I take the land for distribution among poor peasants and soldiers?

The partisan leadership bowed to necessity and left alone the rich peasants and landlords (such as there were in such a backward area); as a result, supposedly after a land reform of some years standing, Mao complained that the Kiangsi Republic's central area remained dominated by rich peasants.[15] The policy remained intact and was, officially, fully implemented, but nothing was in fact done. Hypocrisy covered the gap (as had occurred in reverse in 1926–7: agrarian revolution was the reality, but a reduction in rent and interest payments the official policy).

In Shanghai where the official Party leadership struggled to survive, the politics of the Third Period completed the destruction that Chiang Kai-shek had begun. The line was immediate insurrection, but Chiang's police wiped out even the most modest agitation or strike. Indeed, most Chinese workers were for the moment too intimidated even to undertake quite moderate action. As each generation of leaders failed to implement the line, they were vilified, purged and replaced, so increasing the demoralization. At its low point, Party membership was put at between one and two thousand, and even that was an exaggeration. In the spring of 1933, the Party accepted the impossibility of reconciling the official line with building a genuine worker base in the cities; it chose to remain loyal to the line by fleeing to Juichin, the capital of the Kiangsi Republic. The partisans, the sword of the Party, had become the Party itself, and 'class struggle' became warfare in the areas under CCP control.

Meanwhile, the Party continued to pretend that the Comintern line was being implemented. The Liberated Areas were supposedly only routes back to the worker bases in the major industrial cities. The pretence extended to all areas of the Party's work. But then lying had become a substitute for so much within the Comintern. Falsification was magnified in transmission to Moscow. Thus, in January 1934, the CCP claimed that its membership had increased from 3,500 to 20,000 since 1931, but in Moscow this was transformed into an increase from 300,000 to 410,000.

The Party and its army survived, just. But its effective programme had all but disappeared, so that its very meaning was becoming equivocal. What suddenly created a meaning to fill this vacuum was an outside event. In September 1931, the Japanese expropriated Manchuria, including a particular Soviet interest, the Chinese Eastern Railway. Moscow was alarmed. It was an open secret that Chiang had earlier reached an agreement with the late Chang Tso-lin, the warlord satrap of the Japanese in Manchuria. Under this, Chiang accepted the provincial rule of Chang in return for his recognizing the formal authority of Chiang's government; both agreed on a common front against the Soviet Union. It now seemed possible that Nanking might reach a wider agreement with the Japanese to establish a common front against the Soviet Union (in 1933, the KMT recognized the Japanese puppet State in Manchuria, Manchukuo, in return for Japanese military assistance).

China was once again becoming a serious matter for Moscow. The Chinese Communists were instructed to call for war on the Japanese 'in order to win the liberation of the Chinese nation and to promote the independence and unification of China'.[16] There was no talk of social revolution: the platform was a straight nationalist one. The Party had discovered a new and fundamental rationale. The only radical element left was that the route to national unity lay, the Party said at the time, through the overthrow of the KMT leadership.

In the spring of 1932, the Chinese Soviet Government declared war on the Japanese. It was an empty gesture in military terms, but it provided a symbolic rallying point for Chinese nationalists angry at the temporizing attitude of Chiang's government. Moscow meanwhile pursued other options. In December, while the KMT armies pressed hard to liquidate the Liberated Areas, the Soviet Union reopened diplomatic relations with the Nanking government and subsequently reached a non-aggression pact with Chiang.

The successive KMT military campaigns against the Kiangsi Republic finally succeeded. The Party and its Red Army were driven out on one of the most testing exploits in modern military history, the Long March. Of the 90,000 who were said to have set out, only some 10,000 finally arrived in north-western Szechuan. The survival of the Party was a triumph of the will and of Chinese nationalism, not of class politics. Once arrived in an area remote enough to provide some security, the Party–army had time to lick its wounds. It was safe – but entirely isolated from China proper.

Again, however, outside events served to create and sustain its new role. Moscow's fears of Japanese aggression (heightened by what was occurring in Germany) led the Comintern to use all efforts to unify the contending forces in China in a common national opposition to the Japanese. Moscow now pressed the Chinese Communists to reach a new alliance with the KMT for a united front against the Japanese – and thereby defend the eastern borders of the Soviet Union (a line which in Europe, with a different cast of characters, became the pursuit of Popular Fronts). The CCP was, unsurprisingly, reluctant to follow this injunction, although, as was the custom, no public opposition was voiced. However, that there were differences was clear in the Sian Incident. Two rebel generals succeeded in capturing Chiang Kai-shek in Sian in late 1936. Moscow swiftly denounced the generals as traitors to the national cause but Mao sent a telegram of congratulations.

However, in due course, Mao formally conformed. But when the united front between Nanking and Yenan was finally agreed, the Communists carefully kept the Red Army separate from the KMT forces (to Moscow's intense irritation; the Comintern demanded that all efforts be united under Chiang's direction). This time round, the Party would preserve its independence. Nonetheless, given all the Communist blood spilt only a decade previously, the return to 'alliance' was an astonishing *volte face*.

The Party programme, as we have seen, was only loosely related to practice during the Third Period, so that the changes now required to secure the alliance were not of practical significance. In theory, the KMT was identified as the party of landlords and capitalists, so the CCP's official policy of confiscating land and factories had to be abandoned. As Mao put it:[17]

> We have already accepted a decision not to confiscate the land of the rich peasants, and if they come to us to fight against the Japanese, not to refuse to unite with them. We are not confiscating the property and factories of the big and small merchants and capitalists. We protect their enterprises and help

them to expand so that the material supply in the Soviet districts
. . . may be augmented.

Later, to the rich peasants, was added the 'patriotic landlords' and the
'enlightened gentry'. [18] There were now, for the Communists, no classes
to oppose; the domestic enemies were restricted to those who sided
with the Japanese, regardless of class. Once more the Three People's
Principles were proclaimed with approval, and praise heaped upon the
great leader of the national movement, Chiang Kai-shek.

In the old alliance, the Communists were to bring worker and
peasant support to a national coalition under the KMT, a four-class
bloc. But now they were a parallel nationalist organization, with their
own military forces, territory and State in Yenan (which guaranteed
the independence which they had lacked in the 1920s). For the vertical
alliance of classes was substituted a horizontal alliance of territorial
organizations.

Insofar as classes were involved, the 'excesses' of workers and
peasants were in general to be restrained lest they offend the employers
and landlords and jeopardize the alliance.[19] In the 1930s, with a KMT
government which was increasingly corrupt and incompetent, the
Communists refused to champion popular grievances against Chiang.
They opposed strikes and peasant agitations in the interests of the war
effort. Chiang's fears of the Communist Party were, of course, in no
way assuaged by this concession.

The traditions did not die, but they came to lack a rationale. The
concept of class faded into terms laudatory or derogatory, implying
political attitudes, not elements of a social structure, much less key
items in a strategy for social change. Workers remained an object
of vague but inexplicable sentimental approval; 'proletarian' referred
to the Communist Party itself, not to those at the factory bench
in Shanghai. In fact, what the seventh Congress of the Comintern
identified as the politics of the united front in the 'backward and
colonial countries', in practice survived the lunacies of the Third Period
intact, for they fitted the politics of national struggle. As we have seen,
even earlier the Communists had 'allied' with the rich peasants and
landlords of the Kiangsi Republic out of material necessity long before
this was raised to the level of explicit policy. And national politics fitted
the position of running a territorial State, albeit tiny and backward (in
Kiangsi or Yenan), rather than leading classes. The miracle is that all
this could be achieved within the pretence of Marxism.

When, under the impact of the Cold War, the Soviet Union revived
the politics of the Third Period, the Chinese Communists remained
loyal to their version of the Comintern seventh Congress. Chiang was
no longer part of the national coalition – civil war was required to

drive him and his armies out of the country – but the national coalition survived intact. In 1949, the Chinese bourgeoisie were included in the 'People's Democratic Dictatorship' that supposedly came to power in Peking.

The Soviet Union came to distance itself from guerrilla warfare on the grounds that supporting armed rebellion against the ex-colonial regimes would drive these potential allies into the arms of Washington. The Chinese Party, however, remained committed to the use of violence. Indeed, this was its claim to radicalism. Thus, the CCP's politics combined the class coalition emphasis of the seventh Comintern Congress (which is why Mao had a reputation for being on the Right among Communists) with guerrilla warfare, the armed insurrection of the Third Period. While Moscow-aligned parties settled into the role of Social Democratic parliamentary oppositions, Peking-aligned ones were dedicated, not to fighting the class struggle, but to establishing independent territorial bases, new mini-States, as the springboard for military conquest.

The Japanese invasion created the new Communist Party. It allowed it to escape the role forced upon it by material circumstances: that of being a populist warlord in a backward area. When Moscow was driven by the increasingly threatening international context to abandon the absurdities of the Third Period, the Russians resumed the search for a stable and established ally in China. Stalin had no time for the search for a Chinese revolution; he treated his Chinese co-thinkers with ill-concealed contempt. His entire interest was devoted to established States, not the madcap gamble of revolution. Even quite late in the day, he continued to support the KMT. In August 1945, the Soviet Union and the KMT Government signed an agreement settling their respective interests in Manchuria. At a Foreign Ministers conference in Moscow in December, the Soviet Minister agreed on the need for a 'unified and democratic China under a National Government' (meaning the KMT). Stalin continued to advise the Chinese Communists to 'join the Chiang Kai-shek Government and dissolve their army'.[20]

As the Red Armies swept to power in the Chinese Civil War, the Russian press did not report their successes. And of all the world's powers, the Soviet Union remained loyal to Chiang to the bitter end; only the Soviet ambassador, Roschin, fled officially with the Kuomintang from Nanking to Canton to escape the Communists. There, in the south, the Russians continued their negotiations on mining rights in Sinkiang, embodied in an extended five-year agreement signed in May 1949.

The Chinese Communists remained officially loyal to the Soviet Union and its associates. As a result, Mao could never make explicit the originality of his revisionism. In any case, theory had little to do with his practice, so the analysis of what the Chinese Communists had achieved would have been conceptually difficult for them. Hypocrisy shrouded the reality. Mao once suggested that he did no more than take a 'European' Marxism and Sinify it, but this was to assume the primacy of nationalism, not to explain what had happened. For the CCP not merely related the same set of aims to a Chinese context – to suggest this is merely to express, not analyse, the hypocrisy – but changed the aims. Working-class self-emancipation was not a particularly 'European' concept, but this was not what the Chinese pursued. They aimed at the national independence of China, which was something not only different from but in contradiction to the original purposes. But that was something that could not be admitted. At best, Mao played with words:[21]

> Can a Communist who is an internationalist, at the same time be a patriot? We hold that he not only can but he must be . . . Chinese Communists must therefore combine patriotism with internationalism . . . our slogan is: 'Fight to defend the motherland against the aggression'. For us, defeatism is a crime.

Or again:

> A Communist is a Marxist internationalist, but Marxism must take on a national form before it can be applied . . . If a Chinese Communist, who is part of the great Chinese people and bound to his people by his very flesh and blood, talks of Marxism apart from Chinese peculiarities, this Marxism is merely an empty abstraction.

The statement is a nationalist one and confuses application to a particular society, China, with being 'part of the great Chinese people etc.'. The Marxist component has become no more than a decorative form without function.

Mao's thought, stripped of what appears as Marxist pretence, would have been understood by Garibaldi or Kossuth. They would have understood the search for *military* power and found incomprehensible the emphasis in the Marxist tradition upon class and programme. As with Sun Yat-sen, the programme was a negotiable part of the public relations aspect of the Party, not the instrument by which social interests – the supposed basis of power for a Communist Party – were mobilized to act. With soldiers, social interests were not needed. Nor were they needed where the pure national idea appeared to evoke popular support.

The nineteenth-century national liberators would likewise have understood that social reform would be accomplished only after the military conquest of State power. There was no role for the mass of the population to implement their own reforms directly. Indeed, any reforms would be closely supervised by the State itself. For nothing should be allowed to jeopardize the power of the new State, nor, in the Chinese case, the national coalition of classes. This was quite contrary to the Bolshevik view, where the mobilization of interests was the means of conquering the old State: spontaneous mass reform constituted the heart of self-emancipation. But then national liberation in China meant the liberation of the State, not the self-emancipation either of the world or, indeed, of the Chinese.

In sum then, the triumph of the Chinese Communist Party turned upon the failure of the Kuomintang, the Japanese invasion and the transformation of Marxism into Stalinism in Russia. The KMT made the first efforts to reunify the country, but did so by reliance upon the old elites of warlords, land and capital, including the foreigners. Chiang compromised with the old order and, when the invasion came, with the Japanese. He could neither institute badly needed reforms, nor prevent his followers raiding the assets of the State and the inhabitants of China for private gain, nor champion Chinese nationalism against the invader. For nationalists, the Nanking regime was demoralizing and rotten. That gave the Communist Party the opportunity to replace the KMT. The fragments that survived 1927 never restored the class basis of the Party. For a time, they operated as a form of social banditry in remote areas, but they did not become a peasant party. They constituted a mini-State, a small country, and it was this, rather than a class identity, which secured their independence. The detachment from class interests, and their uncompromising opposition to the Japanese invasion, made credible their claims to speak as the authentic voice of reforming nationalism.

Once in power, all the forces that had shaped the emergence of a powerful nationalism in Russia came to bear in China. The split with the Soviet Union thus became almost inevitable. Furthermore, the forces to establish a cultural homogeneity had far fewer restraints in China than in post-revolutionary Russia. There was no struggle against 'Great Han chauvinism', and the wreckage of Tibet during the Cultural Revolution is melancholy witness to the cruelty of the regime, a cruelty that continues.

11

BRITISH INDIA: OPPORTUNISM AND IMPERIAL POWER

A continuing thread of the discussion so far has been the relationship between the Marxists and national liberation. With South Asia, that preoccupation disappears, and we move to examining the forces which shaped the emergence of Indian and Pakistani national liberation, the creation of Bangladesh, and two continuing struggles for national liberation, one in the Indian Punjab and one in Sri Lanka. However, while the subjective perceptions of the participants and the language change in this transition, many of the preoccupations and forms of explanation remain the same.

One of the sources of nationalist opposition, as we saw earlier, has been resistance to the economic centralization associated with the growth of capitalism, and the administrative centralization introduced by imperial States in order to enhance their capacity to compete with each other. We noted this phenomenon in both the Austro-Hungarian and Tsarist empires, as well as in the Soviet Union. In the British Indian empire and the independent States that replaced it, there are some interesting parallels.

South Asia today can perhaps claim to be the home of more nationalisms, fading into a rich variety of changing communalisms, than anywhere else in the world. Indeed, so swiftly do they emerge, the world at large loses track of the new movements and few are concerned to understand the interests at stake. The political air of India is now so saturated with communalism, it is almost instinctive to accept the unequivocal nature of communal categories; it is easier to describe things as a Hindu–Muslim clash than as gangsters (who also happen to claim loosely to be Hindus) raiding the warehouses of shopkeepers (who also happen to be Muslims).

The revolt of minorities, sometimes with the threat of secession, has been an important bargaining counter in innumerable collisions. However, nationality – whether created on the pretext of religion (as with Pakistan, or the Khalistani movement) or language (an important element in Tamil nationalism in both India and Sri Lanka) or, that weasel word, 'culture', or race (as with supposed Dravidian–Aryan conflicts), or province and language (as with Bangladesh) – is only one principle of the creation of groups for social action. Indians have a multiplicity of groups to choose from – caste and sub-caste, village, district, sub-religion (Sunnis and Shi'ites; Shivaites and Vishnavites), and occupational groups, down to temporary alignments defined by which way a turban is tied or tea is drunk. There is a staggering and endlessly manufactured complexity of forces beneath the surface of the heroic simplicities of established State nationalism. Unsatisfied claims seem to grow far faster than opportunities. It behoves the hungry and ambitious youth, with talent and education but no income, to identify carefully what banner can be used to rally discontents and create movements for resistance and advance. Of course, the majority of banners are no clear guide to the interests at stake – they may be designed deliberately to mislead. Landlords appear as farmers, shopkeepers as Muslims. As in other countries, those who traffic in heroin (as in a recent Pakistani case) can also be patrons of the Boy Scouts.

Divide and rule

The history of British India is long and complex – and its complexities are only now becoming explored in the work of many excellent Indian and foreign historians. Even with heroic oversimplifications, the story can be presented here only in selected and schematic terms. At an all-India level, there is a misleading impression of waves of growth in opposition to the British, but the waves had different forms at different times and in different localities, with complicated cross-currents – anti-Brahminism in some places, regional movements in others, and a continuing saga of peasant revolt that only sporadically and obscurely connected to the national movement. British rule in many parts of the sub-continent strengthened landlordism. Landlords in their turn became moneylenders. The burden on the peasantry increased enormously, symbolized in the concentration of land in fewer hands (and the growth of landlessness) and a vast increase in rural indebtedness. The commercialization of agriculture may also have cut the supply of basic foodstuffs. The incidence of famine seems to have increased. Furthermore, between 1783 and 1900, there were at least 110 important peasant revolts.[1]

The agrarian revolution, however, usually related only accidentally to the growth of the national movement. Nationalism as an important political force was essentially a creation of the twentieth century, rising with vigour and increasing persistence in the periods 1905–8, 1919–22, 1928–34, 1942, and from 1945. The tiny group of British who ran India responded with great tactical flexibility, shifting between the creation and sustaining of strata of loyalists among the population, setting some groups against others, and outright repression. Tactics varied not only relative to the nature of the opposition, but – in the nineteenth century – according to the predilections of different Viceroys and administrations. Thus, Lord Ripon placed great reliance on the stabilizing influence of the English-educated Indians, while Lord Lytton dismissed them as 'Babus, whom we have educated to write semi-seditious articles in the Native Press'.[2] However, by the end of the nineteenth century, there was an emerging consensus that to undercut the opposition required the continuing extension of elective and consultative participation in provincial administrations.

British rule required, both conceptually and in reality, a structure of power based upon the willing collaboration of an Indian establishment. The tiny group of British administrators could not hope to govern without this. On the other hand, to rely exclusively on the traditional rulers would have been to strengthen the resistance to social and economic change. Furthermore, with the passage of time, the traditional rulers whom the British patronized had, as a result, a declining capacity to lead their peoples, and so could be of no help to the maintenance of British power.

The need for collaborators at an all-India level was not great when British power was restricted to certain localities. But, as the British came to dominate the sub-continent, an all-India order required for the first time all-India classes of clients, classes which had hitherto not existed. Macaulay, in his famous 1835 Minute on Education, saw the remedy in the creation of a social stratum of British Indians – 'a class of persons, Indian in blood and colour, but English in taste, in opinions, in morals and in intellect'.[3] In the first instance, this worked, but ultimately the process of change stimulated new ranks of claimants who could not or would not become English. The British Indians, in such a context, would be accepted by neither side.

From this non-communalist strategy, the British moved to formalize their identification of the official building blocks of Indian society – religions, castes, peoples, and, later on, interest groups (businessmen, landlords, princes etc.). Of course, this formulation makes a long and fluid period of shifting alliances far too schematic. Both the Raj and its clients were engaged in opportunistic shifts in relationships as events unfolded.

It would not have been possible for the British imperial administration to programme Indians to react within communal guidelines, but nonetheless it played a decisive role in setting the terms of reference within which Indian politics developed – both in invoking defensive reactions and in rewarding those who agreed to be regarded as first and foremost members of an exclusive communal group. The most important achievement of the British Raj in this respect – and the achievement included the greatest catastrophe in the history of the British Empire, the partition of India – was the invention of the brand-new *political* categories, 'Muslim' and 'Hindu'.

After the terrible shock of the Mutiny (1857–8), the British Raj came to choose religion as a key all-India principle of division. 'The most patent characteristic of our Indian cosmos', the Viceroy, Lord Dufferin, observed in 1888, 'is its division into two mighty political communities, as distinct from each other as the poles asunder.'[4] It was this perception which led to the dominant British opinion of the Mutiny as a rebellion of 'the Muslims', supposedly in British eyes the former ruling power of India (in the Mughal Empire). Lord Dufferin put it in this way: the Muslims were 'a nation of fifty millions with ... *their* remembrance of the days when, enthroned at Delhi, *they* reigned supreme from the Himalayas to Cape Comorin' (emphasis added).[5] Charles Raikes, Collector of Agra, added the popular paranoid flourish:[6]

> The green flag of Mahomed too had been unfurled, the mass of the followers of the false prophet rejoicing to believe that under the auspices of the Great Mogul of Delhi, their lost ascendancy was to be recovered, their deep hatred of the Christian given vent, and they rushed forth to kill and destroy.

After the Mutiny, savage reprisals against Muslims, Palmerston's order that all civil Islamic buildings be razed (a directive fortunately ignored), and numerous other measures, forcibly turned the British view from private fantasy into material fact.

Yet, up to this time, 'India' did not exist for the overwhelming majority of the inhabitants. It was a geographical not a political, social or cultural concept. Those who espoused the complex customs grouped under the terms Islam and Hinduism did not constitute groups (other than in the pure classification sense). Neither had a sense of common identity (or, insofar as they did, it was local or dynastic, not all-Indian) nor did they constitute a social or political community. Nor was the

Mutiny self-evidently Muslim, for Hindu sepoys, infuriated on a caste issue, joined it, while the overwhelming majority of Muslims, including most of the rulers and the militant Islamic sects, did not (most of them were probably unaware that it took place). The overwhelming majority of Muslims had not 'ruled' India at all, nor had any relationship to the Mughal empire, let alone any 'deep hatred' of that tiny group, the Christians.

The myth of 'the Muslims' as a political community was neither simply a mistake nor a fantasy. For it served important political functions: indeed, had the Muslims not existed, the British would have been obliged to invent something similar. For once the Muslims had been invented as an all-India political class, this created the Hindus, both groups by implication locked in battle with each other for hundreds of years until the British, by reason of their sense of justice and wisdom, were able to separate them in a benevolent order.

After the Mutiny, the British with surprising speed turned to explaining it as the result of the backwardness of the Muslims in comparison with the Hindus. The Hindus, it was now suggested, had gained disproportionately from British rule. The remedy was to favour the sons of upper-class Muslim families with special efforts to educate and promote them, an early form of positive discrimination. The case was no less fictional than the account of the Mutiny, and its application was clearly confined to the narrow class of respectable Muslims and Hindus; the overwhelming majority of both religions were excluded from consideration.

The context was changing. In the last decades of the nineteenth century, the British and their empire were under increasing pressures from growing competition between the Great Powers. Economically, by certain key criteria, the United States and Germany were overtaking Britain. In Asia, other imperial powers seemed to be closing in on the British territories. The Russians advanced southwards on both sides of the Black Sea into Ottoman domains, and penetrated Afghanistan and Persia; the French took Indo-China, and a general unseemly scramble to seize whatever was possible was beginning in Africa (and later China). The British reaction was the same as that of their rivals. The Raj attempted to turn Afghanistan into a satellite, seized Baluchistan (1887) and, to block any French advance into south-west China, Upper Burma.

Indian troops were vital in the expansion of British imperial power. They were paid for by the Indian exchequer. Military spending increased from 42 per cent of the Indian budget between 1891 and 1892 to 52 per cent twelve years later.[7] This burden required increased taxation, as also did the reforms needed to expand the output of the Indian domains.

Reform in India included attempts to modernize communications and agriculture. This, and increased taxation, entailed greater centralization. London increased its power over the capital of British India, Calcutta; Calcutta increased its power over the provinces, and the provinces over the districts. The army command was centralized; new tenancy legislation introduced, new laws of contract and land transfer; public works programmes were expanded – in irrigation, public health, forestry, conservancy and education.

The costs were high, but simultaneously the Raj endeavoured to offload part of the burden of meeting them onto municipalities. To be effective, this required a greater degree of Indian participation in the operation of political and administrative power. Anil Seal observes:[8]

> The Raj mitigated its administrative drive by devising new methods of winning the co-operation of a larger number of Indians. Systems of nomination, representation and election were all means of enlisting Indians to work for imperial ends.

Simultaneously, the old strategy of securing collaboration – through British Indians – was producing perverse effects. If the British could have treated their brown Englishmen with equality, it might have worked, but there were always many more white Englishmen threatened by the brown and therefore determined to exclude them. The Raj ultimately depended on its English followers, so, regardless of what might make political sense (and was lauded as the essence of British justice), the rules had to be shaped to embody a highly discriminatory order, not unlike that being developed in South Africa. From the petty irritants – the compartments on trains and steamers reserved for the British, the special protected localities that received the larger share of urban expenditure – to the obstacles to promotion and the crude assertions of superiority and egotism, the beatings, shooting 'accidents', all came to symbolize a hated order. In the last twenty years of the nineteenth century, 81 shooting incidents were recorded, and almost invariably the courts cheated to exonerate the white offenders. The English-educated Indians in the cities were the equals of the British in competence, but excluded from equal treatment. The resentments turned the allies into critics or enemies.

Partly to assuage this smouldering resentment and press for the reforms that would achieve greater equality, A.H. Hume, a retired civil servant, with the support of the Viceroy, initiated in 1885 an association of loyal Indians, the Indian Congress. The first meeting brought together one hundred English-educated gentlemen, representing the only all-India social group. They were, in the main, men of property, lawyers and journalists, with a natural hostility towards

171

the interests of their social inferiors. Indeed, Hume was one of the more radical participants, later leaving Congress in anger at its refusal to take up issues affecting the peasantry. The Congressmen were in favour of reforms that would open to their abilities the positions occupied exclusively by the British. They were Westernized, secular, liberal, exceedingly law-abiding and proudly modern – they deplored as reactionary the Hindu revivalist movements then operating. At the end of the last session of the first conference, Hume proposed three cheers for Queen Victoria.

The Westernized Indians, with their emphasis upon the need to reform, not revive, Hinduism, threatened the position of traditional elites and the non-Westernized intelligentsia (particularly those associated with religion and teaching). To the hurt of the British assertions of cultural and religious superiority were added the betrayals by their hangers-on, the Westernized Indians. In the nineteenth century, this produced strong affirmation of a newly created all-India Hinduism. Thus the British imposition of a fictional religious basis for India was now becoming real, and evoking a new Indian fiction of Hinduism, which would, in time, also become real. The mass of locally defined rituals and practices were now, for the first time, being forced into the form of a single national religion. Since the people who were mainly concerned to create this new religion were drawn from the Brahmin caste, the historical bearers of Hinduism, it was inevitable that this invention of an Indian culture should be heavily dominated by a Brahmin definition of Hinduism. Brahmin scholars made a pre-emptive strike to establish one religion suitable to their interests out of the great complexity of Hinduism, the heart of what was now offered as one culture to parallel the supposed one British and Christian culture. Out of these acts of gross simplification and reduction, a new history had to be invented to parallel the claims of the British – heroes of the past, dragooned in the service of the present, warriors against the domination of 'foreigners' (even though there had been neither foreigners nor Indians before the British).

The revivalists were militant in defining by action their defiance of the British assertion of superiority. Increasingly, through the later nineteenth century, Hindu defence organizations were created to seek, for example, to ban the slaughter of cows, to defend child marriage or the ritual suicide of widows, to ban the use of Urdu script (associated with Islam and the Middle East) as opposed to Devanagri, etc. It was inevitable that this aggressive anti-Western, anti-reform and populist movement should begin to affect Congress. In the hands of a group of Congress leaders of whom the most pre-eminent was Tilak, Hindu revivalism became, to the horror of the original founders, an important strand in Congress, the first to break out of the narrow circle of brown

Englishmen and the politics of what Tilak scorned as 'mendicancy'. As he put it: 'We will not achieve any success in our labours if we croak once a year like a frog.'[9]

Thus, the newly created Hinduism became and was to remain an important force in Congress, particularly at the local level. As Bayley puts it, 'Congress at the local level was sometimes indistinguishable from the movement for the protection of cattle or for the propagation of Hindi, even though this may have been contrary to its secular protestations.'[10]

The invention of the new Hinduism could be speeded by taking on targets less heavily defended than the British. In 1893, there was a major clash between Hindu militants and Muslims on the issue of cow slaughter for the Mohammedan festival of Bakr-Id; 107 were killed. There had been fifteen riots in the 1880s. Of course, the pretexts were frequently only distantly related to the underlying issues – Hindu peasants resisting Muslim landlords; Muslim artisans and small traders facing Hindu big merchants and bankers etc.

The new Hinduism pre-empted the definition of Indian. What the British had imposed upon India, the Hindu militants imposed upon the Muslims. Now the Mughals and their Muslim forebears became no less foreign than the British, even though they had inhabited India as long as those who claimed to be Hindu. Thus, the glorification of Shivaji, the Maratta leader, or of Maharana Pratap, created a new pantheon of *national* heroes, long before the existence of the nation had been conceived. The definition of Indian made 'foreigners' of the non-Hindus. In Bengal, L.A. Gordon notes:[11]

> the Bengali national leaders . . . said they spoke for all Bengalis but the symbols they used and the achievements they referred to were predominantly Hindu . . . to some of the Swadeshi leaders, the Muslims were foreigners, intruders in India, who would be allowed to stay as the guests of temporary hosts, the British, and their long-term landlords, Hindus.

The inventions were not, however, even primarily of Indianness. Jnanabrata Bhattacharyya[12] offers a fascinating picture of how a group of Brahmin pundits fashioned Bengali out of at least six different languages and dialects, heavily larded with words of Sanskritic origin, since the British orientalists had identified Bengali as a corrupt descendant of Sanskrit (and Sanskrit was the language of Hinduism). With standard primers and primary education, the invention became a standard language, driving all others out of respectable usage. To Muslim scholars this seemed an act of war on the syncretic culture they held in common with Hindus (given the enormous variety of forms throughout eastern India), and they in turn then began borrowing names and styles from Arabic, Farsi and Urdu to invent an origin in the Middle East. The changes in language were only part of a general drive to 'purify' – that is, identify one practice as authentic and eliminate all other forms. In a long history of living together (and changing from one religion to the other from time to time), Hindus and Muslims had merged many practices (as with the common celebration of Muharram and Durga Puja) that now had to be sharply differentiated as part of the process of building political forces and private advancement.

Thus, a series of factors came together to provide the basis for the emergence of Hindu and Muslim as political categories: the needs of the British to identify loyal collaborators and to divide potential opponents, the rise of Congress as the voice of the urban middle class, and the assertion of a 'Hindu' nationalism (which implicitly excluded Muslims) as against British nationalism. Beneath this surface, complicated and changing interests sought to employ whatever symbols they could to advance their fortunes. Of course, these were themes in a fluid political context with shifts back and forth and changing alliances. The British could never rest content that they had secured their power, since to many of the nationalists it was always apparent that ultimately the British were the main beneficiaries from the senseless divisions.

The British were on hand to reward those who were loyal to their definition of politics and accepted the label which they ascribed. Eventually, they even created an ideological justification for their preference for Muslims (in stark contrast to the attitudes expressed after the Mutiny). Lord Oliver wrote to *The Times* of 10 July 1926:

> No one with a close acquaintance with Indian affairs will be prepared to deny that, on the whole, there is a predominant bias in British officialdom in India in favour of the Muslim community, partly on the ground of closer sympathy but more largely as a make-weight against Hindu nationalism.

A tiny minority of educated Muslims in north India were quick to seize the opportunities offered to official 'Muslims'. In the very small public class of India in the late nineteenth century, Sir Saiyid Ahmad Khan (1817–98) responded to the opportunities held out by the British and came to be one of the more important champions of the reconciliation of Britain and Islam. The means to achieve this was through fostering scientific education for upper-class Muslim boys. Such a position was flatly contrary to respectable Islamic opinion, but nonetheless British support made Khan the most important representative of 'the Muslims'. In turn, he acted as a vocal public supporter of the British. He began publication of the *Loyal Mohammedans of India* in 1860, and later founded the famous Aligarh College (to which the Viceroy contributed), the precursor of Mohammedan Anglo-Oriental Colleges throughout the sub-continent, as a means of creating a modern educated class of Muslims.

British support for Khan was the beginnings of a strategy. At this stage, favouring Westernized Muslims was intended to counter 'Muslim fanatics', the anti-foreign sects favoured by the lower- middle class (petty traders, small-town mullahs, booksellers, shopkeepers and minor officials). Congress was at this stage far too unimportant to warrant Viceregal attention, let alone a strategy. But the seed was sown. Already Khan spoke as if the Muslims were a nation:[13]

> Now suppose that all the English and the whole English army were to leave India. Is it possible that under these circumstances, two nations, the Mohammedans and the Hindus, could sit on the same throne and remain equal in power? Most certainly not. It is necessary that one of them should conquer the other and thrust it down.

The mischief had been done.

Now a Muslim interest became a formalized political entity, with the right to be consulted. A group of dignitaries appointed themselves the voice of this supposed political force, and the British warmly welcomed the initiative. The Ripon reforms of 1882–3 duly took the first steps to create separate political representation through Muslim nominations to the Viceroy's Legislative Council, and to the Education and Public Service Commissions. It was a fateful first step in legislating the main features of an Indian social structure acceptable to the Raj. The well-to-do, hitherto essentially local (and linked to numerous and changing alliances with people of different faiths but the same social standing), were now being nudged into recognizing the advantages at an all-India level of separating from their former associates and joining a new class, 'the Muslims' (which of course covered only a tiny minority of the people who embraced that faith).

The Muslim was by no means the only invention of the Raj. The social structure was defined exclusively by the British in the interests of their power. As Anil Seal puts it:[14]

> Government was now balancing interests by separating them into categories of its own defining. Who were 'the Mohammedan community in the Presidency of Bengal' or 'the Landholders of the United Provinces', each of whom was to elect one member

to the Governor General's Council? Neither of these bland categories made any sense at the local level in Bengal and the United Provinces; both of them ignored the different interests and rivalries among those groups whom the British bundled together in a phrase.

To these categories were added others – 'Hindus', 'Muslims', 'Sikhs', 'Depressed Castes', and 'an even more improbable category, "the Indian Princes"'. Improbable and inaccurate they might be, but few of that tiny class of Indian notables with political ambitions who could claim membership of one of the categories could afford to ignore them. For[15]

the Raj itself had cut the steps which these politicians had to mount; it had also defined the tests they had to pass. Its administration had carved its people into large administrative blocks; it had set up a system of representing them.

The Raj had done even more. It had created a methodology of politics which ultimately it bequeathed to independent India. Communalism had been made the basis for effective political action as well as a universe of discourse which undercut claims to a higher political purpose, to the creation of an Indian nation. The method was profoundly conservative; if clashes between landlords and landless could be dismissed by the Raj as Hindu–Muslim riots, government was not required to meet the grievances of the landless.

The Raj had instituted a system, based upon an apparently eclectic collection of categories, unrelated to numbers of people. It was no longer enough to have an opinion, a mission and a vote. One must 'represent' a group: community, caste, religion, village, gender, occupation (and, it was somehow implied, representation of one excluded the others). The overwhelming majority of the inhabitants of India were in no way involved. The British identifications also changed the way people perceived the political world; being a Christian had now become a claim to a separate social, economic and political interest.

Representation and privilege for the chosen counterweights went hand in hand. In 1901, for example, the government of the Punjab reserved 30 per cent of the provincial administrative appointments for Muslims. In 1906, a self-appointed group of 35 Muslim luminaries called on the Viceroy, and were immediately accepted as 'representing' *the* Muslim interest. They informed him that a Muslim who represented a district where a majority of the inhabitants were Hindu would be obliged to represent Hindu interests and could therefore not be seen as representing the Muslims; there needed to be special representation. The Viceroy warmly welcomed this blatant piece of special pleading. Subsequent legislation endowed the Muslim voter with two votes, one for general seats and one for reserved Muslim seats.

Yet there were never enough privileges to secure a safe vote. The political exigencies of the operation of the Raj's power could suddenly alienate its clients. For example, in 1905, the province of Bengal was divided. The reasons for this were not directly religious, but the measure did separate a predominantly Hindu west from a predominantly Muslim east. The Viceroy indicated his desire to create by this measure 'wholesome centres of provincial opinion' in the east, 'antipathetic to Calcutta lawyers and babus' (in the west). As if in direct response to this, the Muslim League was founded in December 1906 in Dacca. However, the Raj greatly underestimated the impact. Partition roused an unprecedented scale of urban opposition which included a boycott of British goods, a student boycott of higher education, as well as the famous Bengal terrorist movement. In 1911, the British revoked the partition without consulting 'the Muslim interest'. The Muslim notables involved saw the reversal as a concession to terrorism and Hindu Calcutta: the British had betrayed their trust. Tactics other than reliance on the Raj might now be needed to protect the Muslim interest. In 1912, there were Muslim calls for Indian self-government. The Muslim League and Congress reached an agreement for united activity, the Lucknow Pact.

Meanwhile, the explosion of urban mass opposition to the British in Bengal had caused extreme difficulties for the reformers of Congress. Tilak had pioneered the use of his version of Hinduism as a means of mass mobilization against the British. In 1907, Congress split between reformers and revivalists. Tilak and some of his associates were later arrested, and his followers turned to terrorism as the means to prize the British out of India.

The First World War sharpened all the conflicts that had affected the country in the years leading up to 1914. Increased taxes to pay for the war and India's 1.2 million troops simultaneously increased the burdens on the mass of the population and the levels of inflation. Congress, reunited with Tilak and his followers, was on the brink of becoming the focus of mass nationalism (although it was still not committed to an independent India).

Furthermore, the war raised an issue on which it was possible to build unity between Congress and the Muslim League, thus blocking the British strategy of dividing the two. The Ottoman Caliph was reverenced by educated Muslim opinion, and the long maturing Anglo-French plan to dismember the Ottoman Empire caused anger among some of the Muslim intelligentsia, particularly when, in the war,

Turkey sided with Germany and the Dual Monarchy against the British, French and Russian allies. Congress could with ease support the Khalifat, the movement of opposition to the British invasion of Turkey, precisely because it had nothing to do with issues in India. The movement reached its peak in 1919–20 when Muslim activists were fully involved in common action against the British attempt to extend the draconian wartime regulations, the Rowlatt Acts, into the peace, and against the provisions of the Versailles Treaty which affected Turkey. There were even Muslim calls to end cow slaughter for Bakr-Id in the interests of Hindu–Muslim unity. When the ruler of Afghanistan began a brief war against British India, some 20,000 Muslims are said to have trekked on foot to the mountains to support him (some of them later reached Tashkent in the Soviet Union and became early members of the Indian Communist Party).

The postwar world

The British reply to this failure of their strategy was straight repression, the climax of which was the appalling massacre at Jallianbagh in Amritsar where, officially, 379 unarmed people were shot dead by British forces. Congress was for the first time in the thick of the mass waves of protest which followed. It was now becoming influenced by a new mass leader, who was to become known as Mahatma Gandhi. Congress was at the peak of its power so far, even though the politics of its main leadership had scarcely developed much beyond the old programme of reforms.

However, the British also persisted in the strategy of undercutting opposition by extending the suffrage to wider layers of the middle classes. In August 1917, the Secretary of State for India committed his government to the development of Indian self-government. At the time, it was not seen as a likely accomplishment in the medium term, nor as weakening the British position. The Reform Act of 1919 extended the electorate for provincial administrations to some five and half million voters (under 3 per cent of the population) and, for the imperial legislature, to one and a half million. It repeated the principle of the representation of interests through special electorates at the provincial level – 'the advancing wave of majorities', as Hardy puts it, 'was to be broken up by the rocks of special interests'.[16] The measure, however, was part of a process in which the small class of traditional supporters of the Raj were now being overwhelmed by newcomers from the middle classes.

There were other forces at work. In 1919, what was to be one of the more important Hindu nationalist parties was formed, the

Hindu Mahasabha (later notorious when one of its members murdered Mahatma Gandhi). When the Indian nationalist movement was most active, communalism had little success. But in the 1920s the movement did decline (the membership of Congress went down to a low point of 56,000). There were communal riots in 1920, and, between 1923 and 1926, 72 more were recorded (the largest number before 1946). They were still restricted to the small urban sector, and a key role was played by lower-middle-class youth, those waiting in line to enter the political arena. The British seemed vindicated in their role as peacekeepers and could point to communal clashes as inherent in the Indian social structure (of course, dutiful historians could find riots in the past and identify them as communal, with the sharpened sensitivities of the twentieth century, and so give credibility to the claims of the Raj).

Riots and a sharp decline in the nationalist movement were related also to a long-drawn-out period of economic stagnation, punctuated with a disastrous slump. Bombay was stricken by a wave of major strikes in the textile industry, not unlike what was happening at the same time in Shanghai. In the countryside, the interwar years and the Great Depression increased the hardships of peasant families, and led to a considerable radicalization, as shown in the response to Gandhi's Salt March in 1930. There were demands to end the *zamindari* system and landlordism generally, and for the redistribution of land. Congress which, under Gandhi, identified India with the peasantry, nonetheless kept the real peasants at arm's length and was most reluctant to have a serious agrarian programme. On the other hand, the British sought to keep the peasants and Congress apart with a series of reforms – rent restrictions, tenancy protection. In effect, the peasants were scarcely affected but the landlords were to some extent alienated. In the 1930s, landlords in the United Provinces, it was noted, began to join Congress and the communal parties in order to seek to dilute or oppose Congress' commitment to abolish *zamindari*. Muslim and Hindu landlords united to oppose the UP Tenancy Bill.

Educated unemployment was also a severe problem. The opportunities for the young and ambitious were sharply curtailed in the interwar years. The supply of militants for the nationalists was considerably increased. Now there were also many new potential adventurers willing to risk much in climbing the greasy pole.

The diverse rebellions often employed the name of Congress or, more likely, the Mahatma as their banner, without having any connection with the nationalist movement. Thus, in 1930, a Chittagong group seized the armoury there, declared India independent and fought with dedication against the counter-attacks, all in the name of the pacific Gandhi.

The British returned to the central strategy. New attempts at constitutional reform began with the Simon Commission in 1927. In 1935, a new Government of India Act increased the electorate to over 30 millions, and conceded to Indians the right to form provincial governments. The nationalists assumed that the British were now seeking to enfranchise part of the better-off peasantry in order to emphasize the inability or unwillingness of Congress and its urban leadership to relate to rural issues. There was also a British interest in helping non-Congress mass parties in the Punjab and Bengal. Yet others saw the concession of provincial self-government as a means of making Indians do Delhi's work (Nehru as President of Congress took this view and opposed Congress forming governments).

The 1937 elections were a profound shock for the British establishment. They tested how far Congress could extend its reach beyond the circle of its big-city followers and to what extent communalism had come to overwhelm all other issues. Of the 7.3 million votes reserved for Muslims, the Muslim League won only 321,722 and 109 of the 482 reserved seats. Congress captured 716 of the 1,161 general seats. Thus, the extension of the electorate had not, on the face of it, swamped secular nationalism with 'interests'. But it had swamped 'the Muslims'.

The Muslim League had assumed that Congress would boycott the provincial Ministries, so that, although the League had done badly, it might still inherit a significant share of power. But, in the event, Congress formed the government in six provinces, thereby gaining access to the resources required to secure the loyalties of new supporters. It was the low point for the Muslim League. The overwhelming majority of Muslims had not consented to vote as Muslims. Mohammed Ali Jinnah, the most famous League leader, returned from exile in Britain to take in hand the small clique that constituted the League. Events now conspired to turn his little organization into the leader of a new country.

The leadership of both Congress and the Muslims made occasional efforts to seek measures of unity. Jinnah, for example, in 1928 acknowledged that:[17]

> We are all sons of the land. We have to live together . . . Believe me, there is no progress for India until the Musalmans and Hindus are united.

And again, before the 1937 elections, we find him arguing that only Hindu–Muslim unity could secure independence for India, but, acknowledging the primacy of the British political methodology, such unity required a strong Muslim organization. Without this, Congress would ignore Muslim interests. The 1937 election results changed all this, for now it seemed Congress had grown far too strong. What made it even worse for the leaders of the League was the Congress 'contact' movement.

In the 1930s, Congress had many more Muslim members than the League's total membership. However, among the Congress Muslim leadership and parts of the Congress Left, the fears of a religious split remained strong (and in the event were fully vindicated). Nehru, a lone voice in the leadership, might meditate that[18]

> when we look at the vital problem of independence and of the removal of poverty and unemployment, there is no difference between the Muslim masses and the Hindu or Sikh or Christian masses in the country. Differences only come to the surface when we think in terms of the handful of upper class people.

Yet that handful dominated Congress.

Muslim radicals in Congress denied that Muslims were a political or social group, and campaigned on the basis of class slogans that cut across religious differences. In the late 1930s, they launched a mass campaign to increase the Muslim membership, and had some success in urban areas (in the rural areas, the lack of success was the same as that attached to the recruitment of Hindu peasants).[19] However, much of Congress disapproved of the campaign, and local branches dragged their feet or were positively hostile. The more vocal saw the campaign as just a means to increase the strength of Nehru and the Congress Left. Where Hindu communalists were active in Congress, Muslims were excluded altogether. Thus, just as the British Raj was founded upon a racialist minority – despite all the claims to liberalism and equality before the law – Congress at its base was much more a Hindu communalist organization than its leadership would have cared to acknowledge.

Partition

The Second World War transformed the political options. The grave vulnerability of British power to the Axis alliance was suddenly exposed, particularly as a new Asian Great Power, Japan, swiftly ate into European possessions in South-East Asia and arrived on the borders of India. Radicalization brought masses of newcomers into Indian politics. Congress itself was obliged to adjust its programmes to accommodate them – with policies of agrarian reform, rent reductions, enhanced security for tenant farmers and the abolition of that particular form of landlordism, *zamindari* (but it retained a strong right wing, which included landlords).

The change opened a wider gap between Congress and the landlord interests. Furthermore, it was becoming clear that the British would not survive politically in India, so that the landlord order could no longer rely on British power to protect its position. Suspicions of both the British and Congress led to increased recruitment of Muslim landlords to the League which expressed strong opposition to the mild reforms advanced in the Congress programme. Talbot[20] has given us a picture of League tactics in the Punjab in winning away from the dominant Unionist Party its landlord and gentry interests, with their mass peasant followings, and in skilfully building on the growing rural discontents of the last years of the war. In the 1937 election, the League fielded 7 candidates in 85 Muslim seats and won in two; in 1946, it won 75 seats.

The Viceroy in 1939, Lord Linlithgow, declared India at war with the Axis powers without even nominal consultation of Indian opinion. He further refused any commitments concerning India's constitutional position as an inducement to Congress to collaborate. Accordingly, Congress declared its opposition to the war, its now eight provincial ministries resigned, and the leadership launched a campaign of civil disobedience in protest. The Viceroy responded with massive repression, imprisoning much of the leadership for the rest of the war. After the launching of Congress's Quit India movement in 1942, the repression increased — nearly 1,000 people were killed, 3,000 injured, and by late 1943 92,000 were in prison. Congress was banned.

Jinnah was delighted at this unexpected turn of fortune. The hour of the League — as of Hindu communal parties, and, for other reasons, the Communist Party — had struck. Without the competition of Congress, the League could seek to replace it among sections of the Muslim middle class, in conditions of growing unease at what the British evacuation of India might portend. In elections in 1943, the League won 47 of the 61 seats reserved for Muslims and open for election. It replaced Congress Ministries in Bengal, Assam, Sind and North-West Frontier Province, and made major advances in the Punjab. Now it was the League which had access to those resources needed to bind to itself new layers of Muslim opinion; the All-India Muslim Chamber of Commerce was created in 1944, symbolizing the bifurcation of capitalism itself. The League's alliances were complex, differing in different parts of the country, and relating to different patterns of interest. But it had now become a major national force.

In March 1940, just after the repression of Congress, the Muslim League went beyond the British definition of an interest: to nationality.

For the first time, it espoused the demand for a separate State for Muslims, a 'Pakistan'. Jinnah now made the claim that 'Mussulmen are a nation by any criterion.' There were therefore two nations in India, and Congress could no longer claim to represent a single Indian nation. It also followed, Jinnah explained, that democracy was impossible in such circumstances since Hindu majorities would always swamp the Muslim minority (and, of course, Congress only favoured democracy, he implied, because it would result in a Hindu majority). It was a new argument for a position of opposition to majority votes which Jinnah had espoused before, on the grounds that the Indian electorate was 'totally ignorant, illiterate and untutored, living in centuries-old superstitions of the worst type, thoroughly antagonistic to each other, culturally and socially'.[21] The following month, a conference of Muslim parties in Delhi protested against the concept of 'Pakistan', and declared in favour of a 'common homeland of all citizens, regardless of race and religion'.[22] Jinnah still had far to go to make the British methodology stick.

It is not clear how far Jinnah intended the new claim to be only a part of the bargaining stakes in the negotiations for responsible government, a threat rather than a commitment. But he was obliged to spell out the implications for his followers: a new State with the name Pakistan. Nobody was very clear what it meant nor whether it would ever come about, but it offered an almost messianic focus of hope for many, a vision of a sanctuary for those who were oppressed and afraid. Obversely, it identified by implication the source of current discontents: 'Hinduism', a concept even more mythic than the polity of Islam.

However, the progress of the war brought other changes. A Britain isolated in occupied Europe was completely dependent upon the United States. Washington pressed London to reach an accommodation with the nationalist forces. That aim was made even more urgent by the triumphal advance of Japan's armies to the borders of India, and the known information that considerable numbers of Indian troops and officers had agreed to fight for the Japanese (in what was called the Indian National Army). Concessions were needed, and a prominent Labour leader in the British wartime coalition and a friend of Nehru's, Sir Stafford Cripps, was sent on a Cabinet mission to offer concessions: dominion status for India and the right to leave the Commonwealth. Cripps also offered India's provinces the right to secede from the Union. This surprising replication of Lenin's national self-determination policy was necessary, the British said, to 'force Congress to compromise with the minorities'. In fact, the real problem was that the British had granted the League a right to veto all proposals, so perpetuating British power.

In 1944, Gandhi was released from prison for discussions with Jinnah, and he offered the League a plebiscite in all provinces where there was a Muslim majority. Jinnah refused, acknowledging that he lacked confidence that the League would be chosen in an open vote. He demanded an unequivocal commitment to an independent Pakistan by what he described as the Hindu party, Congress.

The end of the war brought a quite new situation. Soviet power now extended over Eastern Europe, China was engaged in civil war and South-East Asia was expelling its former imperial rulers. India was full of expectation and excitement. When the British authorities foolishly tried to put on trial for treason a number of the former soldiers of the Indian National Army, it became the occasion for a mass anti-British campaign. There was a naval mutiny and an unprecedented wave of strikes and peasant agitations (not, it needs to be said, all on the issue of national independence).

The new British Labour Government, in some panic over its ability to contain the situation, now decided to break the impasse by ordering a British evacuation of India as swiftly as possible. The change was as much in the interests of maintaining the unity of the war-weary British armed forces and peace in Britain as in the interests of India. The elections in December 1945 were sharply polarized. The League campaigned solely on the issue of Pakistan, and now won 439 of the 494 reserved seats in the provincial assemblies (Congress won 930 seats and an absolute majority in 8 provincial assemblies): 'From a cabal of self-interested office seekers, condescendingly seeking the suffrage of their social inferiors, [the League had become] the chosen shepherd of a nation in the making and on the march.'[23]

In March of the following year, a new Cabinet mission reopened discussions which again ended in deadlock. In response, the League announced its first-ever 'day of action' to create Pakistan without recourse to constitutional agreement. The results should have warned the participants that communalism had now seeped out of the conference chambers and soaked deep into India. In the 'Great Calcutta killing', 4,000 died and 15,000 were injured in three days of clashes between Hindus and Muslims. It was a preface to the largest of the achievements of the British and the communalists, the partition of India. The religious armies voted with their feet or were driven by terror. Hindus (and Sikhs) fled from western Punjab and eastern Bengal, and Muslims in the opposite direction, leaving Muslim enclaves in the far west and east of the sub-continent – 10 million fled as refugees, possibly 200,000 died. Of course, a very large number of Muslims remained in India.

The British scuttled, with scarcely a nod towards the protection of those minorities whose defence had for so long been claimed as justification for their rule. At the end, two newly independent States had been created by mass initiative and a nightmare of terror. Contrary to the philosophy of its leading inspiration, Mahatma Gandhi, India had been won by a scale of violence rarely matched before. On the other side, if Jinnah had intended his demand for Pakistan to be no more than a bargaining issue, others had implemented it in blood, and created, in his laconic phrase, 'a truncated and moth-eaten Pakistan'.

Retrospect

A mass of people paid the price of communal leadership, people who had not been seriously involved in any of the earlier conflicts. For, despite the claims, only minorities were involved in the overall issues. The minority of Muslims who fought for Pakistan, who stood to gain from reserved jobs in public employment and in education, won finally a reserved territory and State, but at dreadful cost.

Perhaps the League could have been undercut by Congress if the leadership had been willing to step outside the narrow class interests of its supporters to appeal to wider forces, to the common interests of poor cultivators regardless of religious affiliation. But Congress was a coalition, many of whose members would have been terrified to unsheathe such a weapon even if they themselves or their families had not stood to lose by it. Communalism was a lesser evil than the possibility of social revolution.

Gandhi's attempt to solve the same problem – the creation of almost a new religion, founded in toleration and love – had little real following. Religion for most people was not a philosophy, but a set of conservative social practices. Gandhianism was no more than a tolerated sentimentality for much of the Congress leadership. Its social implications were quite incompatible with operating a modern State. It had no role in the work of the new government, as the Mahatma himself recognized sadly in April 1947:[24]

> Whatever the Congress decides will be done; nothing will be according to what I say. My writ runs no more. If it did, the tragedies in the Punjab, Bihar and Noakhali would not have happened. No one listens to me any more. I am a small man ... Where is Congress today? It is disintegrating. I am crying in the wilderness.

Yet it was Gandhi who selected the thoroughly anglicized and secular Nehru to be his heir, and thus predetermined the nature of the leadership of independent India. By implication, Gandhi accepted that his objectives were utopian, incompatible with a world of competing States. Perhaps he also accepted Nehru's judgement, so at variance with his own public views:[25]

> in the context of the modern world, no country can be politically and economically independent, even within the framework of international interdependence, unless it is highly industrialized and has developed its power resources to the utmost.

The national context of communal division did not spread throughout India. It remained a phenomenon of the political minority, despite the mass involvement in partition. Villages were not partitioned by religion, and Muslims remained an accepted part of the rural social structure, a kind of separate caste where the Hindus were a majority. There were riots, but relatively infrequently and invariably with complex material motives at stake and competing political leaderships – with many other causes.

People were also not usually restricted to membership of one group. They could, to some extent, choose the label relative to the strategy for action. That had been so for a long period. Francis Robinson notes of an earlier time:[26]

> Muslim politicians adopted the Muslim identity when it was useful, and discarded it when it had served their purpose. Being a Muslim was less an article of political faith than a useful weapon in their political armoury . . . They have emphasized issues when convenient and ignored them when not.

In practice, large numbers of Muslims, Hindus, Sikhs, Christians etc. had only the haziest idea as to the meaning of their respective religious persuasion, and constantly absorbed elements from the practices of their neighbours of different faith. In communal clashes, religion supplied the pretexts and symbols rather than the causes. It was a kind of tribal loyalty (not so different from the loyalties of football club supporters) attributable to a different line of claimed descent, a shared common struggle, rather than a different creed.

The electoral reforms introduced by the British up to the Second World War did not extend the vote beyond the middle classes – from the shopkeepers, merchants and moneylenders to the richer peasants. They changed the tone from aristocratic and landed to greater populism, but not to mass issues. The less sophisticated within these classes retained stronger psychological moorings in a religious and caste tradition – or rather, perceived the conflicts of their daily lives in terms of the practices that passed locally as that tradition.

Nehru recognized the class basis of communalism in the 1930s – 'so long as our politics are dominated by middle-class elements, we cannot do away with communalism altogether' (Lucknow, 1936). The issues concerned those who might gain from communal privileges or reservations. Few cared much about the poor Muslim weavers or Hindu tenant farmers. In this they were at one with the Raj which urged enhanced educational opportunities for 'Muslims', meaning a small minority of the Muslims, not education for all.

In times of turbulence, comfort could be derived from half-remembered rituals, symbols and cyphers. But it took ambitious adventurers to turn this heterogeneous cultural flotsam into a purified secular political argument. Once there were privileges to be gained or threats to be avoided, people had often no option but to embrace willingly the identity thrust upon them. So the village priest discovered membership of an all-India secular group, the Brahmins (still masquerading as an ancient social formation, a caste); the humble shopkeeper found an all-India identity as a Muslim (now become transformed into a secular and political attribute). And both might discover unlikely associations, between Cabinet Ministers, rich merchants, temple beggars. As a theory, communalism vastly simplified the understanding of the bewildering complexity of India.

In another sense, it provided an entry point for newcomers to the political world, a transmission belt to the wider society. For many who had previously been excluded could now employ a religious identity as their passport to secular participation. It represented – warts and all – an advance in democratization. Of course, quite quickly communalism turned into an attempt to establish monopoly privileges that oppressed everybody else. But, for many of the oppressed, it offered some protection. It also bequeathed to independent India the potential for endless political permutations and occasional warfare, the despair of Indian nationalists. It imprisoned the public discourse in dangerous stereotypes that tended to become self-fulfilling; if the rebellion of some people in the Punjab was described as a movement of Sikhs, there was a grave danger that treating it as a phenomenon of Sikhism would succeed in converting the interest of a small minority into that of the majority.

In sum then, the intensified competition between the Great Powers in the last quarter of the nineteenth century forced centralization on the Raj, a process enhanced in this century by the needs of two World Wars. That process both evoked resistance and necessitated a steady expansion in the clients supporting the State. The Raj created interests, a set of legitimate corporations to support its power. Each extension of participation, however, became perverse in evoking greater opposition, which was overcome only by increasing still further the participation.

Sooner or later that process would have produced the end of British power. What radically changed the picture was the Second World War. It was this that drove Congress to boycott the process of participation, so opening the way for the League to transform itself into a major political alternative. By the time the League had become a force, the British had no further purpose for it, for they were leaving. The nemesis of empire was partition, a fearful monument to the politics of imperialism and the opportunism of the clients.

12

INDEPENDENT INDIA: A HOST OF DRAGONS WITHOUT A LEADER

*T*HE British in India were an extraordinarily small group, exercising power through the manipulation of social interests which they had in part created, backed by the threat of the use of physical force. But, insofar as it became necessary to employ force for any length of time, they were politically defeated: it became apparent that they could never mobilize sufficient power to hold the country. Bluff was the essence of the British Raj. It was bluff mixed with concessions, mixed with the necessity of extending the perimeter of participation in a vain effort to drown Congress. Thus, paradoxically, the British were obliged to democratize, too little and too late, but nonetheless their strategy forced them to increase participation. In each reform, the forces emerging in the public arena added steadily more complexity to the exercise of power.

Independent India, in important ways, was not dissimilar. Legally, all participated in the political process, but the degree to which they actually did so changed. The exigencies of representative politics and elections reached out steadily more widely through the years to include increasing numbers. The widening perimeter of participation now coincided with a much enhanced rate of economic growth and rapid social change.

The changes were heroic. Independent India inherited some 335 million people, and they had become nearly 800 million by the 1980s. The under 60 million urban dwellers had become 156 million by 1981. And the under 17 per cent who were literate in 1951 had become

36 per cent by 1981. Average life expectancy had increased from 32 years at the time of independence to 57, an extraordinary and splendid achievement.

It is strange that these gigantic changes did not produce greater divisions. If it were true that peoples of different languages or cultures would inevitably be driven to collide, it was remarkable that the country – with, according to the 1961 Census, 197 separate languages (98 Indo-Aryan, 21 Austric, 26 Dravidian, 52 Tibeto-Chinese) – did not fall apart. The appearance of increasing heterogeneity was not a reflection of any new diversity, only of the increasing numbers of newcomers entering the arena of politics.

A key force was the increasing centralization that came with swifter domestic industrialization and the extension of Delhi's power beyond its borders. Despite the continuing endemic poverty among so many millions of people, India was emerging as a Great Power, dominating South Asia in a way few Great Powers dominated their region. Successive reforms, from education to the results of the continuing five-year plans, created a single market, a national division of labour and interdependent patterns of specialization in the production of commodities, underpinned by a national system of speedy communications and a large and growing political audience. One of the by-products of this progress was the greater movement of people, within and between provinces, so that the largest cities became increasingly, by Indian standards, cosmopolitan. In terms of language, religion and culture, a national labour market increased the heterogeneity of the working class in the major cities. Of course, to many of those in the countryside, changes appeared slow and the country immovably sluggish, but this should not mislead us into underestimating how quickly the cities and parts of the countryside changed.

The establishment of State power emancipated rising peasant castes. Just as the British had been required to manipulate and balance between local elites, Delhi was obliged to balance and mediate between new interest groups, particularly the largest: rich peasants dominating power at the State level. The successive incarnations of Congress were now required to relate to different segments of the social structure in different ways, sometimes for periods championing the 'backward' (supposedly castes, tribes and Muslims, but in fact this was a thin disguise for the better-off among these groups), at other times, hinting at the importance of a 'Hindu' block of support as the bedrock of India. Delhi, somewhat remote from the reality of the country and, in some ways, more of a link to the rest of the world, could maintain a semblance of detachment from the complex base of shifting alliances and alignments. Once Ministers and Members of Parliament (the Lok Sabha) left Delhi, they returned to India.

As we have seen, the 1905 and 1917 revolutions in Russia included a diversity of national rebellions as well as agrarian and working-class revolution. There was no revolution in India, but there were similar separatist demands, as well as other major social struggles (including mutiny in the armed forces). There was no internationalist political party to draw these forces together, let alone pursue unity through affirmation of the right of national self-determination. The Communists had long become part of Indian – and Soviet – nationalism.

Thus, the independence movement led to claims by some of the Muslims to an independent Pakistan, by some Bengalis calling for an independent Bengal and some Sikhs for an independent Sikh State. But, in general, the predominant conflict – between Congress and the British – was able, with the exception of the Pakistan claim, to subordinate all these subsidiary collisions. Independence ended this.

It seemed there were almost continuous waves of rebellion. Few ruling orders have been faced with such a persistent war of attrition from below from quite unpredictable sources. The linguistic agitation of the 1950s was a harbinger of the establishment of a *status quo* perpetually wracked by conflict. In 1953, popular pressure led to the partition of the old state of Madras between a Telugu-speaking Andhra Pradesh and a Tamil-speaking Tamilnad. Thus Andhra excluded Tamils from competition for public employment, and both excluded English and Hindi speakers. Three years later, the southern states were reorganized, supposedly to recognize the language distribution. The old Bombay state was partitioned between a Gujerati-speaking Gujerat and a Marathi-speaking Maharashtra. In 1966, the old state of Punjab was divided, supposedly between a Hindi-speaking Haryana and a Punjabi-speaking Punjab, a somewhat transparent cover to achieve a Punjab with a majority of Sikhs (but which, in retrospect, seemed to Hindu communalists only a prelude to the demand for an exclusive and independent Sikh State, Khalistan). The old north-eastern state of Assam disintegrated into a patchwork of new states, but still the agitations continued.

The north-eastern states were afflicted sporadically by agitations against immigrants, identified as Bengalis (supposedly foreigners from Bangladesh, but quite often natives of some standing whose ancestors may have come from what became, after Independence, India's West Bengal). The most savage of these agitations led to the slaughter of many Bengalis in the early 1980s. The student leaders of this movement came to power, forming the Assam state government, and sought to transfer non-Assamese out of public employment and impose Assamese as a compulsory language in all schools (which outraged the native non-Assamese tribal people as well as indigenous Bengalis). The agreement reached with Delhi on ending the agitation included the proviso that immigrants to the state before 1966 were granted citizenship; those entering between 1966 and 1971 were to be registered as foreigners and denied the right to vote; those entering after 1971 were to be expelled (the state government later maintained that Delhi did nothing to implement this accord). At the same time, another student movement in the north of Assam was agitating for a separate state; students in Meghalaya (a fragment of the old larger Assam) pressed for the expulsion of their immigrants (mainly Nepalese), and in Arunachal Pradesh (yet another fragment) others pressed for the eviction of Tibetans and Chakma tribal refugees. Bedlam – if not chaos – from the viewpoint of Indian nationalists, had come again, with all too few to affirm the existence of India and its overriding claims relative to localism, casteism and religion.

It was not the peculiarities of the north-east that explained this process. Everywhere, provinces – states in the Indian Union – and districts aped the prejudices of national entities. Even the sophisticated metropolitan areas had their own versions. In Bombay, the Shiva Sena, a militant Hindu organization with rumoured links to the underworld, was reportedly patronized by Congress in the 1960s as a weapon against Communists in the trade unions. In the 1980s, the Shiva Sena fought the elections to Greater Bombay's Municipal Corporation on the platform of a Maratha Bombay and the expulsion of non-Marathi speakers arriving in the city since 1974 ('or', as the main leader of the organization put it with a frightening casualness, '1970'). On a 40 per cent poll, the Shiva Sena won 70 of the 170 seats and was able to form an administration. There were understandable fears of violence against the non-Marathas. However, the Chief Minister of Maharashtra expressed polite interest in the idea of expelling them, although it was difficult to see how, even if the basic premise were accepted, anyone could verify the claims as to time of arrival. One of the main targets of the Shiva Sena attack were Tamil-speakers from the south. And in the state of Tamilnad from which the Tamils had supposedly come, in the city of Coimbatore, posters appeared threatening violence on 'all north Indians' if any Tamils were injured in Bombay. Briefly – as so frequently in India – the atmosphere was electric with violence; like summer lightning, it was impossible to predict where the next shaft might strike, what insane connection would suddenly destroy this or that bystander.

The communal battles were rarely about secession (at least, for the leadership), rather more about the establishment of bargaining positions. The difference was not always clear, and it was legitimate for the South Block – the Prime Minister's complex of offices in Delhi

– to assume that all bargaining could end in the demand for separation. As we shall see in the next chapter, in the case of East Pakistan, such an assumption had some validity.

The style and the striking unpredictability of violence were not restricted to issues of nationalism and communalism. There were thousands of agitations, a thousand dragons stalking prey both real and imaginary. At each stage, in issues tragic or absurd, the class struggle was interwoven in ways hardly to be recognized. Sharecroppers fought the pitiless greed and brutality of landlords. Workers waged pitched battles and long wars of attrition against employers. Untouchables were required to struggle for years against violence to win the right to use the village well or enter the temple. And occasionally, as in Gujerat in the early 1980s, all the issues came together in a succession of horrifying battles in which caste, religion and class set each other off, with only blood and exhaustion at the end.

At the other extreme, some Bangalore Muslims objected to the use of the name Mohammed in a newspaper article, mistakenly believing it referred to the prophet; Vishnavites battled with Shivaites over the sign that should appear on the forehead of the elephant that led the religious procession; the police and self-righteous citizens attempted to dress a traditional naked religious procession and precipitated a riot. Clashes invoked ancient – and spurious – traditions of collective identity and a history of warfare. The press, ever loyal to the lie, faithfully reproduced the myths. Thus, *The Economist* (6 February 1988), on Hindu–Muslim riots, maintained that they 'have been at each other's throats for centuries'; but 'they' did not exist as a community only a century earlier, and, in not existing, had not been at anybody's throat (though throats were no more secure in those bygone days).

The Sikh issue

It was not, as many surmised, simply unemployment, poverty and a poor rate of economic growth which sustained so many struggles. Certainly, there were from time to time important constituencies of the educated unemployed (especially in Calcutta and Kerala where the Communist parties were strong), and they were occasionally bought off by that classic British imperial tactic of job reservations, positive discrimination for the advanced members of the backward community (a procedure which incited the backward members of the advanced communities to compete by claiming to be backward or by demanding their own tranche of legal privilege). In the late 1970s, the pace of economic growth quickened, yet it seemed only to incite further communal clashes, and opposition from those who were not the beneficiaries of expansion and centralization. In the Punjab, a state which experienced the greatest prosperity in the country as the result of the Green Revolution, there also occurred one of the most ferocious and intractable communal wars.

The demand for an independent State of Khalistan, a State of Sikhs, was a good illustration of the complexity of the issues at stake. The Sikhs, if they could be considered as a nationality, were an unlikely candidate for an 'oppressed nation'. The 1987 per capita income of their state, Punjab, was more than two-thirds above the national average, and the general standard of living was perceptibly better than the rest of India. With under 2 per cent of India's population, the Sikhs supplied in the early 1980s 8 per cent of government employment, 6 per cent of the top civil servants, 5 per cent of the Indian police force, 7.5 per cent of the army. At different times, a Sikh was the President of India, the Chief of the Armed Forces, the Governor of the Reserve Bank; a number of others were generals, and important businessmen.

The Green Revolution transformed rural Punjab, and the farmers of that state, the biggest employers of migrant agricultural labour from the rest of India. Land holdings in the state were relatively equal – although growing unequal – so the rise in income generated from the technical transformation of the cultivation of first wheat, and then rice, was spread relatively widely. Furthermore, from the Punjab district of Jullundur came one of the main streams of Indian emigrants to the rest of the world (particularly to Britain, Canada, the Middle East and, latterly, the United States). The return flow of remittances enhanced local incomes and supported conspicuous consumption.

Yet all these changes affecting 'Sikhs' had little to do with the young and hungry who had neither a farm in the Punjab nor a job in Vancouver, but did have education and ambition. There was little sense in including in the same concept the wealthy businessman, the senior government or police or army official, the comfortable farmer, the starveling school teacher, the hungry writer and the new school leaver without family assets and only his wits to earn a living. The heterogeneity of the inhabitants of the Punjab – both between urban and rural, but even more between urban castes and between rural income groups – was obliterated in the religious concept. Sons of rural families who had been educated out of agriculture might always fit uncomfortably into an urban intelligentsia.

To the misery of unemployment was added the indignity that, with an agricultural boom, half a million non-Sikh migrant workers were drawn annually into the cultivation of the Punjab. Sikh farmers, faced with the seduction of profit, preferred cheap 'foreign' labour, particularly in labour-intensive paddy farming (where four-fifths of them depended on migrant workers), to offering Sikh boys wages appropriate to their status as superior people.

It seemed to be the same with manufacturing. The Punjab had a relatively low level of industrialization, but few Sikhs were said to obtain jobs in the factories. At what was claimed to be the largest bicycle factory in the world at Ludhiana, Hero Cycles, only a fifth of the workforce was Sikh. Whether the employers refused to hire ambitious Sikh youths, or Sikh youths had ambitions which would not allow them to work in such menial tasks at such poor pay – or a combination of the two – there was an audience for resentful 'Sikhism'.

Wealth and mobility spread an acid of secularization, or, rather, divided those for whom religion was a comfort and consolation, and those for whom it was an incitement to rage, a call to arms to defend ancient verities, lineages and destinies, but, above all, a dignity. By whatever route, Sikhism came to be all that a minority of young Sikhs had to constitute their honour, the basis of a fierce self-discipline and willingness for sacrifice in a high cause. The self-abnegation required to inculcate discipline led to contempt for those who did not share this austere code. For a time there was a ferocious campaign of violence to prevent other Sikhs from smoking, drinking alcohol, wearing bras or plucking eyebrows.

A propensity or even predisposition is one thing, behaviour is another. The Sikh militants needed to champion a much wider set of interests among the apparently prosperous peasantry of the Punjab, to be able to lead a crusade, oust the dominant Sikh Party, the Akali Dal, and confront the oppression of Delhi. It was here that the narrow interest of Mrs Gandhi, as Prime Minister, was decisive. She sought to undermine the Akali Dal to the advantage of her own Congress Party by promoting a fiery young Sikh preacher, Jarnal Singh Bhindranwale. He was an ideal instrument to undercut the Akali since, from a position of religious integrity, he could accuse them of betraying Sikh interests to Delhi on a series of disputed issues – the distribution of river waters and the status of some border districts and the provincial capital, Chandigarh. However, his uncompromising stand not only upstaged the Akali Dal: it also provided a focus for rallying the scattered Sikh student and youth forces around the demand for an independent state, the primary task being to build an army both to oppose Delhi and to drive the non-Sikhs out of the Punjab.

From this point, it was Delhi which played the major role. The Punjab was densely occupied by police and troops, and for the first time the issue now entered every village. In Operation Bluestar, the Indian army stormed the most important religious centre of Sikhism, the Golden Temple in Amritsar, which was a sanctuary for the armed militants. This was an act of great sacrilege and the damage done an even greater one. Delhi had nailed the issue of Khalistan on the very nature of Sikhism. The militants fought to the death and Bhindranwale was killed with them. The armed forces then spread out to the villages in Operation Woodrose, designed to arrest and intimidate youths in their late teens. Ultimately, 365 were officially detained without charge in prison at Jodhpur. Bluestar was a blunderbuss and the ensuing campaign of ill-disguised terrorization of the villagers created a mass of new enemies of the Government of India, and, by default, supporters of the Khalistani fighters.

The murder of Mrs Gandhi must have seemed to the religious Sikh a divine judgement. But it was followed immediately by a massive attack on all Sikhs without apparent discrimination. As in all such communal riots, the lower echelons of political parties, the local police, gangsters and hoodlums, all had a share in the spoliation of Sikh properties. Possibly 2,500 died. India's nightmare, a return to the horror of partition, briefly reappeared. Hindu militants dragged all Sikhs off the Bombay express and slaughtered them. Politically, it seemed for a moment as if Delhi might indeed succeed in creating a tragic unity that, left to themselves, the Sikhs could never have hoped to achieve. Sikh families were among those most widespread throughout India, and there was talk of their beginning to stream back to the sanctuary of the Punjab for safety. Fortunately it was untrue.

As noted earlier, there is great heterogeneity of interests among the Sikhs – by caste, occupation, urban or rural location, district and size of farm holding, etc. The political standing of Delhi and the Akali Dal, like that of the British, traditionally depended upon manipulating these differences. But after the murder of Mrs Gandhi the centre turned to treating Sikhs as if they were a single consolidated force, barely distinguishable from the Khalistani terrorists, and standing in sharp contrast to an even more mythical block, the Hindus (represented in the activities of the Punjab Shiva Sena and the neighbouring state of Haryana). The government supposedly now feared a 'Hindu blacklash', and this no less mythic character, it seemed, allowed the betrayal of secularism. For the moment Sikhs had no option in the face of the communalism of the central government but to accept a communal identification.

There was a reversal. A new Prime Minister, Rajiv Gandhi, reached an agreement with a Sikh leader, Longowal, and the centre, in as clear an admission of defeat as there could be, supported the re-establishment of an Akali state government. But the issues remained and, despite the commitments embodied in the Longowal–Rajiv agreement, Delhi took no steps to implement its promises: to release those detained and to set up an enquiry into the circumstances of the Sikh massacre in Delhi. Thus, what had now become the main sources of Sikh anger against the central government remained. The centre continued to try and divert attention by claiming that the Khalistani action was funded and directed from Pakistan. Furthermore, the continued armed actions of the government turned some of these manageable grievances into hatred, which in turn increased the pressure for military measures. Finally, when Longowal was assassinated, the centre took the opportunity once more to despatch the state government.

Delhi then changed tactics and relaxed the repressive regime. In the short term, terrorist killings soared, and arms were once more smuggled into the Golden Temple. However, on this occasion, the retaking of the temple, Operation Black Thunder, was accomplished without destruction and sacrilege – and the Khalistani militants surrendered. For the first time, their prestige as the sole defenders of the Sikhs was damaged. To have kept their place as leaders of a nation, they would have been obliged – as with the earlier defenders of the temple – to become martyrs. The issue could continue for many years, but it was no longer of the same significance.

Delhi's political insecurity was the key factor throughout in promoting and sustaining the Khalistani movement, balancing it against the 'Hindu' vote. Communalism had long since become institutionalized in Indian politics; Delhi depended upon communalism to survive. The majority of Sikhs were probably always opposed to or unenthusiastic or neutral about Khalistan, but the centre's need to use them as a further means of solidifying non-Sikh loyalties forced many of them, in some measure, to accommodate to the leadership of the Khalistani militants.

The Sikh issue has a number of important features. It was not a product of the poverty of a people, for the mass of Sikh farmers were relatively better-off than the rest of India. It showed, however, that it was a mistake to think in terms of an 'oppressed people', for there were invariably some who were oppressed in every people. The Sikhs were among the more secularized groups in India, yet the Khalistani movement was closely interwoven with religious issues; the Golden Temple and the role of priests were fundamental. The reality, however, constantly checked religious zeal. Khalistani students might rail against alcohol (and seek for a brief moment to bomb the liquor shops), but the tide of prosperity between the mid-1960s and mid-1980s pushed up the state's consumption of indigenous liquors by eight times, and of foreign spirits by fifteen times.[1] Paradoxically, it was precisely because of secularization that religion became the sole means left to identify Sikhs: they were being absorbed so swiftly in whatever context – class, locality, occupation – they lived.

Nor could they be regarded as 'exploited' by the rest of India. But the condition of the average was no guide to that of the poor. And indeed the definition of Sikhs as exploited depended upon the behaviour of the central government, supposedly the fist of Hinduism. The national leadership, trapped in far wider political challenges and insecurities, duly obliged by oppressing Sikhs as Sikhs: that was the lesson of the Delhi massacre.

The fate of the movement was not a function of the tenacity of the guerrillas (as Delhi liked to present it), but of the centre's need for communalism. Under such a hammer, a militant Sikhism could hardly fail to grow. Yet still weariness on both sides, other changing needs at the centre, could give relief to the much abused citizens of the Punjab, leaving Khalistan as a nostalgic romantic issue. For the centre would never let go of the Punjab; it would never relinquish territory lightly, but territory along the Pakistan border was especially inalienable. The achievement of Khalistan could only occur with a general disintegration of the Union.

The Sikh revolt was only one of a vast number of rebellions against the Union which, abstracting from the important particular circumstances of each, were partly protests against the continuing economic, social and political centralization of the country, as well as the turmoil of social change and the changing nature of oppression. As the tempo of growth increased in the late 1970s, so did the collisions. Of course, to narrow the focus to communalism, proto-nationalism, is severely to distort the picture. For this was only one expression of opposition among many. However, in the Punjab, it was possible for the discontents of a minority of the young to connect with a broader movement only through the intervention of Delhi, turning the issue – or allowing it to be turned – into a directly communal one. Then the political interests of Congress elsewhere in India encouraged it to behave as a Hindu party, so enforcing a rigid Sikhism upon the Sikhs. Exhaustion – and new pretexts for Delhi's initiative elsewhere – saved the Union.

In the melancholy turbulence of India, the failure of any inter-nationalist Left to be able to offer a different all-India perspective was striking. Class politics had degenerated into merely another concern with a fragment, a special interest, rather than a nationally unifying force. The disappearance of the Communists into Indian nationalism was complete; their debates were preoccupied with the terms of *national* class alliances even where they proclaimed forms of action beyond the bounds of parliament. Stalinism had, quite unknowingly, done its work well in securing the stability of the new Indian order.

13

MORE DRAGONS: PAKISTAN AND BANGLADESH

*T*HE first President of Pakistan, true to his origins in the Indian Congress, saw the new State as a secular one. He told its citizens:[1]

> You are free to go to your temples, you are free to go to your mosques or to any other place of worship in this state of Pakistan. You may belong to any religion or caste or creed; that has nothing to do with the fundamental principle that we are all citizens and equal citizens of one state . . . you will find in the course of time, Hindus will cease to be Hindus, and Muslims will cease to be Muslims, not in the religious sense because that is a personal faith of each individual, but in the political sense as citizens of the State.

Thus, we can deduce (with some surprise) that Jinnah saw the political identity of religious persuasion as being only a temporary one, now to be shed in a common secular citizenship.

It was a utopian aspiration. Muslim communalism in India, itself the creation of that unholy alliance of the British Raj, the minority of Hindu nationalists (as opposed to Indian nationalists) and ambitious adventurers of Muslim origin, now became the incubator for many more competing communalisms. Just as in India, while the area of political participation slowly spread outwards to include many newcomers, the essential form of that participation was that the newcomers should 'represent' a group. In Pakistan, the unity that the fear of Hinduism imposed upon a significant number of Muslims disappeared – or at least, became refracted into a much less significant issue of foreign policy. The Muslim League, the champion of an Islamic political communalism, had served its historic purpose; it now shrank back into being no more than a traditional clique of political notables. Pakistan did not inherit a State apparatus as did India, and the army, overwhelmingly recruited in west Pakistan, proved the sole force capable of supplying authority sufficient to overawe both subsidiary communalisms and other fierce divisions.

The new State was, all agreed, an absurdity. Its western half was divided from its eastern by more than 1,000 miles of actually or potentially hostile Indian territory. It was in the west that the new capital was established, for the class identity of the new ruling order was oriented to the west, not to the east of poor rural labourers. The largest province of the west, Pakistani Punjab, supplied much of the new ruling order. Thus, already in the initial establishment, there was a potential in the west for conflict among the Punjabi upper classes, the Sindhi landlords, imn igrant capitalists from India in Karachi, and Baluchi and Pathan tribal chieftains (with links across the border to Iranian Baluchis and Afghan Pathans). The pressures for greater equality in the distribution of resources to the provinces, for increased provincial autonomy and even secession have been continuous themes throughout the history of Pakistan. Apart from the issue of East Pakistan, there were sporadic struggles in Sind and guerrilla warfare among the Baluchis and Pathans against the forces of the centre.

At different stages, the potential for divisions in the west connected with other more complicated distinctions in the cities, and above all in the great melting pot of Karachi. The Orangi district of western Karachi was a vast shanty town said to shelter a million people, variously Muhajir and Bihari (claiming descent from immigrants from India) and Pathan. Lanes provided the frontiers that circumscribed social intercourse, from friendships to marriage, and occasionally provided the lines of war. The ruling order identified communities, but ethnic or cultural separation was possibly less important than the divisions among competing occupations, and particularly among the segments of a mafia that competed in crime and heroin and arms smuggling: not for the first time, supposedly communal riots might conceal battles for the control of illegal trade between rival groups of gangsters. But occasionally the divisions were connected with politics and aspirations to elements of territorial sovereignty. In November 1987, not long after the Shiva Sen took control of the Bombay Municipal Corporation (on a platform of excluding inmigrants), a party claiming to represent the Muhajirs won the Karachi Municipal Corporation and, now that they had become good natives to a man in this immigrant city, demanded restrictions on inmigration to Karachi to exclude more Punjabis and Pathans. Control of the movement of labour is everywhere the popular symbol of sovereignty.

However, one of the most instructive inventions of a nationality – with a secession of more than half the Pakistani population – occurred in the separation of West and East Pakistan and the creation of Bangladesh. National claims were advanced as rhetorical devices to underline bargaining positions, but the logic – or the accident – of events turned them into ideological routes to separation. Furthermore, the role of outside intervention – so crucial, as we have seen, in the case of secessions in the early years of Soviet Russia – was decisive in East Pakistan. Victory is not certain with outside intervention but, without it, the evidence suggests secession cannot succeed. A subsidiary theme in the account is the astonishing opportunism of the adventurers who led both sides of the collision: political slogans were no more than convenient stepping stones to power, to be abandoned where their efficacy was in doubt.

In the continuous crisis surrounding the creation of the new Pakistan State, at its then capital in Karachi, it is not clear how far the new ruling order thought it feasible to hold the East. The warfare over Kashmir symbolized what was expected to be the continuing hostility of India which controlled the direct route to the East. There is some evidence of a certain scepticism in Karachi; Chowdhury Mohammed, Secretary to the government, is said to have framed a confidential memorandum in 1948 that predicted that the East would break away at some stage. It would therefore be unwise of the West to waste resources there.[2] However, what began as an apparent accident, with time acquired normality; in the end the Pakistan government did commit resources to the East and ran grave international risks in seeking to keep it within Pakistan.

For the economists of the East, the relationship between East and West seemed a prototype of 'internal colonialism'. In 1947, they said, the regional income of the West was slightly below that of the East, but by 1970 the West was 25 per cent above the East. In terms of real per capita income, while the 73 million of the East (in 1970) stagnated, the 60 million of the West were 60 per cent ahead with a significantly higher rate of growth. One of the key mechanisms for this differential performance was seen in Pakistan's international trade. In the early years of the new State, the jute exports of the East earned much of the country's foreign exchange, but the imports of industrial equipment went overwhelmingly to support rapid industrialization in the West. For a time, the East was able to prevent this by continuing its traditional exports of raw jute to the mills of Calcutta (in India's West Bengal), and also purchasing there the bulk of its manufactured imports (considerably cheaper than equivalent goods from West Pakistan both because Calcutta, in industrial terms, was much more advanced than Karachi and because the distance goods for the East had to travel was much less). However, the 1965 Indo-Pakistan border clashes led to the permanent closure of the eastern frontier. Perforce, the East had to set up jute processing at home and export raw jute to mills outside India; and import its manufactured goods from the high-cost source of West Pakistan. On top of this discriminatory trade regime, two-thirds of external aid and national development funds were said to have been spent in the West (West Pakistan's strategic position vis-à-vis the Soviet Union and the Middle Eastern allies of the United States exaggerated this factor). The neglect of irrigation and flood-control works in the East to offset the notorious cyclones was one of the by-products of this regime, and one which continues to plague Bangladesh to this day.

As with the ruling orders of other provinces of the new State, there were continuing clashes with the centre. The East, with its traditional trading and cultural links with Calcutta, was always suspected of being half-hearted in its loyalty to Pakistan, particularly over the issue of Kashmir (on the borders of the West). The resentment of the Bengalis at this situation was exaggerated because they constituted the majority of the population and might claim with some justice to be the nation, even though political, economic and cultural life was dominated by Karachi. That domination was symbolized by an attempt by the government in 1953 to impose the use of Urdu (the *lingua franca* of north India in the Mughal and British periods). A major campaign of opposition in the East warded off the threat to Bengali. At this stage, however, there was no serious evidence that the East entertained dreams of independence.

The sporadic clashes became summarized in the Six Points of Mujib-ur-Rahman's Awami League, which set out the terms for the decentralization of power (with defence and foreign affairs alone reserved to the national government) and the creation of a local militia. The League's leaders were arrested. However, only three years later, the President of Pakistan, former General Ayub Khan, was himself overthrown. It was this event which began an entirely new period in the history of Pakistan.

The creation of Bangladesh

Ayub Khan had seized power in 1958. Although the military moved into the background and a civil order was officially established, it was an authoritarian regime. Ten years after coming to power, the President was faced with the rebellion of one of his former lieutenants, an ex-Foreign Secretary, Z.A. Bhutto, who began an agitation for the restoration of civil rights, the holding of elections, and radical land reform. Perhaps as much to the surprise of Bhutto as anyone else, the campaign elicited a great upsurge of support, particularly in the cities and among the middle and working classes. The East was already engaged in a major campaign to advance Mujib's Six Points and secure the release of the League leadership. A simultaneous revolt in both wings of the country, particularly given the distance between them, posed peculiarly grave difficulties for the regime, which were compounded by the simultaneous threat of guerrilla warfare in eastern India which was ultimately to cause a breakdown in order in Calcutta. The Government of India might be tempted to exploit the discomfiture of Pakistan by embarking on further military adventures across the borders.

The Pakistan military high command selected the President as the sacrificial victim to popular anger. A coup overthrew Ayub Khan in the spring of 1969. Further concessions were required, however. The interim military government promised a return to civilian rule and, then, what in retrospect was a momentous step, the first general elections based on universal suffrage to create a Constituent Assembly which was to define a constitution enshrining greater provincial authority. Perhaps intended to neutralize Bhutto's fiery radicalism in the West, this proved, with the benefit of hindsight, to be a disaster for the interests of the West and of the armed forces. Hitherto, Assembly seats had been divided equally between the two wings of the country; now the more populous East would have a majority.

For Bhutto and his Pakistan People's Party (PPP), there was no question of reaching an alliance with Mujib and the Awami League to secure a democratic order: Bhutto was determined to be Prime Minister. He therefore reversed his position on the demand for democracy (for much the same reason as Jinnah had opposed universal suffrage in British India: because he would not win), and endeavoured to compensate for this reversal by a greater emphasis upon nationalism and a powerful State. He demanded a national commitment to a 'thousand-year war' to liberate Kashmir, a strong central government and army to prosecute this objective, the ending of 'feudalism', and the nationalization of the more important industries and the public transport system. He also hinted at the expropriation of banking and insurance to end the country's domination by the notorious 'Twenty-Two Families'.

In the East, the League continued to champion the Six Points for provincial autonomy (and so oppose Bhutto's demand for a strong centralized government), while the Bengali Left, divided into numerous sects, was in general unable to rise above the radical nationalism which Stalin had bequeathed it under the name of Marxism.

The election results were as catastrophic for the PPP as Bhutto had feared, but also for the military. The Awami League won 167 of the 169 seats allocated to the East, giving it an absolute majority in the Constituent Assembly (of 313 seats). The PPP, the largest party in the West, had easily carried the largest province, the Punjab, and also Bhutto's home province, Sind, but in the combined Assembly it had less than half the Awami League's total. It is rare in politics for events to assume such an oversimplified, almost operatic, form, and to become, apparently, so fateful. The election had trapped in the same corner the Pakistan military high command and its erstwhile scourge, Bhutto; the champion of Pakistan democracy could now come to power only through the agency of the military. On the other hand, as if by accident and wanting only more provincial autonomy, Mujib had emerged as major arbiter of the country's destiny.

On the surface, however, the situation remained courteous. President Yahya Khan congratulated Mujib on the League's historic victory and set the date of 5 March 1971 for the Assembly to meet in the capital of the East. Bhutto, however, had begun a campaign to discredit Mujib's credentials as a Pakistani patriot and to accuse him of being a Bengali separatist. The PPP announced that it would launch a major protest movement of demonstrations and strikes until Mujib-ur-Rahman agreed to compromise on his Six Points (which Bhutto now described as a manifesto of Bengali national independence). Bhutto also threatened that any deputy from the West who dared to travel to Dacca would be punished. On 1 March, the President, without consulting the League, postponed the convening of the Assembly.

The incompetence of this move, so late in the day, still has the power to astonish. The Presidency had so little standing, and the army was so suspect, that cancellation could only pour petrol on the fires of popular fury. All now believed the original setting of the date had been a trick to gain time so that the army's strength in the East could be expanded. To cancel so late, however, was to incite the East. While the date for the Assembly was firm, Mujib had been able to keep his followers in some order, disciplined behind his Six Points. But cancellation opened Pandora's Box.

On 2 March the army was called out to put down demonstrations in Dacca; ultimately 200 people were said to have died. Simultaneously, the army accelerated the movement of troops and equipment from West to East. India had banned the overflight of its territory by Pakistani aircraft, so supplies were diverted to the long route via Sri Lanka; perversely, however, Sri Lanka was simultaneously facing a major internal rebellion, and Indian troops offered support to Sri Lanka's government by guarding Colombo airport – and thus the Pakistani aircraft in transit.

However, Mujib-ur-Rahman moved with extreme caution. At no stage did he defy the President or hint that he might summon the Assembly as sovereign. But he was obliged to do something to keep his hold on the leadership of the movement in the East. He called a general stoppage (a 'hartal'). On 4 March the League staged an enormous demonstration in Dacca, and for the first time slogans demanding independence appeared – with the flag of an independent Bangladesh. Mujib was not moved, however. He said nothing of independence but warned the President privately that he could not control the movement for much longer without concessions which would vindicate his appeals for patience. Two days later, the President duly obliged with the announcement that the Constituent Assembly would be convened on 25 March. But it was too late. At another massive demonstration in Dacca on 7 March Mujib demanded an end to martial law, but also indicated firmly that, while the Assembly would be sovereign, he was not going to use his majority to declare an independent Bangladesh, nor to compromise on Kashmir, nor to reopen trade links with India. The President's concessions to the East were now more than matched by the East's concessions to the West.

The position of Yahya Khan was now becoming insecure. The PPP's resumed agitation in the West to try to force the cancellation of the Assembly was alarming some of the high command, and there were fears of a new coup. On the other hand, Bhutto was not so sure that the President might not be able to strike a deal with Mujib in talks held in Dacca. But the Awami League leader now needed more concessions if he was to divert the growing demands for independence. Leaving one of the meetings with Yahya Khan, he exclaimed to the waiting journalists with some frustration:

These people [the military high command] must come to their senses. Can't they see that I alone can save East Pakistan from communism? If they make a fight of it, I shall lose the leadership within a few years, and Naxalites* will take action in my name. They will even carry my picture at first, to gain the confidence of the people. Then they will take over.

Three days before it was due to meet, the President postponed the Assembly. Dacca was a sea of flags of an independent Bangladesh, but still Mujib held firm, resisting any talk of independence. On the other side of the sub-continent, Bhutto, scenting victory, redoubled his agitation; the PPP seized and occupied government offices and

*'Naxalite' after the rural guerrillas of the Communist Party of India (Marxist–Leninist), operating in the Naxalbari district of Indian north Bengal in the late 1960s.

factories. Those in the East, who felt vulnerable and had the income, began to flee. In the West, Bengalis prepared for the worst.

On 25 March, Yahya Khan vested supreme power in the military authorities of the East and returned to the West. The army fell upon the Awami League with the utmost ferocity as the first step in an attempt to liquidate all forces calling for independence (which covered much of the Bengali intelligentsia). Some claim that in the ensuing campaign some 3 million people lost their lives. The country, already terribly poor, was devastated. 'By the grace of the Almighty', Bhutto proclaimed, 'Pakistan has at last been saved.'

Retrospect

In 1947, Jinnah had given every sign of not being prepared for the independence of Pakistan, that gift that a popular movement had unexpectedly delivered into his hands. But at least he had raised the demand for it. Mujib had steadfastly opposed the demand for an independent Bangladesh. There were no preparations for the military assault. The League did not warn its followers, nor alert the Bengali military and police forces. There was spontaneous resistance – railways and bridges were blown up – and a general refusal to collaborate. But, in terms of a real struggle for national liberation, it was very little. Mujib, to the end, remained loyal to Pakistan. The Secretary of the Awami League and Prime Minister in the Provisional Government of Bangladesh admitted what had been clear throughout: 'there was no thought of secession until the army cracked down on us on March 25th'.[3] Indeed, the Awami League remained dependent upon the Pakistani army to defend it against India – and against the more unruly inhabitants of the East. This dependence increasingly paralysed Mujib between his followers and the military. In the end, he was immobilized. He did not flee to organize his followers; he simply awaited arrest and internment in West Pakistan.

These events did not take place in isolation. The neutralization of Pakistan had been the central aim of Indian foreign policy since 1947. Pakistan, an ally of the United States, had recently arranged a secret flight for President Nixon to Peking in order to negotiate the terms of Chinese support for the evacuation of US forces from Vietnam. From the slit trench of Delhi, the emergence of a US–Pakistan–China axis menacing India on two land sides and, through the US fleets, at sea, seemed a serious threat. In East Pakistan, the National Awami Party of the famous Leftist leader, Maulana Bashani, was known simultaneously for advocating an independent Socialist Republic of Bangladesh and alliance with China. With Mujib interned and the

Awami League in disarray, it seemed possible that the Maulana might replace them and complete the noose round India. Furthermore, eastern India was wracked with Maoist rebellion, and the Communists of Indian West Bengal might be tempted to ally with Bashani's forces in East Bengal.

Thus, a multiplicity of fears impelled Indian intervention. Within a day or two of the Pakistan army's attack in the East, the Indian High Command finalized plans for the invasion of East Pakistan. These were sanctioned by the Indian Cabinet at the beginning of April. The Pakistan military must have guessed that this would happen. Their folly had exposed their alarming vulnerability, for the full weight of Indian armed power could not be resisted for long so far from their bases in West Pakistan. However, the Indians were in no haste, for the political ground had to be prepared. The military governor in Dacca had fully eight months to prepare himself to lead the most catastrophic defeat experienced by any army in South Asia. In the interim, India's Prime Minister could use the flight of between 6 and 10 million refugees from East Pakistan to India as the humanitarian basis for military intervention. The pursuit of virtue and power coincided most excellently.

In fact, the fears of the Indian establishment were largely fantasy, for there was little left of any internationalism on either side of the border. The Indian Communists (CPM), indeed, organized collections for defence funds as the Indian army swept through East Pakistan, little regarding the central purpose of Mrs Gandhi: to break Pakistan, not to liberate the Bengalis. The Indian army swiftly overwhelmed the Pakistanis, forcing a catastrophic surrender upon the luckless General Niazi.

Mujib was interned. Bhutto, now relieved of the burden of a Bengali majority, was able once again to change sides and champion a return to democracy and civil rule. The military and Bhutto, advocates of an advanced military position against India and champions of Pakistani nationalism, had suffered overwhelming military defeat and lost more than half their country to Indian arms. The position of Delhi within South Asia had dramatically changed. There was now no serious check upon its regional domination; Indian nationalism was triumphant. The victory had also shifted the balance of domestic power – Mrs Gandhi was at the peak of her popularity. Her intervention in East Pakistan seemed to have done more for the cause of national liberation than all the exploits of guerrillas.

For the battered newborn Bangladesh, the prospects were grim. To economic disasters – famine and cyclone – was added the military devastation of the country by two armies, particularly in terms of infrastructure and the all-important bridges across the country's complex waterways. As an independent State, there were the additional problems of establishing a stable political order. Mujib-ur-Rahman, discreetly transformed from opponent of an independent Bangladesh to 'Father of the Nation', set up an administration renowned equally for its corruption and it incompetence. He was murdered in 1975 without serious popular protest or mourning.

The achievement of an independent Bangladesh demonstrated a number of important points. The first was the striking speed with which a Bangladeshi nationalism was created. It had no ancient and illustrious past, even though, once the historians were unleashed, an exclusive slice of history could be colonized (a parallel to the exclusive territory of the new State). The concept of Bengal was a quite late invention – beginning as a Turkic administrative division in the Middle Ages, but lacking linguistic or cultural homogeneity until the nineteenth century. And an Islamic Bengal was even later, and implied no separate political order. This is not, of course, to say that Bengalis, particularly in the intelligentsia, have not for long had some sense of shared experience, but this was of no political significance. Bangladesh was a tactic, a short-term reaction to the manifest injustice of the Pakistani regime and the complicated interaction between forces in East and West following the fall of Ayub Khan. Adventurers were on hand to utilize the opportunities as they arose – whether a Bhutto or a Mujib (whose sole principle seems to have been opposition to a secession by Bengal). Despite appearances, there was nothing inevitable about the outcome until India intervened, at which stage the domestic crisis of Pakistan became the means for the implementation of Indian foreign policy. But, in the language of nationalism, the soul of the nation had now to be invented to make inexorable its advance to self-realization in a new State.

India was decisive. The Pakistan army could have held the East, despite the difficulties, almost indefinitely. The demand for national liberation can, with astonishing speed, come to summarize masses of diverse discontents. But translating these into a new State requires the intervention of the world system of States. As Rosa Luxemburg argued, national independence in the modern world requires some measure of imperialism.

14

AND YET MORE:
SRI LANKA AND TAMIL
EELAM

*T*HE island of Sri Lanka (formerly Ceylon) has been inhabited
in modern times by a people speaking two major languages
and practising four religions. Insofar as such statements make
sense, the inhabitants appear to be of common ethnic descent, to some
degree related to the peoples of neighbouring south India (but with
admixtures from Arabs, Portuguese, Malays etc.). About two-thirds
claim Sinhalese as their home tongue (some 11 million of the 1981 15
million population), and Buddhism as their religion. The other third
speak, in the main, Tamil, and are subdivided – in Sri Lanka terms
which mix religious and ethnic labels – into Sri Lankan Tamils (12.5
per cent), Indian Tamils (6 per cent), and Muslims (7.5 per cent). Of
the non-Buddhists, some 18 per cent are Hindus, 8 per cent Christian,
and slightly fewer, Muslim. Language, religion and place of origin thus
constitute both alternative and duplicating forms of classification.

The post-Independence history of Sri Lanka is yet another account of
how these innocent linguistic and religious distinctions – never entirely
clear or exclusive – have been the pretext for the ambitious to create exclusive secular and political groups competing for advantage and power.
For the participants, it has been a hideously destructive process. But it
is also instructive in the methods of inventing new fictitious identities,
'Sinhalese–Buddhist' and 'Tamil–Hindu'. The two (and the 'two' is a
modern concept since, in the past, operative social distinctions followed
different and more complicated lines) shared caste, kinship, popular
cults, customs, sacred places and a single history. As Tambiah puts it,
'the Sinhalese and Tamil labels are porous sieves through which diverse
groups and categories of Indian peoples intermixed with non-Indians.'[1]

Modern secular groups have expropriated old traditions – or, perhaps more correctly, ransacked fragments of traditions – in order to provide symbols for themselves, creating what are now exclusive histories, archaeologies, genealogies and the rest. The competition for power within the 'majority', now created as Sinhalese, has forced a no less spurious unity upon sections of the Tamil minority. Adventurers played and continue to play a key role in this process, predominantly mobilizing groups from the educated middle and lower-middle classes on both sides. The class preoccupation is illustrated in the fundamental issues in dispute: access to higher education, to the professions and trade, and to public employment. Finally, the role of an outside power, again India, has been fundamental. This time, however, Delhi had an interest not so much in neutralizing Sri Lanka (as it had sought to neutralize Pakistan) as in removing a source of possible Great Power intervention in the Indian Ocean. However, Indian involvement immediately allowed the Sri Lankan Sinhalese majority to see themselves as an oppressed minority, facing the millions of India and, particularly, India's 50 million Tamils.

Origins

The British in Sri Lanka did not weight the political system in favour of the communal and interest groups which they identified as constituting Ceylonese society (as they had done in India). While accepting communal proportions, they rejected multiple votes for minorities. The Donoughmore Commission in 1928 went even further – echoing Lenin's original views on federation – and deplored communally elected representatives as:[2]

a canker in the body politic, eating deeper and deeper into the vital energies of the people, breeding self-interest, suspicion and animosity, poisoning the new growth of political consciousness and effectively preventing the development of a national or corporate spirit.

The officers of the Raj in Delhi could usefully have been instructed in this text.

Nonetheless, the British identified the Sinhalese as backward in comparison with the Tamils, a now familiar form of myopia. In reality, a small minority of Tamils from the north and some low-country Sinhalese of the south-west were able to benefit from the expansion of trade and the public bureaucracy. However, poverty and cultivation –

the crucial signs of 'backwardness' – remained the lot of the majority of Sinhalese and Tamils. Mission schools allowed some of the Tamils to escape from a relatively arid agriculture to white-collar employment in commerce and the professions. The use of English was both an escape and a method of excluding competition from the majority of Ceylonese. By 1948, it was said, some 30 per cent of government jobs and of places in the University of Ceylon were held by those of Sri Lankan Tamil origin.

These differential benefits, however, did not seem to create more than normal tensions; the acceptance of class did not spill over into a resentment of communities. Before 1948 and Independence the local communal riots afflicted rich Christians (1883), Muslim traders (1915), Indian Tamils (from 1928) and Malayalees (from 1930), but not Sri Lankan Tamils.

However, as in India, the approach of Independence began to widen the area of participation. The small circle of English speakers who represented the Ceylonese to the British (in many ways, a mirror image of the English colonial mandarins) were now required, if they wished to be successful in the new political order, to build support among the many newcomers who had no competence in the language. What had been a useful means of excluding competition now became a grave weakness, an inability to relate to the new participants. In the 1940s, English-speaking politicians started to learn Sinhalese, to re-adopt Buddhism and to don a pseudo-native dress (of course, this was not only an attempt to locate themselves in Ceylonese rather than English colonial life, but also a cultural rejection of the British and an attempt to create a Ceylonese alternative). As happened in India, however, this creation of a political version of tradition to fit the majority was skewed, in Sri Lanka towards a Sinhalese fiction rather than a Sri Lankan Tamil one. In doing so, the fundamental divisions between the Sinhalese ruling groups were now subsidiary to the division first with the British, and then with the Tamils. In response, the Tamil parties themselves began to affirm a different distinction. However, there is no evidence before 1956 that this found any sympathetic echo among the mass of the Tamils. It was a squabble within the Establishment.

Neither religion nor language socially united all Tamil speakers. The Indian Tamils, brought to Ceylon by the British from the middle of the nineteenth century to work the tea gardens, were of the same language and religion as the Sri Lankan Tamils, but this is no way united them. The class identity of the Sri Lankan Tamil leadership always prevented them from allying with the solidly working-class Indian Tamils of the tea plantations, let alone combining with the vastly much larger group of Tamils in India. One of the first acts of the newly independent Ceylon government was the Ceylon Citizenship

Act of 1948, which excluded the Indian Tamils from Ceylonese nationality, laying it down that half of them should be expelled to India. Two subsequent agreements with India on the issue resulted finally in 600,000 being expelled and 400,000 or so being recognized as Sri Lankan. The Sri Lankan Tamil Members of Parliament supported the 1948 measure. They also supported a bill in the same year which deprived the Indian Tamils of the vote (even though those who were eligible to vote had participated in the elections for the State Council in 1931 and 1935). At the other extreme, the representatives of those Indian Tamils who had been allowed to become Sri Lankan nationals under the settlement with India remained supporters, or part, of the UNP governments in the late 1970s and 1980s which were engaged in a civil war with some of the Sri Lankan Tamils. 'Tamil' therefore in practice came to refer, not to all speakers of Tamil nor to Hindus, but to the inhabitants of the north (and a minority of the east). In practice, it more often referred to the small minority of militant secessionists.

Thus, after Independence, a much larger educated class came to participate in politics. In particular, those who had attended Sinhalese schools provided an important, and growing, constituency for lower middle-class employment and were therefore directly affected by the strong position of Tamils in education. So long as English remained the language of power, the Sinhalese speakers were excluded. For an aspirant political leader, anxious to locate him or herself in the new Ceylon, shaping the political perceptions of this group of newcomers and championing its interests and prejudices was an important route to power.

S.W.R.D. Banderanaike proved in the short term to be one of the most adept at the manipulation of this issue. Westernized and Christian, he became Sinhalese and Buddhist. In rejecting English, he repudiated the old use of the language to exclude most people from the operation of politics and the law. As his wife put it many years later:[3]

> By giving the due and rightful place to the Sinhala language as the official language of the country, we have made it possible for these voiceless millions who speak only that language to play an effective part in the affairs of the country.

By the same token, the 'voiceless millions' who spoke only Tamil were excluded from playing an effective part. Banderanaike himself came to recognize this; dethroning English not only undermined the position of the privileged, it removed the advantage of the English-educated Tamils in education, the professions and trade, to the direct advantage of his supporters. He was more direct still in declaring that the use of Tamil was itself a problem:[4]

> The fact that in the towns and villages, in business houses and
> boutiques, most of the work is in the hands of Tamil-speaking
> people will inevitably result in a fear, and I do not think an
> unjustified fear, of the inexorable shrinkage of the Sinhalese
> language

There spoke the adventurer, attempting to focus diverse fears upon a
particular, and irrelevant, target: what language one might hear.

In 1956, Banderanaike gambled on the issue in a general election. The
campaign of his Sri Lanka Freedom Party (SLFP) was almost exclusively
based on the proposal to make the Sinhalese language (Sinhala) the sole
official medium. His prescience was confirmed in a landslide electoral
victory.

In June, the bill laying down Sinhala as the country's official language
passed through the Assembly (by 56 to 29 votes). By then, the main
opposition party, the United National Party (UNP) had swung into
supporting it. Tamil MPs staged a sit-down protest outside the
Assembly building and there was some violence when it was broken up.
Simultaneously, Buddhist monks led a counter-demonstration against
the clause in the bill which permitted 'reasonable use of Tamil'. Some
of the uglier forces, and some clad in saffron, were beginning to emerge
now that Banderanaike had identified an enemy.

The bill symbolized a new order of politics. After it, Tamil numbers
were steadily reduced in public employment. In the Civil Service, total
employment increased from 82,000 in 1948 to 225,000 in 1970, but
Tamils declined from 30 to 6 per cent of the total. After 1956, there was
a sustained increase in non-civil service public sector employment (to
1.2 million in 1982), virtually all of it recruited from Sinhala-speakers
(though Tamils still held a slightly higher share of senior jobs than their
proportion of the Sri Lankan population). The decline in the private
sector was much less noticeable, and still in 1981, when Sri Lankan
Tamils were 12.6 per cent of the population, 35 per cent of doctors
and engineers were Tamil (although the proportion of all Tamils in
these occupations was very small).

The language bill was a covert attack upon the Tamil middle classes.
It began that sequence of events which ultimately culminated in civil
war. Banderanaike released forces far more violent than he could have
anticipated – just as had Jinnah, Mujib-ur-Rahman and Mrs Gandhi.
They were not simply Sinhalese nationalism, for that very concept
summarized the most complex and violent rivalries: of class, caste,
locality and occupation. In the case of Banderanaike himself, when
he attempted a compromise on the language issue in 1959, he was
assassinated by a Buddhist monk.

The Left proper in Sri Lanka was no better in political approach than further north in India. But if the Indian Communists could claim their nationalism was a product of the evolution of the Comintern and Russia's interests as a Great Power, the strongest left-wing party in Sri Lanka, the Lanka Sama Samaj (LSSP), claimed to be Trotskyist and inimical to the Stalinists. Yet the LSSP proved no less compromising on the issue of Sinhalese communalism, identifying it as authentic Ceylonese nationalism. In 1964, the LSSP – with the Communist Party – was a component in an alliance led by the late Mr Banderanaike's party, the Sri Lanka Freedom Party.

Civil war

Slowly events now began to move towards what, in retrospect, seemed an inexorable advance to civil war, but with a gradualism which allowed the majority of innocent bystanders to be changed, involuntarily, into collective protagonists. The appearance of necessity was illusion, for in fact, along the way, there were many opportunities to reverse the process: choices were made and options rejected.

In 1958, a Jaffna express (Jaffna is the capital of the northern province) was derailed and there were anti-Tamil riots with numerous deaths. In 1961, the Tamil Federal Party tried to initiate a general strike of Tamils in public employment in protest at the language policy. There was scattered violence. The then-Prime Minister, Mrs Banderanaike, declared a State of Emergency and moved troops into the north and east.

In 1965, the UNP sought to check the SLFP by means of an electoral alliance with the Tamil parties, promising in return district autonomy and new language proposals. The proposals were initially defeated in the Assembly, but, when finally passed, were not implemented.

The 1970 election was won by an SLFP-led alliance (again, including the LSSP and the Communists) on a platform of nationalizing the banks. But within a short time it was faced with the most serious mass rebellion in Sri Lanka's history, led by an organization of educated rural Sinhalese youth, directed against upper-caste domination. The rebellion of the Janatha Vimukti Peramuna (JVP, People's Liberation Front) constituted yet another fundamental change in the nature of Sri Lankan political life. For it was a second front, a challenge by Sinhalese youth to the Sinhalese ruling order. The government, with a tiny army, was obliged to expand its defence forces rapidly, and to call upon a variety of powers – particularly India, Britain and China – to come to its aid. During the State of Emergency (which ultimately ended only in 1977 under a new UNP government), it is estimated some 10,000 died.

The rebellion revealed the vulnerability of the *status quo*. Perhaps also it led governments to be more harsh towards the scapegoats of the north as a method of trying to solidify the loyalty of the Sinhalese. Certainly it prompted a rather more constructive official response to the discontents of young Sinhalese than young Tamils had received: new efforts were made to reduce unemployment (60 per cent of the age group 15 to 19 were said to be without work in 1975, and 34 per cent of those between 20 and 29), and to make more space – or at least more talk about the need to make more space – in society for some of the Sinhalese young. In 1972, the 'standardization of university entries' scheme was introduced, a system of special weighting, supposedly designed to favour applicants from more backward areas – that is, Sinhalese. The numbers of Tamils in higher education, it was said, began to fall immediately, and many more sought education abroad, part of the growing diaspora of Sri Lankan Tamils.

At roughly the same time, a few small groups of young Tamils began to talk of the need to end what they saw as the policy of weak compromises pursued by the established Tamil parties – and to take up armed resistance to Sinhalese aggression and strive to achieve an independent Tamil State (the groups included what was to become the leading guerrilla organization, the Liberation Tigers of Tamil Eelam, LTTE). The Tamil militants objected, just as the JVP did, to the upper-class Establishment that ultimately betrayed the youth of both sides. But the politics on each side of the boundary could not unite against a common enemy. The alliance of Tamil parliamentary parties, the Tamil United Front, responded to the growing militancy by, for the first time, publicly opting for secession (Liberation was inserted in the title in 1976, TULF).

Meanwhile in the north, the incidence of violence increased. Both sides were inventing an identity through leapfrogging charges of arbitrary arrests, torture, assassination, acts of inexplicable barbarism by the other side. In 1974, the Tamils claimed that the police made an unprovoked attack upon the Fourth Tamil International Research Conference at Jaffna: nine were killed. The government refused an enquiry even though the conference included strong participation by Tamils from India. In August, there were anti-Tamil riots.

In 1977, the organization of the Indian tea-garden workers, the Ceylon Workers' Congress, was induced to form an electoral alliance with the UNP, which swept to power under Junius Jayawardene in a landslide victory – 51 per cent of the vote brought 83 per cent of the seats. Once again, the government conceded that Tamil could be used as a national language, that district councils would be established and fairer procedures for university entry introduced. In practice, little was done for fear of inciting protests by the self-appointed representatives of the Sinhalese, particularly by the minority of Buddhist monks who were seen as very important leaders of opinion. The fears were not groundless: in August, there were again anti-Tamil riots. This time, allegedly, the police refused to intervene (perhaps 100 were killed).

The new government brought in a number of important changes. First, it introduced yet another new constitution to sustain a presidential form of administration (with Jayawardene as the first President). Second, responsive to the new fashions in economic policy sweeping the world and for the first time in Sri Lanka's independent history, it began to liberalize the economy and orient it towards the export of manufactured goods and expanded tourism. For a time, the formula seemed to work – the national product more than doubled up to 1983 and employment was significantly increased. But then the effects of the civil war and heavy arms imports tipped the balance. Between 1978 and 1987, defence spending increased fifteen times over. Growth faltered, and both inflation and unemployment increased rapidly.

Armed clashes now grew more frequent, and in 1979 the government introduced the draconian Prevention of Terrorism Act and a State of Emergency in the north. The LTTE and other organizations were prohibited. Four battalions of the army occupied Jaffna. In 1982, the State of Emergency was used to justify extending the life of the administration for another six years by simple majority in a referendum.

The police in Jaffna were accused of rioting and looting. In Colombo, there were more anti-Tamil riots, said now to include, with government toleration, police participation (25 were killed). Tamils noted that the President seemed to delay the introduction of a curfew and any official statement; when the statement came, it announced 'The time has come to accede to the clamour and the national respect of the Sinhalese people.'[5]

The guerrilla groups established sanctuaries in Madras, where they set up training facilities; raised money and publicized their aims; and organized the smuggling of arms across the Palk Straits to Sri Lanka. The Chief Minister of Tamilnad, M.G. Ramachandran ('MGR'), gave benign protection to this activity since it was thought to contribute to his political standing as a protector of world Tamil interests (Indian Tamil sympathies were strained, however, when the guerrillas accidentally detonated a bomb at Madras airport, killing 32 people). At various stages, MGR is said to have contributed the equivalent of nearly £2 million to the guerrilla groups. Since at this stage he was one of the few state-level allies of Rajiv Gandhi's government in Delhi, his benevolence perforce carried the support, or at least the toleration, of the Government of India. Thus, already India as the dominant power of the region was involved, and on the side of what the Sri Lankan government saw as treason (simultaneously Delhi waxed furious at the alleged Pakistani support for the Sikh Khalistani movement).

Challenge and response

Options now seemed to close in. The old Sri Lanka, the fertile land of serendipity, was beyond recall. A tiny force of 1200 troops 'occupied' the north. In practice, this meant the use of as much terror as was feasible – from the safety of fixed barracks – to make up for the paucity of forces. But the barracks, in turn, were ideal fixed targets for the free-ranging guerrillas. Charges and countercharges of violence became a self-reproducing sequence of reprisals in which it was no longer possible to say who was right and who wrong – or, indeed, to say exactly what happened.

A mass murder of 53 Tamils in Colombo's main prison was the signal to launch that unholy alliance which seems always to be at the heart of communal (and race) riots – small-time gangsters, petty traders, local political organizers, policemen and even soldiers, with their legion of hangers-on, eager for spoils. In the Sri Lankan case, also, some of the Buddhist monks led the ultras. They fell upon the Tamils of Colombo, supposedly in righteous indignation at the insult to 'Sri Lanka' and 'the Sinhalese', but more often to line pockets, liquidate rivals, open up job vacancies and seize properties and the stocks of warehouses. The assault had been prepared with some thought, and the connivance of the authorities was required to allow this act of public punishment (as in the attack on the Sikhs in Delhi). Possibly 350 Tamils were murdered (the Tamils claimed 2,000 deaths). Something over 125,000 were made homeless, fleeing, where they could, to India, and where they could not, to refugee camps. Part of the attack was also upon Indian businesses (which were not particularly Tamil).

The issue had now become an international one. Delhi was aware of the flow of arms and military advice to the Sri Lankan government from Israel, Britain, China and others. Thus, as well as the external involvement (always a paranoid preoccupation in Delhi), there was the danger that the war in the north would become linked to the revived JVP agitation in the south to produce a general social collapse, with yet more opportunities for outside intervention threatening India's security. The Indian Prime Minister's offer to mediate between Colombo and the guerrillas was accepted. Delhi insisted that only a political compromise, without the threat of force, could hope to reach a settlement.

Meanwhile the savageries continued, both between the warring forces and upon an increasing number of non-combatants; 2,000 were said to have died in 1986. The tiny military forces in the north were slowly being driven out. In May, the government's counterattack to re-establish control of Jaffna was repulsed. The guerrillas were increasingly coming to constitute the administration of the north, and encroaching on the eastern province where only a minority were Tamil; their aim appeared to be to terrorize the non-Tamils into fleeing, much as the Khalistani militants in the Punjab sought to drive out all non-Sikhs.

In May 1987, Colombo made one last effort to restore its position with land, sea and air offensives on the guerrilla strongholds of the Jaffna peninsula. The gossips said Jayawardene had reason to fear his overthrow unless he made a determined bid to achieve victory (and a coup might have been popular given the economic stagnation and the decline in social spending). Increased military activity was flatly contrary to Indian advice, and Delhi expressed outrage at what it saw as making a bad situation much worse.

As a gesture of reproof, the Indian government supported the despatch of a flotilla of relief supplies across the Palk Straits to Jaffna. However, a Sri Lankan naval force turned them back – to the fury of the Indian government and newspapers (some of which spoke darkly of the need for a 'Cyprus solution'). In reprisal, supplies were now dropped by air, supported by an aggressive display of India's Mirage fighters over Sri Lankan air space. The Paramount Power was not to be flouted.

However, irritations aside, Delhi could not afford to undermine Jayawardene. It was the best government they had. The Tamil rebellion was no immediate threat to India (indeed, it was a useful barb to prod the Sri Lankan government towards ends Delhi approved). But it could incite Sinhalese nationalism. The opportunities for chauvinist adventurers seemed limitless, and India was the natural target; for the Sinhalese militants, the Tamil rebellion was no more than the spearhead of Indian imperialism bent on expropriating the Sinhalese.

The Indian Prime Minister began shifting to the middle ground, to support for Jayawardene. In return, the Sri Lankan President made concessions to the Tigers. In June, the Jaffna offensive was halted, and in July the terms of an agreement with India were finalized. The east and the north districts were to be merged in a Tamil homeland, governed by autonomous district councils, modelled on the Indian federal constitution. However, within a year, a referendum was to be held in the east to determine whether a majority favoured the continuation of the merger with the north. The Sri Lankan army would evacuate the north and the guerrillas would give up their arms. The Indian army would control the Straits of Palk to interdict the movement of arms and guerrillas, close the Madras bases and training camps, and supervise the surrender of guerrilla arms and the maintenance of order in the north. In the fine print, Jayawardene's concession – and Delhi's wider purposes – were indicated: henceforth, India was to meet Sri Lanka's needs for military supplies and advice, Sri Lanka's Trincomalee naval base was not to be made available to any other power without Delhi's agreement, etc.

On the surface, it was an extraordinary deal. Jayawardene had at one stroke eliminated the Madras sanctuaries and supply points, sucked the Indian army into policing the north (at Delhi's expense) so that the Sri Lankan troops could be diverted to combating the JVP in an increasingly disordered south, and driven a wedge between India and the Tigers: if the guerrillas wished to fight, they would now have to fight the vastly superior military might of India. He had achieved this with only minor concessions, for the autonomous district councils had been offered before. The referendum qualification to the merger proposal robbed it of any value, for two-thirds of the population of the east was non-Tamil and expected to vote firmly against rule by the Tamils of the north.

However, Jayawardene's shrewdness vis-à-vis the north was out-weighed by its effects on chauvinism in the south. For a section of the UNP Cabinet (already anticipating the imminent retirement of the President and the selection of his successor), for the SLFP and for the JVP, the agreement had voluntarily surrendered to India a major part of Sri Lanka and permitted it to be held by Indian troops. Now the rebellion of the south increasingly superseded that of the north.

There were violent demonstrations of protest, organized by the SLFP and with much support from Buddhist monks. The JVP stepped up its campaign. The universities were closed. A curfew was introduced on 29 July. In two days of rioting, 40 people were said to have been shot dead. When Rajiv Gandhi arrived in Colombo to sign the agreement, palls of smoke hung over the city from the barely suppressed street fighting. A Sri Lankan sailor, part of the guard of honour, earned his place in the annals of Sinhalese nationalism by lunging at the Indian Prime Minister with his rifle butt.

The Tigers, understandably, felt themselves betrayed by India. Their chief leader, Vellupillai Prabhakaran, was held in Delhi, and initially refused to agree to the terms of the agreement. The Tigers had been politically outmanoeuvred by Colombo. Once the prestige of the Indian government had become attached to the peace accord, and of the Indian army to peacekeeping in the north, the guerrillas could win only if there was a radical change in Delhi or an Indian evacuation.

Indian troops moved swiftly into the north to be welcomed by the war-weary inhabitants with garlands. Meanwhile, 75,000 of the Sri Lankan military forces were deployed to the south. The guerrilla groups relinquished some arms, but few observers doubted that most of them were retained – despite successive Indian extensions of the time limit. There were savage clashes between different Tamil groups and continued efforts to terrorize the non-Tamils of the east into fleeing. By October, Indian troops were engaged in fierce battles with the guerrillas; they sought to take Jaffna and there was heavy destruction and loss of life. By the end of the year, there were some 50,000 Indian troops in the north and east. Nonetheless, the district council elections were held, and despite a Tiger boycott (with threats of death to all who participated) a reasonable poll brought to power non-Tiger former guerrillas.

However, attention was now increasingly focused on the south. Jayawardene's retirement was followed by presidential and Assembly elections. The JVP sought to undermine them by a campaign of systematic murder of government officers and candidates. Despite the slaughter, the elections were held and a UNP majority achieved (amid much accusation of poll rigging).

The new government swiftly set about trying to repair some of the damage. The Indians were induced to start moving out. The new UNP President Premadasa persuaded both the JVP and the Tamil Tigers to re-enter talks in a temporary respite.

The nightmare continues, however. Its most vivid symptom is the scattering of Sri Lankan Tamils round the world, a legion of new additions to the Stateless and homeless. Nor was it simply the condition of Tamils. For the savagery of warfare among the three minorities – Tamil, southern Sinhalese youth and the Colombo government – has raised the spectre that Sri Lanka, like Lebanon or, for a long period, Uganda, might become so demoralized and broken-backed that no social order would be capable of re-establishing normal conditions. Some estimated 30,000 had been killed, many of them by the increasingly brutalized armed forces.

The long-term effects of short-term political calculations of advantage in an unstable social and political context had been devastating. Playing the Sinhalese chauvinist card in the mid-1950s set off what became an apparently inexorable drift to civil war and foreign occupation. At each stage, efforts to accommodate both Tamil and Sinhalese educated youth were sacrificed by the Colombo government to securing an exclusive political base among the Sinhalese – without success, since all the concessions, including the astonishing recognition of the JVP by the government in 1987, came to nought and the JVP cadres continued their attempt physically to liquidate the official political leaders.

Yet there was room in the universities for both Tamils and Sinhalese if places were expanded. The country desperately needed all the talents it had, without alienating one group. There was room in the professions, trade and public employment if the economy expanded. But successive governments were more preoccupied with securing their own base among the Sinhalese rising groups at virtually any cost – or rather, in the political auction, preventing themselves being pushed out by their rivals. If the Tamils had not existed, Colombo would have had to invent them. And, in an important sense, it did. It was Colombo that forced the inhabitants of the north to become different, to cease to be Sri Lankan and become exclusively Tamil.

It was chauvinistic nonsense on both sides to pretend that there were ancient reasons for the divide. The illusion of collective self-identity of a minority of Sinhalese and Tamils was created very quickly – and, with some optimism, could by the same token be liquidated. Of course, the claims were often hypocritical; Sinhala might be solemnly recognized in the constitution as the official national language, but in practice English remained the language of the rich and powerful, the required speech of those who aspired to upward mobility, and as solid a barrier as ever to the participation of the majority of Sri Lankans, whatever their home tongue. But then that was not the real issue. In the foreground was the struggle of adventurers to corral an exclusive constituency as the basis for their own advance. In the background stood the hungry with nothing but the labels of their membership of a group to advance their right to be fed.

The Indians changed matters decisively. They had no interest in breaking up Sri Lanka as they had broken Pakistan. On the contrary, their strategic interest lay in shoring up the Colombo regime and tying it closely into their own foreign policy. Their intervention proved that the Tigers were not Indian Quislings. And it allowed the Sinhalese to see themselves as an oppressed minority in the wider picture of southern India, a minority whose right of national self-determination was threatened by Delhi. The Tigers had tried to use India as a means of winning, but, in the end, had been defeated. While they were immensely successful in holding the Sri Lankan forces at bay and beginning the process of pushing them out, no realistic assessment could see them as winning against the Indian forces. The politics of chauvinism blocked any possibility (outside the nightmares of Colombo) of the Tigers and the JVP allying, which was the one condition for either succeeding.

In the long history that lies behind the civil war in Sri Lanka, we can see multiple layers of oppression generating nationalist responses – the British on the Ceylonese, the Sinhalese ruling order on the Tamil (and both, for a time, on the luckless Indian Tamils), the established on the young outsiders. And this is to make no mention of the more complex caste, sub-class, locality and occupational issues within these blunt categories, let alone the underlying patterns of exploitation. Structures forced reactions of national liberation, mediated by the tactical decisions of the powerful. The minorities who ruled the country invariably chose to make their own power secure at the expense of a united Sri Lanka. And those who claimed to embody Sri Lankan nationalism, by their decisions, were inevitably driven to betray it to Indian intervention. If the gods had wished to destroy, the madness of Sri Lanka's rulers gave them every opportunity.

Part IV

CONTRADICTIONS

15

PERVERSE NATIONAL LIBERATION

WE now move to consider a quite different topic. Hitherto, the protagonists have been quite clear: a major dominant power and a people in rebellion against it and pursuing the creation of an independent State. But this part is concerned with two quite different issues. First, a case of national liberation – if defined as the creation of a new State – that imposes subordination on the inhabitants of a territory, not emancipation. Second, an account of some of the forces that today increasingly limit the role of both established nationalism and national liberation. Both are contradictions of the trends examined so far.

National liberation is not invariably an advance in popular power. We have seen this in the case of the origins of Pakistan where Jinnah was obliged to oppose democracy in British India. There is a class of movements which are the reverse of the struggle for majority rule, or rather, which gain greater democracy for some at the cost of destroying it for others. In many of these cases, the hideous oppression of one minority is translated into the hideous oppression of another. The clansmen, driven off the Scottish Highlands by an alliance of lairds and sheep herders,[1] proved, like so many of their fellow immigrants to North America, a pitiless hammer of the Red Indian clansmen. The Boers, heavily defeated by the British, proved no less cruel in their treatment of the inhabitants of southern Africa. The British convicts, transported in appalling conditions to Australia, had little compassion left for the aboriginal peoples. And the Zionists, spurred by the terrible pogroms of the Tsars (and later by the Holocaust) had no time for the rights of self-determination of

225

the inhabitants of Palestine. Brute oppression of minorities – in the name of the right of national self-determination of the majority – seems continually self-generated. Currently, in Yugoslavia, the Serb majority supposedly finds intolerable the autonomy of an impoverished Albanian minority in Kosovo; in Bulgaria, the government sought to force its Turkish minority to adopt Slavic names; and in Roumania, the State apparently sought the cultural destruction of its Hungarian minority, only, fortunately, to destroy itself.

The number and diversity of cases is vast, and each highly specific. Here we restrict attention to one only, Zionism and Israel, because of its fame but also because it offers both definition and contradiction of the case for national liberation.

Jewishness

Once significant numbers of Jews in Europe and North America relinquished a loyalty to Judaism – as they did with the increased opportunities for assimilation that came after the Enlightenment – the definition of a Jew became a problem. Adherents to Judaism continued to define Jewishness in terms of a religious faith, but in time that definition came to exclude the overwhelming majority of those who called themselves Jewish but were agnostic or atheist (let alone Catholic, Protestant, Hindu or Buddhist). For, in all respects except religion, Jews are identical to non-Jews in the countries where they live. Contrary to non-Jewish prejudice, there are no distinguishing physical attributes – colour of hair, skin, eyes etc. German Jews are indistinguishable from other Germans, as Chinese Jews are from other Chinese, Indian from other Indians, Ethiopian from other Ethiopians. There is no culture or language in common. Never has a group which claimed to be one people covered such heterogeneity. Only the myopia of non-Jewish Europeans and Americans allowed them to identify the thoroughly Polish culture of Polish Jewry as the authentic Jewishness, in order to suggest this as the cultural identity of all Jews.

In practice, the European non-Jews originally defined and subsequently redefined Jewishness by determining the conditions of life of those who were called Jews, by preventing or permitting assimilation and forcing or dissolving a separate communal existence. Of course, the non-Jews did not exist as a single force (that is the communalist myth), but as a complicated structure of classes within which Jews played an important, albeit involuntary, role in securing the power of some interests at the expense of others. As with all oppressed minorities, it is the social and political need of 'the majority' which demarcates the boundary and the internal nature of the minority and enforces membership. The needs of the gentiles – or at least some of them – would have obliged them to invent the Jews if they had not existed. Indeed, as we shall see later in the case of Japan, anti-semitism can exist without Jews (which is flatly contrary to the Nazi thesis that anti-semitism existed only because of the nature of Jews).

However, given the overwhelming role of the context, it would have been less than human if at least some of those persecuted as Jews had not come to feel they must possess something in common which explained the hideous character of their oppression. It is always a temptation, faced with persecution, to blame oneself; at least such blame gives one a vital role in the action, and preserves a sense even if mistaken that there is some order of justice in the world.

The greatest concentration of Jews in the modern period was in the two great empires, Tsarist and Austro-Hungarian, both of them, as we have seen, in the late nineteenth century wracked by a diversity of nationalist claims. Thus, one of the responses to anti-semitism by a few of those who called themselves Jewish came to be the assertion of a Jewish nationalism, arguing that Jews in fact shared a common culture, language (Yiddish), ancient social tradition, religion and biological descent.

The implausibility of these claims was less important than the anguish they represented in a market filled with the cacophony of new claims to an independent national existence. For, in fact, the cultures of different Jewish communities were no more than a variation of the local non-Jewish cultures – Polish, German, English, Italian, Greek etc. Yiddish was not the language of Jews outside a particular part of Eastern Europe (even if it was a *lingua franca* in much of Eastern Europe). The social traditions differed from the traditions of the non-Jews no more than the variations within the non-Jews of any particular country. Judaism was embraced by only a minority of the minority, and even then in a host of sects. However, the claims were no more absurd than those made on behalf of other minorities: all reacted to the nature of the denials of their national existence. The problem in the case of the Jews was that, unlike many other minorities, they had no historic territory as the basis for a State.

The claim of biological descent, the ultimate vindication of the existence of a people, is also the least demonstrable. It is possible that a majority of those who today call themselves Jewish are descended from ancestors who did not; and a majority of the descendants of those who in the past did call themselves Jewish do not now do so. It is as unclear for the Jews as for the non-Jews what validly constitutes 'the same people' through time, even though this is the basis for the claim to continuity, the claim that we are the same as our biological ancestors but different from the biological descendants of other ancestors.

The argument is academic. For, of course, Jews, like Slovenians, English, Chinese and so on, exist today, whether or not they have anything in common with a people in the past from whom they claim a descent. But, by all ordinary criteria, the European Jews are as European as the rest of the inhabitants of Europe, with no closer a relationship to the ancient inhabitants of Palestine (whose descendants may have been an important source of those today called Palestinian Arabs). The importance is the present miseries which make for such inventions, rather than the inventions themselves. It is the context of oppression which makes the claim to ancient and exotic lineage a comfort.

The successive transformations of the social roles of Jews are a fascinating dimension in the history of the empires of the Middle East, the Mediterranean and Europe.[2] In late-medieval Europe, the predominant Jewish role seems to have been defined in ways which corresponded to that of other trading minorities – for example, the Armenians in India, Copts in Egypt, Chinese in Indonesia. It might be said that these groups, unlike the Jews, had an original territorial home base. But the idea of a 'home base' is a modern conception. The overwhelming majority of the descendants of migrants retain no links with the land of their forebears, nor sense of loss.

Europe fashioned a different identity for many of the European Jews in the modern period. In Western Europe, assimilation was the norm, so that the Jewish communities which exist today are in the main relative newcomers to the countries where they live (migration has preserved the Jewish identity as a kind of overlay of foreignness). In Eastern Europe, the Jewish communities were very much larger, particularly in Poland, and had moved on or been driven out from the original complex of activities (trading, tax farming, rent collecting) to manufacturing and farming. Despite the obstacles, some of the Polish Jews had become assimilated, militants of, for example, the Polish national liberation movement in the 1860s. Most, however, were not permitted to be assimilated. The emergence of a non-Jewish Polish capitalism and its close collaboration with the Tsars led to increasing restrictions on the growth of Jewish capital and ultimately produced its ruin. Jewish workers sought survival in petty artisan activities, but were again pushed out. Thus, the largest Jewish community in Europe was economically ruined. At the same time, the Tsars were increasingly using discrimination against the Jews as a means to cement the loyalties of the non-Jews. This came to include physical attacks culminating in the terrible Tsarist pogroms. Economic and social persecution inflicted a deeply demoralizing crisis upon Polish Jewry. It is here, in this agonizing process of systematic oppression, that a new version of Jewish identity was fashioned and spread westwards with the streams of refugees, finally to the Americas (Jewish emigration from the Tsarist and Austro-Hungarian empires between 1880 and 1929 has been estimated at some 4 million; the Jewish population of the United States rose from a quarter of a million in 1880 to 1.5 million in 1914).

What began as a reaction to persecution by fellow-Poles or Russians ended as a desperate struggle to survive, to retain an identity as part of a stubborn resistance to liquidation. Now a history was required because Polish Jews were denied their rightful role as Poles in Polish history, Russian Jews in Russian history. Of course, virtually everyone is excluded from a 'role in history' – our ancestors were usually far too obscure to feature in the story of the great. National histories give a vicarious participation to the members of the nation. Not even this was permitted to the Jews, now forever defined as permanent foreigners in their native lands.

What is seen today as Jewish identity was fashioned in the period of rising Great Power nationalisms, of imperialism, forcing all those left outside the incorporation of peoples to invent their own nationalisms. The obverse of the pogrom was Russification, the attempt to impose a homogeneity on those inside the dominant nationality, the contrast with the heterogeneity of those outside. The Jews were not just scapegoats. They were much more fundamental – the anvil on which 'Russianness' was forged. It was this role in the fashioning of the modern State in Eastern Europe which distinguished the Jews from the descendants of all other trading minorities. It was a role in the European drama over which they had no control or influence, and which, paradoxically, affirmed more clearly than ever before their fundamental European character.

Anti-semitism

What was this special role? The enforcement of a national 'homogeneity'* turns upon the existence of a different and hostile homogeneity, 'the foreigner'. Generally, foreigners can be portrayed as agents of a foreign State, anxious to subvert or conquer the true nation (whose superiority is demonstrated by the desire of its neighbours to conquer it). The vital mirror to the nation's unity is the unity of the hostile foreigners, feverishly plotting the downfall of the nation.

However, more important than the obvious foreigner were those who appeared to be natives but secretly were not. Thus, in the hysterical fantasy of nationalism which accompanied the fashioning

---

*Henceforth, we shall omit the irritating inverted commas. They are there to indicate that the criteria of homogeneity are themselves part of the nationalist fiction, and not something independent of it.

of modern States and the increased Great Power rivalries of the late nineteenth century, that group of Poles, Russians and, later, Germans who called themselves Jewish were ideally placed for the role of the enemy within. This was nothing to do with snobberies about origins, low-level prejudice or discrimination. The pogrom is part of the high-level historical drama, an almost deliberate invention of a ruling order to vindicate its rule. The needs of the State determine the entire phenomenon, and the specific characteristics or behaviour of Jews, their culture or predilections, were as irrelevant to the role the State required them to play as were the characteristics or culture of the Vietnamese to the behaviour of the US armed forces in Vietnam. The innocence of the victims was irrelevant to their function. The ferocity embedded in the processes of social change and national competition, in the repression of classes and peoples, was now inflicted upon a single target (of course, there were other scapegoats – gypsies, homosexuals, other minorities, but they were not required to play this supreme role in the European drama).

The existence of discrimination in several European countries allowed the anti-semites to fit the pogrom into a general fiction of universal prejudice, so that then the supposed universality of the prejudice justified the pogrom. The '"idea" of the Jew replaced the analysis and perception of concrete situations'.[3] And universal anti-semitism supposedly implied that it was not caused by local factors but was the result of the intrinsic nature of the Jews themselves, their existence now and throughout the entirety of history. Thus, both time and place were merged to leave only two ahistorical concepts, Jew and non-Jew. The Jews, by the cruellest act of all, were made responsible for anti-semitism, and for the pogroms against them. It followed that relations between Jew and non-Jew must always and everywhere be a problem. An ideology was born which now dredged the past and the present for anecdotal demonstrations of the thesis, regardless of the preposterous character of the basic fantasy.

The ideology was not created, nor could it survive, in a social vacuum. It had to be connected to specific interests – for example, the desire of Polish capitalists to eliminate part of domestic competition or the hatred of Ukrainian peasants for tax and rent collectors. Thus anti-semitism, like nationalism, refracted a multiplicity of other conflicts: between peasant and landlord, peasant and urban trader and money lender. The complex role of Jewish inhabitants allowed anti-semitism to possess great flexibility in connecting diverse interests and concealing them in the righteous indignation of the true patriot.

The ideology gained depth and reputation from a subterranean tradition of political thought that seemed to link the ages in a common condition. It culminated in, for example, the book *The Protocols of the meetings of the Learned Elders of Zion*. The original French forgery was plagiarized by the Tsarist police in a Russian edition at the time of the pogroms, and became a basic component in the world view of the Nazis. The work is so absurd, it is difficult to know why it would need to be exposed. But each recurrence of political anti-semitism leads to its republication (witness its reissue in Britain in 1978 by 'British Patriot Publications'). It is said a gold-bound volume is available in Saudi Arabia where opposition to Israel is ill-distinguished from anti-semitism. At the level of the Protocols, mere prejudice is remote – the Jew has become a collective Satan, bent on the destruction of the world.

The 'Jewish Question' for Hitler explained the crisis of the Weimar Republic. Germany was crushed simultanously between two foreign enemies – the German Communist Party and trade unions, both controlled from Moscow, and foreign banks, working through Germany's debts, with bases in New York, London and Paris. Both forces, Hitler argued, were controlled by 'the Jews' in a single conspiracy. Within Germany, members of the same conspiracy controlled the banks, and thereby much of non-Jewish ('German') business and the State.

It was not just an account of economic problems. On the contrary, it was an alternative methodology of politics. Things of the spirit, not economics, were supreme, and culture was the product of the essence of a race, its means to protect and enhance its genius. The means to destroy a race was to force its members to interbreed with other races and subvert its culture and morale. It was here, Hitler argued, that the Jewish role was so evil. Jews had deliberately infiltrated the main organs of cultural life in order to destroy the German family, to demoralize it and so encourage miscegenation. The Jews refused to intermarry with non-Jews for they knew that this would destroy their racial superiority, but they used all methods to encourage non-Jews to marry outside their 'race' in order to destroy their racial character and so control them. Thus, in Hitler's words,[4]

> by breeding a generally inferior human mishmash, by way of a chaotic bastardization . . . [the German people] ultimately would no longer be able to do without the Jews as its only intellectual element . . . His [the Jew's] ultimate goal is the denationalization, the promiscuous bastardization of other peoples.

Hitler thus gave the mythic Jews a role which was breathtakingly ambitious. This was no question of prejudice, but the casting of anti-Christ in the great drama of the European State, in the struggle for domination. The Holocaust provided so terrifying an application of this secularized religion, it has left much of the world shell-shocked. For it is not just the numbers that are so shocking – after all, half those who died in concentration camps did not call themselves Jewish – but that so gross an injustice should be inflicted upon those who were entirely innocent: simply by the accident of birth.

Soviet history did not, for Jewish people, attain anything comparable to the horrors of the Holocaust, but official anti-semitism, portrayed as anti-Zionism and without the full conspiracy case, nonetheless played some role. As we have seen, the immediate post-revolutionary period saw a general flowering of Jewish culture – as with other minorities. With the ending of all legal restrictions on movement, there was greatly increased migration to the cities. Later, however, during the faction fight in the Party, it was noted that numerous Jews were prominent in the opposition. During the NEP, Jewish merchants flourished (of course, non-Jewish merchants flourished too and there were far more of them). With the decisive defeat of the opposition by the followers of Stalin, an active campaign against 'Jewish nationalism' was one of the elements in the general destruction of what were identified as local nationalisms. Then, reversing the consistent Bolshevik view of the question – that the Jews were not a nation – Stalin in 1928 decreed the establishment of an autonomous Jewish region in Birobidzhan, a particularly inhospitable area on the borders of Manchuria. It is said some 40,000 Jews were settled there during the 1930s.

From 1937, a campaign of enforced cultural assimilation was launched in the Soviet Union at large, and, as with the Muslims and Christians, this led to the gradual closure of the minorities' schools, courts, newspapers etc. Finally, Birobidzhan was purged; something of the order of a quarter of the population were said to have been arrested. The Second World War led to a reversal of this policy in the interests of 'national unity' (a clear difference from the Nazi order). But after the war it was resumed, and now the target was 'rootless cosmopolitans' (much closer to the Nazi formulation) and 'bourgeois nationalists'. In the great Slansky trial in Czechoslovakia at the end of 1951, 11 of the 14 Party leaders on trial were Jews. And in the 1953 'doctors' plot' in Moscow, 7 of the 9 accused were Jewish. The association of Israel with the United States allowed anti-semitism to be presented now as anti-Zionism and part of the Cold War. However, since the death of Stalin, political anti-semitism, with some fluctuations, has become marginal, retreating into an occasional – rather than a systematic – social prejudice.

Prejudice requires there to exist people who call themselves Jews. But the role of Satan does not – indeed, it may be easier to sustain the fantasy where there are no real Jews to contradict the myths. Political anti-semitism can flourish without any Jews. Journalists have noted the development of anti-semitism in Japan where it has no history. Masami Uno's *If you understand the Jews, you can understand the world: a 1990 scenario for the final economic war* is said to have sold 680,000 copies. It seeks to demonstrate that the United States is under Jewish control, and this fact explains the forcing up of the value of the Yen in the 1980s, unemployment in Japan, South Korea's undercutting of Japanese exports and numerous other issues. His *If you understand Judea, you can understand Japan* (selling, it is said, 181,000 copies) presented a well-rehearsed postwar Nazi argument that the Holocaust did not occur in Nazi Germany, but was invented by the 'Jewish' media so that Israel could extract reparations. Eisaburo Saito, a member of the Upper House of the Japanese Diet, has published *The Secret of Jewish Power to Control the World* (which includes the bizarre claim that Lenin, Guevara and Richard Wagner were Jews). Den Fujita, President of McDonalds of Japan, has produced *The Jewish Way of Blowing a Millionaire's Bugle*. These are only the more noteworthy titles of what are said to have been over 100 works on 'Jews' published in Japan in the mid-1980s.

The anti-semitic case still has a life of its own. But it is, as always, determined by the needs of those who invent and propagate it – in this last case, elements of the Japanese ultra-conservatives. It has no relationship at all to anything done by those who call themselves Jewish. However, what partially brings these two phenomena, the real people and a fantasy, into some alignment is a particular reaction and accommodation to anti-semitism by a minority of Jews: Zionism.

Zionism

In the context of the diverse national claims within the empires of Eastern and Central Europe before the First World War, it was understandable that some Jewish intellectuals would react to anti-semitism with an affirmation that the Jews also were a nation. They would then see the Jewish question as arising from the lack of a territory on which Jewish nationalism could be made effective. Such a case accepted the anti-semitic accusation that Jews were foreigners, and gave up any attempt to affirm that, wherever they were, they were as much natives as anyone else. The Zionist embraced the hostility of the anti-semites and turned it into a virtue, indeed, a vanity.

From this small beginning, a case was developed almost as a mirror image to anti-semitism (as all defensive national claims develop as mirror images of the oppressing force). The Jews were now identified as a different race which must preserve its purity against assimilation (let alone miscegenation). Thus, one of Hitler's main planks was incorporated in Zionist assumptions from the outset. For many Zionists, assimilation was treason to racial integrity. Nahum Goldmann, a one-time president of the World Zionist Organization, thought assimilation a graver danger than persecution (and this was *after* the Holocaust):[5]

> The danger represented to the survival of the Jewish people by the integration of Jewish communities into the peoples among whom they live is greater than that constituted by external threats, anti-Semitism or persecution.

The countercase was much more powerful. Jews had long lived without persecution in most societies for most of the time; furthermore, the majority had, wherever it was feasible, assimilated without difficulty. But, in the shock and horror of the pogroms, deep pessimism and even paranoia were understandable. As Laqueur puts the view in characteristic form:[6] 'nowhere in Europe were the Jews accepted as fully belonging to the community', the word 'fully' giving him complete power to interpret reality as he wished. Yet probably the majority of those who had considered themselves Jewish two centuries earlier had produced descendants who considered themselves German; it was not that they were 'accepted' for no one had any idea whose ancestors had called themselves what.

Zionism was nationalist, modern and secular (rabbis and religious Jews tended to oppose it). It included all the social and political currents of the Europe of its times. Some of its members were socialists, anti-imperialists and Marxists (a Zionist party applied to join the Third International). From its Russian source, it absorbed a Tolstoyan agrarian populism, and from the socialists, an emphasis on the primacy of labour, workers and peasants.

In conditions of severe persecution and the approaching break-up of empire and World War in Europe, the idea of a home for the Jews, a sanctuary, had an understandably powerful appeal. Yet all the great hopes were confronted by the problem that no empty territory existed, it seemed, upon which an independent Jewish State could be constructed. Theodor Herzl, the founder of Zionism, rightly identified the only real possibility of achieving a Jewish State as being through the territorial ambitions of one or other of the Great Powers. The heyday of European nationalism – including Zionism – was also the heyday of imperialism. In most European foreign offices, the disintegration of the Ottoman empire, the 'Sick Man of Europe', was expected through much of the nineteenth century. It was this prospect which came to inspire Zionist hopes of finding a home: in Palestine.

Herzl was a great admirer of the famous British imperialist of southern Africa, Cecil Rhodes. He wrote to him to invite his support for a project of colonization in the Middle East:[7]

> You are being invited to help make history ... This cannot frighten you ... it does not involve Africa but a piece of Asia Minor, not Englishmen but Jews ... I turn to you ... because it is something colonial.

He reasoned that a new Jewish State in the Middle East would 'form a portion of the rampart of Europe against Asia, an outpost of civilization as opposed to barbarism'.[8] At the first Zionist Congress in Basel in 1897, the organization committed itself to securing a Jewish homeland in the then Ottoman territories, in a land already inhabited by the Palestinians.

Herzl was tireless in his efforts to find a Great Power which, in pursuit of its imperial interests, would launch his new State for him. He tried to persuade Kaiser Wilhelm to support his efforts to establish German culture in Palestine. To Joseph Chamberlain, he urged the case for safeguarding the strategic interests of the British Empire and the route to India. To the Ottoman Sultan, he offered a new economy in Palestine which would replenish the treasury in Istanbul. And to Von Plehven, the Tsar's Minister of Police and director of the anti-semitic pogroms in Russian Poland, he urged that the advance of Zionism would weaken the attractions of revolution in Russia. For, as he put it with frankness, 'The governments of the countries where anti-semitism flourishes have the most interest in granting us this sovereignty.'[9]

By the end of the century, a few first steps had been taken; funds were collected for a Jewish colonial bank and a Jewish National Fund was created to purchase land for immigrant settlers. From the beginning, there were clashes between the newcomers and the existing inhabitants. In 1901, the local administration authorized the formation of a Jewish militia to protect the settlers. In 1911, the first Palestinian political party was created, with Muslim, Christian and Jewish members; one of its aims was to resist Zionist colonization.

However, all this could have been absorbed in time. The modest flow of Jewish immigrants could not have come to constitute a serious political force. The Zionists would have kept their dreams of a future State, much as black nationalists dreamt of a return to Africa, or Rastafarians of a mythic Judaea in Ethiopia. What changed the picture was the break-up of the Ottoman Empire under the impact of the First World War and the short-term needs of British imperialism.

Imperialism

Each major power had long prepared for the end of the Ottoman domains. The Russians continually extended their rule southwards, and vied with the Austro-Hungarians in the Balkan peninsula. The French advanced in north Africa, and tried to create a client State in Lebanon. In 1876, the British took control of the Suez Canal and consolidated their predominance in Egypt. The Germans planned a railway to Baghdad, and later became the ally of Turkey in the First World War. All three powers dabbled in Palestine. The competition was intensified by the discovery of oilfields in Persia. From the turn of the century, the British discreetly patronized Arab nationalism as a force to replace the Ottomans. By 1914, they aimed to create an Anglo-Arab front to resist what was becoming a Turkish–German axis. In this context, the idea of a stable European colony in Palestine had some attractions.

The conception of a Jewish enclave in Palestine was not at all new. It had been proposed by Lord Shaftesbury in 1839; by the British Consul in Beirut, in 1860; by Napoleon III's personal secretary, at the time of a French expedition to Syria; and in 1902 by Joseph Chamberlain. In 1844, a society had been created to pursue this aim, and the Rothschild family took it upon themselves to finance a slow trickle of migrants. But all this was very marginal.

It was the First World War which brought the unlikely ambition closer to realization. The British did take Palestine. British Jewish volunteers formed four battalions of the Royal Fusiliers, and fought there alongside the locally recruited Jewish League. In fomenting a generalized Arab revolt, London began to find the idea of a stable Palestinian colony an increasingly attractive short-term tactic, provided it could be achieved without cost.

This was the background to the extraordinary Balfour Declaration of November 1917. On the surface, this stated British government policy, but it was contained in a private letter to Lord Rothschild (a letter not made public until 1920 lest it incite other Great Powers to take counteraction, and the Palestinians to object):[10]

> His Majesty's Government views with favour the establishment in Palestine of a national home for the Jewish people, and will use their best endeavours to facilitate the achievement of this object, it being clearly understood that nothing shall be done which may prejudice the civil and religious rights of the existing non-Jewish communities in Palestine.

The statement was also extraordinary because it was conceded without an apparent *quid pro quo*. The British government apparently accepted as valid the preposterous claim that groups of British, Poles, Russians, Germans and so on had a right to territories in the Middle East that were already occupied. It was also supreme hypocrisy, for Balfour was long gone when the cheque was cashed, and no one was required to defend 'the civil and religious rights of the existing non-Jewish communities'. But then Balfour, in a confidential Foreign Office memorandum of 1919, made no bones about his indifference to at least one of these rights, that of being consulted:[11]

In Palestine, we do not even propose to consult the inhabitants of the country ... The four Great Powers have made commitments to Zionism, and Zionism (whether it is good or bad, right or wrong) has its roots in ancient tradition, in immediate needs and in hopes for the future that are much more important than the desires and prejudices of the 700,000 Arabs who presently inhabit Palestine.

The British were speculating. They gave away nothing of substance; little would be lost if nothing came of the idea. Certainly there was no reason to assume a benevolent motive, as, for example, does Walter Laqueur[12] –

It [the Balfour Declaration] was on the whole a self-less act, perhaps the last time that an individual succeeded almost single handedly in inducing the government of a major power to take a decision irrespective of national interest.

The Zionists, had they been of a religious persuasion, might have detected the hand of a divine providence in Balfour's decision. The opportunity now existed, with the protection of British arms, to create a buffer State, a counterbalance to Arab nationalism, 'a little loyal Jewish Ulster in a sea of potentially hostile Arabism' as a later observer called it.[13]

However, unknown to most of the participants, the sunset of European imperialism was already approaching. The fostering of a Jewish State was one of the last acts of colonialism. There were plenty of precedents at the time for Europeans to drive out the native inhabitants – in the Americas, Australia, South Africa, the Rhodesias, Kenya etc. But they were in the past, in a ruder age. Nonetheless, in the interwar period, the Great Powers continued to behave no less arbitrarily in refashioning the political landscape to suit their interests – the British carved out Iraq from the Mesopotamian provinces of the Ottoman Empire and installed Feisal as King (later creating an Emirate of Transjordan for his brother). It was taken for granted that Great

Powers had a right – if not a manifest destiny – to seize the lands of inferior peoples and use them as they saw fit.

The colonization of Palestine, however, wandered into a different epoch that, even in the 1930s, augured the end of empire, indeed, turned empire increasingly into an outrage. Laqueur is insensitive to the changing moment, and gives a weak vindication in terms of the Zionist colonization: 'Zionists are guilty of having behaved like other people, only with some delay due to historical circumstances.'[14] Of course, most people did *not* expropriate the land of others, but it is characteristic that Laqueur's focus is the behaviour of the imperialist powers (disguised as 'other people').

The Zionists were less ruthless than the British up to the Second World War, for they lacked the power to be so. When they were most ruthless, they had arrived in anti-imperialist times that transformed their behaviour into something shocking, as in Golda Meier's careless observation:[15]

> It wasn't as if there had been in Palestine a Palestinian people that felt itself such, and that we drove out to take its place. They didn't exist.

Even Balfour admitted to 700,000 in 1920, alongside 56,000 Jews.

The State of Israel

No States have been born of an immaculate conception; by now, the conditions of Israel's birth are not necessarily relevant to its current status. Zionism, in creating a State through whatever injustices, created itself as a nationalism. But its method of self-invention is a peculiar one in being so interwoven with the operation of the interests of the Great Powers – first the British, and latterly the Americans. Despite the Balfour Declaration, there was far to go before Israel could be created. At numerous points in the early years, the trajectory could have been changed. At the beginning, with so few Zionists (far fewer than the number of Palestinian Jews), they needed great powers of circumspection to survive.

Arab nationalism flourished throughout the interwar years. There were continual movements of opposition to Zionist encroachment, and riots in 1920, 1921, a general strike in 1925 (to greet Balfour's visit to Palestine), 1929, 1933 and, most massively, 1936 (when, it is said, 2,000 were killed). British commissions of inquiry duly reported that a main issue in each collision was Palestinian opposition to the creation of a national home for Jews. What was elsewhere in the

Middle East directed against British or French power, in Palestine was deflected into intercommunal strife, which in turn drove the mass of non-Zionist Jews, in self-defence, into support for the Zionists. For Zionism, British military power was in this period decisive; without it, Zionism would have been extinguished and this would have made possible a common movement of Palestinian nationalism combining Arabs, Jews and Christians.

Outside events also shaped the definition of the Zionist community. Initially, the early settlers embraced a form of colonialism found in east and southern Africa: Jewish landowners depended upon cheap Arab labour. But the arrival of a flood of penniless immigrants, the children of ruined Polish shopkeepers and artisans, created a new labour supply. Arab workers, it was said, worked harder, however, and for less. A strategic decision was required (with an internal struggle to define a populist rather than a landowning Zionism) on whether class or nationality should prevail. A Zionist 'labourism' emerged to subsidize Jewish employers to employ Jews, to 'produce Jewish' and to 'buy Jewish', boycotting Arab labour and products. Sometimes, the campaign involved the physical destruction of the produce of Arab workers. A Labour member of the Knesset recalled in 1968 the embarrassment this caused:[16]

> It was not easy in the 1930s to explain to our comrades in the British Labour Party why we had to pour petrol over the tomatoes of Arab women.

The Histadruth (General Confederation of Jewish Workers in Palestine), created in 1920, was the trade union instrument to enforce a segregation to protect European labour from competition with Arab workers. Later, after the formation of Israel, the arrival of 'Oriental' Jews provided a further domestic supply of cheap labour. After 1967, an increasing number of Arabs came to be included within the Israeli economy.

The Zionist project was fragile; few had any clear idea of a future State. The Holocaust changed this; now the need for a sanctuary became extreme. It seemed also that the Zionist thesis of the implacable hostility of the non-Jews was overwhelmingly vindicated.

With the onset of the Second World War, the alarms of the British grew. In the First World War, they had exploited Arab nationalism against the German–Turkish axis. In the Second, Palestine became an issue pushing Arab nationalists in the opposite direction. In 1939, the British promised the independence of Palestine within ten years, with some form of democratic representation. Hitherto, the Zionists – like the Muslim League in British India – had opposed any moves to majority voting lest this lead to the Zionist minority being outvoted. Talk of independence now made the problem of numbers crucial. All efforts had to be bent to increasing Jewish immigration. Yet, at just the time when the need for a sanctuary for Europe's Jews was greatest, the British, to woo Arab support, limited immigration to 75,000 a year.

There was another grave problem. European Jews showed reluctance to migrate to Palestine. Between 1935 and 1943, Jewish emigration from Germany was some 2.6 million but, of these, only 9 per cent chose to settle in Palestine. The opportunities for assimilation in the Americas raced far ahead of the Zionist promise. Indeed, Palestine was hardly credible as a sanctuary when German arms reached Greece and the borders of Egypt. The Zionists tried to persuade the Allies to oblige homeless Jews to go to Palestine. Ben Gurion, for example, opposed a scheme to admit German Jewish children to Britain:[17]

> If I know that it would be possible to save all the children in Germany by bringing them over to England, and only half of them to Eretz Yisrael, then I would opt for the second alternative. For we must weigh not only the life of these children but also the history of the people of Israel.

The political conjuncture in Palestine had, on a far smaller scale, further echoes of British India. In both, the ambitious minority, conjured by the needs of empire, finally precipitated a British evacuation before any real settlement had been achieved. However, the Pakistanis did not aspire to seize the whole of India, and the terrible agony of the exchange of populations left no permanent residue of an expropriated majority. Palestine, on the other hand, assumed an insoluble form, a permanent injustice to reproach the world.

The new United Nations intervened to seek a settlement to end the civil war. The 1947 partition plan divided Palestine into a State with 55 per cent of the territory and a narrow Jewish majority (but containing 400,000 Arabs) and one containing 725,000 Arabs and 10,000 Jews. The Zionists had only a few cards to play if they were to create their homeland, and they played them with outstanding brutality and vigour. 800,000 Palestinians were terrorized into flight – 'a miraculous simplification of the tasks of Israel', as Chaim Weizmann put it. The land was confiscated, the villages razed, to underline that this was a permanent settlement and the Arabs were not to be allowed to return to their homelands. The cruel irony of this change of roles was not lost upon the more thoughtful Jewish intellectuals. I. Smilansky (S. Yizhar) wrote a story, *Khirbet khiz'eh*, to describe the feelings of a

Jewish soldier creating a homeless people so that the Jews might find a home.[18]

The British had calculated that the intervention of the armies of the Arab League (themselves guided by British military officers) would prevent this outcome. But Israel and Abdallah of Jordan outwitted them by partitioning the proposed Arab State. In any case, the League's armies were in no position to take on the larger Israeli military and paramilitary forces. Furthermore, the League was not fighting for its very existence. By early 1949, Israel held four-fifths of Palestine, and at long last a homeland had been achieved. However, the forced diaspora of the majority of Palestine's inhabitants established a permanent threat to the security of the new State. It took two more wars for Israel to recreate the old Palestine and at a cost of permanent militarization, a Cold War with its Arab neighbours, and ultimately the destruction of its northern neighbour, Lebanon. By the Six-Day War of 1967, Israel acquired the West Bank on the River Jordon and the Gaza Strip, bringing the total of Arabs now inside Israeli territorial control to one million.

The homeland still required the continued support of the Great Powers – in the postwar world, the United States. But the transfer of colonial patronage was not instantaneous; Israel had to earn its position. The US National Security Commission in a 1958 memorandum noted that the corollary of opposition to Nasser and Arab nationalism 'would be to support Israel as the only strong pro-west power left in the Middle East'.[19] The 1967 Six-Day War convinced Washington of Israel's capacity to humiliate Arab nationalism; 'Israel', a State Department memorandum concluded, 'has probably done more for the United States in the Middle East in relation to money and efforts invested than any of our so-called allies and friends elsewhere.'[20]

However, not until the Arab oil boycott of the 1970s did this become almost a principle of American foreign policy. Early on President Reagan formulated the view of the US government:[21]

> Israel is 'combat ready' and has a combat-experienced military ... a force in the Middle East that is actually of benefit to us. If there was no Israel with that force, we'd have to supply that with our own men.

Israel's usefulness to the United States was not restricted to the Middle East. It came to be an important exporter of arms, a support to regimes which were thought to be too unsavoury for the direct association of Washington, but nonetheless vital to American interests (for example, South Africa, Chile, Taiwan, Somoza's Nicaragua and, most notoriously, Iran). In turn, the US made Israel the recipient of the largest share of its aid – an estimated 48 per cent of US military and 35 per cent of civil aid between 1978 and 1982.[22]

Without this financial support, it is difficult to see how Israel could have survived in its present form. It would have been obliged to reach some accommodation with the Arabs. The process of change has not ceased, however, for now that Israel contains a major Arab population – and one engaged in almost continuous rebellion, the Intifada – the issues of 1948 have returned. But to a quite different people; today, the Jews of Israel are a territorial nationality with little cultural or social relationship to the wider diaspora. Ironically, the idea of a Jewish homeland proved to be a mechanism not to preserve old Jewry but to assimilate Israelis – this time, into an ordinary State, subject to all the competitive pressures of other States. Those Akiva Orr calls 'Hebrew-speaking Gentiles', secure in their national identity, have almost nothing in common with their forefathers or with those who claim to be Jews in other countries.[23]

On the other hand, the mythic significance of Israel for the wider diaspora has grown. The Six-Day War seemed to alert important sections of the non-Israeli Jews to the possibility of a new devastating destruction inflicted upon the Jews of Israel. Even some Jews for whom Israel had been a matter of indifference discovered a symbol of hopes and fears, a secular devotion that somehow replaced the absent Judaism. While very few were sufficiently moved to emigrate to Israel, the country became a focus for a dying identity. Thus, perversely, the Zionist promise of Israel as a means to prevent, or at least delay, assimilation did have some success, but only for Jews who did not become Israelis.

The oppression that created Zionism was in Europe, not Palestine. But it was in Palestine that the Zionists sought their revenge, and upon Palestinians, a scapegoat that, like all scapegoats, was innocent, unconnected to those that inflicted damage upon the Jews. Of course, the Zionists intended no such revenge; the Palestinians were only an obstruction to the realization of homeland. But then, political anti-semitism was also not about the particular people who called themselves Jews; it was about fashioning a majority of non-Jews.

In the end the Zionists failed in their main project, for the majority of Jews found their real homeland outside Palestine; there are twice as many Jews in the United States as Israel, and more – at least for the moment – in the Soviet Union. History cheated the Zionists. They thought, by energy, ruthlessness and drive, to create the promised land in Palestine and so recreate a Jewish people, but they created only a small military State, already dominated by a minority of the orthodox in religion. They entered, not emancipation, but the tyranny of a system of competitive States. For the Israelis, founded upon a continuing injustice, survival is an unremitting struggle. Paradoxically only for some of the Jews at large is the original Zionist vision green, but then, only because it is far away.

16

NATIONAL LIBERATION AND A WORLD ECONOMY: ECONOMIC NATIONALISM

*B*EFORE 1914, Marxists were protected from the full force of the nationalist case by the way in which they identified the 'national' as primarily a matter of the cultural–linguistic concerns of a group. On the other hand, the world of work and production – the economy – was 'international', and characterized by an inexorable drive towards the creation of an integrated world economy. The political, the State, must inevitably follow the evolution of the economy. In the first instance, this was towards the partial and distorted internationalism of empire (dominated by modern capitalism, as opposed to the archaic empires of Romanov and Habsburg). It was the second drive which created and sustained the international 'horizontal' divisions of class, a world bourgeoisie and a world working class, as opposed to the territorially restricted remnants of pre-capitalist society, the 'vertical' orders of community and nationality.

The diagnosis contained the assumption that the national issue had come to an end in the more advanced areas of capitalism, in Western and Central Europe and North America. There, economic integration had created a polity and a class structure which made redundant any aspiration to national separation. Outside Europe and North America, in the 'colonial and backward countries', economic underdevelopment ensured that the national question was still paramount. The old empires of the Russias and Austro-Hungary were a kind of transitional zone between the advanced and the backward, for here some elementary economic development had already integrated the territories of many nationalities even though separate national cultures still survived. It was therefore possible, in the transition to a bourgeois or socialist society, to aspire to keep what were seen as the great economic merits of large multinational territories. The condition for this was a satisfactory accommodation – short of separation – of the nationalism of the backward nations within the empires.

In the global empires of Britain, France, Holland, Belgium and the rest, multinational economies would disintegrate on the rocks of nationalism. Here, the right of national self-determination also included implicitly a right of economic self-determination. Of course, cynics might argue that this different approach was merely a Bolshevik trick to justify simultaneously retaining intact the empire of the Russias while seeking the destruction of the empires of the anti-Bolsheviks. This would have been an unfair comment since the Bolshevik position was formulated long before the exigencies of directing State power came to discipline the party with the *Realpolitik* of international relations.

Before 1914, the debates on the national question in the Second International also took place in isolation from the necessities of running States. Perhaps this is why so few recognized the reality that had emerged in the advanced countries in the preceding forty years: the material basis of the world economy was national (or imperial) not international. The illusion of international integration was fostered by the existence of a small number of national–imperial centres, particularly one, the British. Today, however, the world economy is characterized by a multiplicity of national centres and multinational markets. The illusion of inexorable internationalization was one the Marxists shared with – perhaps even acquired from – the 'cosmopolitan bourgeoisie' of the early Victorian years.[1]

The Marxists had in common the assumption of an integrating international economy. Thereafter they divided. The Luxemburgists argued that, so far as the working classes were concerned, internationalization had already eliminated the national question in Europe, East and West; only reactionaries, trying to prevent the workers seizing power by raising divisive national issues, would now demand the right of national self-determination. At the opposite extreme, the followers of Otto Bauer saw the national as an eternal social formation, but nonetheless one which could be accommodated politically without jeopardizing the international economy: by conceding 'personal cultural autonomy' (in education, language and culture, regardless of the territorial distribution of the members of the nationality, a distribution which would inevitably be determined by the needs of the international economy). Lenin accepted the importance of the national issue, but argued that in conditions of democracy and the complete equality of nations, the material benefits of belonging to a large country would ensure that peoples would freely choose economic integration in a centralized State (although, as we have seen, he later conceded both the principle of federation and elements of cultural autonomy for national groups).

In retrospect, this distinction between culture and economics can be seen as mistaken. Even before the First World War, the movements of national liberation were not simply reactions to cultural or linguistic oppression (although these might be important symptoms of a general condition), nor to a denial of political rights. They were just as likely to be movements to reject economic exploitation and domination. The centralization of activity implicit in the idea of economic integration was also a subordination of peoples to market forces that derived from sources outside the national boundaries, and that could provide a basis no less valid for national liberation. Indeed, underlying the power of Lenin's famous work on imperialism is a conception of the fusion of political subordination and economic exploitation in the colonies which implicitly accepted that nationalism was also about economic issues.

After the Second World War, national liberation became explicitly and emphatically a struggle for national *economic* independence – a movement to halt, reverse or eliminate economic integration. The right to political self-determination now needed to be also an assertion of economic self-determination. The Marxists would have regarded this extension of the case as entirely utopian – as well as reactionary.

The almost invariable inclusion of radical economic nationalism in the programme of national liberation makes the post-1945 period the most nationalist of all. It followed a period of the most ferocious European nationalism, culminating in the World War itself, representing for E.H. Carr the 'bankruptcy of internationalism'.[2] For both more and less developed countries, the political order was no longer seen as subordinate to economic forces: on the contrary, the political seemed to determine the economic, to fashion a national economic order regardless of external markets.

At this point, the argument moves from the realm of national liberation as ordinarily understood – a political movement for the creation or conquest of State power – to the nationalism of established States (the transition we have already examined in the case of Russia). The conditions here are quite different – as the national liberators swiftly discovered on coming to power.

The disciplines of a world order

The 'discipline' of a movement for national liberation is imposed by the nature and behaviour of a single enemy, the established State or empire against which the national liberators struggle. The target is relatively simple and identifiable, sometimes as a dictator, a family or a racially or culturally distinct group. But a new State faces a very different and much more complicated set of imperatives, a multiplicity of competing States. Furthermore, States are so unequal in terms of their power, it seems even perverse to call them all equally 'States' (some of them are far smaller than medium-sized companies or cities in the larger countries).

The world order of competing States sets the terms of competition, not the new State itself. The terms include a certain level of military preparedness and of the civil basis for such a defence effort (which might include, in some circumstances, measures of agricultural and industrial self-sufficiency). Of course, the majority of States cannot realistically defend themselves against the most powerful among them, but they are not usually required to do so, only to defend their national independence against local rivals, to deter potential and actual attack, and to promote national interests abroad. The price of failure in this endeavour can be the loss of national independence (the country is expropriated or controlled by another) or the liquidation of the national order by competing neighbours or domestic revolution (as, for example, has occurred in Lebanon).

The defence of national independence requires the domestic production of as much as possible of what is needed to survive, reducing 'dependence' upon the rest of the world. According to the country's access to resources, this ambition implies industrialization and economic development, both to create an independent means of supply and, what has become a twentieth-century aim, to foster the social conditions for popular support. However, the pursuit of this development imposes a new and extraordinary set of disciplines on top of those laid down by a competitive world order. Industrialization promotes an unprecedented centralization. Thus, paradoxically, the disciplines of a world order can enforce domestic conditions that, disregarding the final results, might seem far more onerous than those sustained by the old order, before national liberation. National emancipation thereby becomes the means to compete more effectively, to de-emancipate.

The issues are powerfully affected by the changing context. Not only does this influence the terms of competition, the standards of technology and the productivity of labour. It is also important in determining the potential for, and the limits to, domestic growth. In this respect, the years after the Second World War were in striking contrast to those in the interwar period. The possibilities of growth up to the 1970s were very much greater. The national revolutionaries in this period were the unwitting beneficiaries of this generalized growth, while they claimed that these economic successes were the result of their defeat of imperialism and the establishment of political independence. Thus did the world of politics claim its ascendance over the world market.

Economic nationalism

The countries that emerged from the European empires (including the much earlier cases in Latin America) almost universally embraced a particular form of economic nationalism. In policy terms, this consisted of sustained government efforts to promote investment in industry either as part of the public sector or in the hands of national companies (rather than foreign). These efforts were supported by controls on imports (to create a monopoly market for domestic producers), on capital (to cheapen the supply and discriminate in favour of priority sectors and national companies) and on finance (to control exchange rates to cheapen priority imports and to control interest rates to cheapen capital, often with the nationalization of commercial banks). There were many other local priorities – to force foreign companies to divest majority shareholdings (or to nationalize them) and reduce or eliminate expatriate staff, to buy local inputs, to prevent foreign-registered companies repatriating local profits and oblige them to divulge their technical secrets; to eliminate foreign companies in the exploitation of natural resources (particularly in mining and oil extraction); to appropriate offshore fishing and prospecting rights by extending territorial waters; to expel or control minorities, usually important in the business classes (as with Indians in Burma, Uganda, etc.; Chinese in Indonesia, the Philippines and Malaysia); to secure agricultural self-sufficiency ('When you lose control of grains, you lose your independence,' as Egypt's Minister of Agriculture and Food Security put it in 1983);[3] to secure as swiftly as possible self-sufficiency in steel production and, where realistic, heavy industry generally. All assumed that it was feasible to create an independent national economy and that the distinction between foreigner and native was clear and important.

The case was not new (although it was more extreme than ever before). There were experiments with such tactics in the eighteenth and nineteenth centuries as means to accelerate economic development (and the expansion of military power). Thus, just after the creation of the United States, Alexander Hamilton identified industrialization and controlled trade as the means to counter the economic domination of Britain. Friedrich List in the first half of the nineteenth century advanced a programme to accelerate German economic development by closing the national borders to imports, with the State undertaking such external trade as might be required. Both programmes were to counter British domination, expressed through London's self-interested advocacy of free trade, the means to perpetuate British superiority in manufactured exports. Bismarck, the architect of imperial Germany, introduced a very diluted form of List's scheme in the 1870s. Hamilton and List, however, saw nationalist policies as temporary tactics, and the level of Bismarck's tariffs were slight in comparison with what came later. Indeed, Hamilton did not favour discrimination against foreign capital, arguing:[4]

> Rather than treating the foreign investor as a rival, we should consider him a valuable helper for he increases our production and the efficiency of our businesses.

These earlier examples had no influence after the Second World War. Then the more important inspirations were the claims of Soviet planning in the 1930s and the policies of the Western powers in the Great Depression and the war. For in Europe and North America, State intervention reached an unprecedented level, and established an almost universal form of State capitalism. Even those, like Keynes, who had been devoted – and were later to return – to economic liberalism, perpetuated the pessimism that flowed from the breakdown of the world economy in the 1930s and embraced the same ideology in which the State was to supersede the market. For example, in 1943, Keynes echoed List's proposal on external trade:[5]

> I am a hopeless sceptic about a return to nineteenth century laissez-faire ... I believe the future lies with: (1) State trading for commodities; (2) international cartels for necessary manufactures; (3) quantitative import restrictions for non-essential manufactures.

The economic nationalist programme was no longer – as it had been for Hamilton and List – a temporary tactic to accelerate the economic development of a backward power. It had become the universal norm. The national and the political took priority over the economic, the operation of markets and open competition.

For many observers, the State domination of the economy represented a great step forward in the control of capitalism. It might not be the conquest of the ruling order by the proletariat nor an international movement against all States, but it seemed that, under representative government, the ballot box could tame capital. It was this junction point between anti-capitalism and nationalism which provided a means whereby socialists could come to accept an established order of competing States and the priority of defending their own State. In the years after 1931, the intellectuals of the industrialized countries remained enamoured with this form of economic nationalism in which State power was identified, for at least some of them, as socialism. No less so in the developing countries, the intellectuals remained in thrall to an ideology which was presented as a set of general truths although it was only a by-product of a weak position in the interwar slump and the protectionism of the more advanced which forced the less advanced also into protectionism.[6]

However, in the former colonial empires, the nationalist indictment of capitalism seemed more securely based. It was agreed across a broad range of opinion that native capital could not repeat the process of economic development that had occurred in Europe. On the Left, Fanon, an influential writer of the 1960s, argued that the allies of colonialism were the landed classes whose interest it was to prevent the growth of capitalism; the capitalists were 'compradors', no more than brokers between foreign interests and the domestic market. Furthermore, they retained close links to the landed interest. Thus, native capitalists would neither transform society nor even fight imperialism.[7] Moreover, all were agreed that foreign capital could not develop a country; its interest was only in draining resources out of it, whether as raw materials or as profits, in servicing its home production base, and not in expanding the local economy. Finally, the Great Depression seemed to offer unequivocal evidence that development could not come through exports, through using the world capitalist market; the terms of trade were permanently fixed to discriminate against the exports of the less developed, and the governments of the more developed would sooner or later ban those imports. In sum, economic autonomy – even autarky – under the direction of the State was the sole means available to develop economically.

The reality

The reality was different. As the world entered a phase of extraordinary growth from the late 1940s on, the dominant powers were obliged, if they were to share in this growth, to unwind much of the structure of economic nationalism and to free capital. Commodities, capital and finance were progressively decontrolled.[8] What began hesitantly in

Europe in the immediate postwar years, spurred by the efforts of the United States to secure outlets for its exports and capital as well as allies in the rivalry with the Soviet Union, spread from the Atlantic economy to the Pacific, and from there in the 1970s to a larger and larger part of the developing world. Those economies that grew most swiftly in the postwar period were, it seemed, more often those capable of exploiting a world market, not of concentrating on a domestic economy. In the early 1970s, a crisis in the international monetary system led to the floating of all major currencies, an outcome remote from the assumptions of the Bretton Woods order: a new world economy had been created. World markets, privatization, a hostility to governmental intervention became an ideology as all-embracing as economic nationalism had been earlier.

Freeing national economies meant integration: the emergence of production systems which spanned many countries, so that exports and imports became flows linking geographically separate points in a single manufacturing process. Many factors combined to produce this result, including the search for low labour costs in conditions of great labour scarcity in the developed countries, the elimination of trade barriers, radical changes in the conditions of production in developing countries (in the quality of the labour force and of infrastructure), innovations in transport and the costs of movement, etc.

However, government ideology did not change as quickly as the system. Economic nationalism did not disappear; there were fights every inch of the way, against what seemed to be a loss of national sovereignty in the economic field. Liberalization was the result of attempts to solve particular problems, not of a general intellectual conviction, let alone a coherent strategy.

With the return of slump and stagnation, protectionism became more general. Nevertheless, unlike the 1930s, the structure remained open – with some exceptions (agriculture, textiles and garments). That degree of openness seemed to be the precondition for any growth. Furthermore, the advanced economies had become, in significant respects, dependent upon imports to sustain their output, so that generalized import controls were now self-destructive.

The areas of ambiguity remained. Were the subsidiaries of Japanese-registered companies in the United States Japanese or American when they operated in Europe? Should 'British' helicopters, electrical equipment or chocolate be owned by foreigners? Did it make any difference to anything of substance who owned such things? Did commodities or capital or companies have any nationality? A single commodity might now be manufactured in part in many countries; capital was bleached of nationality when it swam in the global tides; and the ownership structure of large companies made it generally impossible to say with ease to which State they should be loyal. The fictions persisted to cause unease, anxiety, panic, but reality continued to undermine them.

For developing countries, the changes were also dramatic. By the late 1970s, nationalist defences were being partially dismantled almost everywhere because, it seemed, they did not defend national economies, but they did jeopardize the capacity to grow. And for those countries, as in Latin America, rich enough to resist the new fashions, debt in the 1980s broke their opposition. They too were obliged to internationalize.

With sustained growth in the world economy and liberalization, new national centres of capital grew swiftly, and, as a result, the world distribution of manufacturing capacity changed. In 1950, US companies produced 76 per cent of world output (excluding the Eastern bloc), and in 1979, 28 per cent (a share which included the growing importation of inputs into manufacturing). As late as 1957, North America and Europe produced 97 per cent of world manufacturing output (again, excluding the Eastern bloc); by 1979, this was down to 65 per cent. Even in the period of slow growth and recession, the change continued. The old established manufacturing powers, of Europe and North America produced 64 per cent of the value added in world manufacturing in 1970, and 54 per cent in 1985.

It was an extraordinary shift, and while those who captured an increasing share of output were a quite small group of newcomers (of which Japan was the most important), the change demonstrated that the distribution of manufacturing was not an immovable phenomenon: the rich, or those supposed to be so, were not ever richer, and the poor poorer. The assymetry in the effects of world growth that so many development economists had detected in the 1950s was an illusion (or at least required radical revision to accommodate both the Newly Industrializing Countries and Sub-Saharan Africa). Furthermore, exports – and exports of manufactured goods – rather than autarky were the recipe to participate in this transformation.

Nor, contrary to the pre-1914 Marxist perception, was growth a function of the size of a country. New patterns of specialization made room for fast processes of economic growth for very small economies, including the two remarkable city-States, Singapore and Hong Kong. Indeed, in these two cases, growth proceeded without any control of imports, the local currency or the foreign ownership and management of capital.

Thus, the emergence of a single global economy undermined the assumed relationship between the old programme of economic nationalism and national liberation. Insofar as national liberation had promised material improvements for the mass of the population to be achieved through a reduction in external links, it seemed no longer possible to achieve such commitments. Political and economic aims diverged; economic integration appeared to have resumed the inexorable forward march that the Marxists had identified before 1914. But now it was not an integration trapped within empires, but an integration organized by impersonal and non-national markets.

There is, of course, still far to go. There will be many reverses. States are involved to different degrees, at different times and speeds; the Eastern bloc entered the process only late in the day, and it is not clear that the domestic institutional structure of, say, the Soviet Union, will allow it to participate fully in the world marketplace. On the other hand, the emerging structure of the world economy seems already to be beyond the point of no return. Europe, North America and Japan constitute an integrated and integrating block of such economic power, it is almost impossible for the rest of the world to resist the process of interlocking. The governments of the advanced bloc can themselves only resist the process at the expense of their own economic power and prosperity.

In sum, the processes of internationalization in the world economy seem now to be set so firmly, it is hardly conceivable that they could be reversed. Neither protectionism, nor Europe's integration in 1992, nor a free trade area encompassing the United States, Canada and Mexico, nor an East and South-East Asian economic federation including Japan, seem capable of supplying the means for national or regional economic isolationism.

Thus, if politics were no more than a reflex of economics – as some of the cruder Marxists seemed to imply – the world ought to be within sight of the end of nationalism as a political force. On such a reading, it might survive as a cultural–linguistic concern, but the economic and political issue would be over for all except the economically least developed. Such an eventuality would once more restore the pre-1914 theorizations.

Labour

However, there was one area where the liberalization of the world economy received little attention. Here no successive rounds of tariff negotiations sought to secure increasingly free movement, no IMF or World Bank offered loans to support structural adjustment. In the field of labour, there was a stark contrast to the treatment of the other elements of the world economy. Workers were not commodities, capital or finance, for they had minds, and their minds were basic factors in supporting national State power, a key element in popular nationalism. Was it here that one might find the main source of resistance to internationalization, the last defenders of national power?

During the earlier phase of sustained growth, in the forty years before 1914, there had also been a powerful element of internationalization. Then, there had also been large-scale migration of labour in response to a changing geography of demand. But it was also in that period that, in the advanced countries of north-western Europe, the incorporation of the mass of the population in the 'nation' occurred. Till then, the aristocracy and later the propertied classes had constituted the nation. The incorporation of the working class implied that its interests − security of employment, improved incomes and public welfare, health and educational services − should be issues of national concern. Furthermore, the importance of employment was now seen not so much in terms of the material hardship which its absence inflicted upon people, but rather the injustice of this punishment for those who had laboured so long and loyally for the nation. In this context, control of immigration, it was deduced, was the method to protect jobs by reducing competition for work, a permanent aim of trade union organization. This would create a national closed shop: native jobs for native workers. Thus, there was a paradox; while trade, finance and capital were increasingly liberalized, the first steps were being taken to restrict the movement of labour.

Political leaders were swift to champion the cause, to solicit workers' support for controls on imports (to protect domestic business) in return for controls on immigration. Thus, in Britain, the apostle of imperialism, Joseph Chamberlain, sought to vindicate the 1905 Aliens Act before his Limehouse audience in the following terms:[9]

> You are suffering from the unrestricted imports of cheaper goods.
> You are suffering also from the unrestricted immigration of the
> people who make those goods.

His audience could not be expected to catch the faulty logic in the spoken word; for, if the makers of British imports moved to Britain, the imports would cease.

The growing nationalization of the mass of the population, including the working class, could not leave the socialists untouched. As Carr put it, 'The socialization of the nation has as its natural corollary the nationalization of socialism.'[10] The tension in the transition from one to the other was an endless source of equivocation. The older ethic of internationalism collided head-on with the new imperative of defence of the nation's jobs. A speaker at the 1904 Congress of the Second International proclaimed,[11]

We socialists, free of any racial or colour prejudice, keep in our heart a limitless hope in the future of those so-called 'inferior people' [of the colonial empires]. What they are now, we have formerly been ... from now on, the workers of the civilized countries will have to secure themselves against the deadly competition of colonial labour.

The same point was put more bluntly by a British trade union leader, Ben Tillet, welcoming the Jewish fugitives from Tsarist persecution: 'Yes, you are our brethren and we will do our duty by you. But we wish you had not come.'

The most heroic accomplishment of the social incorporation of Europe's workers came in the First World War. Then, 10 million died, 20 million were wounded and some 20 million civilians perished of famine or disease. After such a spectacular act of incompetence, Europe's ruling classes still survived intact, their crimes smothered in mass loyalty. Each nationality decided that the villains they knew were preferable to those unknown. By 1914, Carr wrote, with some oversimplification:[12]

Whatever ideals of international class solidarity they [the European masses] might profess, their immediate interests were identical with those who were supposed to be their opponents at home. The will to defend a privileged position in which all social classes shared had welded together each of the great Western nations into a community of economic interests strong enough to appeal to all emotions of an aggressive nationalism.

There were many threads of causality in this process of incorporation and the creation of a popular nationalism. For workers, there were profound material and social differences between countries; it made a great deal of difference to be born a worker in Paris or in Moscow. On that foundation, the more conservative working-class leaders could lead their followers in a transition from the demand to overthrow the existing order to one to defend it against foreigners. The First World War vividly illustrated the power of this exit from revolution. The ruling orders had a strong interest in supporting these translations of purpose. On the other hand, in an era of increasingly aggressive competition between the Great Powers and what already seemed to be the arrival of total war (where much of the population had to be conscripted to serve the war machine), it was impossible to maintain social stability, let alone persuade a significant proportion of the adult males to die – or risk death – for the government, without a much greater degree of consultation and care. Furthermore the demand for labour was changing; high productivity required a greater degree of psychological participation on the part of the workforce, and this necessitated education, elements of health and welfare provision, a popular culture.

More and more, those who had been required traditionally to be, at most, silent by-standers of a history fashioned by the minorities of the powerful, now came to constitute an involved audience whose cheers and groans, like the counterpoint of some Greek chorus, punctuated an action which they saw as their own. Their work, it was now acknowledged, made history possible; their lives were required to defend an order that was supposedly both personal and national.

The population had become an object of policy. The State intervened in the practices of the household to influence the reproduction of the labour force and to ensure its physical quality and education. For the size, composition and skill of the population had become a measure of national power and therefore an objective of public management. The distinction between the true-born native and the foreigner now became a matter of reinforced concern, an issue of legal dispute and definition. By the time of the First World War and immediately afterwards, the regulation of immigration had become an important element of national politics in almost all the advanced countries.

The interwar reactions to the Great Depression continued the process. Governments created, more or less explicitly, corporatist programmes in which labour, capital and the State were allied to ensure social order, founded, supposedly, in a mutual concern for the whole society. A complete economic programme underpinned national loyalty; autarky and, in particular, the control of imports were justified in terms of saving jobs. Indeed, the promotion of a multiplicity of interests was now regularly advanced in terms of defending or expanding employment. Unemployment was a *national* injustice rather than simply a severe hardship. Indeed, the protection or expansion of jobs had become a universal hypocrisy (without necessarily having any effect on government policy).

By the time of the Second World War, virtually all the inhabitants of the Great Powers were completely absorbed in one or other national collectivity. Even those supposed champions of internationalism, the Communist parties, as we have seen, outshone the patriots whenever Moscow permitted them to do so.

The creation of the unified mass State entailed the absorption of the 'individual'. Of course, the individual as a social atom had, in the later nineteenth century, been superseded by the Individual, the comfortably-off respectable citizen standing in contrast to the faceless crowd of non-individuals, the masses. Now all became individuals and therefore none, for none could now stand against the State. In a time of war, individuals, their persons and possessions, were at the complete disposition of the State. In May 1940, the British Parliament authorized the government to make regulations 'requiring persons to place themselves, their services and their property, at the disposal of His Majesty' for any purpose arising from the war. The State had now, it seemed, completely fused the national elements – government, capital, people and the classes into which they were divided – in a single whole.

Border controls

The process of enforced homogenization within particular countries necessitated increased differences between them. In this process, the symbolism of the border became enormously enhanced. Before 1914, passports were generally not required in order to cross international frontiers in the Americas and Europe. Within countries, the freedom to move was an essential element in the creation of unified markets.

After the First World War, the freedom to move between countries was appropriated by the State as one element in population control. Controls intensified until the border became a veritable stockade, maintained as if to repulse permanent waves of invasion. Consider this description of the frontier between East and West Germany as it existed before 1989:[13]

> marked by parallel metal trellis fences with contact mines between them; until recently, some sections were equipped with SM-70 automatic shooting devices . . . Immediately to the east of the fence is an anti-vehicle ditch, then a tracking strip to detect footprints and other tracks, then a relief road to provide the guards easy access, and finally another fence outfitted with electrical and acoustic warning devices. . . . Border guards have standing orders to shoot to kill anyone within fifty yards of the metal trellis.

While this is an extreme case, each country now surrounds itself with greater or lesser intimidatory barriers. Furthermore, States do not hesitate to take powers to maltreat non-natives within their boundaries when it suits national policy. No wonder the frontier becomes a matter of such emotion, associated with the joy of returning or of escaping: the line that divides the privileged from the benighted, those who are supposedly to be protected and those who may be freely insulted. Under medieval serfdom, each serf was tied to a piece of land and to a particular lord; now every inhabitant is expected to be tied to one national soil and one government, or to be an outcaste. The first system was designed to prevent inhabitants escaping; the second to prevent both escape and entry.

The tighter the border controls, the larger the numbers of those who fit nowhere. The most victimized in this intensified colonization of populations are those who are without the requisite documents, the exiled or refugees.[14] In the nineteenth century, by and large, boundaries were open to those driven to flight. Refugees were no different from other migrants and no special provision was required.

After 1945, there were some 45 million displaced persons, most of them in Europe, and finding places for them to go took an army of agents and years of work. It was only the beginning. Now all States are to some extent involved in the process of controlling populations. Most recently, possibly a million boatpeople have left Vietnam (and continue to do so), Rohini Bengalis have streamed across the Burmese border to Bangladesh, and others into Indian Assam. Between 6 and 10 million fugitives left East Pakistan for India at partition. Several million Afghans have scattered into Iran and Pakistan. The internecine savageries of Central America have driven a sad horde northwards. By the 1980s, Africa had attained the doubtful distinction of having more refugees than any other continent.

Earlier, refugees were welcome as a supply of able-bodied workers, the cost of whose upbringing and education had been met by another country (migration could thus be represented as a net transfer of human capital from one country to another). Monarchs were willing to bribe and even to kidnap to obtain scarce skills. Bodies meant power. In retrospect, it seems a sensible policy in competitive conditions. It would seem similarly sensible to accept with some eagerness the cheaper goods made elsewhere as a means of improving local livelihoods.

Yet, in our own times, the opposite is the reaction; both people and goods are described as invasions. Immigrants are supposedly the carriers of a wide range of social ills – unemployment, poor housing, low skills, criminality, without mentioning medical illnesses. For refugees, the milk of human kindness runs thinner and thinner. Governments have now invented the concept of 'economic migrant', as opposed to 'refugee', as a dodge to escape responsibility by separating the undeserving from the deserving poor – as if the search for work were morally reprehensible. The rules are constantly revised to escape past obligations; the British, for example, have spent much ingenuity and legal sophistry in betraying the trust of British passport holders in the former territories of their empire (most recently by abandoning the citizens of Hong Kong). Sea captains were urged not to fish boatpeople from the sea since they could guarantee no way of getting them off their ships (the next ports of call would not accept them); airlines were fined for bringing into Heathrow those whose claims to asylum were subsequently rejected. When even these tricks did not serve to deter the boatpeople arriving in Hong Kong, policy was shifted to 'compulsory repatriation'. Thailand pushed the boats back into the sea. By dint of cheating, bullying and betrayal, the tide of refugees flowing into the industrialized countries was kept to the minimal levels.

The cruelty of this endeavour was only exceeded by its irrationality. For as Hong Kong debated the introduction of compulsory repatriation and expressed panic at the city's stock of 56,000 (1990) Vietnamese refugees, employers estimated that there already existed 200 to 250,000 vacancies for mainly unskilled workers in construction, manufacturing, retailing, hotels and other service sectors.

Border controls are expensive to administer, arbitrary in effect and apparently economically irrational. There is little evidence that controlling the inflow of goods, capital or workers saves jobs, reduces unemployment or achieves other desirable economic objectives. Indeed, there is some evidence of the reverse.

In an integrated world economy, the import of inputs makes possible domestic output, and so sustains – and, if the price of imports falls, increases – domestic employment. Given that, under competitive capitalism, the composition of national output is constantly changing, the pattern of imports must also change, without this necessarily being a matter for alarm. Cheaper imports make possible improved consumption for the inhabitants; and cheap goods can have an especially desirable effect for the poor. Furthermore, cheaper inputs can entail increased national output. To prevent cheaper imports is therefore to sacrifice the interests of the majority (and sometimes the poorest) to the defence of the profits of a tiny minority. Nor does control of imports contribute to saving jobs. The overwhelming proportion of job losses derives from rationalization, not import competition.

There are no stronger arguments for discriminating against foreign capital. Despite widespread fears, there is no systematic evidence that companies with headquarters abroad (if that is the definition of a foreign company) behave differently from those with local headquarters, whether in terms of employment, exports or government revenue. If businessmen are primarily guided by the expected profit rate, then they will tend to behave in the same way, regardless of their national origin. Some people have argued that companies tend to locate their highest-value activities and their research and development close to their headquarters, reserving lower-level branch assembly plants for foreign locations. The picture is not clear. There are, of course, anecdotes to illustrate that companies are biased towards their home base, but the anecdote does not demonstrate that there are in fact consistent differences in behaviour. On the face of it, however, this would seem unlikely; profitability remains the prime criterion.

Many people seem to believe that controlling labour inflows is a pre-eminent attribute of sovereignty. As we have seen, Bombay Municipal Corporation and the state of Assam both wanted to expel immigrant workers just like the government of Estonia (1988–9). Some of Moscow's citizens adopted the same attitude towards the 700,000 workers brought into the city over the preceding fifteen years. But they were brought in because they were of an age and skill to do the work Muscovites could not, or – at the wage offered – would not, do. Without that work being done, it is likely that the rate of unemployment among Muscovites would have been higher.

The argument – that controlling the inflow of labour will protect the jobs of native workers – seems to be both universal, and universally wrong. The labour force is not a simple homogeneous supply, nor is labour demand fixed. The workforce is a package of complementary skills in a state of constant change. Preventing the immigration of labour where there are specific shortages can lead not to the defence of existing jobs, but to increased unemployment. Too few building workers means others of higher skill cannot be employed because the workplaces cannot be built. Too few nurses means workers must take time off to care for their sick dependants. If mothers who are computer programmers cannot find help in caring for their children, they cannot work. Insofar as governments are successful in increasing the skills of the domestic labour force, tight immigration controls may then lead to a shortage of unskilled workers. Either the unskilled jobs involved become prohibitively expensive or the work is not done at all. In the end, total employment will tend to be less.

The labour force is a bundle of skills in another sense. Workers are not automatically able to flow into other occupations. Doctors cannot become bus drivers, nor old miners twenty-year-old shorthand typists, even if they are in the same geographical localities. This lack of interchangeability means that labour scarcities in some jobs coexist with unemployment in others. Insofar as the scarcities are not met from other sources, unemployment can stay high or absenteeism increase.

Those who favour immigration controls sometimes also suggest that, without control, there would be an unlimited flood of new workers arriving. They point to the populations of India or China as if all those millions were poised and ready to migrate if controls were for a moment weakened. There is no evidence, however, that controls are the key factor in deciding whether people migrate or not. For hundreds of years, there were no restrictions and no resulting large-scale movements. There are cases now where movement is possible, but people do not take the opportunity. Thus Spain offers citizenship to immigrants from Latin America after two years' residence, but only 50,000 – out of several hundred million – have seized the opportunity. Italy is ready to grant citizenship to the many Argentinians who can demonstrate Italian descent, but few have taken up the offer.

Today, with a very much larger world population and much easier means of travel it might be thought that the argument for free movement has been changed. Liberal migration rules were, it might be said, not hypocritical only where countries enjoyed the 'natural protection' of relative isolation because of transport difficulties. However, the overwhelming majority of people are still unable to migrate because they do not have the means to pay for the transport required. And the minority that move only do so because there is a real prospect of employment at the other end. With high unemployment, immigration of workers ceases.

It is social and political persecution which drives refugees to flee, not the inducement of a high demand for labour abroad. In practice, however, the distinction between refugee and economic migrant is not at all clear. The decision of refugees to flee could never be unrelated to the prospects of survival abroad. The 'problem' of refugees is self-imposed by the host government insofar as it forbids them to work. The Hong Kong government's complaints over the burden of the Vietnamese boatpeople only occur because it insists on their internment and forbids them to fill a small part of the high demand for labour in the colony.

For ordinary migrants, the evidence suggests that what determines movement is not controls but the demand for workers. But if labour demand is high enough to induce immigration, other things being equal, it will be high enough to minimize unemployment. When unemployment is high – that is, jobs are scarce – migrants do not migrate; indeed, the natives are likely to emigrate. The perverse effect of control is to force people to rush to immigrate before the controls are introduced, and then force them to settle at the destination (in case, if they leave, they will be refused the right to re-enter). Thus controls increase the numbers, albeit temporarily, of those who are obliged to settle.

Movement of workers, both domestically and internationally, is almost certainly vital for any type of dynamic modern economy. For there are always likely to be geographical discontinuities between where workers are trained and where there is work appropriate for their skills. In some parts of the world, for the foreseeable future, there will also be a scarcity of unskilled workers. There has to be immigration, especially where there is full employment, if economies – and the incomes of the majority – are to grow.

This is not at all a new argument; it is the stock in trade of properly liberal economists. Yet the behaviour of governments is everywhere perverse, particularly those which claim to be liberal. The present US and British governments may have liberalized many markets, but on labour they have proved to be as illiberal as their predecessors. Immigration controls, it seems, exist not for defensible economic purposes, and certainly not to defend the jobs of the natives, but as one of the means of distinguishing natives from foreigners, giving the former a certain measure of modest privilege. The policy is not the result of nationalism. It is the main means of demonstrating a nationalism that, in an otherwise integrating world economy, would be lacking. The popular foundation of the State is the loyalty of its inhabitants, and without some means whereby governments can demonstrate a concern for their citizens (rather than for markets), some privilege which attaches to being a native, loyalties become strained. Thus, the political conditions for a world divided by States come directly into conflict with the imperatives of an integrated world economy.

However, the picture is not quite so simple. Whenever there is increased growth in the industrialized countries, the prospect of labour scarcity rises quite quickly, particularly in specific grades of skill, and this impels movement, whether legal or illegal. Population stability requires relative economic stagnation.

Furthermore, demographic logic is now catching up and threatens to propel more radical change. The populations of the developed countries are ageing. Between 1980 and 2030, the number of those aged over 65 will double, reaching some 21 per cent of the whole. Switzerland will have the highest proportion, 29 per cent, but West Germany will have reached 26 per cent. Simultaneously, those in the active age groups will decline, and this will be exaggerated by the increasing time devoted to acquiring higher-level skills (that is, not participating in the workforce). Three problems arise from this process:

(i)   In a nationally isolated economy, the burden of meeting the costs of the growing proportion of the aged will fall on fewer and fewer workers in the active age groups.

(ii)   The decreasing size of the workforce will, other things being equal, make it increasingly difficult to man the national economies on the same scale of operations.

(iii)   The continued upgrading of skills could increase the scarcity of unskilled workers at the wages on offer, thus threatening existing employment levels for the skilled.

Take the case of West Germany. The 1987 Census shows that the number of people over the age of 65 increased by 18 per cent during the previous decade to over 15 per cent of the total, while the number of those under 15 – the future wage-earners – declined by nearly 40 per cent to 14 per cent. Whereas there were two workers for every pensioner in 1987, there could be more pensioners than workers by the year 2030. The problem would be exacerbated insofar as more training and military service took people out of the labour force, and workers chose to work only part-time (the fastest-growing sector of women's employment). Yet, in political terms, the government continued to prevent immigration; indeed, in 1983–4, it offered DM 10,500 to each Gastarbeiter willing to leave the country. There was, the government said, considerable hostility towards immigrants, brought to a head by the official policy of accepting all who claimed to have a German grandparent; *perestroika* released some 300,000 ethnic Germans from Poland, the Soviet Union and Roumania (with a possible total number of some 3–4 million) for migration to West Germany. Many more flowed in in 1989 and 1990 from East Germany. There were voices urging that such an inflow of relatively young workers would do much to improve the age structure of the workforce, but they were lost in the tide of xenophobia.

The same set of problems was beginning to affect Japan, where the ruling orders have traditionally relied more on xenophobia to instil loyalty in their subjects. The growth in the numbers of the aged (and their increasing longevity) has been accompanied by very low birth rates, extending periods of education and a buoyant demand for labour. The rapid expansion of Japanese manufacturing activities abroad – largely due to the high value of the yen – relieved some of the labour scarcity. But there are a mass of jobs which cannot be relocated abroad – including farming, fishing, government, construction, restaurants and services – and many of these cannot be done at the levels of wages now current. However, the government has always set its face against immigration on the grounds that this would weaken that mythic racial homogeneity which is the supposed source of the Japanese genius. There is thus an impasse between the political ethic and the pressures of the labour market, particularly the demand for cheaper immigrant labour from small labour-intensive businesses. In the short term, illegal immigration is taking place from South-East Asia, Pakistan and Sri Lanka, Taiwan and Korea. In the medium term, the government is considering reorganizing the labour force, increasing the employment of women and the elderly, and relocating more activity abroad. But it is not at all clear that this can ensure a supply of labour adequate to sustain the economy. Japanese internationalization in commodities, capital and finance will have to be followed by labour.

Europe and Japan are peculiarly afflicted by these problems. Furthermore, the socially tolerated climate of prejudice is a disincentive to the settlement of immigrants. In the United States, on the other hand, immigration controls are much less effective, more obviously a hypocritical gesture to a battered American nationalism. There is thus a much greater volume of legal and illegal immigration. Indeed, in 1987 more legal immigrants entered the United States than in any year in the country's history. Furthermore, as immigration increased, unemployment declined – the number of jobs has grown consistently faster than the supply of labour. Indeed, a free-market economist might argue that it is because the supply of labour has increased that there has been a sustained expansion in the economy and thus a disproportionate growth in jobs.

There is also a stronger opposition to controls. Parts of intensive US agriculture have been traditionally dependent upon seasonal immigrant labour (particularly Mexican illegal immigrants), although this is less true now. So also is a substructure of the sweated trades – garment and shoe making, restaurants and hotels, petty services. Some bankers even favour the entry of Mexican migrants so that their remittances assist Mexico to service its debts. The economic case, that tighter control of immigration will damage the economy – as expressed editorially in the *Wall Street Journal* – is also better developed. This also applies to the mix of the labour force. The sweated trades are only the most striking case of the shortage of unskilled labour. One study estimates that, with a growth rate of 3 per cent and half a million immigrants annually, the United States will still face a shortage of 5 million workers by the year 2000, the majority of them unskilled. In the case of high-level skills, the United States has continued a relatively liberal policy, recruiting from the world at large. For example, some 15 per cent of the staff of the leading twenty universities were born outside the country, compared to 4 per cent in Europe. Furthermore, foreigners are overrepresented in important growth sectors of the economy (aerospace, electronics, computer software, advanced health care etc.).

The national options open to governments to meet the problem of a changing age structure of population are limited. To meet the growing burden of pensions, workers can accept higher levels of taxes, pensioners can accept lower pensions, and more old people can be induced to stay at work. None of the options are likely to please those concerned, particularly when it is acknowledged that these options exist only because of the attempt to isolate the economy demographically: a pensioner must be obliged to work solely to keep out of the country a young unemployed worker who could do the work instead. But if the economy is integrated with the rest of the world, the age structure is transformed. In sum, the disproportionate production of different types of skills in different parts of the world economy, combined with different patterns of specialization in the production of goods and services in different places and at different rates of growth, impels measures for the redistribution of workers. Young workers are now overproduced in developing countries and underproduced in developed; the unskilled follow the same pattern. Furthermore, there may be some degree of overproduction of highly skilled workers in developing countries – there are 9 million new graduates each year in South and South-East Asia, and 3½ million in North America, Europe and Japan.

Much may be done to redistribute work and stimulate appropriate innovations in technology in order to ease labour shortages without migration. Yet it still seems likely that the problems will need more radical responses – through as sustained a reduction in controls on immigration as has taken place in trade. Then, the most important single remaining material foundation to established political nationalism will have been subverted. The worst outcome of the process would be continued efforts by governments both to promote growth and to prevent immigration. For then it is likely that illegal immigration will be the area of greatest expansion, adding to the problems of austere labour regimes the terrors of illegal status. Such a result would increase political nationalism in the short term, with expanded opportunities for the unscrupulous to make their fortunes from persecuting illegal workers.

The phenomenon of the collision between the labour market and demographic policy is not restricted to the advanced economies of Europe, North America and Japan. For similar problems will afflict the Soviet Union and Eastern Europe insofar as they are able to sustain high rates of growth. The issue in terms of internal migration has already been noted in the case of Moscow. In the capital's textile industry where conditions are said to be particularly bad, two-thirds of the labour force are non-Muscovites. However, the Soviet Union has within its borders its own developing countries and, provided workers can freely migrate, the industrial machine can be manned for some time ahead.

The main issue in China, also, is internal rather than international migration, so it is not directly relevant to this account. However, it again illustrates the collision between the labour market and government demographic policy. On the one hand, China possesses unlimited supplies of unskilled labour; on the other, it has tightly controlled immigration into the cities and, until recently, has enforced a policy of limiting families to one child. Projections of the population already show the rapid ageing of the urban population. In the past, the government has relieved the situation by admitting temporary unskilled labour on short-term contracts.[15] But high rates of growth make this supply of workers insufficient to meet the urban demand for particular sorts of labour (while not necessarily eliminating underemployment in other sectors). Illegal immigration – and a considerable reduction of controls – have gone some way to ease the pressures, but now the government has permitted a second child (to families where the first was a girl!).

Singapore is another example where the government has consistently endeavoured to prevent immigration while maintaining one of the highest rates of economic growth in the world. The Chinese majority is not now reproducing itself, and there is a decline in the proportion of young workers available. In 1980, for each pensioner, there were 9 in the active age groups; this is projected to be 6 by 1991 and 1.5 by 2030. The government has pursued the most ruthless policy to eliminate immigration and raise the skill levels of the native labour force. Labour costs were forced up by edict in order to drive out low-skill immigrant activities. This was a powerful contribution to a major economic crisis when labour costs exceeded Singapore's nearest competitors and exports started to decline. The government drew back and resorted to heavy taxation on employers of immigrants, which the Chamber of Commerce retorted would precipitate a strong increase in wages as employers chased a limited supply of workers. The government has for long urged its graduate women to produce more children, but it is now making it impossible for them to work since they cannot hire help with their children at tolerable cost. The drive to create a high-skill, low-employment enclave is thus flawed in several ways. The shortage of unskilled labour could become severe, relieved only by illegal workers, yet most recently the government has begun a campaign to seize, flog and expel illegal immigrants.

The control of labour mobility has become a key element underpinning nationalism in the more developed countries. The arguments for such control suggest that, without it, the natives will be swamped, facilities will deteriorate and native employment will be affected. As we have seen, the case neglects to note that immigration occurs only where employment, and therefore incomes, are rising. The function of control seems to be rather more ideological than economic. Perhaps this ideological function is too important to permit overt relaxation. Nonetheless, economic growth will force an increasing degree of hypocrisy, the worst recipe for the mobile worker. For, on the one hand, his or her work is vital to maintain national economic growth and high employment levels for the natives; on the other, not only is this contribution not recognized, the illegal immigrant is terrorized as the scapegoat to sustain national unity. The contradiction between maintaining economic growth and seeking to prevent labour mobility and so generating artificial labour scarcities can only be overcome by a black economy.

The methods by which each country reproduces its labour force are only accidentally related to future labour demand, so it is inevitable that there will be over- and under-production of particular skills, which themselves are exaggerated by the growth of specializations. Migration is the means whereby these disproportions are overcome, and people are enabled to escape from poverty. Thus, a future labour force in any particular locality is likely to be increasingly cosmopolitan; the great cities of the United States, particularly of California, are possibly already the most advanced in this respect.

Conclusion

All governments are, to a greater or lesser degree, obliged to be economically nationalist. But the specific form of economic nationalism discussed here, embodied in what has become known as a strategy of import-substitution industrialization, began for the less developed countries as a defence against the Great Depression and the reactive efforts by the industrialized countries to cut their imports, and became a means to accelerate the development of a relatively backward country in a system of competing and very unequal States. It is founded upon creating a monopoly market for domestic producers so as to redistribute resources away from consumption and in favour of investment and manufacturing. In its heyday, both more and less developed countries shared this economic ideology, albeit for different reasons. It was most explicit in theories of corporatism. For all, economic and political nationalisms were fused in a single loyalty.

However, the quarter of a century of unprecedented growth in the world economy after 1950[16] created a new structure which apparently broke down economic nationalism and forced international economic integration. In an important and new sense, a single world economy has emerged from the national parts, most clearly so in the developed countries. To ensure growth and thus their own power, States are obliged to accommodate to this new phenomenon, which implies systematic decontrol of external trade, capital and financial movements. The process is still far from complete, and not all are equally involved, but there are grounds for thinking integration is now too far advanced to be reversed. What is left as the heart of economic nationalism in the developed countries is the control of population movement, a simplification of economic nationalism which makes for an obsessive, and irrational, preoccupation with national origins.

However, the set of problems now emerging in the developed countries is leading to a divergence between the politics and the economics of immigration. What began as a defence of domestic employment has become transformed into a means of enforcing political loyalty, but at increasing economic cost. Immigration controls impose an economically disastrous degree of rigidity upon the creation of a labour force appropriate to a changing national economy, and the problems are likely to grow worse. Of course, the heterogeneity of countries supplies some basis for the privilege and disprivilege of native and foreigner, but the ideological structure created upon this foundation goes far beyond it. Countries – both developed and developing – are going to need more labour of greater diversity of skill (as well as adequate supplies of unskilled workers) than can be reproduced from their home populations. They will also need it to pay the pensions of those who are currently workers – which gives the natives an interest in permitting immigration.

The Economist (2 April 1988) proposed an agreement similar to the General Agreement on Tariffs and Trade for migrant labour, and urged developing countries to make concessions on current negotiations in the GATT in order to secure an easing of immigration into the developed countries, which it saw as helping them through the remittances from their workers abroad. However, the developing countries are not required to plead for concessions, for the emerging needs of the developed – to find young workers and diversified skills – will grow increasingly urgent. Thus, a vital element in the emergence of an integrated world economy – the creation of a cosmopolitan workforce – will be further advanced.

17

THE PAST AND FUTURE OF NATIONALISM

NATIONALISM today provides the framework and language for almost all political discussion, and for obvious reasons. Politics is concerned with the attainment and employment of power in society, and power is usually vested in particular institutions, of which government is by far the most important. So it is inevitable that politics is most commonly preoccupied with questions concerning the State, an institution defined by national power: a territory, a share of the world's inhabitants and output.

So all-pervasive are the assumptions that the most important questions concern national power and the interests of governments that it is difficult to detach ourselves from them. Yet nationalism had a beginning and, conceivably, could come to an end.

Furthermore, up to 1914, there was always a strong rival tradition of international liberation, based upon the conception of an international class alignment and strongly hostile to what was seen as a reactionary diversion. Even among the Social Democrats who had, despite all their previous claims, apparently collapsed into nationalism with the outbreak of the First World War, internationalism remained a powerful inspiration when they regrouped themselves in the Socialist International after the war. The October 1917 revolution drew around itself the majority of the most uncompromising internationalists. In theory, the Russian revolution had nothing at all to do with national liberation; it was the first step towards an international workers' republic and could have occurred, in principle, in any country. The conversion of the Russian revolution into a purely Russian event, and the Soviet State into a conventional Great Power, came later and, when it did, inflicted irreparable damage on the tradition of internationalism. Simple nationalism won the day, albeit clad in the borrowed language of Marx and internationalism.

Yet, despite the frightening scale of the problems, Lenin had been the most successful of all the Marxists in translating the general position of internationalism into the specifics of an alliance with national liberation. But even he underestimated the processes transforming Russia, and overestimated the capacity of his fellow Communists to penetrate the opaque quality of nationalism and its complicated and changing social interests. In the key cases, Communists could not take over the nationalist movements. The aspiration of the second Congress of the Comintern – that the Communists might turn national rebellion into permanent and international revolution – was stillborn. Even if the perspective had been closer to reality, the nature of the colonies and the Stalinization of Communist parties – their subordination to Soviet foreign policy – made it impossible for them to succeed.

The successes came only – and not always then – when the Communists could scrap their intellectual baggage of class politics and themselves become nationalists. They did not ally with nationalism, they allowed themselves to be taken over by it. The remarkable achievement of Mao in China was to exploit the opportunity provided by the Japanese invasion to undercut the claims of Chiang Kai-shek to embody Chinese nationalism, and in order to facilitate this, to abandon the programme of class warfare. Mao presented the Communist Party as the only true nationalists, and founded the doctrines (if not the practice) of China's revolution upon an alliance of all China's classes. As we have seen, the line laid down by the seventh Congress of the Comintern encouraged European Communist parties in the same direction, to form national coalitions of all classes and bring their trade-union following to support the political *status quo*. Again, they did not ally with nationalism, but abandoned what was left of their original aims in order to subordinate themselves to the defence of the *status quo* against the threat of fascism.

Today, the majority of those who call themselves Marxists, particularly in the developing countries, are predominantly nationalist. Thus has the system successfully subverted its opponents and, through nationalism, converted them into its defenders, if not the ruling order of this country or that. Lenin's language has, in the years of sterling service it performed for Moscow, become transformed into a simple support for the right of national self-determination anywhere. As a result, it always attracted some of the more uncompromising nationalists, whether in Communist parties or in the groups to the left of the Communists. Few noted that Lenin's original line – the attainment of 'complete democracy' and the 'full equality of peoples'

– was never attained in Stalin's Russia. The Stalinist order rode roughshod over any genuine national aspirations, thus storing up for *perestroika* a new settlement of the national question.

Modernizing States

The more the historical research, the greater becomes the constituent complexity of each appearance of national liberation. The chameleon changes so swiftly, it is difficult to believe it exists as one creature. Here we have had the temerity to collapse these complexities into three types. It is perhaps worth summarizing their character.

In the first, which we might call, schematically, the 'French–English' case, modern States were a by-product of the rivalries of the European powers. Here monarchs, through the circumstances of domestic structures of power and external situations, were able to centralize their authority over extensive territories, breaking down the elaborate restrictions of local particularism. They created the bureaucracies and armies with which to extend their reach, and deliberately fostered an expanding commercial capitalist economy as the financial basis for their power. Nationalism – in this case popular loyalty to the State – was forced upon a section of the population, and embodied in an expansionist, aggressive drive both at home and abroad. The French were always more advanced than the English in the creation of the modern State, and their example was enormously influential among rulers throughout Europe. Perhaps it was precisely this measure of advance which evoked its own contradiction: the passionate belief in a free French nation which seized the Parisians and turned nationalism from being an instrument for their own subordination into a weapon with which to beat the Bourbons.

The task of 'modernization' was never completed. The reforms, in time and with vested interests, were reconverted into restrictions. Liberation in one period turned into inhibition in another, requiring yet more reforms. The reform movement, to repeat, was driven by the competition between States in which it seemed that rulers must reform or their power would be overwhelmed by, or at least made subject to, other States. Thus, most major European States at different times – given the particular energies, propensities, anxieties and domestic opportunities of their rulers – made sporadic attempts to create what we have called loosely 'modern States'. The Swedes made consistent efforts over a long period. The Spanish, Russian and Austro-Hungarian emperors all at various times endeavoured to create new orders capable of mobilizing resources for a sustained defence of their territories. But so often their successors proved uninterested in the task, or the forces of inertia in the old social orders, particularly an obstructive aristocracy and an immovable pattern of inherited land ownership, checked the process and in some cases even reversed it. Despite all the efforts – and cruelties – of a Peter or a Catherine, by the end of the nineteenth century, Tsarist Russia had become more antiquated in comparison to its rivals. We have seen in the case of the Habsburgs of Austro-Hungary not only the scale of the obstacles, but the ways in which a reforming monarch could incite precisely the forces of opposition he most wished to exorcize. On the other hand, even without a comparable economic base, Frederick of Prussia could supersede the British in the fashioning of State power as a weapon of European aggrandizement.

There was a second type which proved of much greater significance in the long term and which provided much of the nineteenth-century standard account of national liberation. The inhabitants of the Netherlands and of the British colonies in North America fashioned the sense of being national groups in the process of struggle against imperial domination. The rebels began with an essentially conservative defence of established rights against the attempt by their respective rulers to create new forms of taxation. This was not initially an affirmation of the right to national self-determination. In the American case, the struggle itself made public a new and dazzling doctrine, a secular ideology of national liberation and the rights of man (which went on to become a contributory stream to the French events of 1789). Here it was possible to see something like a nation plausibly existing before the achievement of a State, indeed, creating a State. For the Netherlands, that process took nearly a hundred years; and it was war that broke down the internal divisions separating the citizens and allowed a unified military effort. In the United States, there was still far to go – and a civil war – in the creation of Americans; and the country was protected by distance from the disturbing rivalries of Europe which could otherwise have interrupted the creation of an American nationalism.

Thus, the crude idea that the modern State and nationalism were created by the rise of capitalism (meaning the capitalist class rather than the system in which they played a key role) needs amendment. Indeed, we might with equal truth say that the expansion of capitalism was in part produced by the rivalries of kings, the competition of States. In the struggle for dominance, monarchs fostered capital as an ally, a source of finance and of supply – to the point where capitalist interests came to dominate the society and colonize the State as the instrument of their overall interests (with or without a bourgeois revolution). Elsewhere, if capital was allowed to pursue its purposes through an alliance with the local pre-capitalist orders, it did so. The Ruhr accepted the Kaiser and a Junker State. The British, French and other merchants sustained the Ch'ing dynasty in its decaying years.

In formal terms, in a context of rivalries, once a measure of centralization was introduced, other competing States were obliged to emulate it in order to defend themselves, just as competing monarchs copied each other's innovations in weaponry. In eighteenth-century Europe, the French State and the British economy were powerful examples. In the nineteenth century, the twin aspirations – and they were rightly hardly distinguished – were adopted by almost all the powers of Europe. Performance, however, was very different.

A plurality of States created the possibility of collaboration to limit the more destructive aspects of competition, a Concert of Europe. After the great blood-letting of Napoleon's crusade for national self-determination, a European State system emerged, including both modern and archaic powers, not only to curb France, but to limit change generally by restraining the ambitions of rising powers in the interests of the established, and by collaborating to suppress revolution.

The year of revolution, 1848, was stalemated. This was a crucial turning point in the European movement for national liberation. The German liberals were by now too weak vis-à-vis the modern State of Prussia, and too intimidated by the prospect of popular – and possibly socialist – revolution, to risk everything. The Ruhr traded the supposed historic demand for a democratic republic in return for an unimpeded opportunity to make profits under Prussian auspices. On the other hand, having prevented a revolutionary unification of Germany in 1848, the system permitted the Kings of Prussia to assume the imperial rule of Germany, and the rulers of Savoy, the monarchy of a new Italy. The decline of the Turkish empire imposed an intolerable strain, however, for the greed of the established powers was hardly controllable in the contest to divide up the old empire in the Balkans, the east Mediterranean and North Africa.

With these growing rivalries in the late nineteenth century, a new phase in the 'nationalization' of the population occurred in Western Europe. Through education, elements of popular welfare and health provision, but above all through the extension of the suffrage, the mass of the population of each country were solemnly inducted into the nation. There was now an articulate audience for sagas of national loyalty, a source of unprecedented tax revenue and an equally unprecedented potential source of military manpower.

If the Balkans and the eastern Mediterranean could not be included in the agenda of the State system of Europe, how much less was this possible for Asia and Africa. The Great Powers now knocked the rest of the world into convenient administrative dependencies. In doing so, they created a third type of nationalism – the defensive reflection of imperial dominance. The process was slow, interacting with the changing tactics and needs of foreign rule. Furthermore, the growth of national feeling was powerfully mediated by the concepts imposed by the imperialists. For, as we have seen, their rule required the creation of supporting interests to offer loyalty and tax payments, concepts created to differentiate those who ruled and those who were required to obey. They thus defined classes, tribes, castes, communities and interests, exclusive building blocks of their power. There were rewards for those who accepted this definition, and sanctions for those who did not. In the Indian case, the British attempts to reform their administration and increase local taxation (a rationalization itself impelled by the growing rivalries of the Great Powers) led them to offer greater participation to the indigenous population and to create those clashes whose existence supposedly vindicated their presence.

It was not purely invention, nor, usually, conscious or cynical manipulation. The British used the materials that came to hand to build the imperial dwelling. They took existing distinctions to disaggregate India, but in doing so they transformed their meaning, so that they could just as well have invented them completely. There are, after all, thousands of social and religious distinctions, and they are in general of no great importance to the State. They are elements of an innocent heterogeneity, without implications for anyone except those directly involved. There are a multiplicity of social groups, and people are members of many at the same time. The selection of what label was to assume *political* significance and what the form of that significance would be was the prerogative of the imperial officials. Once chosen, the label, regardless of its provenance, became a social and economic category, but above all a political one. Muslims, whose scattered groups shared nothing in common apart from worship in a mosque, certain customs of birth, death and marriage, and perhaps for a minority a tradition of Koranic scholarship, were fully integrated with those of other confessions in specific localities; but now they were fused by the ideologists of the Raj into a separate nation. The invader chose the concepts – Muslim, black, Kikuyu – and enforced the homogeneity of those identified.

It was not at all a unique procedure, nor particularly new. For had not the earlier Muslim rulers of India in like fashion invented the term 'Hindu' to describe all non-Muslims? The French imposed the concept of Berber on the warring tribes of North Africa's mountains to stand in contrast to the coastal Arabs (imperialists displayed a continuing Lévi-Straussian fascination with simplified dichotomies). Even today the Californians have invented 'Asians' and grouped beneath the term the amazing diversity of Koreans, Vietnamese, Chinese, Japanese, Filipinos, Indians and so on. In Britain, 'black' forces together Jamaicans, Pakistanis, Nigerians and any others that the supposedly homogeneous British choose. In time, perhaps, those so rudely – and without consultation – yoked together by ignorance and prejudice will come to feel they have a common identity, experience and culture.

In sum, groups were created and enforced by empire, transforming distinctions which were a very restricted selection from inherited differentiations into the divides of a new colonial society. In India, the British created a complexity in order to deny that the concept 'Indian' had any *political* significance. Even so, they were obliged to acknowledge that Indians were those excluded from power. Elsewhere, they could not avoid creating a class of the subordinates, whose common inferiority could become a nation in rebellion. Once corralled within the concept, common oppression could become the basis for inventing a social homogeneity to underpin the arbitrary 'us' that vindicated the divide with 'them'. An obscure collectivity could thus come to realize that it potentially had power to overthrow the colonizers. Perversely, what the imperialists fashioned as a weapon of domination proved a double-edged sword which could be turned against them.

The fact that the basic concepts which define and sustain the existence of a nation are forced upon a subordinate people shows the error in the attempt to define objective criteria for nationality – as both Otto Bauer and Josef Stalin did. The symbols chosen to identify a people are contextually determined and quite arbitrary. If the imperial order insists that the subordinate class is black or Buddhist or Bantu-speaking, these become the basis for a defensive nationalist reaction. There are no grounds for denying that a people are a nationality if they say they are. But the concepts are specific to the context; they are not the basis for a general science of nationalism.

The nationalist movement in the European colonies was not the voice of a rising capitalist class. Many of the imperial possessions lacked capitalists of any significance; and where they existed they were often seen as foreigners (for example, the Chinese in South-East Asia). Indeed, the modern national liberation movements were usually as hostile to capitalism as they were to workers. They were voices of a future modernizing State rather than existing profit-makers, and drawn from the urban middle classes, the salariat of empire, rather than other groups.

The imposition of concepts, however, is only one side of the picture. The content that filled these concepts was not necessarily determined by imperial aims. The labels of group identity often summarize complicated and contradictory issues, and do not self-evidently indicate the interests at stake. Take, by analogy, the campaign against Salman Rushdie's *Satanic Verses*. In Bradford, the book stirred up a long-simmering anger at the racialism and discrimination of British society. In Islamabad, it was a counterattack in the general elections which had just brought a woman to the premiership and defeated the conservative forces, identified with Islam. In Teheran, Ayatollah Khomeini used the issue both to advance his claims to the leadership of all Muslims and to signal that the concessions made to 'moderation' in the ending of the war with Iraq had come to an end, while his son exploited it to advance his challenge to the established heirs. The ruler of Saudi Arabia was obliged to respond to separate his Sunni followers from Shi'ite temptation. In Bombay, one mullah was competing with another for the influence of a community. And so on: a multiplicity of interests found the book of value in advancing their claims and in mobilizing other interested parties. They did so under the common banner of Islam. Yet the overwhelming majority of Muslims showed no interest in the issue. In what sense can we say that this was a single *Muslim* reaction, implying that Islam itself was the key to the behaviour of these diverse events, rather than the opportunistic employment of inherited concepts to achieve other purposes?

Modern historians are engaged in a splendid mining of the sources of Indian nationalism. The research underlines the point that the claim to a nationality is not an indication of a passive identity, a given inheritance. It is taking up a weapon in the struggle for power, a weapon which offers a diagnosis of present discontents, the identity of the enemy, the allies with which to fight, and the nature of the remedy. In the struggle between Congress and the British Raj, whether or not 'Indians' existed as a political conception was a key issue in dispute. Congress won on this score not because it was correct in its judgement that Indians existed, but in the gamble that the British had half-created them – and they could be fully created in action.

Thus, we cannot say in general what any particular nationalism means in isolation from the specific conflicts of a given situation. The nationalist tradition can swing from the extreme right to the extreme left, can be the voice of landlords or landless, employers or workers, contradictory coalitions of one thing in one place and another elsewhere, or none of these. Here it may mean peasant against merchant, there Buddhist against Taoist. Only a detailed analysis will allow us to say what the underlying significance of nationalist claims is.

Of course, one can say with reference to Marxists that all national liberation is reformist, or formally to a greater or lesser extent conservative. For even the most revolutionary nationalist takes for granted a world order of national States, and aims only to overturn the local ruler while leaving the system intact. Nationalism may seek to liberate the citizens of one country, but this is to settle for much less than universal self-emancipation. Indeed, as we have suggested earlier, this fact has allowed the world order to nullify many of the historical ambitions of national liberation.

The precipitation of the struggle is yet another area of complexity. As we have seen, where an imperial regime has traditionally administered a population in separate language or ethnic groups, then rebellion can be set off by attempts to rationalize the administration and its financing which lead to a reduction in traditional liberties. However, major economic changes, flowing from the centralizing effects of the introduction of a market economy, can also be important in promoting national rebellions, particularly where the regime concerned is suffering from a loss of morale. Interwoven are the struggles of farmers or capitalists against imports, of white-collar and professional staff against foreigners competing for jobs, of students operating in an educational system dominated by criteria of excellence derived from the metropolitan country and so on.

It would be premature, at the time of writing, to draw any conclusions about the meaning of current events in Eastern Europe and the Soviet Union, and, in particular, whether they constitute a fourth type of nationalism. It still seems unlikely that the Soviet Union will break up, but in conditions of very rapid change such an opinion could be outdated even before this book is published.

Some preliminary observations might be worth making, however. First, in Stalin's Soviet Union, selected national differences were entrenched in the administrative and political organizations of the republics and regions. All Lenin's original fears in this respect have now been realized – 'estrangement' has, apparently, survived the years. This is particularly so since the main part of Lenin's programme – the establishment of complete democracy and equality of all peoples – was in no way realized. On the contrary, the national minorities became one of the many foci for cruel persecution. In such circumstances, general assimilation became impossible. In the absence of most other political distinctions over such a long period of time, the national became initially the main focus for all the diverse discontents released by Gorbachev's reform programme. Furthermore, the reform programme itself, in attacking the corrupt inheritance of the previous order, particularly in Central Asia and the Caucasus, replaced many of the local Communist leaders there; those leaders in turn organized, or turned a blind eye on, popular resistance against the intervention of Moscow. In crucial cases, the armed intervention of Moscow then inflamed opposition.

Secondly, each separate struggle covered a vast diversity of different issues. The Tajiks attacked what they saw as an invasion of Armenian refugees jumping the queue to gain access to desperately scarce housing (so the answer to nationalism was a housing policy) or receiving privileges above the poorly paid Tajiks. They also resented the low prices Moscow offered for their cotton, as the Azeris complained of low prices for Baku's oil. Estonians and Armenians opposed the siting of polluting nuclear power stations in their midst (so nationalism required an environmental response). In the Baku pogroms against Armenians, some saw the hand of the security police and discredited party leaders, facing elections they were likely to lose, not the Shi-ite frenzy that some commentators were quick to suggest. In Yerevan, in the same way, a Party leadership sacked by Moscow was seen as the organizer of the demonstrations. In the Baltic Republics, with a standard of living higher than in the rest of the Soviet Union, the nationalists wanted to stop Russian immigration and create free trade zones to emulate Scandinavian levels of living. There were few common threads other than the attitude to Moscow, and each rebellion required different responses.

Thirdly, the appalling performance of the Comecon economies meant that there was much popular support for the operation of free markets. Of course, this was never as much as Western political leaders and newspapers liked to pretend, but the dominant economic orientation was strikingly at variance with that espoused by decolonizing movements in the postwar period. Market capitalism, it seemed, had at least temporarily attained an unprecedented popularity. It did so without any significant class of private capitalists (the same condition that existed in many of the decolonizing developing countries), as a kind of abstract aspiration to rejoin a world market. Of course, it was also partly a recognition that the world market was the source of both the crisis of the Comecon economies, their incapacity to sustain the same trajectory of economic change, and a proposed programme of remedies. It remains to be seen how long this embrace of capitalism continues to be popular.

The phase of political empire is now past, with the possible sole exception of the Soviet Union. The other imperial powers have been pushed out of the rest of the world, and have learned to entrust its administration to new independent States. Economic domination by no means ceased – indeed, it increased – but it no longer required political control. In retrospect, we can see the period between 1848 and the 1960s as the great age of nationalism and its rebellious reflection, national liberation, with the greatest period in this century, particularly after the Second World War. The times included both the unprecedented horrors of two World Wars, the unbridled clash of European nationalisms, and the destruction of empire, leaving behind some 170 or so States.

Decolonization, however, also brought to the rest of the world the order of the system of States. Once empire had been broken up, it became very much more difficult to create new States unless this change was regarded as appropriate by the governments of the world. The existing States created institutions to police and guide the processes of acceptable change. Furthermore, new States, no matter how poor, clung tenaciously to what they had won, permitting no further fragmentation except in very extraordinary circumstances. National liberation retreated from the demand for secession to no more than a threat to strengthen a bargaining position, to define a defensive politics. The Quebecois decided that secession from Canada would be an economic catastrophe; they did so without relinquishing any rights to reproach English Canada for its oppression.

Furthermore, the experience of sovereignty tempered the enthusiasms of the liberators. It seemed that, after all the sacrifices, all the travails, required to come to power, freedom had proved elusive. The new State acquired a host of new constraints that flowed from becoming a competitor in a world order. The sovereign State was only an archaic theory. The reality was a continual struggle to survive as one component in a system, subject to the disciplines generated in the world at large. Indeed, some governments might feel themselves to be little more than impotent brokers between turbulent and unreasonable social forces at home and the turbulent and unreasonable forces of a world economy and polity. Even in the case of the heroics of forced development, we can now see with the benefit of hindsight that this was not a means to achieve economic independence, only a stronger competitive position in the world order, not a means to end dependence, but in certain respects to increase it. All roads led back to Rome.

The point at which State power was attained was the transition from one condition to another. Beforehand, in the struggle for national liberation, it was possible to dream about what the liberators would achieve with State power, to imagine a future utopia of order, plenty and universal peace. Once in office, immediate hard practical issues swiftly eliminated such sentimentality – or, at least, did to it what normal society did to religious belief, reduced it to the world of private fantasy, without practical implication. The saints who led the national struggle, the Gandhis, gave way to the men of affairs, the Nehrus; Gandhi was reserved for pious invocations, for statues and celebrations, for romantic films, daydreams that were neither history nor a guide to the future. Where the saints continued in office – as Sukarno did in Indonesia or Khomeini in Iran – they often led their countries to the brink of ruin.

Participation in a world order enforced a new kind of nationalism. This was no longer defensive, reacting to imperial domination, but could as easily be aggressive. In a system of unequal States, subordination of the weaker did not lead to a neat divide between dominant and dominated, so much as a hierarchy. Indian reaction to British control and then, as an independent State, to the Great Powers at large, was reproduced in Delhi's domination of South Asia and Sri Lanka's domination of the Tamils. And the chain was reproduced down to the street-corner bully or the chauvinist football player whose strutting and threats of violence mocked the pretensions of State power. What Lenin identified in the Soviet Union as Great Russian chauvinism was not simply a Russian problem; each State had its local variant.

States and economies

In the post-1945 period, changes in the world economy further transformed the context for national economic independence. The period when the greatest number of new States was created was precisely the time for unprecedented growth in the world economy and the integration of the economies of the dominant powers; the process of political fission coincided with that of economic fusion. The logic of economic internationalization seemed to resume developments taken for granted by Marxists before the First World War and which had persuaded the Luxemburgists that the demand for the right of national self-determination was utopian.

For developing countries, the immediate policy implication was that rapid economic growth seemed to be associated – although not invariably so[1] – with a country's capacity to exploit the world market, rather than the growth of domestic demand. From the 1960s, an increasing number of developing countries began to participate in the process of integration. The package of governing policies was steadily changed. As in the developed countries, the old corporatist coalition of government, capital and labour, where it had existed, was scrapped along with the external economic controls; governments became preoccupied not so much with domestic collaboration as with external markets and competition. The structural supports of the old domestic alliances, a large public sector, measures of welfare provision and planning, were replaced by measures to institute market mechanisms. Indeed, it seemed as if never before in the history of capitalism had the fictions of open market competition attained such astonishing intellectual hegemony. So much so that the new fashions continued beyond the era of high growth to the years of relative economic stagnation and recession.

There were other implications that would take considerable time to absorb. For example, in the nineteenth century, it was generally thought – among that small minority who considered such questions – that new national States must be large – a view held in common by Marx and Engels, John Stuart Mill and Friedrich List. Commentators were scornful of the petty principalities of Germany, and 'Balkanization' was a term of derision for the inevitable squabbling of small States. Even as late as the Second World War, E.H. Carr deplored any general decolonization on the grounds that most of the resulting countries would be too small.[2] The economic advantages of large and, if necessary, multinational groupings in terms of the concentration of capital, the size of market and labour force, and, above all, the productivity of labour were thought to be self-evident.

However, in an economically integrated world – as opposed to a world consisting of separate national economies – these advantages are less clearcut. A Hong Kong or a Singapore can, within an international division of labour, attain the highest rates of growth of labour productivity. Indeed, were Hong Kong burdened with the vast hinterland of China, it could never have hoped to develop as swiftly as it did. The importance of size is not now in the economic field, but in terms of a State's political and military weight in the world. This point was recognized perceptively by Eric Hobsbawm,[3] arguing that the principle of the formation of States had now become detached from the necessities of a territorial economy; he feared that this would lead to a proliferation of divisive petty nationalisms.

The prospect is not so alarming as Hobsbawm feared in 1977. We are far from the utopian world of Norman Macrae[4] where power has trickled down from States and multinational corporations to the little platoons. Even if the ambitions of economic independence make no sense and virtually all countries are dependent upon a world division of labour, governments cling tenaciously to their existing territories and inhabitants, making the price of secession extraordinarily high. There is some dissociation between large concentrations of capital and governments; 'national capital' in the developed countries is increasingly difficult to identify. Perhaps a cosmopolitan bourgeoisie is emerging which lacks any strategic nationality (that is, firms are loyal to a government in behaviour, as opposed merely to the managers being of a particular nationality). But still governments, even the weakest in some cases, retain particular powers – the power of the expropriation of the assets of corporations. The monopoly of the use of physical violence in a given territory gives them a power of sanction. Of course, the conditions in which the power would be sensibly used, and in conditions of the great inequality of States, qualifies the right heavily.

The role of the State is being reshaped. It is less and less the leadership of a discrete national segment of the world's capital, relating to a relatively autonomous domestic market and currency area. Rather, governments are coming to administer part of a world economy, junction points for transactions which begin and end their life outside the country concerned, and which form a national specialization that has meaning only within an international division of labour. The State manages a territory, supervises the reproduction of part of the world's labour force, ensures that the domestic environment is hospitable for international capital and competes for its share of that capital. Mere size of country in this context is not necessarily important.

The issue of size of country was analogous to that of size of capital. Marxists – and many others – took it for granted that capital was concentrated. The indices of concentration were at least threefold – an increasing share of the world's capital was concentrated in fewer hands, the size of average production units increased, and there was increasing geographical concentration of activity. It was also assumed that as time passed the capital intensity of production increased. As the system opened from a national-based one to an integrated world, all four propositions came under question. With the decline of national economic barriers, great masses of much cheaper labour became actually or potentially available for production in an open world market. This must change the relative pricing of the factors of production, transforming the parameters which determine the development of technology. New centres of national capital have appeared (so, other things being equal, reducing the concentration of capital in fewer hands). The average size of plant in many sectors has for long appeared to be declining, reversing what seems to be a very old trend within capitalism. New geographical centres of production have begun, often coinciding with the precipitate decline of old established ones. And finally, labour-intensive production in many sectors has become very much more competitive than automated plants. What had been seen as the inexorable, indeed necessary, drive of the system to centralization now seems to have been reversed, at least while the rest of the world is absorbed. All this transforms the prospects and the shape of what national economic development might be.

However, governments and the existing concentrations of capital remain dominant in the system and will not easily be reduced. The integration, as we have noted, of finance, capital and manufacturing has not been copied in the field of labour. There, enforced national isolation of people remains a vital political support for national governments. Indeed, the peculiar hysteria over immigration (and not just in the developed countries) seems to compensate for the erosion of sovereignty in other fields. However, even here, as we discussed in the last chapter, there are features of the world economy which impel some reduction in controls on the movement of people. Although this will in no way abolish the real material differences between countries which underlie part of nationalist differentiation, the cosmopolitanization of labour forces will go some way to weaken some of the elements of cultural nationalism (even if, in the short term, it may lead to their exaggeration).

The control of population is not the only issue, however. A new set of concerns has emerged which strengthen one form of nationalism: the defence of one's homeland against environmental pollution. The emotional content of the Green movement is sometimes not very different from the reaction to immigration – opposition to an invasion of alien elements. However, the environmentalists are defensive, not offensive, and are acting in reaction to the growing integration of a polluting world. It is the creation of an integrated power-generation network in the Soviet Union which has led to the location of nuclear power stations in Estonia, Armenia and, above all, the Ukraine (with Chernobyl) and provided key targets in the nationalist campaigns. But, of their nature, Green issues require greater international collaboration, not less. At Bhopal, the lack of a common legal framework which could penalize Union Carbide equally in India and in the United States demonstrates the need, not for India to expel all foreign capital, but to move towards a common international legal order. The much lesser problem of acid rain, produced in Britain, damaging vegetation in Scandinavia and Germany likewise calls for an international regime capable of penalizing the British government. The lack of effective common political organizations thus makes the slow progress to an international order highly accident-prone, despite the power of the structural features which impel economic integration.

This book has been preoccupied with identifying the material factors determining the emergence and continuation of nationalism. The conditions for the rise of nationalism were seen in a set of competitive modernizing States that fostered capitalism. This began a process which impelled the incorporation of the mass of the population. The sole effective alternative, the internationalism of the socialists, was destroyed, first in 1914 with the incorporation of the sections of the Second International in their respective warring countries, and second, in the subversion of the Russian revolution, turning internationalism into Russian nationalism.

Two World Wars and an unprecedented slump obliged the State to initiate policies on employment and welfare which offered further material support for a fully nationalized population. The continued inter-state competition and inequality reinforced division of the world's peoples into nationalities.

However, part of that material basis is now weakening, even though the international competition continues. If key elements of economic activity are being integrated, even labour forces may become more cosmopolitanized. We have striking examples of large-scale assimilations taking place in this respect – in the Americas, Israel and Australia. Nevertheless, while these processes show a genuine and remarkable intermixing (including intermarriage) they take place only in the context of a new national identity. However, the salient point is the relative ease with which past national identities can be superseded, for it indicates the potential for internationalization.

With increased international migration, quantity can become quality. To the panic of ruling orders, an increasingly cosmopolitan labour force increases the heterogeneity within, and decreases it between, countries. Migration subverts the artificial cultural homogeneity which States have instilled in their citizens. Indeed, already the ruling orders of the world – who prattle of the need to protect their national culture as the vindication for immigration controls – have attained a quite striking cultural homogeneity in ways of life. National cultures, insofar as they exist, tend to be left to the lower orders. Furthermore, a world culture is emerging, to which the United States has made the largest, but by no means the sole, contribution (so that the world culture is mistakenly identified as American). The greater the movement of peoples, the more that culture will come to be fashioned by people from many other sources.

The key to the continuation of nationalism, however, is not the presence or absence of cultural differences, much less the wishes of the world's inhabitants. It lies in the competition between what are still overwhelmingly the paramount political institutions, States. Here the problems are much more severe. There have been numerous innovations to embody an international order – from the international political and sectoral agencies of the United Nations to regulatory bodies and the world's bankers, the International Monetary Fund and World Bank. Regional federations, of which the strongest is the European Community, are similar institutions for eroding the sovereignty of States. It is still the case, however, that sovereignty remains vested at the national level. And it is difficult to see any dramatic change in this state of affairs, short of a very long period of slow erosion in which the economic order tries to draw the political into alignment. While this is so, rebels will almost inevitably gravitate towards national liberation as a key form of revolt.

History played a trick on the Marxists. The apparent sophistication of their method did not protect them from being hoodwinked. The theory of a world capitalism, the abolition of State and nation and the emancipation of civil society, was turned into an ideology of nationalism, with a much enlarged role for the State and a more complete subordination of society. State capitalism was justified as the means to establish political and economic independence, yet it did not even achieve this. Autarky proved no more than the prelude to incorporation in the world order once again, an incorporation required if rates of economic growth and modernization were to be sustained. The assertion of a separate national identity became no more than a detour back to reunification in an international culture. The Israelis discovered this paradox in their transition from being homeless Jews to, in Akiva Orr's phrase, 'Hebrew-speaking gentiles'. Zionism was only a special route to what it abhorred, assimilation.

The Left could have saved itself from being manoeuvred into this position had it held hard to its original aim: universal freedom. But too many remained loyal to the temporary means, the State and the public sector. Too many substituted for the self-emancipation of workers their access to the power to govern society and improvements in publicly supplied welfare. They thus became the last quixotic defenders of a world of national State capitalisms, replacing the tyranny of the market with the dictatorship of the bureaucracy.

NOTES

Chapter 1: Introduction

1. Otto Bauer, see extracts in Tom Bottomore and Patrick Goode (eds), *Austro-Marxism*, Clarendon Press, Oxford, 1983.
2. Tom Nairn, *The Break-up of Britain: Crisis and Neocolonialism*, New Left Books, London, 1977.
3. Nicos Poulantzas, *State, Power and Socialism*, New Left Books, London, 1978, pp.93–4.
4. Régis Debray, 'Marxism and the National Question', Interview, *New Left Review 105*, London, 1977, p.25.
5. Sami Zubaida, 'Theories of Nationalism', in G. Littlejohn et al., *Power and the State*, Croom Helm, London, 1978, p.69.
6. Ernest Gellner, *Nations and Nationalism*, Basil Blackwell, Oxford, 1983.
7. Aidan Foster-Carter, 'Listen class to the latest version of history', *Far Eastern Economic Review*, Hong Kong, 24 December 1987, pp.57–8.
8. David Morgan, *The Mongols*, Basil Blackwell, Oxford, 1986.
9. See contributions by J.E.G. Sutton, D.W. Cohen, G.S. Were and I.N. Kimambo in B.A. Ogot (ed.), *Zamani: A Survey of East African History*, East African Publishing House (new edition), Nairobi, 1974.
10. John Breuilly, *Nationalism and the State*, Manchester University Press, Manchester, 1985, pp.167–74.
11. See Edmund Burke III, 'The image of the Moroccan State in French ethnological literature: a new look at the origin of Lyautey's Berber policy' in Ernest Gellner and Charles Micaud (eds), *Arabs and Berbers*, D.C. Heath, Lexington Mass., 1972, pp.175–99.

12. John Waterbury, 'Tribalism, Trade and Politics: the Transformation of the Swasa of Morocco' in ibid., pp.231–57.

13. Benedict Anderson, *Imagined Communities: Reflections on the Origins and Spread of Nationalism*, Verso, London, 1983.

14. Gellner, *Nations and Nationalism*.

15. Maxime Rodinson, *Cult, Ghetto and State: The Persistence of the Jewish Question*, translated by Jon Rothschild, Al Saqi Books, London, 1983, p.173.

16. Amilcar Cabral, *Return to the Source: Selected Speeches of Amilcar Cabral*, Monthly Review Press, New York, 1973, p.78.

17. Claude Lévi-Strauss, *The Savage Mind* (*La Pensée Sauvage*, 1962), Weidenfeld and Nicolson, London, transl. 1966, pp.16–36.

18. Kenneth Brown, 'The impact of the Dahir Berbere in Sale' in Gellner and Micaud, *Arabs and Berbers*, p.209.

19. Partha Chatterjee, *Nationalist Thought and the Colonial World: A Derivative Discourse*, Zed/United Nations University, London, 1986, p.101.

20. F. John, *Das Deutsche Volkstum*, Lübeck, 1810, translated in L. Snyder (ed.), *The Dynamics of Nationalism: A Reader*, Princeton University Press, Princeton NJ, 1964, p.129.

21. Cited by Michael Edwardes, *Nehru: A Political Biography*, Penguin, London, 1971, p.214.

22. Karl Deutsch, *Nationalism and its Alternatives*, Knopf, New York, 1969, p.25.

23. Nirmal Sengupta (ed.), *Fourth World Dynamics: Jharkhand*, Authors' Guild Publishers, Delhi, 1982, p.254.

24. Anderson, *Imagined Communities*, pp.51 ff.

25. Leon Trotsky, *The War and the International*, Young Socialist Publication edition, Colombo, 1971, pp.vii–xii.

Chapter 2 The European Origins of the National Idea

1. *Nationalism*, Royal Institute of International Affairs Report, London, 1939, reprint by Frank Cass, 1963, pp.8–9.

2. Samuel E. Finer, 'State- and Nation-Building in Europe: the role of the military' in George Tilly (ed.), *The Formation of Nation States in Western Europe*, Princeton University Press, Princeton NJ, 1975, p.128.

3. George Tilly, 'Reflections on the History of European State-Making' in ibid., p.42.

4. H. Trevor-Roper, 'The general crisis of the seventeenth century' in *Religion, the Reformation and Social Change*, Macmillan, London, 1967, p.68.

5. J.E.E.D. Acton, *Essays on Freedom and Power*, republished by Thames and Hudson, London, 1956, pp.146–7.
6. Hugh Seton-Watson, *Nations and States: An Enquiry into the Origins of Nations and the Politics of Nationalism*, Methuen, London, 1977, p.162.

Chapter 3 Marx–Engels: The Springtime of Nationalism

1. F. Engels, 'The Festival of Nations in London', 1845, *Collected Works of Marx and Engels* (hereafter, *CW/ME*), Lawrence and Wishart, London, various years; 6, p.6. See also Speeches on Poland, 29 November 1847, ibid., 6, pp.388–90.
2. 'The German Ideology', 1846, *CW/ME*, 4, p.55.
3. *New York Tribune*, 24 April 1852, p.6.
4. Letter to the editor of *Commonwealth*, 160, 31 March 1866, *CW/ME*, 20, p.155.
5. Ibid., p.156.
6. 'Po and Rhine', 1859, *CW/ME*, 16, p.254.
7. *New York Tribune*, 8 August 1853 in *Karl Marx on Colonialism and Modernisation*, edited with an introduction by Shlomo Avinieri, Anchor Books, New York, 1969, pp.132–9.
8. Letter to *Commonwealth*, 31 March 1866, *CW/ME*, 20, p.156.
9. *CW/ME*, 6, pp.488–9.
10. Engels, 'The Frankfurt Assembly debates the Polish Question', 1848, *CW/ME*, 7, p.351.
11. *CW/ME*, 6, p.549.
12. Speeches on Poland, 19 November 1847, *CW/ME*, 6, p.388.
13. F. Engels, *The Condition of the Working Class in England*, Panther edition, London, 1969, p.299.
14. Engels, letter dated 23 May 1956, *CW/ME*, 40, p.50.
15. Letter of the Association Démocratique de Bruxelles to the Fraternal Democrats in London, signed by Vice President Marx, published in *Northern Star*, 4 March 1848, *CW/ME*, 6, p.641.
16. 'On the Jewish Question', 1843, *CW/ME*, 3, p.147.
17. Letter to Engels, 30 December 1867, in *Ireland and the Irish Question*, Progress, Moscow, 1971, p.148.
18. Letter to Kugelmann, 29 November 1869, *CW/ME*, 43, p.390.
19. Marx to Engels, 10 December 1869, *CW/ME*, 43, p.398.
20. Marx to Meyer and Vogt, 9 April 1870, *CW/ME*, 43, p.474–5.
21. Marx, 1870, in *Documents of the First International*, III, Lawrence and Wishart, London, n.d., p.405.

22. Engels to Marx, 24 October 1869, *CW/ME*, 43, p.363.
23. In *Ireland and the Irish Question*, p.332.
24. Marx to Engels, 1 December 1851, *CW/ME*, 38, p.498.
25. Engels to Marx, 23 May 1851, *CW/ME*, 38, p.363.
26. Letters of Marx, 24 March 1863, and of Engels, 11 June 1863, *CW/ME*, 41, pp.461–2 and 477.
27. Cited in E.H. Carr, *The Bolshevik Revolution, 1917–1923*, Penguin, London, 1966, p.422.
28. 14 May 1872, in *Documents of the First International*, 1963, V, p.297.
29. Cited by R. Rosdolsky, *Engels and the 'Non-historic' Peoples*, translated and edited with introduction by John-Paul Himka, *Critique* 18–19, Glasgow, 1987, p.170.
30. Cited by Horace B. Davis, *Nationalism and Socialism: Marxist and Labour Theories of Nationalism to 1917*, Monthly Review Press, New York, 1967, p.41.
31. 'The foreign policy of Russian Czarism, 1890', in P. Blackstock and B. Hoselitz (eds.), *The Russian Menace to Europe: A Collection of Articles, Speeches, Letters and News Despatches by Karl Marx and Friedrich Engels*, Free Press, Glencoe Ill., 1952, p.53.

Chapter 4 The Heyday of Theory

1. Editor, *Fabianism and Empire: A Manifesto by the Fabian Society*, Grant Richards, London, 1900, pp.23–4.
2. Congrés socialiste internationale d'Amsterdam dès 12–20 aôut 1904, *Rapports*, Brussels, 1904, pp.36–82.
3. xv, 1, p.110, cited in Davis, *Nationalism and Socialism*, pp.94–5.
4. *Neue Zeit*, xv, 2, 1896–7, p.651, cited in ibid., p.95.
5. *Evolutionary Socialism: A Criticism and Affirmation*, translated by Edith C. Harvey, Independent Labour Party, London, 1909, pp.172–3.
6. Congrés socialiste internationale tenu à Stuttgart du 16 au 24 aôut, 1907, *Compte Rendu*, Brussels, Veuve Desiré Brismée, 1908, pp.216–28(I), and 284–322(II).
7. For details, see Robert A. Kann, *Multinational Empire: Nationalism and National Reform in the Habsburg Monarchy, 1848–1918*, II, *Empire Reform*, Columbia University Press, New York, 1950, pp.150 ff.
8. *Das Selbstbestimmungsrecht der Nationen*, Vienna, 1916, p.36, cited in ibid., p.135.

9. In *Marxismus, Krieg und der Internationale*, J.H.W. Dietz, Stuttgart, 1917, extract translated in Bauer, *Austro-Marxism*, p.198.

10. See his *Die Nationalitäten Frage und die Sozialdemokratie*, Volksbuchhandlung (Marx Studien ii), Vienna, 1907.

11. In the Bottomore and Goode extract, Bauer, *Austro-Marxism*, p.107.

12. Cited by Charles C. Herod in *The Nation in the History of Marxian Thought, the Concept of Nations with History and Nations without History*, Martinus Nijhoff, The Hague, 1976, p.215.

13. Bauer, *Austro-Marxism*, p.114.

14. *Neue Zeit*, xiv, 2, 1895–6, p.466, cited by Tony Cliff in *Rosa Luxemburg*, Bookmarks, London, 1983, p.58.

15. 'The question of nationality and autonomy', cited by J.P. Nettl, *Rosa Luxemburg*, Oxford University Press, London, 1966, I, p.848.

16. Ibid.

17. In Horace B. Davis (ed.), *The National Question: Selected Writings of Rosa Luxemburg*, Monthly Review Press, New York, 1976, p.139.

18. 'The Russian Revolution, 1918', in ibid., p.84.

19. 'Was Wollen Wir?' in ibid., p.88.

20. In O.H. Gankin and H.H. Fisher (eds), *The Bolsheviks and the World War: The Origins of the Third International (a collection of documents)*, Stanford University Press, Stanford, 1960, pp.219–20.

21. 'Der Verbote', in ibid., p.507.

22. 'Finis Poloniae?' *Neue Zeit*, ii, 1895–6, pp.484 ff. and 513 ff.

23. Speech at the Mainz Congress of the German Social Democratic Party, 17–21 Sept. 1900, cited in Nettl, *Rosa Luxemburg*, p.176.

24. Ibid., p.852.

25. 'The national question and autonomy' in Davis, *The National Question*, p.112.

26. *Selected Works of Lenin*, 4, Lawrence and Wishart, London, 1936, p.266.

27. 'The Russian Revolution, 1918' in Davis, *The National Question*, p.297.

28. Ibid., p.299.

29. *Collected Works of Lenin*, Progress, Moscow, various years (henceforth, *CW/VIL*), 2, 1964, pp.95–121.

30. *Iskra*, 15 July 1903, *CW/VIL*, 6, pp.457–8.

31. Ibid., p.458.
32. Ibid., p.480.
33. Ibid., p.452.
34. Ibid., p.335.
35. Ibid., pp.486–7.
36. *1903:Second Congress of the Russian Social Democratic Labour Party*, translated and annotated by Brian Pearce, New Park, London, 1978, p.77.
37. *CW/VIL*, 20, p.26, and ibid., 21, p.408.
38. '4 July 1914', *CW/VIL*, 43, p.410.
39. Tony Cliff, *Lenin*, Vol.2, *All Power to the Soviets*, Pluto Press, London, 1976, p.257.
40. *CW/VIL*, 41, p.319.
41. Ibid., 19, pp.499–500.
42. Ibid., 20, pp.45–46.
43. Ibid., 22, p.423.
44. Ibid., 22, p.339.
45. Ibid., 20, p.50.
46. Ibid., 20, p.34.
47. *Selected Works*, 4, p.308.
48. *CW/VIL*, 20, p.396, and 22, p.145.
49. Cited by James M. Blaut, *The National Question: Decolonising the Theory of Nationalism*, Zed, London, 1981, p.67.
50. *CW/VIL* 24, p.73.
51. Ibid., p.300.
52. See Joseph Stalin, *Marxism and the National Question*, *Selected Writings and Speeches*, International, New York, 1942.

Chapter 5 The Tsar's National Minorities

1. Seton-Watson, *Nations and States*, p.82.
2. Ibid., p.87.
3. In R.P. Browder and A.F. Kerensky (eds), *The Russian Provisional Government of 1917: Documents*, Stanford University Press, Stanford, 1961, p.1501.
4. Ibid., p.1480.
5. *CW/VIL*, 24, p.302.
6. Cited by Cliff, *Lenin*, Vol.2, p.252.
7. Cited by Richard Pipes, *The Formation of the Soviet Union: Communism and Nationalism, 1917–1923*, Harvard University Press, Cambridge Mass., 1964 (revised edition), p.68.

Chapter 6 National Liberation in Practice

1. The tasks of the revolution, 9–10 October 1917, *CW/VIL*, 26, p.62.
2. 22 November 1917, ibid., p.344.
3. March 1919, *CW/VIL*, 29, p.169.
4. *CW/VIL*, 26, p.449.
5. '12 December 1917', cited by Jesse Clarkson, *A History of Russia*, Random House, New York, 1961, p.636.
6. Stalin had made a similar point in his 1913 tract:

   The Transcaucasus Tatars as a nation might assemble, let us say, in their Diet and, succumbing to the influence of their beys and mullahs, decide to restore the old order of things and secede . . . will this be in the interests of the toiling strata of the Tatar nation? Can social democracy remain indifferent when the beys and mullahs take the lead of the masses in the solution of the national problems?
   Sochineniya iii, pp.52–3, cited by Carr, *The Bolshevik Revolution*, I, p.270.

7. *Sochineniya*, iv, pp.31–2, cited ibid., p.272.
8. Ibid., Note 3, p.272.
9. Leon Trotsky, *Stalin*, Pioneer, New York, 1946, p.257.
10. 'March 1918', cited by Alexander A. Bennigsen, and S. Enders Wimbush, *Muslim National Communism in the Soviet Union: A Revolutionary Strategy for the Colonial World*, University of Chicago Press, Chicago, 1979, p.42.
11. *Zhizn' Natsional 'nostei*, 38(46), 38(47), and 42(50), in Carrère d'Encausse and Hélène and Stuart R. Schram, *Marxism and Asia, 1853–1964*, Allen Lane, London, 1965, p.178.
12. Cited by Carr, *Bolshevik Revolution*, I, p.274.
13. *CW/VIL*, 29, p.170.
14. *Sochineniya* iv, pp.22–3, cited in Carr, *Bolshevik Revolution*, I, p.294.
15. Cited by Pipes, *The Formation*, p.122.
16. For example, see *CW/VIL*, 36, 21 January 1918, p.473.
17. 3 December 1919, *CW/VIL*, 30, pp.193–4.
18. League of Nations, *Report on Economic Conditions in Russia, with special reference to the famine of 1921–1922 and the state of agriculture*, c.705.M.451, Geneva, 1922, II, p.1.
19. *CW/VIL*, 32, p.160.
20. G. Safarov, *Revolyutsia i Kul'tura*, Tashkent, 1934, 1, p.10, cited by d'Encausse and Schram, *Marxism and Asia*, p.32.

21. Pipes, *The Formation*, p.167.
22. Cited by Chantal Lemercier-Quelquejay in S. Enders Wimbush (ed.), *Soviet Nationalities in Strategic Perspective*, Croom Helm, London, 1985, p.39.
23. *Zhizn' Natsional 'nostei*, 38(46), 1919, translated in Bennigsen and Wimbush, *Muslim National Communism*, p.131.
24. A. Denikine, *The White Army*, London 1930, p.156.
25. Cited by Pipes, *The Formation*, p.160.
26. Resolution, April 1923, Appendix to Joseph Stalin, *Marxism and the National and Colonial Questions*, International, New York, 1935, pp.279–87.
27. *Bolshevik Revolution*, I, p.273.
28. *CW/VIL*, 33, pp.65–6.

Chapter 7 Great Russian Chauvinism

1. *Bolshevik Revolution*, I, p.389.
2. *The Formation*, p.277.
3. *Pravda* 10 October 1921, cited by Walker Connor, *The National Question in Marxist-Leninist Theory and Strategy*, Princeton University Press, Princeton NJ, 1984, p.50.
4. *CW/VIL*, 29, p.194.
5. *Sochineniya*, v, pp.244–5, cited Carr, *Bolshevik Revolution*, I, p.375.
6. Bennigsen and Wimbush, *Muslim National Communism*, p.64.
7. Cited by Pipes, *The Formation*, p.279.
8. Cited by Carr, *Bolshevik Revolution*, III, p.273.
9. Patriotica, *Smena Vekh*, Prague, p.59, cited by Isaac Deutscher, *Stalin: A Political Biography*, 2nd edition, Oxford University Press, London, 1967, p.243.
10. *Sochineniya*, v, p.244, cited in Carr, *Bolshevik Revolution*, I, p.376.
11. *Odinnadtsatii sezd RKP(b)*, cited by Cliff, *Lenin*, IV, p.199.
12. Cited in Bennigsen and Wimbush, *Muslim National Communism*, p.161.
13. Ibid., p.86.
14. Ibid., p.168.
15. *CW/VIL*, 33, p.127.
16. 6 October 1922, ibid., p.372.
17. Pipes, *The Formation*, p.273.
18. See L.D. Trotsky, *The Stalin School of Falsification*, Pioneer, New York, 1937, pp.66–7.
19. *CW/VIL*, 36, pp.605–11.

20. Ibid., p.606.
21. Ibid., pp.608–9.
22. *CW/VIL*, 45, p.608.
23. Translated by Pipes, *The Formation*, p.290.
24. Cited by Bennigsen and Wimbush, *Muslim National Communism*, p.83.
25. *Sochineniya*, v, pp.264–5, cited by Pipes, *The Formation*, and Carr, *Bolshevik Revolution*, I, pp.378–9.
26. *CW/VIL*, 33, p.279.

Chapter 8 Russia and the National Question at Large

1. *Sochineniya*, iv, pp.164–5, cited in Carr, *Bolshevik Revolution*, III, pp.236–7.
2. *CW/VIL*, 31, p.412.
3. Jane Degras (ed.), *The Communist International, 1919–1943 (Documents)*, Cass, London, 1971, I, p.38.
4. *Bolshevik Revolution*, III, p.464.
5. *Inprecor*, 8 October 1924, p.768.
6. *Sochineniya*, vi, p.144, cited in E.H.Carr, *Socialism in One Country*, Macmillan, London, 1964, III, p.667.
7. *Second Congress of the Communist International*, New Park, London, 1977, I, pp.181–2.
8. Ibid., p.116.
9. The original typescript, with Lenin's amendments, is included in G. Adhikari (ed.), *Documents of the History of the Communist Party of India*, People's Publishing, New Delhi, 1971, I, pp.173–7.
10. *Baku: Congress of the Peoples of the East*, New Park, London, 1977, p.31.
11. Cited in E.H. Carr, *The Interregnum*, Macmillan, London, 1954, pp.167–8.
12. *Inprecor*, 103/121, 23 June 1923, cited by Chris Harman, *The Lost Revolution: Germany 1918 to 1923*, Bookmarks, London, 1982, p.252.
13. Demetrio Boerstner, *The Bolsheviks and the National and Colonial Question (1917–1928)*, E. Droz, Geneva, 1957, p.180.
14. d'Encausse and Schram, *Marxism and Asia*, pp.199–200.
15. Carr, *Socialism in One Country*, p.54.
16. *Inprecor* 10, 14 January, 1926, p.126.
17. *Sochineniya*, vii, p.58.
18. J.D Stalin, 'Principles of Leninism', April 1924, in *Sochineniya*, vi, pp.142–5, cited in d'Encausse and Schram, *Marxism and Asia*, pp.185–6.

Chapter 9 Postscript

1. 9 June 1927, in *Inprecor* 19, 17 June 1927, pp.1319–20, cited in E.H. Carr and R.W. Davies, *Foundations of a Planned Economy, 1926–1929*, Macmillan, London, 1969, vol.1, p.9.
2. Theodore Draper, *American Communism and Soviet Russia*, Macmillan, London, 1960, p.315.
3. *CW/VIL*, 31, p.148.
4. E.H. Carr, *The Twilight of the Comintern, 1926–1935*, Macmillan, London, 1982, p.89.
5. 'For the Alliance with the Middle Classes', *Oeuvres de Maurice Thorez*, II, vii, Editions Sociales, Paris, 1952, pp.113–21.
6. Carr, *Twilight*, p.407.
7. *Oeuvres*, 3, xiv, pp.180–1.
8. *Writings of Leon Trotsky 1939–1940*, Merit, New York, 1969, p.72.
9. ECCI, Manifesto on the 22nd Anniversary of the Russian Revolution, November 1939, in Degras, *The Communist International*, III, pp.439–40.
10. Ibid., p.471.
11. See Bohdan Krawshenko, 'The Great Famine 1932–1933 in Soviet Ukraine', *Critique* 17, 1986, pp.137–46.
12. Alexander R. Alexier, in Wimbush, *Soviet Nationalities*, p.72, Note 20. On the Russian volunteers, see C. Andreyev, *Vlasov*, Cambridge University Press, Cambridge, 1987.
13. Vedemosti' Verkhovnogo Soveta SSSR, 38, 2 September 1941, cited by Tony Cliff, *Russia: A Marxist Analysis*, International Socialism, London, n.d., p.220.
14. Russian Institute (ed.), *The Anti Stalin Campaign and International Communism*, Russian Institute, Columbia University Press, New York, 1956.
15. *Current Digest of the Soviet Press*, Columbus, Ohio, 23/14, p.3.
16. In 'Aniversario y Balance', in *Amanta* 17, 1928; see also his *Siete Ensayos de Interpretación de la realidad peruana*, Lima, 1958.
17. Notes on a lecture, Political Club, Peking University, 13 May 1924, *Hsin Min-kuo tsa-chih* (*New Republic*), I, 6, June 1924, in d'Encausse and Schram, *Marxism and Asia*, pp.219–22; see also Maurice Meisner, *Li Ta-chao and the Origins of Chinese Marxism*, Harvard East Asia Series 27, Harvard University Press, London, 1967, p.191.
18. Ibid., p.177.

19. 'The Principles of Nationalism, 1910', in Adrian Lyttelton (ed.), *Italian Fascism: from Pareto to Gentile*, Harper, New York, 1975, p.146.
20. Kita Ikki (1884–1937), *Outline for the Reconstruction of Japan*, 1924, cited by Richard Storry, *The Double Patriots: A Study of Japanese Nationalism*, Chatto and Windus, London, 1957, p.38.
21. 'Foundations of Leninism, 1924', included in *Problems of Leninism*, Progress, Moscow, 1945, p.64.
22. Cited by Chris Harman from *Perestroika* (the speeches of Mikhail Gorbachev), in 'The storm breaks', *International Socialism* 46, March 1990, p.10.

Chapter 10 The Wider World: China

1. See Harold Isaacs, *The Tragedy of the Chinese Revolution*, Secker and Warburg, London, 1938; Conrad Brandt, *Stalin's Failure in China, 1924–1927*, Cambridge University Press, London, 1958; R.C. North, *Moscow and Chinese Communism*, Stanford University Press (2nd edn), Stanford, 1963.
2. Harold Isaacs, 'Conversations with H. Sneevliet' [Maring], *China Quarterly* 45, January–March 1971, p.102.
3. *The Fourth Congress of the Communist International*, London, 1923, pp.222–3.
4. Degras, *Communist International*, II, p.5.
5. C. Martin Wilbur and Julie Lien-ying How, *Documents on Communism, Nationalism and Soviet Advisers in China, 1918–1927*, Columbia University Press, New York, 1956, pp.376–7.
6. Cited by Carr and Davies, *Foundations*, p.747.
7. Unpublished speech, cited by Vuyovitch as a challenge to Stalin at the 8th ECCI Plenum, May 1927. Stalin did not deny the authenticity of the speech; see Isaacs, *Tragedy*, p.185, and Carr and Davies, *Foundations*, pp.756–7, note 2/9.
8. Cited by Patrick Haithcox, *Communism and Nationalism in India: M.N. Roy and Comintern Policy, 1920–1939*, Princeton University Press, Princeton NJ, 1971, p.72.
9. Carr and Davies, *Foundations*, p.883.
10. Wilbur and How, *Documents*, p.44.
11. January 1930, in *Selected Works of Mao Tse-tung* (henceforth *SW/MTt*), Foreign Languages Press, Peking, 1965, I, p.123.
12. 20 December 1964, in *Miscellany of Mao Tse-tung Thought, 1949–1968*, Joint Publications Research Service, Arlington Virginia (mimeo), n.d., p.421.

13. *SW/MTt*, I, p.97.
14. Cited by L.P. Deluisen, former Soviet adviser to the Chinese Communist Party, in memoir, translated in *Chinese Studies in History*, VII/4, Summer 1974, p.41. Mao makes the same point in Stuart R. Schram (ed.), *Mao Unrehearsed: Talks and Letters, 1956–1971*, Penguin, London, 1974, p.97.
15. See Conrad Brandt, Benjamin Schwartz and John H. Fairbank, *A Documentary History of Chinese Communism*, Athenaum, New York, 1967, p.219.
16. Cited by Carr and Davies, *Foundations*, p.346.
17. Mao Tse-tung, *China: The Long March towards Unity*, CP USA, New York, 1937, p.75.
18. *SW/MTt*, II, p.278.
19. Ibid., p.446.
20. Vladimir Dedijer, *Tito*, Cape, New York, 1953, p.322.
21. 1938. *SW/MTt* II, p.196.

Chapter 11 British India: Opportunism and Imperial Power

1. Ranjit Guha, *Elementary Aspects of Peasant Insurgency in Colonial India*, Oxford University Press, Delhi, 1983, p.13.
2. Anil Seal, *The Emergence of Indian Nationalism: Competition and Collaboration in the Later Nineteenth Century*, Cambridge University Press, London, 1968, p.134.
3. Cited by Percival Spear, *India, Pakistan and the West*, Penguin, London, 1960, p.163.
4. *Report on India Constitutional Reforms*, 1918, para. 41, p.91, cited by Bipen Chandra, *Communalism in Modern India*, Vikas, New Delhi, 1984, p.26.
5. Ibid., p.26.
6. Cited by P. Hardy, *The Muslims in British India*, Cambridge University Press, Cambridge, 1972, p.63.
7. Sarkar, Sumit, *Modern India 1885–1947*, Macmillan India Library, Delhi, 1983, p.16.
8. 'Imperialism and Nationalism in India', in John Gallagher, Gordon Johnson and Anil Seal (eds), *Locality, Province and Nation: Essays on Indian Politics, 1870 to 1940*, Cambridge University Press, Cambridge, 1973, p.10.
9. Sarkar, *Modern India*, pp.99–100.
10. C.A. Bayley, *The Local Roots of Indian Politics: Allahabad, 1880–1920*, Clarendon Press, Oxford, 1975, p.132.
11. *Bengal: The Nationalist Movement, 1876–1940*, Columbia University Press, New York, 1974, p.35.

12. Jnanabrata Bhattacharyya, 'Language, Class and Community in Bengal', *South Asian Bulletin*, 7, Albany NY, 1987.

13. Cited by C.H. Phillips (ed.), *The Evolution of India and Pakistan, 1858 to 1947, Selected Documents*, Oxford University Press, London, 1962, pp.188–9.

14. In Gallagher et al., *Locality*, p.14.

15. Ibid., pp.17–18.

16. *The Muslims*, p.200.

17. Uma Kaura, *Muslims and Indian Nationalism*, Popular, Delhi, 1977, p.45.

18. S. Gopal (ed), *Selected Works of Jawaharlal Nehru*, Orient Longman, New Delhi, 1976, Vol.8, p.123.

19. Mushirul Hasan, 'The Muslim Mass Contact Campaign: Analysis of a Strategy of Political Modernization', in Richard Sisson and Stanley Wolpert (eds), *Congress and Indian Nationalism: The Pre-Independence Phase*, University of California at Berkeley and Los Angeles, 1988, p.206.

20. See I.A. Talbot, 'The 1946 Punjab Elections', *Modern Asian Studies*, 14, Pt.I, 1980, pp.65–92.

21. *Speeches and Writings*, edited by Jamil-ud-Din Ahmed, Lahore, 1960 edition, I, p.89.

22. Hasan, 'The Muslim Mass Contact Campaign', p.211.

23. Hardy, *The Muslims*, p.236.

24. Speech, 1 April 1947, New Delhi; in *Collected Works of Mahatma Gandhi*, 87, p.187, cited in Chatterjee, *Nationalist Thought and the Colonial World*, p.116.

25. J. Nehru, *The Discovery of India*, John Day, New York, 1946, p.413.

26. *Separatism among Indian Muslims: The Politics of the United Provinces Muslims, 1860–1923*, Cambridge University Press, Cambridge, 1975, pp.353–4.

Chapter 12 Independent India: A Host of Dragons without a Leader

1. G.K. Chanda, *The State and Rural Economic Transformation: The Case of the Punjab, 1950–1985*, Sage, New York, 1986, p.325.

Chapter 13 More Dragons: Pakistan and Bangladesh

1. Jinnah, *Speeches and Writings*, II, pp.403–4.

2. Cited by T.S. George, 'The cross of Bengal', *Far Eastern Economic Review*, 17, 24 April 1971, p.57.

3. Tajmuddin Ahmed, *The Times*, London, 24 May 1971.

Chapter 14 And Yet More: Sri Lanka and Tamil Eelam

1. S.J. Tambiah, *Sri Lanka: Ethnic Fratricide and the Dismantling of Democracy*, I.B. Tauris, London, 1986, p.6.
2. Cited by Satchi Ponnambalam, *Sri Lanka: The National Question and the Tamil Liberation Struggle*, Tamil Information Centre and Zed Books, London, 1983, pp.52–3.
3. Cited ibid., p.70, footnote 40.
4. *Towards a New Era: Selected Speeches*, Colombo, 1961.
5. Cited by Tambiah, *Ethnic Fratricide*, p.27.

Chapter 15 Perverse National Liberation

1. See John Prebble, *The Highland Clearances*, Penguin, London, 1969.
2. See S. Dubnov, *A History of the Jews from the Beginning to Early Christianity*, translated from the fourth Russian edition by Moshe Spiegel, S. Brunswick, Newark NJ and London, 1967; Abram Leon, *The Jewish Question: A Marxist Interpretation*, Pathfinder, New York, 1970; Ilan Halévy, *A History of the Jews*, Zed, London, 1987; Rodinson, *Cult, Ghetto and State*.
3. Halévy, *A History*, p.130.
4. *Mein Kampf*, by Adolf Hitler, unexpurgated edition, two volumes in one, Hurst and Blackett, London, 1939.
5. *Le Monde*, 13 January 1966, cited by Nathan Weinstock, *Zionism – False Messiah*, translated and edited by Alan Adler, Ink Links, London, 1979, p.26.
6. Walter Laqueur, *A History of Zionism*, Holt, Reinhart and Winston, New York, 1972, p.591.
7. Cited in *Our Roots are Still Alive*, New York, 1981, p.24.
8. Theodore Herzl, *A Jewish State*, London, 1896, p.29.
9. Ibid.; examples and citations from Halévy, *A History*, p.152.
10. Laqueur, *Zionism*, pp.400–1.
11. FO:371/4183/2117.132187, cited in *Our Roots*, p.29, and Halévy, *A History*, p.182.
12. *Zionism*, p.594.
13. Ronald Storrs, *Orientations*, London, 1946, p.345.
14. *Zionism*, p.596.
15. Interview, Israel Television, August 1973, cited by Halévy, *A History*, p.171.

16. Ibid., p.184.
17. Cited by Lenni Brenner in *Zionism in the Age of the Dictators*, Croom Helm, Beckenham Kent, 1983, p.149.
18. See the discussion in Akiva Orr, *The UnJewish State: The Politics of Jewish Identity in Israel*, Ithaca Press, London, 1983, pp.220 ff.
19. Cited by Rose, *Israel*, p.21.
20. *US News and World Report*, 19 June 1967, cited ibid., p.22.
21. *Middle East Observer*, February 1981, cited ibid., p.20.
22. Cited in Noam Chomsky, *The Fateful Triangle: The US, Israel and the Palestinians*, Spokesman, London, 1983, p.10.
23. On Israeli identity, see Orr, *UnJewish State*.

Chapter 16 National Liberation and a World Economy: Economic Nationalism

1. As identified by Charles Jones in his *International Business in the Nineteenth Century: The Rise and Fall of a Cosmopolitan Bourgeoisie*, Wheatsheaf/Harvester, Brighton, 1987. The national qualification is explicit in Jones' formulation (p.28):

   Sons of British and European manufacturers and merchants travelled the world in search of export markets, and often settled in some foreign trading port only to develop a business quite tangential to the original family concern. The mercantile diaspora embraced all the trading and manufacturing nations: Catalans, Basques, Germans, Danes, Chinese, Parsees, Jews, Armenians, Portuguese, Greeks, Dutch, North Americans, Scots and English. The outcome was a cosmopolitan trading community centred on London in which nationality was often blurred . . . Miscegenation also played its part.

2. *Nationalism and After*, Macmillan, London, 1945, p.17.
3. *Financial Times*, London, 4 October 1983.
4. The argument repeated by Jean-Jacques Servan-Schreiber, *Le Défi Americain*, Maspero, Paris, 1967.
5. Keynes' biographer explains the memorandum to P. Lieschig (October 1943) as one arm of pursuing 'both lines', the liberal and the *étatiste* – R.F. Harrod, *The Life of John Maynard Keynes*, Harcourt Brace, New York, 1951, pp.567–8.
6. The case is outlined in more detail in my *The End of the Third World: Newly Industrializing Countries and the Decline of an Ideology*, I.B.Tauris/Penguin, London, 1986/7.

7. See Franz Fanon, *Wretched of the Earth*, MacGibbon and Kee, London, 1965.

8. This is a considerable simplification. For more detail, see my *Of Bread and Guns: The World Economy in Crisis*, Penguin, London, 1983.

9. Cited by Harold Pollins, *An Economic History of the Jews in England*, Associated Universities Presses, London, 1984.

10. *Nationalism*, Royal Institute of International Affairs, p.20.

11. Congrés socialiste internationale d'Amsterdam dès 14–20 août 1904, *Rapports*, Brussels, 1904, p.47.

12. *Nationalism*, p.231.

13. Alan Dowty, *Closed Borders: The Contemporary Assault on Freedom of Movement*, Twentieth Century Fund Report, Yale University Press, London, 1987, p.205.

14. See Carole Kismaric (with commentary by William Shawcross), *Forced Out: The Agony of the Refugee in Our Time*, Human Rights Watch and J.H. Kaplan Fund, in association with William Morrow & Co., W.W. Norton, Penguin and Random House, New York, 1989.

15. See Chapter 8, 'Temporary and Contract Labour: the 'Worker-Peasant System', in my *The Mandate of Heaven: Marx and Mao in Modern China*, Quartet, London, 1978, pp.108–16.

16. The detail and implications of this period are discussed in my *Of Bread and Guns*.

Chapter 17 The Past and Future of Nationalism

1. See my *Of Bread and Guns*.

2. *The Conditions of Peace*, Macmillan, New York, 1942, pp.63–4.

3. 'Some reflections on the break-up of Britain', *New Left Review*, 105, September–October 1977, pp.3–24.

4. *The 2024 Report: A Concise History of the Future, 1974–2024*, Sidgwick and Jackson, London, 1984.

INDEX

Abdallah, King, 241
Acton, Lord, 36
Adler, Max, 54
   Victor, 54, 55, 61
Afghanistan, 128, 170, 178, 258
Africa, 7, 9, 15, 170, 252, 258, 273 *see also individual countries*
   North, 7, 236, 274
agreements
   Anglo-Soviet (1921), 117, 118
   India-Sri Lanka, 212, 218–19
   Longowal-Rajiv Gandhi, 196
   migrant labour, 268
   Persia-USSR (1921), 119
aid, 202, 242
Akalı Dal, 195, 196
Akselrod, 66
Albania, 141, 142
Aleksandr, 66
Alexander III, 76
Algeria, 42, 134
America, Central, 258
   Latin, 248, 252, 261
   North, 2, 35, 42, 244, 249, 252, 253, 265, 272, 284
Anderson, Benedict, 9, 19
d'Annunzio, Gabriele 142
anti-Semitism, 66, 77, 92, 227, 229–33, 235, 242
Arabs, 51, 228, 236, 238–42 *passim*
   League, 241
Argentina, 261
Armenia, 10, 50, 65, 81, 84, 92–3, 102, 108, 124, 140, 141, 146, 277, 278, 283
Asia, 116, 121–4 *passim*, 126, 151, 166–88, 253, 263, 265, 273, 274 *see also individual countries*
   Soviet Central, 81–2, 94–5, 102, 106–7, 118, 137–41, 277
Ataturk, Mustafa Kemal, 118, 119, 155
Australia, 225, 284
Austria-Hungary, 19, 35–8 *passim*, 41, 47, 50, 54–8, 133, 166, 227, 229, 245, 271, 272
Ayub Khan, President, 202–3, 208
Azerbaijan, 81, 92–3, 102, 107, 108, 140, 141

Bakunin, Michael, 47
Balfour, A.J, 237, 238
Balfour Declaration, 236–8 *passim*
Baltic States, 62, 75, 85, 89, 136, 139, 140, 147, 278 *see also individual headings*
Balkans, 66, 273
Baluchistan, 170, 200
Banderanaike, S.R.W.D., 212–13
   Mrs S. 212, 214
Bangladesh, 166, 201–8, 258
Bashanı, Maulana, 206–7
Bashkiria, 85, 94, 98
Bauer, Otto, 3, 54, 56–7, 59, 63, 66, 69, 71, 245, 275
Bayley, C.A., 173
Bayturson, Ahmed, 95
Bebel, August, 61
Belgium, 42, 245
Bengal, 208 *see also* India
Ben Gurion, David, 240
Berbers, 7, 274
Bernstein, Edouard, 53
Bhattacharyya, Jnanabrata, 173
Bhindranwale, Jamal Singh, 195, 196
Bhutto, Z.A., 202–8 *passim*
Birobidzhan, 232
Bismarck, Otto Eduard Leopold, Prince von 36, 70, 249
Blum, Léon, 134
border controls, 257–67
Borodin, M.M., 154
Bosch, Anovna, 60
Breuilly, John, 7
Brezhnev, Leonid, 140, 146
Britain, 3, 5, 11, 12, 15, 19, 35, 39, 42–6, 49, 50, 52, 66, 89, 90, 93, 117–20 *passim*, 122, 126, 135, 136, 155, 214, 217, 235–7, 239–41 *passim*, 245, 249, 258, 262, 272, 273, 283 *see also* England
   in India, 53, 167–89, 274–6
   in Sri Lanka, 210
   Aliens Act (1905), 254
Bukharin, N.I., 60, 67, 85, 87, 96, 113, 130
Bulgaria, 141, 226
Burma, 170, 248, 258
Byelorussia, 50, 65, 108

303

FOR THE BEST IN PAPERBACKS, LOOK FOR THE

In every corner of the world, on every subject under the sun, Penguin represents quality and variety – the very best in publishing today.

For complete information about books available from Penguin – including Puffins, Penguin Classics and Arkana – and how to order them, write to us at the appropriate address below. Please note that for copyright reasons the selection of books varies from country to country.

In the United Kingdom: Please write to *Dept E.P., Penguin Books Ltd, Harmondsworth, Middlesex, UB7 0DA.*

If you have any difficulty in obtaining a title, please send your order with the correct money, plus ten per cent for postage and packaging, to *PO Box No 11, West Drayton, Middlesex*

In the United States: Please write to *Dept BA, Penguin, 299 Murray Hill Parkway, East Rutherford, New Jersey 07073*

In Canada: Please write to *Penguin Books Canada Ltd, 2801 John Street, Markham, Ontario L3R 1B4*

In Australia: Please write to the *Marketing Department, Penguin Books Australia Ltd, P.O. Box 257, Ringwood, Victoria 3134*

In New Zealand: Please write to the *Marketing Department, Penguin Books (NZ) Ltd, Private Bag, Takapuna, Auckland 9*

In India: Please write to *Penguin Overseas Ltd, 706 Eros Apartments, 56 Nehru Place, New Delhi, 110019*

In the Netherlands: Please write to *Penguin Books Netherlands B.V., Postbus 3507, 1001 AH, Amsterdam*

In West Germany: Please write to *Penguin Books Ltd, Friedrichstrasse 10–12, D–6000 Frankfurt/Main 1*

In Spain: Please write to *Alhambra Longman S.A., Fernandez de la Hoz 9, E–28010 Madrid*

In Italy: Please write to *Penguin Italia s.r.l., Via Como 4, I-20096 Pioltello (Milano)*

In France: Please write to *Penguin Books Ltd, 39 Rue de Montmorency, F-75003 Paris*

In Japan: Please write to *Longman Penguin Japan Co Ltd, Yamaguchi Building, 2–12–9 Kanda Jimbocho, Chiyoda-Ku, Tokyo 101*

The End of the Third World

Newly Industrializing Countries and the Decline of an Ideology

South Korea has a growth rate which puts Japan and West Germany – not to mention Great Britain – to shame . . .

The Third World will always be hopelessly poor and underdeveloped, such are the comfortable Western clichés which have been shattered for ever. Malaysia, Singapore and Indonesia have all changed rapidly from underdeveloped societies into advanced economies – a process which took decades, even centuries, in the West – while Brazil and Mexico have made immense strides in the same direction. It is high time we stopped making facile generalizations about 'the Third World'; instead, as Nigel Harris shows in this important sequel to his very successful *Of Bread and Guns*, we must tease out the factors which have left some countries desperately backward while others are catching up with us *fast*.